GOVERNING SECURITY

GOVERNING SECURITY

THE HIDDEN ORIGINS OF AMERICAN SECURITY AGENCIES

Mariano-Florentino Cuéllar

STANFORD LAW BOOKS

An Imprint of Stanford University Press

Stanford, California

Stanford University Press
Stanford, California

© 2013 by the Board of Trustees of the Leland Stanford Junior University.
All rights reserved.

Printed in the United States of America on acid-free, archival-quality paper

Library of Congress Cataloging-in-Publication Data

Cuéllar, Mariano-Florentino, author.
Governing security : the hidden origins of American security agencies /
Mariano-Florentino Cuéllar.
pages cm
Includes bibliographical references and index.
ISBN 978-0-8047-7069-9 (alk. paper) --
ISBN 978-0-8047-7070-5 (pbk. : alk. paper)
1. United States. Federal Security Agency. 2. United States. Dept. of
Homeland Security. 3. National security--United States. 4. Internal security--
United States. I. Title.
HV8139.C84 2012
355'.033073--dc23

2012031603

Typeset by Bruce Lundquist in 10/15 Sabon

Table of Contents

List of Tables and Figures

TABLES

FIGURES

Preface and Acknowledgments

IN MID-JUNE 2009 I attended a White House meeting to discuss a problem that was causing increasing concern within the federal government. I was then serving on the staff of the White House Domestic Policy Council. I had just wrapped up a discussion of a new statute revising the decades-old Food, Drug, and Cosmetic Act, and thus changing the responsibilities of the Food and Drug Administration (FDA). With food and drug law still on my mind, I rushed down two flights of ornate stairs in the Eisenhower Executive Office Building and into a large conference room just as the meeting was getting started. I will never forget it. The World Health Organization had just declared the existence of the first human influenza pandemic in more than forty years. Spreading with unusual speed, a new H1N1 influenza virus had reached 120 countries and territories in eight weeks. A previous flu pandemic in 1968 had caused approximately one million deaths. Four decades later, previously healthy young people were becoming severely ill. In the United States, the disease had already progressed across the nation from California.[1] Given the potential consequences, American health officials braced for a crisis that could overwhelm the health care system.

The discussion then unfolding touched on far-reaching plans being drawn up to deal with possible school closures, vaccine and hospital bed shortages, and economic disruptions. I remember hearing from worried public health officials that possible mutations could render millions of vaccine doses worthless. Ultimately the virus did not mutate, and Americans were spared the most severe consequences then contemplated. The Centers for Disease Control nonetheless estimate that up to 89 million U.S. cases of H1N1 influenza occurred between April 2009 and the following spring. Nearly half a million Americans were hospitalized.[2]

Two massive federal agencies shouldered the primary responsibility for protecting Americans from this threat: the Department of Homeland Security (DHS) and the Department of Health and Human Services (HHS). In the months that followed the pandemic influenza declaration, these agencies answered countless questions about the virus, how they were working together to stop it, how they would spend the $6 billion or so that Congress appropriated for pandemic response, how they would implement the Stafford Act's provisions governing federal disaster relief operations, and how they would shoulder the rest of their wide-ranging responsibilities while managing the pandemic response. Never once did the two secretaries address the more basic questions of why their agencies existed in the first place, or why these organizations had been entrusted with their precise legal responsibilities to keep Americans safe.

Where did these agencies come from, and what do their origins tell us about how Americans govern themselves? It is a testament to the power of agencies to shape the public imagination that citizens eventually come to think of them as part of the natural order of things, whether in the midst of a crisis involving pandemic influenza or in other moments when people come into contact with them. If it is not lost entirely on the public that these agencies are forged by humans and not by nature, it is probably also true that people often treat the agencies as a permanent fixture—much like the faces chiseled into the cliffs of Mount Rushmore. In fact, when Americans fly on commercial airliners or cross national borders, they can hardly avoid coming into contact with one of those two agencies—the one forged in the shadow of the September 11 terrorist attacks. And when parents take their children to the doctor for a vaccine or purchase food at a supermarket, they do so in a world indelibly shaped by a different federal organization that employs tens of thousands and also endeavors to protect the lives of millions every day.

Governing Security investigates the hidden origins of those two agencies: the Roosevelt-era Federal Security Agency (FSA) (which gave rise to the present-day Department of Health and Human Services) and the more recently created Department of Homeland Security. You will discover in the pages to come that these agencies' stories converge on more than the word "security" in each of their names. Beyond their similarities as large federal agencies burdened with nearly impossible security missions, distinctions will also emerge. In the course of exploring the convergence and contrasts of these two security agencies, I will draw on perspectives from public law, American political development, and organization theory to address some persistent puzzles about their origins and to deliver a new take on debates about national security.[3]

The central thesis that emerges concerns the relationship of *two different kinds of security problems.* Put simply, the idea is this: from the response to Katrina to social security policy to immigration and foreign affairs, the impact of public law in our country depends in large measure on how key players go about securing control of the nation's public organizations, and (in turn) on how organizations are then used to define the contested concept of the nation's security. These problems, moreover, are interconnected through legal interpretations, the work of public organizations within the executive branch, and public attitudes about the role of government. In effect, Americans end up choosing goals not through an elaborate technical process but in lively and overlapping settings where the public is reacting to courts deciding on the scope of presidential power, civil servants at the FDA or FEMA (Federal Emergency Management Agency) are setting priorities, and White House advisors are adjudicating whether agencies protecting communities from risks should be consolidated.

The project of governing security is thus one that is as much about high-minded national aspirations as it is about competitive pressures to achieve political advantage. Specifically, the two interconnected dynamics that are the primary subject of this book—the process of defining the scope of security and politicians' competition to secure control of the bureaucracy—are linked to each other through public organizations, whose power includes shaping the scope of security and whose own structure is in turn shaped by debates about the federal role in providing security. The problems of controlling executive power and defining security are also linked to each other through law and legal interpretations. These regulate the structure, control, and performance of agencies, and the perceptions of the mass public (which can translate into political support and simultaneously affect agency missions as well as the scope of federal power). Hence, political control of public agencies can facilitate policymakers' efforts to shape public perceptions of security and agency capacity to carry out their legal responsibilities. Meanwhile, the future development of these agencies—

and debates about the scope of security—affect the dynamics of political control over public organizations. Central to the argument is the idea that the meaning of the concept "national security" is not fixed, but has instead been given life through choices about the architecture of public agencies such as the FSA and DHS, political strategies, and legal interpretations.

Just as societies make choices about the architecture of public agencies, scholars make choices about the questions they will investigate. For some scholars, the right question to investigate is the one that can be answered with their preferred methods. Much as I admire the scholar who leverages exogenous shocks to create a clever quasi-experimental design, I confess that this project grew around a compelling series of puzzles about organizations, law, and security that have left me no choice but to leverage a variety of methods and literatures. You will find here the results of long days in archival reading rooms. You will read the results of efforts to gather budget data from long-forgotten legislative reports, and analyses of terms used in presidential speeches. The result is an argument built on cautious inferences from history, informed by theoretical insights from the study of public organizations, the case law and commentary grappling with long-standing separation-of-powers questions in American public law, and the institutionally oriented literature attempting to explain the development of the American state.

If it is true that I wrote this book in part to contribute to those scholarly literatures, it is even more true that I wrote it to satiate my own desire to understand how we govern through complicated organizations that no one entirely comprehends. Let me illustrate with an example. If one stands just north of the border between the United States and Mexico, it is simple enough to locate the United States geographically in relation to what appears to be a timeless border, and perhaps just as simple to collapse the distinctions between land, laws, people, and public organizations that constitute a nation. In fact, public organizations are at the core of a far more complicated reality—and their work is all the more remarkable because through their routine functions of patrolling borders, screening food supplies, stamping passports, and operating schools, they make it possible for individuals to think of nation-states as natural features of their world (or even, in some relatively prosperous countries, to all but take for granted the functions performed by the state). For some of us, the ability of organizations to play this role begs the question of how they evolve, and what we might learn about ourselves when we analyze how our fears and dreams are reflected in public organizations.

These are the reasons why I sought to understand the intersection of law, organizations, and security—and from there it was but a very short step to the FSA and DHS. The more I studied these agencies, the more I sought to discover. As a matter of legal and political history, what emerged struck me as quite a compelling story about how the United States created legal and organizational arrangements designed to further the nation's security. Among other things, I came across many statements from policymakers showing that the early fights over the Federal Security Agency in the late 1930s implicated not only classic inter-branch conflict about presidential prerogatives but also arguments about the case an ambitious president was making to the nation regarding an expansive conception of "security" as broad-based risk management with implications for families and farmers as well as for fighting forces. I found plenty of evidence of strategic discussions deep in the White House on how executive reorganization could recalibrate the power of the presidency relative to Congress. I learned how White House and Federal Security Agency officials worked together to channel federal funds into secret research on offensive biological weapons. I found evidence that Roosevelt's reorganization efforts, though not necessarily motivated by simple concerns over financial efficiency (which was the legal prerequisite Congress established for using his reorganization powers), created an agency with increasing capacity to implement risk management and economic security policies that Roosevelt greatly supported. While my investigation of DHS was more challenging because of limited access to archival resources, an analysis of the agency's early history also reveals continuing debates about the scope of the agency's security-related mission and the order of its priorities.

Bringing some of these ideas to light remained a priority, and became possible only because of the generous support of extraordinary colleagues, friends, and family members. Dara Cohen and Barry Weingast collaborated with me on some early research on the Department of Homeland Security that is included in portions of Chapters 5 and 6, and Connor Raso worked with me on a project that generated some of the ideas included in Chapter 7. Lively conversations with Barry, my friend and graduate school dissertation advisor, were also enormously helpful in developing the argument. At Stanford Law School, I will be ever grateful to Larry Kramer; even in the midst of his work as dean, he focused some of his energy on encouraging me to stay focused on this project. Pam Karlan's friendship and insights have done much to inspire my scholarship over the years, and this project is no exception. My Stanford Law School colleagues Joe Bankman, Richard Craswell, Michele Dauber, Richard Ford, Barbara Fried, Deborah Hensler, Dan Ho, Mark Kelman, Michael McConnell, Jane Schacter, Al Sykes, and Robert Weisberg have been kind, time and again, with their wisdom and insight. I am also grateful to the staff of the Stanford Law School library, including the incomparable library director, Paul Lomio, and the indefatigable Erika Wayne and George Wilson. Across the Stanford campus, I have been lucky enough to be a member of the Center for International Security and Cooperation (CISAC) at Stanford's Freeman Spogli Institute for International Studies. Through CISAC I have also gained friends and colleagues who have greatly enriched this project. I am particularly indebted to Scott Sagan, Lynn Eden, David Holloway, Paul Stockton, and David Kennedy (who offered some particularly helpful reactions at a CISAC seminar where I presented an early version of my research). And I will be ever grateful to Suzanne Keirstead.

Beyond Stanford, I benefited from the reactions of a number of scholars who have also been generous with their feedback, including Malcolm Feely, Matthew Stephenson, Rachel Barkow, Jacob Gersen, Jerry Mashaw, Daniel Carpenter, and David Zaring. Two anonymous reviewers also offered helpful comments. John Ferejohn and Lewis Kornhauser at NYU Law School were kind enough to host a long workshop on an earlier version of this project. There I received stimulating ideas from their students and from political scientists Sandy Gordon and Bernard Grofman. I also benefited greatly from opportunities to present portions of the manuscript at Berkeley, Hastings, and Cornell. My editor, Kate Wahl, of Stanford University Press, has been an indispensable ally without whom this book would still be a stack of marginally legible notes on napkins. I benefited enormously from the work of helpful staff at Archives II in College Park, Maryland, who helped me find a trove of files on the War Research Service (reading through them immediately brought to mind the theme music from a scene in *Raiders of the Lost Ark* when Indiana Jones discovers the Ark). Similarly helpful were the staff at the Franklin D. Roosevelt Presidential Library in Hyde Park, New York, and at the Harry S. Truman Presidential Library in Independence, Missouri.

Not far from the Truman Library in Independence is a granite and limestone monument to the American soldiers who fought in World War I. On a cold December afternoon, when I was close to wrapping up the archival work for this book at the Truman Library, I drove out to Kansas City to see the monument. Built into the hill from which the monument rises is a museum describing the families and towns the soldiers were leaving. At nearly every turn, the pictures and documents on display underscored how the soldiers' achievements were built in some sense on the relationships with family, friends, and mentors that shaped their lives. In a similar vein, I will always feel a special appreciation for Mary Schroeder and Lawrence Friedman, both of whom taught me more than they know about being a lawyer and being a scholar (Lawrence might be surprised by the "lawyer" part). I thank my friends Jose Luis Rojas and Delia Ibarra for their unfailing support of this project and its author. I am blessed with two parents who shared their dreams and helped my brother, Máximo, and me forge the means to make ours come true. Most of all, I am grateful for my wife, Lucy, and our children, Mateo and Ria. They are my dream come true—a dream capable of making even me stop thinking about governing or security. For that remarkable feat and far more, I dedicate this book to them.

List of Abbreviations and Acronyms

AMA   American Medical Association

APHIS   Animal and Plant Health Inspection Service

ATF   Bureau of Alcohol, Tobacco, and Firearms

CBP   Bureau of Customs and Border Protection

CIA   Central Intelligence Agency

CIS   Citizenship and Immigration Services

CWS   Office of Community War Services

DEA   Drug Enforcement Administration

DHS   Department of Homeland Security

DOE   Department of Energy

DOJ   Department of Justice

EIS   Environmental Impact Statement

EPA   Environmental Protection Agency

FAA   Federal Aviation Administration

FBI   Federal Bureau of Investigation

FDA   Food and Drug Administration

FEMA   Federal Emergency Management Agency

FSA   Federal Security Agency

FTC   Federal Trade Commission

GAO   Government Accountability Office

HEW   Department of Health, Education, and Welfare

HHS   Department of Health and Human Services

HSA   Homeland Security Act

HSARPA   Homeland Security Advanced Research Projects Agency

HSIS   Homeland Security Impact Statement

HSO	Homeland Security Office
HUD	Housing and Urban Development Agency
ICE	Immigration and Customs Enforcement
ICS	Incident Command System
IEEPA	International Emergency Economic Powers Act
INS	Immigration and Naturalization Service
NAACP	National Association for the Advancement of Colored People
NHTSA	National Highway Traffic Safety Administration
NIH	National Institutes of Health
NLRB	National Labor Relations Board
NSA	National Security Agency
NSC	National Security Council
OIRA	White House Office of Information and Regulatory Affairs
OSHA	Occupational Safety and Health Administration
PEOC	Presidential Emergency Operations Center
PFO	Principal Federal Official
PHS	Public Health Service
SEC	Securities and Exchange Commission
SSB	Social Security Board
TSA	Transportation Security Agency
WRS	War Research Service

GOVERNING SECURITY

The Twin Problems of Governing Security

A GRAY DAWN BEGAN TO BREAK over New Orleans on Monday, August 29, 2005, as Hurricane Katrina ripped into the Louisiana Coast. It was 6:10 a.m.[1] At that moment, as thousands of people stuck in the Crescent City were still scrambling to find shelter from the storm, the winds were powerful enough to make even the waters of the mighty Mississippi River reverse course to flow away from the ocean.[2] Less than two hours later, a barge broke loose from its moorings, smashing into New Orleans's Industrial Canal. Before long, millions of gallons of water were spilling onto the residential streets of the Lower Ninth Ward and St. Bernard Parish. Upon learning of the breach, the National Weather Service predicted flash floods of up to eight feet of water. The water did not reach the Superdome, where ten thousand refugees had gathered. But the hurricane did. Shortly after the flash flood warning, Katrina tore two holes in the roof of the arena. Elsewhere in the city, water from multiple canal breaches mixed with fuel and industrial runoff. By early afternoon, the breaches were well on their way to placing much of New Orleans under a muddy soup of polluted water, and no fewer than eight Gulf Coast refineries had shut down.[3]

Severe though these consequences were, they did not come as a complete surprise to some public officials. The preceding Friday, three days before Hurricane Katrina struck, Governor Kathleen Blanco had declared a state of emergency in Louisiana.[4] She authorized National Guard commanders to call up to 2,000 reservists to active duty.[5] Governor Blanco ordered an additional 2,000 Guardsmen to active duty the next day.[6] On Sunday, August 28, the state adjutant general, Major General Bennett C. Landreneau, established five task forces to conduct aviation search-and-rescue missions, to deliver food, water, and other supplies, and to help the Corps of Engineers repair storm levees.[7] National Guardsmen also helped implement contraflow—the use of all lanes of the highway system for outbound traffic only—by directing traffic and erecting barriers.[8] Not to be outdone, New Orleans mayor Ray Nagin followed suit on Sunday, declaring his own state of emergency and directing legal counsel to explore whether the mayor could legally force recalcitrant individuals to leave town without facing liability.[9] While state and local officials across much of Louisiana were scrambling to determine how best to protect their citizens and the delicate infrastructure of a region that partly sat below sea level, other Gulf states such as Mississippi also declared states of emergency and began efforts to protect the security of their residents.[10]

On Saturday morning, however, President George W. Bush was, ironically, focused on a different sort of security issue altogether. In his weekly radio address, the president covered the challenges faced by U.S. foreign policy with respect to the Middle East peace process and the Gaza Strip.[11] Although the president had also declared that a "state of emergency" existed in Louisiana and ordered federal agencies to assist state and local authorities, several reports indicate that two key officials in charge of managing that effort—Homeland Security secretary Michael Chertoff and Federal Emergency Management Agency director Michael Brown— did not mobilize the National Guard at that time.[12] Indeed, on Tuesday, several hours after Katrina hit the Gulf Coast, President Bush proceeded with a previously scheduled speech in San Diego discussing the history of America's involvement in World War II and calling on the nation to continue supporting the deployment of American soldiers to Iraq.[13] Even as the president addressed events thousands of miles beyond American shores, a different cluster of security issues was emerging along the Gulf of Mexico. There the looming disaster posed risks to the American energy infrastructure, and to hundreds of thousands of people, in the path of the vast storm. The people and infrastructure of the Gulf Coast region—as richly demonstrated by the infamous British Petroleum oil spill five years later—were all the more exposed because they found themselves in a fragile, low-lying region of bayous, refineries, and oil rigs crisscrossed by canals and by the waters of the Mississippi.

By Tuesday, August 31, fully 80 percent of New Orleans was underwater. Tens of thousands of its residents had themselves flooded into downtown seeking shelter.[14] For five days, about 20,000 people waited inside the Ernest N. Morial Convention Center in New Orleans, turning it into a squalid urban refugee camp.[15] Conditions inside the convention center rapidly deteriorated, reflecting inadequate security policies and insufficient numbers of security personnel.[16] Observers in the region at the time described problems involving young men from "rival housing projects" who brought guns with them and put them to people's heads.[17] Later, "a gang broke into the locked alcohol storage areas . . . [a]nd before long, there were scenes of gangsters drunk, groping after young girls."[18] Youths hot-wired electric utility carts and forklifts, driving them recklessly through crowds of people.[19] Just over a mile away, nearly the same number of people had taken shelter under the torn roof of the Superdome, where refugees faced hunger, squalor, and racial tensions.[20]

Three miles from the Superdome in the direction of Lake Pontchartrain, floodwaters reached the edge of Tulane University's historic campus, stopping just short of the university's main library on Freret Street.[21] Among the government documents in the university's library system was the Homeland Security Act (HSA), the 187-page statute that provided the blueprint for the creation of a new cabinet-level agency focused on the country's interrelated security challenges. Among other things, the law conferred upon the superagency the responsibility for preventing and mitigating disasters such as the one that was at that moment bringing New Orleans to its knees. And while the HSA unquestionably defined the new agency's mission to encompass disasters like the one that was on the verge of flooding Tulane's library, it also—indeed, perhaps inevitably—left a considerable amount of discretion to the executive branch in defining precisely how security priorities should be understood and implemented. In effect, the problems posed by both the floodwaters at the edge of Freret Street and the complicated statute housed in Tulane's library implicated the role of federal bureaus such as FEMA and the Coast Guard, and the priorities of the new cabinet-level Department of Homeland Security (DHS), which was imbued with the legal responsibility for helping Americans manage threats to their security at home.

Actually, the performance of what was then a recently forged cabinet agency poses a stark organizational irony. Despite the fact that DHS was created precisely to improve the nation's capacity to manage disasters, reasonable observers would find it all but impossible to describe the early response to Katrina as a success.[22] A year after Hurricane Katrina devastated the Gulf region, former FEMA director Michael Brown claimed that there was no federal pre-disaster planning because President Bush and Department of Homeland Security secretary Michael Chertoff did not release funds to allow the federal agencies to coordinate a response.[23] Yet Brown himself waited five hours after Katrina struck Louisiana's shoreline before asking his superior, Secretary Chertoff, to authorize sending about 1,000 employees of DHS to the region.[24] The FEMA director also gave them two days to arrive, a decision suggesting that FEMA hardly grasped the full scale of the disaster in New Orleans.[25] Reacting in part to uncertainty regarding the federal role,[26] Brown discouraged state, local, and private efforts to help in the critical hours after the hurricane struck.[27] While Secretary Chertoff was the pivotal national official in charge of emergency response (and of FEMA itself), he failed to activate the national response plan until late Tuesday.[28] Over time, the Coast Guard—a bureau that had been transferred to DHS—continued rescuing people from the rooftops of city districts swelling with toxic floodwaters and earned plaudits from many observers. But despite this effort and the work of thousands of DHS employees, the roles of FEMA and DHS itself provoked continued concern among lawmakers, state and local officials, and the public as the tense days of the initial recovery gave way to the longer-term challenges of reconstruction. These and countless other examples of staggering failure in the federal response contributed to the scale of a tragedy that cost the nation thousands of lives and more than $150 billion.[29]

The survivors who experienced those costs most directly witnessed the destruction of one of the country's most iconic urban communities. Even for Americans who have never set foot on the Gulf Coast, Katrina's consequences will undoubtedly appear to be unique in the nation's history. The human toll and the economic costs reinforce this conclusion, along with the particular set of individuals and circumstances involved. In the days that followed the devastation wrought by the storm itself, Katrina cast a long shadow over the reputations of certain officials and even entire agencies. That shadow also raised for many Americans—including those who weathered the days after the storm at the Morial Convention Center and the Superdome—the question of whether it was all but impossible to expect that federal officials would prioritize the security of thousands of relatively poor residents hard-pressed to leave the Crescent City.

But the detailed analyses of the Katrina response that emerged over the following year tell a more complicated story. In that narrative, ineluctable and related questions arise about the organization of the executive branch and the scope of the executive branch's responsibility for governing the security of the nation. In that story, organizational problems and trade-offs involving security priorities loom large in a drama also implicating the personalities of those involved in running FEMA, the difficulties overcome by the Coast Guard, and the physical and metaphorical breakdown of entire cities. Boxes and lines on a sterile organizational chart are unlikely to explain all the activities of Coast Guard commanders, disaster response experts, or military commanders. Still, the enormous potential of organizational structure to shape the world is reflected in the fact that it is largely the product of laws allocating jurisdiction across agencies. Indeed, within organizations, formal structure can itself become a form of law, binding groups to each other in a specific way. If it is true that few legal arrangements (whether concerning organizational structure, criminal liability, or anything else) are entirely self-enforcing, it is also true that jurisdictional rules, reporting relationships, and response plans can create expectations and guide the behavior of many thousands of public officials.

In part because of this, when explaining what happened during the Katrina response, a host of observers emphasized the consequences of a complicated and recently imposed organizational structure, coupled with choices that downplayed the relative importance of national disasters in the mission of DHS and FEMA. According to some observers, the reorganization of FEMA under DHS took away its "status as an independent, cabinet-level agency. [I]t became a small part of a large department with much broader objectives."[30] After September 11, 2001, FEMA began transferring its focus away from natural disasters and toward the development of antiterrorism capabilities, a trend that accelerated as DHS was being created.[31] FEMA director Brown and DHS secretary Chertoff both stated publicly that they had not been entirely aware of the conditions in New Orleans, even though the media had provided graphic and nearly continuous coverage for days.[32] Subsequent reports indicate that local, state, and federal government officials were unclear about what role to play, and this confusion "exacerbated the pain, suffering, and frustration of disaster victims."[33] Under the National Response Plan, a Principal Federal Official (PFO) is a person "designated by the Secretary of Homeland Security to facilitate federal support to the established Incident Command System (ICS) Unified Command structure and to coordinate overall federal incident management."[34] In fact, several failures in the appointment of the PFO took place before the Hurricane Katrina disaster. DHS secretary Chertoff should have appointed a PFO on Saturday, two days before the hurricane reached land, but instead he waited until Tuesday, one day after the storm had reached land. Chertoff's testimony before the House of Representatives indicated that he was confused about the role of a PFO and had appointed Brown without understanding the scope of a PFO's duties.[35] The uncertainty in roles and responsibilities resulted in the absence of a unified command structure, diluting the capacity of federal officials to leverage available resources.[36]

Running through the story of the Katrina response, then, is a theme that may hold still-larger implications for the country. It concerns how the nation fills the gap between the general imperative reflected in the Homeland Security Act of providing security to the nation and the pressures that arise when a threat like Katrina confronts citizens, civil servants, lawmakers, and presidents. That gap forces us to consider how the nation defines its security priorities, and at the same time, how public officials work and even compete to secure control of the complex organizations that stand between citizens and the threats they face. If we use the existence of this gap to consider the larger social, legal, and political dramas implicated in the Katrina episode, we can readily discern *two* sets of questions that should spark interest among scholars, citizens, and policymakers. First, in a world of complex risks, competing lawmakers and organized interests, and differing ideologies, how do agencies acquire their particular structure within the larger context of law and politics? Why, for example, is FEMA within DHS, and what does that mean? Indeed, why is there a FEMA at all rather than (for example) two or three separate agencies disaggregating natural disaster recovery, civil defense, and flood prevention responsibilities? A second question has perhaps even more far-reaching implications: How do agencies involved in security define that concept for purposes of pursuing their priorities and even defining the kind of risks that the state will manage for its citizens?

This book is about how profoundly our lives have been shaped by these questions. It is also about why these questions turn out to be so thoroughly entangled. The national debates and legislative choices that forged DHS constitute a vivid example of how an advanced industrialized country such as the United States decides how to organize and define its security. In the chapters to come, we will learn how this process is driven not only by differing ideas about the value of some organizational forms over others or distinct views about where natural disaster risks rank relative to threats of terrorist attacks; it is also driven by pluralist political realities that set the stage for struggles among lawmakers, organized interests, and presidents to secure the ability to govern organizations. But first, we can benefit from considering a largely forgotten episode of American history from a time when the nation faced equally stark questions about the scope of security and the allocation of control over executive power.

FROM DHS TO FSA:
ORGANIZATION, SECURITY, AND EXECUTIVE
POWER IN THE ROOSEVELT ADMINISTRATION

Three-quarters of a century before Katrina and DHS, a different irony was playing out against a backdrop of sweeping legal and political change. During the 1930s the administration of Franklin Delano Roosevelt spurred major growth in the federal state by stressing government's role as guarantor of the nation's security.[37] With security as a lodestar, administration priorities led to now-familiar statutory changes catalyzing financial regulation, retirement and unemployment benefits, food safety policies, and energy rules. As the New Deal matured, security-related rationales taking subtly distinct forms—emphasizing international, geostrategic concerns—also bolstered the case for expansive federal power and even blended with the more expansive domestic risk-reduction ideas in the period before World War II. In 1939, for example, the administration wove together multiple strands of its security trope while using a sliver of legal authority for executive reorganization to forge a colossal new Federal Security Agency (FSA). It then proceeded to justify the executive branch's new legal architecture by arguing that the ability to respond to international threats depended on the strengthened domestic capacity provided by the FSA to implement the law effectively in domains such as health and education.[38]

But for all its success in reconstructing the national agenda around an expansive conception of security, by the late 1930s the administration was losing the capacity to secure its own control of the outsized federal state it had created. In *Humphrey's Executor v. United States*,[39] the Supreme Court refused to let the president fire a Federal Trade Commission (FTC) official whose term had been fixed by Congress,[40] thereby eviscerating presidential power over an ever-multiplying empire of independent commissions and opening the door to even greater congressionally imposed limits on presidential power. In the process, the Court rejected the view that proper presidential supervision of the executive branch under Article II depended on the power to fire senior officials, an idea central to the Court's conception of executive power articulated in *Myers v. United States*,[41] decided just a few years earlier.[42] Meanwhile, Congress was increasingly designing the structure of agencies like the Social Security Board (SSB) to disrupt presidential control,[43] blocking White House staff expansion and refusing to grant reorganization authority, which the Roosevelt administration considered essential to securing control of a rapidly growing federal state.[44]

In at least one respect, the story of the FSA evokes the challenges faced by the nation in creating DHS and responding to the Katrina disaster. The FSA, too, illuminates the fertile intersection of two "security" problems: the control that politicians seek to secure over agencies with expansive legal powers, and the security that modern nation-states promise citizens when justifying why public bureaucracies must be given such powers in the first place. Time and again, whether the subject is the Roosevelt-era FSA or the Bush-era DHS, these two security problems turn out to be deeply enmeshed in the web of federal regulatory power. Bureaucratic control helps executive branch officials and their lawyers promote a particular definition of security through legal interpretations, public communications, legislative initiatives, and discretionary decisions. Security concerns, meanwhile, shore up public justifications for organizational changes affecting political control over implementation of the law. By understanding how these two problems intersect, we can grasp underappreciated tensions coursing through public law—such as how agencies shape public perceptions about the laws they implement, how the definition of "security" has changed as the architecture of the executive branch has evolved, and how to understand the consequences of forging the modern-day DHS.

The link between these themes is an extended case study—the first ever—on the remarkable legal and political history of the FSA, an account that at times will diverge sharply from what happened with DHS and at other times will offer eerie parallels. Placing the FSA in the larger context of its bureaucratic brethren, our exploration of the life and times of that agency will show how politicians exploit reorganizations, particularly during or in anticipation of national security emergencies, to reshape agencies' legal mandates by controlling their bureaucratic power.[45] It shows how changes in the organization of political officials, civil servants, and government bureaus can enhance presidential control. Simultaneously, such changes can repackage regulatory activities in relation to the concept of national security, bolstering the political coalitions supporting those functions. These dynamics have typically escaped scholarly attention among academics specializing in bureaucracy, whose work in recent years has tended to focus on elucidating how politicians reorganize government to satisfy a preexisting public demand or to deliberately sabotage agency activities.[46] Nor have scholars in the developing field of national security law fully investigated questions about the scope of national security rather than the surveillance, detention, emergency, or foreign affairs powers deployed in the name of security.

Although the FSA has been all but forgotten, even cursory scrutiny reveals it to be among the more important bureaucracies created in twentieth-century America. It was the gangly and occasionally brash adolescent—equal parts wartime soldier and audacious dreamer—that matured into the federal government's sprawling health, welfare, and civil defense apparatus. The agency was born amid a tangle of administrative changes enshrined in statutes as the New Deal morphed into the American response to World War II. Its litany of statutory responsibilities at once confirms what has today become a familiar picture of federal functions, encompassing medical research, civil defense, social security, federal education assistance, weapons development, and food and drug regulation. But the list also scrambles modern sensibilities about the line dividing conventional national security functions from domestic regulatory activities.

President Roosevelt began blurring that line nearly two and a half years before the Pearl Harbor attacks.[47] On April 25, 1939, he delivered a long-expected announcement about his plans to reshape the architecture of the executive branch.[48] The change in architecture had been on the president's agenda for more than twenty-four months, but the specific changes he had in mind had become possible only three weeks earlier, after Congress grudgingly gave the president limited reorganization powers. Thwarted in an ambitious effort to create a cabinet-level Department of Public Welfare the previous year, the Roosevelt White House nonetheless announced that it would use its more modest reorganization power to unify half a dozen bureaus involved in health regulation, economic security, and education in the new Federal Security Agency. From then on, the FSA expanded steadily. By 1943, the FSA's bureaus included the Public Health Service (PHS), the Social Security Board (SSB), the Office of Education, the Food and Drug Administration (FDA), the Office of Community War Services (CWS), the War Research Service (WRS), and nearly a dozen other organizations.[49] By 1953, the agency became the Department of Health, Education, and Welfare (HEW).[50] And by the 1970s, HEW's budget accounted for nearly half of federal nondefense expenditures, dwarfing the national budget of every country except what was then known as the Soviet Union.[51]

To observers situated in the early twenty-first century, however, the name of the Federal Security Agency foreshadows DHS more than it does a welfare agency. Legal history readily demonstrates how the meaning of "security" is versatile. Until the current economic downturn, the term elicited concepts of economic risk reduction more easily in the 1930s than in recent years. As will become clear, however, some aspects of the FSA's work nonetheless fit readily with more modern applications of the term, presaging its subsequent evolution. It was the FSA that facilitated the re-settlement of Japanese Americans.[52] It was the FSA that laundered White House funds and funneled them into secret biological weapons research even though the United States had signed a treaty outlawing such activity.[53] FSA officials presided over the rapid growth of a national system to train workers for war-related occupations. They set up record-keeping systems to assist a national military draft. The agency's inspectors prevented food contamination while insisting that their mission was essential to the performance of the military, and they sought to limit the spread of sexually transmitted diseases among military personnel. And the agency performed these tasks while it continued—and expanded—its role of issuing social security benefit checks, providing medical services to underserved American communities, screening new drugs, and printing books for the blind.[54]

As the FSA's origins recede into history and are replaced by public scrutiny of episodes like the disastrous DHS Katrina response seven decades later, however, scholars too have remained blind to certain puzzles about its birth, which are also reflected in the story of the birth of DHS.[55] *Why*, for instance, did President Roosevelt create the FSA at all, particularly when doing so involved such an expenditure of scarce political capital and resulted in the removal of some bureaus from agencies where they were already supervised by trusted political lieutenants? The meager scholarly literature on the subject, much of it written at the time of the merger or shortly thereafter, speculates that the president's interest was in more "efficient" government, without defining the concept or considering the more directly political implications of the White House move. *Why* did the agency so pervasively mix social welfare, regulatory, and national security functions, years before the United States became embroiled in World War II? Indeed, *what* was meant by the reference to "security" used to justify expansive legal powers in the early years of the FSA? And how did the FSA's creation affect the work of its bureaus?

The challenge in addressing these questions arises not only from the limited amount of scholarly attention they have received, but also from the fact that we may not always be able to take the public statements of federal officials at face value. For example, despite Franklin Roosevelt's willingness to explain the immediate consequences of creating the FSA in terms of financial and administrative efficiency, he was also perfectly willing to disparage those arguments in private. Small wonder, too, since the efficiency-focused explanations that so heavily draw on prescriptive scholarship in a "public administration" tradition suffer from limitations. First, they are provided with little or no empirical support. Second, they do not consider the full scope of the FSA's legal powers, or the president's special concern for these functions. And finally, they do not place the discussion in the political context of the times, including the battle over Roosevelt's reorganization plans and the developing war-related rhetoric of the administration.[56]

In the pages that follow, the answers will emerge from a more nuanced and theoretically informed investigation of history. In the process, we will learn something about health policy and public organizations—but far more about the battle to define security in the American state.

OVERVIEW OF THE ARGUMENT

Americans listening to one of President Franklin Roosevelt's fireside chats on a cabinet-sized radio in the late 1930s were not, of course, heavily concerned with organizational charts or statutes about executive power, any more than the waterlogged residents of New Orleans in the early twenty-first century were. Indeed, Americans in the 1930s might have scarcely imagined the eventual birth of the Internet. They would have been hard-pressed to imagine the spectacular growth of East Asian economies, or perhaps even the fall of the Soviet Union. They might have been just as surprised, however, at what remains the same in the early twenty-first century. For all that has changed over the course of six or seven decades, in many respects Americans today share a common reality with their forebears from the late 1930s. First, they face multiple sources of insecurity: from financial instability, natural disasters such as Hurricane Katrina, and potential external threats. Second, their government is characterized by the competition to secure control over the organizations that implement the laws that regulate markets and public health, provide services, manage security risks, and otherwise shape people's lives.

At the core of our exploration will be the under-appreciated connection between these two security dynamics—how our nation defines the scope of security through statutory enactments and the architecture of the executive branch, and how presidents, White House aides, lawmakers, civil servants, interest groups, and political actors work within the law to secure control over public organizations. The book offers major case studies about two agencies charged with promoting (and in the process, defining) American security: the now little-known Federal Security Agency and the all-too-familiar Department of Homeland Security. Both cases showcase how much of law and policy pivots on defining the scope of national security during and after a crisis. Both also indicate the stakes in battles to forge the structure of the organizations charged with implementing our public laws, whether they involve disbursing social security benefits, safeguarding public health, or preventing terrorist attacks. As examples of how our nation defined security and then reshaped the federal government to address that definition, these examples prove enormously revealing.

So powerful has been the recent and understandable focus of our government on counterterrorism that we can easily forget how less than a generation ago policymakers questioned how much to define terrorism as a major geostrategic threat. Earlier still, Franklin Roosevelt's New Deal gave meaning to the concept of security through a confluence of public rhetoric and government programs advocating an expansive definition linking public health, government benefits, and national preparedness in agencies such as the Federal Security Agency. The animating principle behind that agency nicely illustrates, and served to advance, Roosevelt's vision of government as a bulwark of security for citizens facing a panoply of threats: domestic crime, adulterated food, financial instability, public health issues, and dictatorships hostile to democracy. The question of how to define national security, perhaps endemic to the nation-state, also runs through more-recent debates about whether environmental protection, response to natural disasters such as Hurricane Katrina, immigration policies that enhance our standing in the world, or public health goals can be properly understood to fit within the modern nation-state's promise to provide security to its citizens.

How those questions are answered depends heavily on the second dynamic described in this book, reflecting the competition of political players (particularly in the executive branch) to secure control over the public organizations through which laws are implemented. These fights sometimes play out in the executive branch or in Congress as compromises are forged to allocate authority among agencies or to create new bureaucracies of staggering size and power, such as the Department of Homeland Security. Competing agendas to secure control over public organizations also animate fundamental legal developments involving separation of powers. This domain of legal doctrine—with executive branch legal interpretations sometimes driving outcomes at least as much as court decisions do—establishes some of the rules of a political game that often involves the creation, dissolution, transfer, restructuring, and conflict over the authority of public organizations. Both political strategies and legal interpretations shape how presidents, White House staff, agency leaders, lawmakers, and organized interests seek to secure control of federal bureaucracies. And these developments shape how society implements different interpretations of national security. Debates about national security, in turn, can provide different actors in the system with an opportunity to increase their control over the functions of government—as did President Jimmy Carter, for example, in his successful effort to frame the creation of an executive department focused on energy policy as a national security imperative.

The book further contends that these two dynamics—defining the scope of security and politicians' competition to secure control of the bureaucracy—are linked to each other through public organizations (whose power includes shaping the scope of security and whose own structure is in turn shaped by debates about the federal role in providing security), law (regulating the structure of, control of, and performance of agencies), and the perceptions of the mass public (which can translate into political support and simultaneously affects agency missions as well as the scope of federal power). Hence, political control over public agencies facilitates efforts to shape public perceptions of security as well as the future development of these agencies, and debates about the scope of security in turn affect the dynamics of political control over public organizations. Central to the argument is the idea that the meaning of the concept of national security is not fixed but is instead given life through choices about the architecture of public agencies and legal interpretations.

Although the argument draws support from a number of historical episodes over the last century as well as theoretical work in law and political science, the book primarily makes its case by telling the stories of the two major government agencies whose origins illustrate the entanglement between the scope of security and the competition to secure political control of agencies. The FSA was a preeminent public organization bridging the latter New Deal and the emergence of the Cold War state. Although the budget of its successor agency eventually dwarfed that of most nations on earth, the FSA has been almost entirely neglected by scholars and is unknown to the public. Telling its surprising story is one of the book's major contributions. The other is the story of the latter-day DHS. Both the agency's importance and its failures have become all too familiar to scholars and educated laypeople. Less familiar are the curious twists involved in the agency's origins, its concomitant parallels to and differences from the Roosevelt-era Federal Security Agency, and underappreciated dilemmas about the scope of security that were raised behind the scenes during the department's response to Hurricane Katrina or in the work of bureaus such as the Coast Guard.

To link the case studies with the book's core argument, I explore certain unresolved puzzles about the history of these agencies. I consider why Roosevelt decided to expend political capital on executive reorganization despite his decision to back down on the fight for judicial reorganization. Why was it not enough for loyal but separate cabinet secretaries to oversee the bureaus from which the FSA was ultimately forged? I then ask: How did the creation of the FSA affect the day-to-day work of administering statutory programs? And in a more recent context, why did the Bush administration also decide to undertake an effort to reshape security policy through DHS? Why did Bush and his advisors switch, moreover, from opposing the creation of DHS to supporting it? By addressing these puzzles in light of the book's theoretical perspective, we can learn something about how the concept of security has changed over time and how it is given meaning through organizational choices as well as legal interpretations.

The book's theoretical perspective, in turn, is meant to link fights over how the public understands the role of government, choices about the architecture of public organizations, and developments involving the law's implementation and interpretation. It reflects some simple but important ideas informed by developments in organization theory, political economy, and the law. Politicians seek to advance competing agendas within the bounds of legal and institutional rules that are frequently difficult to change. These agendas often turn on efforts to shape the law's implementation by having an impact on the massive public organizations that epitomize the advanced industrialized nation-state, such as the Federal Security Agency, the Department of Homeland Security, the Department of Energy (DOE), or the Federal Reserve. Less commonly appreciated by scholars and educated laypeople, however, are two additional factors: the impact of crises on political conditions and the potential for public organizations to reshape what the public expects from its government.

By juxtaposing the story of these agencies and a theoretical backdrop emphasizing the importance of agency structure, crises, and goal-seeking behavior by individuals, the book will also make several additional contributions to public law, American political development, and security studies consistent with its broader argument. *First*, the book addresses the aforementioned historical puzzles about public organizations and the laws they implement. Readers will learn why Roosevelt sought to use his scarce political capital in the late 1930s on an uphill battle to get executive reorganization authority and create the new Federal Security Agency, despite the fact that loyal political allies were already overseeing the key bureaus that he shoehorned into the new organization. The book addresses how the creation of that new agency affected the work of public bureaus handling some of the core components of Roosevelt's domestic agenda. It sheds light on why President Bush oddly switched from disfavoring the creation of a cabinet-level homeland security department following the September 11 attacks to offering a plan for such a department that actually exceeded the size and scope of previous proposals made by congressional advocates of reorganization. Tying together the answers to these puzzles is the reality that the concept of national security has a contested scope, and fights about that scope raise core questions about the law and the role of the nation-state itself.

Second, the book makes theoretical contributions for scholars of law and political science, centering on the project's new account of how public organizations shape the law by affecting public perceptions (about matters such as the scope of national security, or the immediacy of external threats). A related contribution involves developing examples of how and why politicians sometimes have incentives to invest in the capacity of public organizations to do their job effectively rather than (as some scholars have argued) simply taking credit for reshaping agency architecture without being concerned about agency performance (or, in some cases, affirmatively seeking to sabotage such performance).

Third, the project sheds light on separation-of-powers disputes. It showcases how Roosevelt responded to setbacks in the courts by pursuing executive reorganization, and how the Bush administration later sought to structure DHS to facilitate a considerable degree of de facto presidential control. The book also argues that principled solutions to such disputes will elude courts, lawyers, and the public if they fail to consider the extent of presidential control achieved through reorganizations. In contrast, many judges and scholars underscore the value of simple, unchanging rules in this context.

Fourth, the project offers some underappreciated historical insights about Franklin Roosevelt and the New Deal, and about the creation of DHS three-quarters of a century later. The book describes how Roosevelt used incremental strategies to reshape legal and political realities in response to political difficulties with Congress. It chronicles how the White House used its funds to secretly support biological weapons research disguised as a public health initiative. The Bush administration, meanwhile, seemed far less interested in using reorganization as an exercise in enhancing state capacity. Whereas officials in the Bush administration and their allies in Congress felt strongly concerned about gaps in state capacity in certain areas—most notably the cluster of functions concerned with terrorism prevention—they were far less concerned about overall state capacity as it related to environmental protection, public health, and even (initially) natural disaster preparedness. These decisions were reflected in choices about how to design the statute creating DHS, the Homeland Security Act, as well as choices about funding and organizational priorities affecting how laws under the purview of DHS were implemented.

The pages that follow also highlight some surprising parallels (as well as differences) between Bush and Roosevelt. Both presidents reorganized the executive branch to enhance their control of federal bureaus and promote their particular visions of risk regulation. But the substantive visions of security that each pursued through his work to re-forge the executive branch were in stark contrast—with Roosevelt articulating a vision of the nation-state as an active regulator of risk and provider of public services that would ultimately strengthen (according to him) the nation's capacity to withstand external threats, and Bush focused on articulating a more circumscribed vision of geostrategic security and counterterrorism. These historical precedents emphasize how much the future of the nation-state is likely to pivot substantially on how societies interpret laws and structure organizations to choose among competing visions of national security.

In light of such parallels, though, the overall resemblance of different security agencies should not be overstated. Even without thinking of security in the expansive fashion that Franklin Roosevelt did, no two American security agencies are exactly the same. In scrutinizing agencies such as the FBI and the National Security Division of the Department of Justice (DOJ), the Department of Energy, and the Department of Defense (DOD), it is clear that each has a distinctive story. And while it is not my goal to address the fate of each of these agencies through the Cold War and thereafter, the approach developed here holds important implications beyond the FSA and DHS. Whereas agencies have some role in helping Americans manage domestic or external risks, one can expect presidents and lawmakers to compete for control of these entities. One can anticipate the high stakes that arise when agencies define the scope of their security-related missions, and when crises serve as inflection points for policymakers seeking to reshape the agencies that implement the law.

Ultimately, the spike of interest in the concept of homeland security is furnishing opportunities to remake the domestic regulatory state similar to those that Roosevelt had in anticipation of World War II. Today's world of elaborate infrastructure problems, global non-state actors, and mature regulatory agencies renders the historical context different. The George W. Bush administration's narrow substantive definition of security, with implications that tend to cut against expansive regulatory activity in domains such as environmental protection or federal involvement in providing health services, is also different.[57] But the cycle epitomizing fundamental conflicts over the architecture of law is not: policymakers mold law by defining security and then seek to command the implementation of that law by securing control over bureaucracies.

CHAPTER 2

Rethinking Law, Security, and Organizational Structure

THE CRISP, CLOUDLESS SKY on the eastern seaboard of the United States on September 11, 2001, was almost precisely the inverse of what the Gulf Coast experienced in the hours before Katrina struck. If anything, the bright blue September skies that morning made what unfolded later in the day all the more shocking. By mid-morning, approximately 3,000 people had been killed in an audacious series of terrorist attacks. Millions more were affected in the months that followed—months that eroded the nation's sense of security and reshaped its immigration rules, its financial markets, and its executive branch institutions. In fact, the pressing domestic issues that confronted the White House immediately following the attacks offer a compelling example of the intimate bond between physical security threats and the web of domestic activities carried out by the federal government.

Beginning almost immediately after the attacks, White House Deputy Chief of Staff Joshua Bolten began convening a "domestic consequences" group scrambling to organize federal emergency assistance, to oversee allocation of federal assistance and analyze options for compensating victims, to reopen financial markets, and to shoulder competing pressures regarding whether and how to return civil aviation, ports, and land borders to something close to normal operations.[1] Far-reaching consequences also affected millions of Americans in the wake of the Katrina disaster in 2005, and millions ranging from Vietnamese American fishermen to the families of oil workers were affected in the wake of the Deepwater Horizon/ British Petroleum oil spill in 2010. In all these cases, drastic changes in the well-being of large numbers of Americans forced public agencies and ordinary citizens to mobilize even as people struggled in far-flung corners of the nation to continue their daily routines.

Universities were not immune to the effects of these disasters. Students and faculty at New York University found their entire neighborhood cordoned off after the 9/11 attacks. The Katrina disaster left much of Tulane University underwater, its students scattering to campuses across the country for months. In a more intellectual sense, however, scholars at universities have long been interested in the issues of national security, organization theory, and public law that were so powerfully implicated in these disasters. The 9/11 attacks galvanized concerns about the organization of security, spawning not only scholarly work to understand how rivalries between the FBI and the Central Intelligence Agency (CIA) (for example) could exacerbate the risks faced by Americans but also bipartisan commissions and lengthy government reports. But scholars writing in all of these fields have only scratched the surface in areas to which this book makes lasting contributions. Authors have focused enormous attention on the New Deal, and some scholars (particularly David Kennedy) have generated fascinating work about how the Roosevelt administration approached risk regulation. Nonetheless, authors have had almost nothing to say about the history of the FSA or its subsequent development into one of the major agencies of twentieth-century America. One can find a lot more about the origins of DHS, though gaps still remain in terms of understanding the consequences of this merger. A rich literature, associated with the work of scholars such as McNollgast, Terry Moe, Jerry Mashaw, Sharyn Epstein, David O'Halloran, and Amy Zegart, discusses how institutional rules and legal enactments shape the competition for control of agencies. While this work generates important insights about issues like how competing political goals can generate dysfunctional agencies, it evinces a relatively rigid separation between scholars of legal doctrine, historians of institutional development, and specialists in examining mass political behavior. Some scholars writing about "homeland security," Stephen Flynn being perhaps the most articulate in this regard, have made a case for a more expansive concept of security pulling together geostrategic defense, counterterrorism, infrastructure protection, and natural disaster response. These projects have had little to say, however, about the historical context of these debates or how legal interpretations and political agendas affect them.

In contrast, this book is ambitious in scope because it straddles a host of academic distinctions to make a more far-reaching (yet historically grounded) argument. In particular, it will illustrate the extent to which the meaning of security is heavily contested in the modern nation-state (in contrast to how the academic field of security studies and the parallel domain of national security law both largely take as a given what we mean by security). It will provide exhaustive case studies of how changes in organizational structure shape agency mandates and (ultimately) the law's implementation. We know exceedingly little about the full range of consequences of organizational design on law and policy. In contrast to conventional abstract treatments of separation of powers, this book will address larger questions about public law in the context of specific organizational changes (e.g., it will discuss how Roosevelt tried to mitigate losses in the courts by reorganizing executive branch agencies and playing up national security concerns). And finally, in the process, the project will provide rich details about the origins and early operations of DHS—even in crucial episodes such as the response to Hurricane Katrina—and about the history of the FSA—an agency whose existence was the culmination of a decades-long fight to create a health agency and which became the conduit for federal budgets larger than those of nearly all countries on earth. To understand those details, however, we need to start by surveying some of the intellectual territory at the fertile intersections of law, political science, and organization theory.

Admittedly, some of this project addresses scholarly—and in some cases specialized—questions of history, legal principle, and organization theory. Ultimately, though, it speaks to contemporary social and political concerns in three ways. First, the way we define national security will affect risk regulation, civil liberties, and ultimately the scope and future of a nation-state that increasingly justifies its raison d'être in terms of securing its citizens. Second, our ability to manage pollution and global warming, to educate, to frustrate terrorist mobility, to control crime, to protect the food supply, and to build a world-class immigration system (among other challenges) all depend perhaps more than anything else on our capacity to build effective, complex public organizations. Third, American democracy's aspirations are supposed to be reflected in its legal commitments. The meaning of those commitments depends not only on court decisions or even legislative enactments, but on organizational realities such as what department has jurisdiction over disaster relief, or how political appointees interpret their organic agency statutes. An insightful new book addressing the interplay of constitutional, statutory, and administrative decision making helps put these points in context. In *The Republic of Statutes*, William Eskridge and John Ferejohn upend many settled ideas about how law develops, and in particular how constitutional change occurs.[2] Central to their argument is the importance of statutory implementation and administrative practice in shaping long-term legal commitments in domains ranging from monetary policy to civil rights. My account, in turn, offers a story of how law and politics forge the organizations that play such a preeminent role—sometimes with surprising results—in that process of statutory and administrative elaboration. In a fashion, statutes are to the U.S. Constitution what organizations are to statutes—the means through which principle becomes concrete.

ORGANIZING GOVERNANCE

Observers from Max Weber to modern judges and political scientists have readily appreciated politicians' interest in delegating the execution of legal mandates to agencies. Nearly every one of government's legal responsibilities is implemented through such agencies. Bureaucratic structures seem inherent in the very essence of many of the state's legal responsibilities—such as distributing public benefits in accordance with statutory criteria or monitoring private sector behavior for compliance with statutory rules.[3] The difficulties associated with closing military bases illustrate another rationale for delegation, as that allows politicians to achieve desired goals without bearing the full political cost themselves.[4] It is also conceivable that politicians may leverage the capacity of agencies to amass expertise and, in the process, solve complicated technical problems important to the politicians' goals. These routinely accepted rationales for delegation have something in common. They recognize that a defining feature of the modern administrative state—in both the United States and most non-failed states—is the delegation of legal power to agencies by strategic politicians.

In contrast to our relatively clear picture of why agencies exist at all, we have a much blurrier image of why they are structured as they are, why their structures or jurisdictions change over time, and what effect bureaucratic structure actually has on legal mandates. The uncertainty arises not from a lack of potentially compelling explanations but from questions about which of the conventional rationales proves particularly compelling in explaining the fate of a particular agency and its legal mandates. More fundamentally, one might question whether the existing approaches provide a sufficient explanation for all the important bureaucratic phenomena that merit investigation. This chapter surveys those approaches and provides a conceptual map for updating them to better explain the trajectory of the FSA and similar entities. We begin with a brief (re)formulation of why public agencies that are charged with the regulation of risks—whether they involve conventional national security and counterterrorism or other functions—occupy a central role in the modern American state.

Regulations can protect fragile ecosystems and save lives. They can also affect the economic interests of businesses, industries, and regions. Whether the goal is counterterrorism, drug enforcement, or environmental protection, regulations become meaningful through the work of public agencies. The more prominent the role of regulatory bureaucracies in managing the environment, shaping public priorities, affecting the costs of doing business, and calibrating risks, the greater the effort politicians and organized interests will make to control public agencies.[5]

Consider, for example, the agency that perhaps survived the Katrina response with its reputation in the best condition: the Coast Guard. The captains, crews, regulators, maintenance workers, and analysts who work for the agency demonstrate not only the complexities of overlapping environmental, safety, and homeland security responsibilities, but also the stakes riding on regulatory decisions. An example: the cruise ship industry contributes more than $11 billion to the American economy and about 170,000 jobs.[6] The industry also generates vast quantities of waste. The extent to which the industry degrades its surrounding environment depends to a substantial degree on the content and enforcement of federal regulations. So does the extent to which the industry remains as lucrative as it has been.[7] Not surprisingly, the industry has explicitly decided to become increasingly involved in politics as a means of ensuring attention to its concerns.[8] Its representatives have made extensive political contributions, and devoted particular attention to reining in Coast Guard regulatory enforcement.[9] Political controversy has also enveloped a range of other facets of Coast Guard regulatory activity. In 1994, for instance, Louisiana representative Billy Tauzin sought to legislatively invalidate Coast Guard regulations that imposed higher liability standards on companies involved in spills of oil and toxic materials, asserting that the absence of regulatory relief would make it all but impossible for some shippers to operate.[10]

These examples help explain why politicians and organized interests seek to affect the performance of regulatory agencies such as the Coast Guard. But it is not always easy for them to do so. Civil society groups, trade associations, and members of the public often support the goals of regulatory programs. Armed with public support for regulation, legislators and agency officials may gain the political ammunition to resist cutbacks in environmental, health, and safety policies.[11] When Ronald Reagan became president, for instance, he explicitly announced his opposition to an elaborate regulatory state and appointed a number of administrative officials who shared this view. Even with the administration's relative popularity, the high-profile deregulatory policies of Reagan appointees encountered considerable resistance. In some cases, litigants seeking stricter regulatory enforcement used the courts to stop agencies from watering down regulatory provisions. For example, the Reagan-era leadership of the National Highway Traffic Safety Administration (NHTSA) sought to roll back passive-restraint rules to improve automobile safety, but insurance companies and consumer groups persuaded the courts that the agency was acting arbitrarily in doing so.[12] In other cases, high-profile officials who were particularly explicit about their efforts to curtail regulatory programs paid a political price for appearing to overstep the bounds of their authority. Reagan administration Environmental Protection Agency (EPA) administrator Anne M. Burford, one such official, eventually resigned under pressure as a result.[13]

NAVIGATING WITH A CLEAR DIRECTION VS. HIDDEN COURSE CHANGES: ORGANIZATIONS, REGULATION, AND ACCOUNTABILITY

The high-profile public battles over regulation that characterized the Reagan administration reinforce the idea that presidential administrations are supposed to be accountable to the public in part on the basis of what they choose to say and do about regulatory policy. In principle, the existence of accountability justifies a number of familiar features of the regulatory state, such as an extensive role of the White House Office of Information and Regulatory Affairs (OIRA)[14] and the presumption that agency legal interpretations are entitled to deference.[15] Justice Scalia cites accountability when excoriating courts that fail to defer sufficiently to agency legal interpretations.[16] Justice Rehnquist, too, echoed the accountability fugue in the passive-restraints case, in which the Supreme Court invalidated the Reagan administration's move to dilute automobile safety regulations. Dissenting from the majority opinion, Rehnquist praised the alleged virtues of the executive branch's accountability for its regulatory decisions. In his view, the Reagan administration was simply carrying out publicly ratified choices when it sought deregulation at NHTSA and EPA.[17] Rehnquist did not persuade the majority in the passive-restraints case with this argument. Nonetheless, judges, lawyers, and scholars have often found such assertions to be persuasive over the years, and have repeated the mantra of presidential accountability in a host of regulatory contexts. Given the importance of passive restraints in automobiles, reductions in air pollution, marine safety, and the potential costs of regulation, voters are supposed to respond to changes in regulatory policy when making political choices.

But do they? Upon closer inspection, the basic story of how the public monitors executive branch regulatory policy brushes over a host of complexities. It is doubtful, for example, whether voters routinely appreciate the full complexity of regulatory decisions at NHTSA, EPA, FEMA, or the Coast Guard. Moreover, because of political opposition engendered by regulatory policy changes, presidential administrations may aspire to hide what they are doing. By moving less publicly, politicians interested in ratcheting down regulatory enforcement can minimize the risks inherent in directly taking on policies that the public and organized interests might want to protect if the changes were more readily apparent. In short, accountability of politicians—and particularly the executive branch—for regulatory policy changes has become a foundational assumption of modern American public law. Yet accountability can be costly to those who must shoulder public scrutiny for regulatory changes. Consequently, we should expect that some politicians craving changes in regulatory policy will look for strategies that avoid such public scrutiny.

The risk of unwelcome public attention forces politicians to navigate through a dilemma when seeking major cuts in regulatory activity while attempting to minimize public opposition: how might regulatory activity be discreetly diluted? One tactic is to simply avoid public confrontation, instead using appropriations riders in Congress. Lawmakers allied with Microsoft sought to use such a tactic to stifle antitrust enforcement by the Justice Department.[18] In some cases, even appropriations riders can draw so much attention that their sponsors fail to achieve their goals. But by using a technical change in appropriations, Microsoft's supporters leveraged the substantial power of appropriations subcommittees and avoided taking an explicit position against the substance of the antitrust laws that Microsoft was accused of violating.

Policymakers can also use changes in agency structure or missions to affect governance. If they modify an agency's mission, place it in a new bureaucratic context where political appointees emphasize new priorities, or load it with new responsibilities but restrict its resources, a de facto change in regulatory policy may become possible. In response to such changes, bureaus' organizational cultures may evolve. Political appointees with different goals can reorient a bureau's priorities. Bureaus shouldering new responsibilities can become a locus of fierce internal competition for limited resources, playing out amid signals from political superiors as to what priorities can fall by the wayside. Such possibilities led the Roosevelt administration to seek removal of the Public Health Service from the Treasury Department in the late 1930s.[19] The bureau's health-related missions were among Treasury's lowest priorities. When President Roosevelt encountered an increasingly hostile congressional coalition blocking his efforts to strengthen the Public Health Service, he turned to a more subtle approach: enhancing what the bureau was able to accomplish by placing it in a new entity that would be more supportive of its health-focused mission. Decades later, between the 1970s and the 1990s, legislators hostile to another Treasury agency—the Bureau of Alcohol, Tobacco, and Firearms (ATF)—used a different organizational tactic to shape bureaucratic activity. Because lawmakers succeeded in pressuring ATF to assume additional responsibilities for investigating federal gun cases without corresponding increases in resources, they effectively diluted firearms-related regulatory activity.[20]

Wary of even the scrutiny generated by these indirect tactics, politicians may discover unique opportunities to pursue budgetary and bureaucratic changes affecting regulatory policy in the midst of a national crisis, or in its immediate aftermath. If crises by definition focus attention on some national problems rather than others, they may provide cover for politically difficult substantive changes in agency mission or otherwise subtly affect regulatory functions. As public attention shifts to focus on matters such as the energy crisis (in the 1970s) or counterterrorism (in the early 2000s), the political constraints that keep the status quo in place begin to loosen. Hence, legislative action becomes possible in response to the new political circumstances, though such action ordinarily would have been blocked by watchful lawmakers trying to protect existing arrangements. Bureaucratic resistance may become easier to overcome. The result can be a new organizational structure, changed budget priorities, and new responsibilities imposed on bureaus, changes that together forge a new context for administrative action.

BUILDING BLOCKS FOR A THEORY OF LAW AND ORGANIZATION: STRATEGIC ACTION, DIVIDED CONTROL, CRISIS, AND CULTURE

How then do public organizations evolve, and how might they be subject to political control? Casual observers of organization theory might be forgiven for assuming that we already know much of what there is to know about how organizational structure affects the implementation of legal mandates. There is little doubt that beginning in the latter half of the twentieth century, scholars greatly clarified our understanding of organizations. We know, for example, that politicians may use the creation of an agency as a means of satisfying a public demand for action on a particular issue[21] or that they may deliberately set up mechanisms designed to impede organizational effectiveness.[22] It is also clear from a substantial body of research in institutional sociology and social psychology that organizations may spontaneously develop internal routines and cultures that take on a life of their own, leading individuals and groups to interpret the law in accordance with certain patterns that may or may not correspond to prescriptive standards about those legal mandates.[23] In more recent years, political scientists and scholars in law and economics have shed light on how bureaus may be understood to be part of a principal-agent dynamic, where politicians make decisions about how to structure organizations and what powers to give them in accordance with their expectations of how those powers will be used.[24] While all of these perspectives reveal important features of what could be called the organizational logic of legal mandates, case studies of how organizations develop and how they carry out their legal mandates may shed light on crucial questions that remain.

To better understand some of the most prevalent approaches seeking to explain the impact of developments in bureaucratic structure on legal mandates, we might begin by asking how those approaches would explain a *change* in bureaucratic structure such as the one that created the FSA. Policymakers prefer to treat structural changes as a means of achieving prescriptive benefits, as implied in executive branch statements extolling the creation of DHS, the Department of Energy, and the Office of the Director of National Intelligence.

But policymakers' claims should be regarded with considerable skepticism. Many legal mandates prove far too ambiguous to let lawmakers or executive branch officials easily discern *what* organizational changes should be treated as achieving prescriptive benefits. Consider, for example, the new Food, Drug, and Cosmetic Act passed during the New Deal enhancing the power of the FDA; the Social Security Act and its technical complexities; or authority for the PHS to fight infectious diseases. Moreover, history and theory give us considerable reason to question the prescriptive justifications policymakers give for changes in bureaucratic structure. President George W. Bush, for example, pursued the creation of a vast homeland security bureaucracy despite the misgivings of many of his advisors who believed such a move could threaten bureaus' abilities to undertake even security-related functions.[25] The initial structure of the Defense Department served the interests of the military services at the expense of those of the larger public.[26] And even when there is little political disagreement, the costs and benefits of reorganization are often highly uncertain and counterintuitive.[27]

As an alternative, one prominent line of scholarship assumes that structural changes primarily involve benefits of symbolic position-taking with no real effect on the implementation of legal mandates. James Q. Wilson's work is one example and even discusses the creation of HEW itself—with no empirical support cited.[28] This perspective proves especially attractive to those who would consider the development of the state—and of the law—to be most readily controlled by broad social forces. Hence, at one level, the contrast between the views of those who think organizational structure has a limited impact and those who think it is central comes down to a contrast between the sort of macro-level determinism associated with Marx and the focus on hierarchy and organizations reflected in Weber's canonical writings.[29] Even for those who consider the development of law and policy to arise in a more dynamic context, there may be reasons to question whether bureaucratic structure tends to prove more than window dressing in light of broad social forces or large-scale political trends. Neorealism in international relations, for example, consistently questions the impact of internal bureaucratic politics and, by implication, of differences in bureaucratic structure.[30] Other scholars might agree that changes in agency structure are associated with symbolic position-taking activities but emphasize that their impact is to create a dysfunctional agency;[31] and still others suggest that formal organization spreads along with ideas that become fashionable—regardless of whether they advance political agendas or prescriptive goals.[32]

There is plainly some overlap among these approaches in terms of both how they are deployed as explanations and how they might be defined in principle. But each nonetheless reflects a somewhat distinct focus in explaining structure, and, accordingly, each is often deployed as a sort of dominant organizing principle to interpret how developments in structure affect the implementation of legal mandates. Because this analysis is a detailed case study of a major public agency, the focus is on the more fundamental question of whether existing approaches sufficiently explain how a major portion of the federal government developed. We can begin addressing that question by evaluating the extent to which some of the dominant approaches give a convincing account of bureaucratic structure in a variety of contexts—in particular, in the evolution of the FSA.

What soon becomes clear is that the preceding approaches seem to explain some, but not all, facets of organizational structure. If there is a problem with assuming that changes in structure will generally enhance efficiency, there is also a problem with assuming that reorganizations are purely symbolic. Although institutional sociologists rightly caution that informal routines and cultures may occasionally dwarf the importance of formal lines of authority, other scholars have shown structural changes to matter in a variety of contexts. The creation of DHS led to cuts in Coast Guard environmental activity.[33] The Carter-era Department of Energy, a creation rich with opportunities for the administration to reap symbolic rewards, also centralized power over the Strategic Petroleum Reserve and redistributed control over the national laboratory system.[34] In short, while questions about the precise impact of structural changes remain to be addressed, it seems more sensible to assume that structural changes will have *some* effect than to assume they will have none (at least in the absence of context-specific information suggesting that the structural changes are entirely a sham).[35]

Similar problems beset the proposition that changes in bureaucratic structure tend to be motivated by the goal of, and inexorably lead to, creating organizational dysfunction. It is surely true that not all agencies are built to attain a demanding standard of success or efficiency. An agency lacking the capacity to enforce the laws under its jurisdiction or otherwise poorly designed to achieve its putative goals may arise as a result of legislative efforts to harmonize competing priorities. In some cases legislative coalitions may deliberately seek an agency that lets them claim credit for addressing a problem but lacks the structure or resources necessary to create political problems. It is one thing to accept that such agencies arise; it is quite another to imply that organizational dysfunction is unavoidable. Some changes in bureaucratic structure are not plainly dysfunctional, such as the creation of the Joint Chiefs of Staff or the Federal Reserve Board. It is not clear why the Roosevelt administration would *want* some of the agencies and programs for which it had fought so hard—including the SSB, the FDA, and legacy New Deal agencies such as the National Youth Administration or the Civilian Conservation Corps—to be "dysfunctional." Even defining what counts as "dysfunctional" is beset by conceptual difficulties similar to those associated with defining "success" in the implementation of legal mandates.[36]

Finally, there is a problem with explaining structure primarily through the spread of ideas that become popular among the public or policymaking elites and are adopted without conflict. This perspective may explain why dysfunctional states in African nations have science ministries when they have essentially no science going on, but it does not account for the intense strategic activity and political conflict surrounding structural questions in many advanced industrialized nations. The creation of the FSA, for example, was part of a long-term struggle over whether health, welfare, and security responsibilities would be concentrated in a single, powerful agency. It strains both theory and historical analysis to assume that all of this reflected the diffusion of ideas; nor can that rationale fully account for the striking differences that persist in bureaucratic structure across nation-states.[37]

Whatever those differences might be, it is hard to separate the political activity surrounding legal choices about organizational structure from the idea that political actors engage in strategic action. In the American system, for example, eager new lawmakers from politically polarized districts, seasoned Senate committee chairmen secure in their reelection, recently confirmed agency commissioners, White House advisors, and lawyers representing organized interests often differ in what they want from government. Their very ideas about ultimate goals may be confused or uncertain. But in the contested arena of the regulatory state, what these actors have in common is an impulse toward strategic action. It is all but impossible to make sense of organizations without assigning a central role to the strategies that political actors use to pursue their goals. Too much is riding on who supervises an organization, which officials make ultimate judgments of fact and value, whose legal advice is considered authoritative, and who controls the purse strings to assume that choices about organizational structure only occasionally or intermittently provoke strategic behavior.

As used here, the term "strategic behavior" simply suggests that legislators, executive branch officials, and organized interests seek to achieve concrete goals through changes in structure. Precisely *what* those goals are may vary to a considerable degree. Some participants, such as legislators imposing procedural requirements on administrative agencies, may be interested simply in improving their ability to monitor what bureaucratic organizations do. The National Rifle Association's interest in the responsibilities of agents at the Bureau of Alcohol, Tobacco, and Firearms may stem from its keen sense that a bureau whose budget is held constant while the organization is shouldering additional responsibilities may be less able to carry out regulatory activities.[38] Regardless of the content of its goals, however, the challenge of achieving its objectives may encourage participants in the bargaining over bureaucratic structure to act in ways that are at odds with their public pronouncements.

Scholarly observers and legal practitioners commonly recognize that statutes and regulations are shaped by strategic action. But why would bureaucratic *structure*—in effect, the rules governing where in the *United States Government Manual* certain bureaus appear and what officials are listed as being in charge of them—be subject to strategic activity? After all, it is not difficult to think of examples of organizational realities' failing to conform to bureaucratic structure. Despite the fact that former FBI director J. Edgar Hoover was nominally a subordinate of the attorney general, he stopped behaving like one soon after becoming director.[39] Conversely, nominally independent agencies such as the Federal Reserve Board and the National Labor Relations Board (NLRB) may be subject to political influence through appointments and appropriations.[40] With these examples in mind, some observers may be skeptical about the importance of bureaucratic structure. They might even deploy a simple political "Coase theorem," implying that bureaucratic changes are unlikely to have much importance, perhaps only reflecting preexisting distributions of political power. In effect, they would suggest that perhaps—other things being equal—formal bureaucratic structures do not matter much in a world where organized interests, legislators, and politicians have some mix of interests and powers to direct what public organizations actually do.[41] This conclusion might be bolstered by a particularly expansive reading of the work on institutional sociology and social psychology emphasizing the limits of formal structure in reshaping norms, routines, and informal networks that arise within organizations.[42]

Yet formal bureaucratic structure is the legal backdrop against which the policymaking game is played. Though formal structure rarely tells the whole story of organizational power over legal mandates, most participants in the drama of governance proceed on the assumption that hiring decisions, policy priorities, budget requests, office assignments, and future career advancement all depend to some extent on formal lines of bureaucratic authority. Politicians and interest groups engage in bitter fights over whether an agency should be a commission or a typical administrative agency, whether a position should be subject to Senate confirmation, or whether, for example, the U.S. Biological Survey should be an independent bureau of the Interior Department or a subsidiary office of the U.S. Geological Survey.[43] The recurrence and intensity of these fights suggest something other than mass delusion about the importance of bureaucratic structure. Moreover, existing work in political economy and sociology suggests that structure can have effects by conditioning residual decision-making rights and shaping expectations (both internal and external) regarding accountability. Even the territory of modern administrative law suggests that structure is likely to matter because it determines who decides how to interpret an ambiguous legal mandate.[44]

In effect, arguing that lines of organizational jurisdiction are entirely inconsequential is likely to be as difficult as arguing that lines of geographic jurisdiction are inconsequential. The relevance of bureaucratic structure is also supported by theories grounded in sociology, political science, economics, and psychology. Broadly speaking, institutional sociology, political economy, and social psychology approaches all suggest that formal lines of authority, jurisdictional limits, and formal hierarchical arrangements should be expected to change how legal mandates are carried out. The effects may not be salutary, intended, or obvious. Nonetheless, from an intellectual perspective, it is a radical position indeed to suggest that formal organizational structure should routinely have no effect on how legal mandates are carried out.[45]

Politicians have repeatedly treated structure as particularly important in the context of health, education, and security. Major legislative fights occurred in connection with Roosevelt's reorganization plans over Truman's efforts to elevate the FSA to cabinet status and (earlier) over whether to create a federal health department. Moreover, while there is next to no scholarship specifically on the FSA or even on the development of HEW, what little is known suggests that the FSA's existence was eventful and perhaps even momentous. Between the late 1930s and the early 1950s—when HEW became a fixture of the president's cabinet—the FSA's bureaus matured. The FDA and the Social Security Administration radically expanded their budgets.[46] The National Institutes of Health (NIH) effectively began their modern existence as the premier funders of federal intramural medical research.[47] And the public heard countless times from high-level presidential appointees how intimately connected the federal government's health and welfare functions were to the overall success of the American national security effort.[48]

Now consider the implications of divided political control, and how it interacts with the fact that the ultimate social welfare implications of organization are often ambiguous. If strategic action is a recurring feature of the process shaping bureaucratic jurisdiction over legal mandates, then divided control is nearly always its corollary. Even dictators rarely have an entirely free hand in shaping their bureaucracies. Despite the fact that FDR himself was often accused by political elites of seeking dictatorial powers through reorganization, the reorganization powers he sought in 1938 would have been exercised in the shadow of legislative control. This was even more true of the powers he obtained under the 1939 reorganization bill, which were subject to a one-house congressional veto. It is now widely understood that lawmakers share power over bureaucracies with the executive through their control of substantive statutory mandates, budgets, oversight activity, and procedural requirements. Indeed, presidents pursue reorganization in part to bolster their interests in the midst of lawmakers' efforts to assert their own power.[49]

But the reality of divided control is important beyond the confines of legislative-presidential interaction. With so much at stake in decisions about organizational structure, bureaucratic officials and organized interests often support fragmented control, with one agency controlling initial regulatory decisions and another commanding enforcement. Hence, the Department of Health and Human Services—the principal descendant of the FSA—decides on chemical exposure limits for workers while the Labor Department's Occupational Safety and Health Administration (OSHA) enforces those provisions.[50] Even when political pressures do not explicitly favor divided control, fragmentation of legal responsibilities becomes commonplace given preexisting bureaucratic divisions and the enormous complexity associated with some legal mandates. Thus, anti-money-laundering policy is best understood not as a federal function designed to achieve a coherent goal, but as a mix of statutory decisions controlled by prosecutors, rulemaking choices governed primarily by regulators, and investigative decisions mostly in the hands of criminal investigators. Because it is such a common feature of the allocation of bureaucratic authority, divided control is both a contributor to pressures for change in structure—as presidents and organized interests maneuver for advantage—and a constraint on how those changes are implemented.[51]

It is not impossible to anticipate how bureaucratic structure will affect the success of legal mandates. But given the breadth of many such mandates, along with the political divisions about what counts as "success," it becomes extremely difficult to connect particular structures to some defensible concept of "success." The difficulties are complicated by the gaps in our knowledge of bureaucracy. Together these factors should make one skeptical of bald assertions, such as those frequently made by FDR, about the capacity of reorganization to promote "efficiency" in the strict sense of the term. One must recall that there is considerable uncertainty about the extent to which particular types of bureaucratic structures will contribute to "effectiveness" in achieving consensus goals associated with the implementation of legal mandates. Even when a probability exists that a particular structural change—such as centralization of functions—will have a given impact, key audiences, such as members of the mass public, may not appreciate the extent to which desired effects are contingent on complex factors such as the nature of congressional organization. Given the pervasive reality of divided control of bureaucracies, there are strong reasons to question the conventional prescriptive case for reorganization. Organizational changes carry relatively certain costs. In contrast, prescriptive benefits are contingent on potential complexities arising from the impact of organization on an agency's legal activities. Adjudication of immigration benefits, for example, will probably experience different responses than an agency's regulation of an economically powerful industry will.[52]

If external pressure can affect how agencies are structured and how they implement their legal responsibilities, the same is true of an elusive but important concept involving the internal life of an organization—the concept of organizational culture. The work of any organization is shaped by the shared assumptions of the people who work within it. The intelligence professionals who make up the bulk of the workforce in the CIA may harbor stark disagreements about the value of clandestine tradecraft relative to analysis of raw intelligence, but it is easy to imagine them developing a set of shared assumptions about the importance of intelligence and counterintelligence in an adversarial world. In contrast, even if the State Department employs hundreds or even thousands of people charged with keeping its facilities, information, and people secure, its culture may lead it to tolerate the routine use of foreign contractors to build embassies—in some cases resulting in facilities that are severely compromised.[53]

James Q. Wilson offers a definition that neatly sums up the core of the concept. He defines culture as "a persistent, patterned way of thinking about the central tasks of and human relationships within an organization," and analogizes it to the role that personality plays for an individual.[54] Social scientists have widely documented the significance of culture in organizations, even as some scholars occasionally question the analytical precision of the concept.[55] For close observers of public and private organizations, it is difficult to fully explain what happens in organizations without some reference to organizational culture, used in the same sense that an individual's personality or a nation's culture might be cautiously used as one lens through which to understand behavior. As Wilson puts it, "we find it hard to explain how exactly Italians differ from Germans or introverts from extroverts, but we do not doubt that there are important differences."[56] Indeed, both psychologically oriented social scientists and economists have worked hard in recent years to develop individual-level foundations for "organizational culture," spurred no doubt by the somewhat vague nature of the concept coupled with the deeply held sense that it references something important about the life of organizations.[57]

Different organizational cultures can also raise the stakes when security-related functions are transferred entirely out of one agency and into another. Consider as an example one author's description of the consequences riding on the transfer of the "Indian Office" from the U.S. Army to what was then the Home Department and is now the Department of the Interior:

[In the Home Department,] the Office of Indian Affairs was deeply committed to avoiding Indian wars in the West. It distrusted the army, and tended to disbelieve cries of wolf from the settlements, believing that the whites' problems with the Indians were their own doing. They liked the idea of treaties, the more the better. They liked the notion of an enduring peace, in spite of the headlong rush of settlers onto Indian territory who wanted peace only if it meant complete capitulation by the Indians. The army knew better, but could do nothing about it.[58]

This picture is, of course, misleading inasmuch as neither the Home Department, nor the Army, nor the Office of Indian Affairs was a monolithic entity. The decisions of individuals and smaller groups write much of the story of any organization. Nonetheless, an identifiable organizational culture—supported by a mix of formal institutions and informal incentives—is part of what makes it sensible to envision, however cautiously, an organization as a single entity.

Whether policymakers and agency managers work in an agency with a dominant culture or in one with a range of competing cultures, they obviously need not take the culture they find in a particular organization as set in stone. If policymakers recognize they can have an impact on agency activities in ways that can advance their agenda, they might seek to affect culture in a variety of ways. As with the Indian Office and the Home Department, they may seek to move a bureau from one agency to another in order to affect its culture. They could seek formal change in agency missions in a manner that favors the selection of some workers over others, or that alters likely promotion paths of individuals already hired. They can try to empower some subcultures over others. Recall that even within the CIA, for example, spies and intelligence analysts evolve different expectations about what their agency should value and what trade-offs it should tolerate. They can try to rebrand an agency to nudge the expectations of external constituencies regarding a particular agency, thus changing the incentives of operators and managers within the agency. In short, the presence of organizational culture can influence the behavior of strategic politicians seeking to shape the law's implementation, or the public's understanding of a major governmental function such as the provision of security. We might investigate whether there is any historical record suggesting that politicians understand how shaping organizations can affect culture, and how a distinct organizational culture can have effects (ranging from subtle to profound) on the trajectory of legal arrangements and public expectations.

THEORETICAL REFINEMENTS: CAPACITY-BUILDING, COALITION EXPANSION, AND ENDOGENOUS CRISIS

Although the histories of agencies such as the FSA and DHS may readily seem to confirm the importance of some of the preceding dynamics, they may also provide an opportunity to develop refinements on the approach described above. Such refinements may be especially helpful in addressing the persistent puzzles about the creation of these organizations.

Just as politicians may sometimes reap rewards by appearing to address a problem while creating an agency that will fail to do so, in other cases their goals could give them a great stake in the ability of a bureaucracy to carry out complicated tasks. Whether those tasks actually fulfill a president's publicly asserted goals is not the primary issue. The point is to recognize that politicians may have a good deal riding on building bureaucratic capacity. For example, Dutch politicians recognize how their fortunes are tied to the success of the nation's levee system and have every reason to bolster the capacity of that bureaucracy to perform effectively.[59]

Most statutory mandates are naturally subject to more controversy. The PHS's forays into rural health inspired as much support among poor farmers as they did scorn among private doctors' associations, who saw such moves as the first step of a campaign to nationalize health insurance. The Food, Drug, and Cosmetic Act continues to this day to mean one thing to government regulators and another to pharmaceutical companies. But even—and perhaps especially—when there is an absence of political consensus, presidents or their aides may seek additional resources to enlarge the layer of superiors overseeing an agency's functions, so these can be better controlled or (in some cases) protected from political attacks.[60]

If a president persuades Congress to create a new layer of executive branch officials above the bureaus that carry out the government's work and the president can fill those ranks with loyal personnel, he can better control how agencies carry out their functions. He can cement emerging political coalitions by ensuring that agencies carry out their missions in a favorable manner. He can use the new layer of appointees to blunt the influence of legislators and organized interests seeking to assert control over agencies. He can align existing bureaus—such as the PHS, which was originally a minor office of the Treasury Department—under new superiors who will devote more time and energy to using the bureau's resources and building a distinctive organizational culture, thereby facilitating the development of statutory proposals or policy initiatives advancing presidential goals.

These opportunities do not guarantee that executive branch officials will want bureaus to work as effectively as possible: recall that even defining effectiveness beyond extreme cases like the levees in Holland soon becomes taxing. Moreover, building up agencies with new bureaus, leaders, and resources is not without risk. As the experience of FEMA in handling Hurricane Katrina indicates, the creation of a new superagency such as DHS can be associated with major setbacks in performance.[61] Likewise, bureaus such as the National Park Service can use new resources to bolster their independence from politicians. Despite these risks, some politicians may have good reason to enlarge bureaucratic capacity while protecting agencies from legal changes that would set them up for failure. Faced with opponents who would rather keep bureaucracies weak and difficult to monitor, proponents of bureaucratic capacity should be especially inclined to take advantage of windows of opportunity for political change that emerge during (actual or imagined) crises.[62]

COALITION EXPANSION AND AGENCY STRUCTURE

Why did the Roosevelt administration entrust so many defense-related functions to the FSA? The answer may depend on whether changes in bureaucratic structure have the capacity to alter the public's responses to political appeals. The loading up of the FSA with defense functions may also shed light on how *politicians*, such as Roosevelt, Jimmy Carter, and

George W. Bush, use agency reorganizations to affect the distribution of power among policymakers, thereby reshaping the implementation of legal mandates.

Most work on bureaucratic structure has little to say about the reactions of the public at large except, perhaps, to note that politicians can gain some political credit by making structural changes to soothe preexisting public demands. Yet the position-taking opportunities associated with bureaucratic structure at least show that bureaucratic matters can occasionally break through the public's inattention barrier. Because questions of structure may register with voters, we might ask whether changes in agency jurisdiction can nudge the public's demand for particular policies rather than merely follow those demands. Consider: if a grant program for funding youth education and community centers is run by the Justice Department rather than the Department of Housing and Urban Development, how might public perceptions about those grant programs change? Presumably, the answer depends on the underlying mechanisms through which individuals form opinions and on the extent to which linking community grants with crime control can evoke more favorable associations among politically relevant constituencies. The possibility of such an effect, however, is enough to suggest that politicians could use organizational structure, like legal doctrine, to carry on a conversation with the public and elites about the essential nature of particular government programs. Such a process could implicate several of the building blocks just mentioned, especially position-taking, expertise, and forging political coalitions. This makes it important to answer the question of whether it is possible for the politics of structure to have an "epistemic" dimension relevant to conflict over the merits of particular legal and policy functions alongside the more conventionally acknowledged policy control dimension.

In contrast to situations where politicians support reorganization in response to preexisting public demands—as with Richard M. Nixon's creation of the EPA, Carter's design of the Department of Energy, or Bush's campaign to forge DHS—an alternative strategy would deploy reorganization to foment public demand for a particular statutory mandate. First, the reorganization itself could deliver a means of generating media attention, which is one reason that organizational changes are also useful to politicians who want to assuage a concern already present among the public.[63] By the same token, politicians can use the attention to focus concern on a new issue that advances their political agenda. Second, some proportion of voters may become more supportive of statutory mandates if politicians supply a new version of what political scientists describe as a "policy metaphor": a narrative to organize the relationship between widely shared concerns and policy prescriptions. Not everyone is amenable to new policy metaphors. Some—indeed, perhaps most—members of the public may expend considerable cognitive effort to resist such appeals. But just a few people taking another look at energy law as a component of environmental policy, for example, or food safety as a component of national security, may tip the scales in favor of more aggressive regulatory expansion. Third, policy elites favoring one agency mission over another may have a harder time deciding whether to withhold support for an entire agency when doing so may also restrict the functions they value[64]—a point developed in more detail below.

Executive branch officials might achieve an additional benefit by mixing functions in a new bureaucracy. By modifying the bundles of adjudication, expenditures, investigation, and legislative activity undertaken by bureaucracies, executive officials could fashion a new relationship between bureaucracies and more conventionally rational—but skeptical—political elites such as lawmakers. The key idea is that weaving national security functions into the fabric of a domestic agency changes the political game for legislators who would have preferred to cut administrative and regulatory programs. Once mixing has occurred, the lawmakers' choice is beset by two new complications: the possibility that by cutting domestic programs the legislators are genuinely hobbling defense, which may run counter to their own political goals; and the risk that even if such adverse effects never materialize, some members of the mass public might now ironically punish the legislators for cutting defense-related programs. In short, creating bureaucracies could involve *more* than just passively exploiting a crisis such as an impending or actual war. The very act of creating the bureaucracy can help reshape how the public understands the role of government, the scope of a crisis, and the nature of the "security" that the resolution of the crisis would presumably entail.[65]

ENDOGENOUS CRISIS

While agency architecture can drive the law's implementation, natural disasters, national security emergencies, or an economic crisis such as the Great Recession of 2008 can in turn shape agency architecture. But what does "crisis" actually mean? Upon closer inspection, there may be more to crisis than the simple idea of an unexpected, exogenous shock.

If crisis can be the handmaiden of legal change, we should also expect certain factors to drive lawmakers' or executive branch officials' capacity to argue about the presence of a crisis. Undoubtedly some of what seems to be a crisis in retrospect reflects an exogenous shock, such as an unexpected, sharp upswing in the number of Haitian asylum seekers requesting entrance to the United States, an economic recession, or a terrorist attack. As a variation on this theme, rapidly crumbling political fortunes faced by a coalition or an individual political actor can also spur action because of further expected deterioration that could occur in the absence of some response. Nixon's firing of Archibald Cox and other Justice Department officials may be an example.[66] Separate from the underlying shock itself, officials in a presidential administration, lawmakers, and other political actors can use their agenda-setting power to coax public attention toward the conclusion that a crisis is under way. Senator Estes Kefauver's hearings on the dangers of thalidomide and drug safety in the early 1960s are an example: even though the FDA had in fact blocked the drug from being sold in the United States, the senator leveraged public concern over the episode to create a crisis atmosphere contributing to statutory expansion of the FDA's power.[67] Finally, a position taken by actors external to the political branches, such as organized interests, can contribute to the public perception that there is a crisis—particularly if the position is unexpected.[68] Think of a Supreme Court opinion taking a position on the quality of evidence about global warming,[69] an oil company unexpectedly acknowledging the existence of global warming,[70] or an individual from a party historically opposed to immigration reform proposing a guest worker program.[71] By the same token, public officials' desire to pursue politically costly legal changes such as the creation of new bureaucracies, or even the use of controversial interrogation techniques, could play a role in fostering public perceptions that the country faces a particularly difficult period.[72]

Because the true nature of a crisis is difficult to observe, members of the public may find themselves drawing inferences from the behavior of politicians. The more that public officials are willing to shoulder the costs of a particular legal change or policy prescription, the greater the perceived magnitude of a crisis may be among the public. Each of the foregoing choices could help political actors foster an impression that a crisis is afoot. Yet these actors often face a devilish trade-off between facilitating desired policy change by fostering a perception of crisis and paying the political costs associated with being viewed as not effectively or appropriately managing that crisis.[73]

These dynamics should underscore the difficulty of deciding when exactly a genuine crisis fully emerges, in prescriptive terms. To a considerable degree, the contemporaneous or even historical perception that a crisis has occurred probably emerges endogenously from political choices made by presidents, executive branch officials, lawmakers, courts, and organized interests. By contrast, the prescriptive analysis of what counts as a crisis depends on a combination of close scrutiny to a specific temporal and policy context—the number of lives affected after a natural disaster, the extent of a slowdown in credit markets, or the extent of exposure to toxic contaminants after an industrial accident—and a sense of the goals of the evaluation. Because such evaluations are difficult in a world of limited information and of voters with cognitive constraints, one should expect considerable room for politicians to play up the crisis theme in pursuit of achieving the desired legal architecture for agencies charged with governing.

ORGANIZATIONS OR NATIONAL SECURITY ORGANIZATIONS?

Crises often focus particular attention on organizations responsible for sensitive national security, defense, or emergency response functions. In the United States, these agencies account for a vast proportion of the overall federal budget. If our primary concern is understanding how the United States or similar countries address their security goals through legal arrangements and the organizations designed to implement them, how much can we learn from theoretical approaches designed primarily to explain the organizational structure and performance of generic agencies, rather than bureaus specifically focused on security? Earlier I suggested that the distinction between security and non-security functions may be far from clear-cut, and indeed may be blurred by strategic political action or even a genuine recognition of the interrelationship between domains such as geostrategic power and domestic pre-college education policy. But such blurring does not necessarily preclude the existence of sharp distinctions in the organizational realities faced by traditional security agencies such as the Army or the National Security Council (NSC) when compared to conventional domestic agencies.

In a widely noted book and related articles, Amy Zegart has articulated a compelling case for recognizing important organizational distinctions between national security agencies and non-security agencies.[74] Zegart starts by drawing a distinction between national security agencies and "domestic" agencies. In the context of domestic agencies, she observes, interest groups are plentiful, powerful, and varied.[75] In contrast, she posits, interest groups are relatively new in the national security context and do not wield much power.[76] Moreover, domestic agencies afford extensive information on their activities, and thus the cost of congressional oversight is lower, whereas for national security agencies information is not widely available.[77] Finally, in domestic politics interest groups drive the politics, bureaucrats are not particularly influential, and Congress oversees even relatively routine operations.[78] This state of affairs, she argues, stands in sharp contrast to the norm for national security agencies, in which the president is the principal actor and the policy issues lie primarily within a domain where the president is traditionally treated as preeminent.[79] Proceeding from these premises, Zegart then traces the outline of her theory of national security agencies. First, she expects the executive branch to drive initial agency design, and agencies to reflect primarily the conflict between contending bureaucrats and the president. As a result, agencies should for the most part not be well designed to promote national interests.[80] As agencies mature, she expects the executive to drive agency evolution, with Congress exercising only sporadic and ineffectual oversight because legislators have weak incentives and blunt tools.[81] Finally, she posits that an individual agency's evolution can be explained by three factors (in order of importance): initial agency structure, the ongoing interests of relevant political actors, and exogenous events.[82]

Zegart nicely explains why presidents rarely if ever get precisely what they want from the design of security agencies. And she makes a good case for proceeding with some caution when comparing agencies with traditional domestic functions to the bureaus with core responsibilities for traditional national security functions such as counter-intelligence and/or military strategy. Bureaucratic interests unquestionably affect, and in many cases burden, the resulting structure of the agencies she analyzes. These agencies' emphasis on external threats facing the nation almost certainly exert an impact on the organizations' political context. Indeed, if the Roosevelt administration was drawn to the goal of identifying some of its domestic agencies with national defense functions, it was probably because of the recognition that defense-related functions could garner support from lawmakers, organized interests, and members of the public who might not care nearly as much about social security or education policy.

Still, a close analysis of these conventional national security agencies also reveals strong grounds to recognize a deep continuity in the organizational logic of agency structure across the (conventionally understood) security and non-security domains. Although Zegart's work illuminates some important specific cases (accounting for the development of the modern Joint Staff in the U.S. Department of Defense, the Central Intelligence Agency, and the National Security Council [NSC]), an alternative conclusion might emphasize three observations. First, because the boundaries of the national security domain are in fact contested, political efforts to describe an agency's work as essential to national security amount to a lottery ticket, rather than a guarantee, that political actors will treat its functions differently. When a president argues that a new energy initiative has implications for our (conventionally understood) geostrategic security interests, the debate may evolve, but there is no guarantee that the agency's fate will be resolved in a particular way. Second, the organization of security agencies may not be simply the result of a unique set of dynamics applying to national security agencies. Instead, politicians will almost certainly use structure precisely to impact the public debate regarding the relationship of particular organizational functions to security—and perhaps even to impact the public's understanding of which policy domains involving the management of risks are so important that they merit the "national security" label. In addition, although Zegart's account provides quite compelling examples of organizational dysfunction exacerbated by bureaucratic infighting, we might expect a different outcome in at least some situations where (for example) presidents heavily invest their political capital to achieve long-standing policy goals.

So the questions raised by Zegart's insightful account of national security agency organization converge in some sense on the large issue of precisely how much the paradigmatic security agencies differ from the broader web of regulatory and service provision agencies in a pluralist democracy. Military officials and intelligence professionals may differ from food safety inspectors or education policy experts when it comes to advocating for particular organizational structures. In some cases, important legal distinctions exist between defense-oriented agencies and the full range of executive bureaus. The president, for example, is not exactly the "commander in chief" of the Federal Communications Commission or the Federal Reserve Board.

What is not so clear is whether such uniqueness overwhelms the fact that all federal agencies exist within the same larger constitutional and political system. On this issue, Zegart makes a case that agencies such as the Department of Defense are sufficiently distinct from entities such as the Food and Drug Administration to merit a distinct theoretical model. An alternative premise would be to recognize that the powers granted even to conventional national defense and security agencies touch on domains that are enormously valuable to businesses, local politicians, and civil society organizations concerned about matters such as political developments in the Middle East or civil liberties.

True, the logic of external engagement in agency structure may at first seem to apply more to agencies straddling the divide between conventional national security problems and domestic concerns. But a reasonable answer would observe that even the U.S. Department of Defense mixes functions. Deep inside the Pentagon, an assistant secretary for homeland defense worries not only about how the United States would weather a nuclear attack but also about how in the future military assets can help prevent the disaster that befell New Orleans when Katrina hit the Gulf Coast. Elsewhere in the building, civilian and military officials oversee the complex financial arrangements leveraging the civilian health system to provide medical care for military personnel. Procurement decisions planned in a different corridor can catalyze or crater local economies. In this account, the enormous stakes involved in matters such as military base closures are not so much an exception as part of a larger pattern involving competition to shape the structure, agenda, and decisions of agencies. The stories of the FSA and the DHS in the chapters ahead may provide some perspective on whether significant engagement from external constituencies turns out to be a routine part of the history of these agencies.

SHAPING LAW BY ALTERING ORGANIZATIONAL EVOLUTION AND THE PROSPECTS FOR AUTONOMY

Most of the theory presented so far develops the idea that external conditions affect organizations implementing the law, and that those external conditions generally have far-reaching consequences even for agencies charged with missions generally described as involving national security. The FSA and its bureaus depended on external support. External constraints could interfere with agency plans, whether they involved new regulations expanding food safety inspections or secret biological weapons programs. Nor are agencies such as the FSA or DHS unique in this regard; no account of the law's implementation works without considerable attention to the external context.

But if agencies are largely a product of their environment, so too are they occasionally capable of shaping that environment to some extent. Agency officials can facilitate or impede the adoption of legislation reshaping the organization's architecture, as when Congress sought to cut off nuclear security functions from the rest of the Department of Energy in the mid-1990s.[83] Civil servants can lay the groundwork for subsequent statutory changes and in some cases even use limited legal authority autonomously to pursue goals later mandated by statute. FDA employees are a case in point, having articulated and accepted innovative legal arguments to pursue efficacy testing of drugs before it was required by statute.[84] These examples merely illustrate how external pressures on agencies can coexist with, and in some cases are even premised on, attempts to control the autonomous agendas of agency staff.

47

So what happens when the possibility of autonomy and the reality of external pressure intersect? Across the constellation of interests within and around an agency, it remains possible that some players will be all too aware of an agency's potential capacity to acquire a greater measure of autonomy over time, as it builds an external constituency of support or acquires an ever stronger reputation for technical competence. After all, not all agencies are in the same position to protect themselves from external interference. For example, the Federal Reserve Board—sitting firmly at the more autonomous end of the spectrum—acquired its relatively more independent status gradually, thereby becoming harder to challenge over time.[85]

If lawmakers, executive branch officials, and organized interests recognize that budgets and formal organizational constraints could affect agency behavior in the present, they could also recognize that an agency's capacity for autonomy over time depends on a host of factors that could be controlled in the near term. Potentially important but subtle variables contributing to autonomy over time, such as the cohesion of an agency's internal culture, may depend on factors that can be controlled by external actors in the near term, such as where in the larger scheme of government an agency is located (for example, whether a parent cabinet agency supports a bureau's overall mission or views it as peripheral), what an agency's capacity is to generate technical knowledge (thereby affecting whether the organization can use a reputation for scientific or technical competence to bolster autonomy), and whether it is overseen in its early phases of development by political officials sympathetic to the agency's likely trajectory as it gains independence. Accordingly, we might examine the history of the FSA and the DHS to see if the structural moves that created it could have contributed to changes in the relative autonomy of its bureaus over time.

FROM THEORY TO HISTORY: LOOKING AHEAD

Our theoretical exploration has helped us map the terrain in which agencies operate, and just as important, the environment in which agencies are forged. Virtually no function of the modern nation-state takes place without agencies. Hence the question of how agencies will be organized becomes enormously important. No hardwired feature of our constitutional scheme or inviolable logic of public administration automatically determines what minimal responsibilities the U.S. Department of the Treasury should possess, or how national defense and public health functions can be bundled together. As lawmakers, executive officials, civil servants, and external constituencies shape agency organization, they also tend to affect what these agencies do and how they do it.

In light of these realities, theory helps make sense of the world so we can decide what is worth investigating and understand the context of what we learn. Our brief theoretical survey helps motivate the historical investigation to come. From our theoretical survey we have gleaned some general principles to understand how agencies are organized and how the process of organization affects the law's implementation. We have reviewed the importance of political competition and the consequences of changes in agency structure. Yet there is much we do not know yet about how precisely agencies are organized, and what consequences arise. We can also benefit from learning a great deal more about agencies whose functions are tied by policymakers to the concept of "security," and perhaps especially about those agencies whose functions straddle the conventional distinctions between security and non-security functions.

Finally, we have generated some tentative predictions concerning how organizations implement the law, and these are worth investigating in the pages to come. We have reviewed, for example, why we might expect lawmakers and executive branch officials to use crises as a means of advancing their organizational agendas. Those policymakers will often have reason to act strategically in shaping security agencies to achieve long-held goals. Their strategies should reflect the reality that even if security agencies sometimes operate in a different environment, they are subject in large measure to the same broad mix of competition and external pressures that affect conventional domestic agencies. Moreover, while the political process often yields dysfunctional agencies, sometimes the result of organizational changes will be a combination of culture, structure, and resources that allows agencies to advance their missions with a degree of competence and partial autonomy. With these preliminaries on the table, we can return to the surprising history of the long-forgotten FSA.

CHAPTER 3

Arming Democracy

Designing Federal Security

EVEN THE SINGULARLY OPTIMISTIC Franklin Delano Roosevelt could have a bad turn. By late 1938, the disappointed president would have been hard-pressed to deny that he was having one. Gone were the heady days of the early New Deal coalition, when Roosevelt had created the massive National Recovery Administration, the Agricultural Adjustment Act, and dozens of agencies, and had undertaken major banking reform. The administration had drawn down its reservoirs of political capital. Roosevelt's infamous judicial reorganization plan, already tarred as a "court-packing plan," had been defeated. And the legislature had also dealt him a blow by rejecting his executive reorganization plan.[1]

The administration's plan to give the president control over where bureaus would fit in government had been soundly defeated, as had his plan to create a new Department of Public Welfare around the nascent SSB.[2] His party controlled the legislature, to be sure, but the increasing prominence of an alliance between conservative Southern Democrats and Republicans had greatly complicated his efforts to reshape the structure of government.[3] The government was growing, the president explained to legislators. No one could be expected to administer it efficiently with such a vast number of regulatory commissions and independent agencies. The New Deal's legislative opponents even made the point themselves often enough; where they differed with the president was in recommending a thorough pruning of government agencies—eliminating regulatory and administrative bodies instead of consolidating their powers. After all, scores of administrative agencies were initially described as temporary, and there were other pressing matters besides domestic social welfare and regulation—such as the deteriorating international security picture in Asia and Europe—that seemed to command the nation's attention.[4]

And it was not only legislators that Roosevelt had to worry about, for the torrential arguments over reorganization had flowed from legislative debates into the public sphere. Civic organizations opposed to the New Deal had made the president's quest for executive reorganization a centerpiece of their campaign against him.[5] "Dictatorial" was increasingly the label given to the president's aspirations, and the drive for reorganization was allegedly the quintessential evidence of that.[6] So successful had these associations been in drumming up opposition to reorganization that it seemed difficult to imagine that the president's legislative agenda could recover from this low ebb.

Two years later, President Roosevelt had confounded his opponents. Not only did he possess much (though not all) of the reorganization authority he craved, but he had immediately used it to create an agency focused on health and social welfare that was—in some respects—even more ambitious than the one he first proposed. The new Federal Security Agency lacked cabinet status and was short of funds in 1940. But within its bureaus lay the seed of elaborate legal machinery that would become a quintessential twentieth-century bureaucratic institution.[7]

SOME PUZZLES AND THEIR CONTEXT

In the midst of mounting political difficulties, Franklin Roosevelt allocated a considerable amount of his political capital to fight with Congress for power over the executive branch. At the other end of Pennsylvania Avenue, lawmakers vigorously resisted the president's stratagem for much the same reason that the president wanted those powers in the first place: in effect, public law in modern nation-states is largely about what bureaucratic institutions do. And because law is nearly always administered through such massive public bureaucracies, the history of the federal government is in some measure the story of how its bureaucracies grew in statutory power, budget, and administrative scope. Nearly all of the major agencies in the federal government have interesting stories, capable of revealing subtleties about the emerging American state. But the FSA merits special attention, even when considered alongside the panoply of "unorthodox" administrative formulas that Roosevelt's minions routinely deployed to control the law's execution during the New Deal.

First, it eventually spawned the massive Department of Health, Education, and Welfare. Even at the time of its creation, the FSA was among the largest agencies, in terms of both appropriations and employees, despite the fact that it lacked cabinet status. By understanding developments in that important context, we may learn something more about how presidents control bureaucratic functions amid legal constraints imposed by congressional enactments as well as substantive statutory mandates.

Second, efforts to create an agency to centralize health, welfare, and security activities were shrouded in controversy in this country. Theda Skocpol discusses failed efforts to create such an agency in the nineteenth century.[8] Roosevelt, dragged down by the court-packing fight, failed at his first attempt, in 1938, to create such a cabinet-level agency. In effect, Roosevelt's predecessors had failed, and even the politically dexterous president was rebuffed when he attempted to pursue the matter directly. Afterward he tried to do the next-best thing, by creating an independent, non-cabinet agency. The evolving bureaucracy eventually came to encompass even more than what Roosevelt himself had initially sought to include within it. Nor did the fighting over the FSA stop during the Roosevelt administration. Later, once the FSA made the idea of a unified health, welfare, and security agency a reality, President Harry S. Truman marshaled the agency's resources to promote his national health insurance plan. Yet, partly for that reason, he failed to obtain support for cabinet-level status from the Republican Congress. Though Truman was unable to elevate the agency to cabinet status, President Dwight D. Eisenhower eventually succeeded in 1953, making that the first major legislative achievement of his presidency.[9]

By contrast, the British forged a Ministry of Health by 1919, on the heels of a costly victory during World War I. Through it, the British radically reshaped local control of social services and promptly began advocating for expanded health benefits.[10] But beyond changing the lines of authority for *existing* functions, creation of a new ministry was understood by some observers as changing the government's capacity to reshape the legal determinants of health policy. Wasting little time in displaying his ambitions for the new ministry, Dr. Christopher Addison (the new health minister) explained: "The object of the new ministry is, of course, to provide better health services throughout the country, and we are now working on our health programme; and various proposals will be submitted to the consultative councils at no distant date."[11] The presence of these controversies and the trajectory of health, security, and welfare policy in comparative perspective suggest that it is important to understand the story of the FSA and its progeny in order to explain important legal and policy developments involving health, welfare, and security.[12]

Third, the story of the FSA illuminates the elusive content of the term "security," a now ubiquitous concept defining a major category of government responsibility. As the analysis below suggests, the use of the term to anchor the agency's name and so many of its functions was no accident. It was not a mere reference to an established social security bureaucracy; "security" had often been used to describe the goal of economic relief programs, but it had also been deployed in connection with defense-related activities. The concept itself remained ambiguous, waiting for policy entrepreneurs to fill in the blanks. Fights about how to do so have been central in the creation of other major federal agencies, such as the modern Departments of Energy and Homeland Security. By tracing the progression that transformed the FSA from a scattered cluster of bureaus into the preeminent domestic policy agency of twentieth-century America, we can learn something about how the content of "security" was written by political actors and how it may yet again be rewritten.[13]

These puzzles reveal deeper gaps in our knowledge about the effect of bureaucratic structure on the evolution of the law. Lawsuits sometimes turn on how legal authority is divided across public bureaus.[14] Lawmakers struggle to control that allocation.[15] Lines of organizational jurisdiction over legal mandates may determine who has power to interpret and implement the law as much as lines of geographic jurisdiction define the boundaries of nation-states or localities.[16] Yet we know little about precisely how changes in bureaucratic structure affect the implementation of legal mandates, how presidents control the immense powers of a sprawling executive branch, and how the competition to shape the meaning of concepts such as "security" among the public and legislators may play out in the intricate boundaries that are created by politicians to allocate bureaucratic jurisdiction over the legal powers of the federal government. Closing some of these gaps depends in part on closely scrutinizing the institutional choices consolidating power in agencies such as the FSA.

· · ·

The first few pages of the FSA's own history were written in what was, from President Roosevelt's perspective, a political environment that was becoming increasingly difficult to control.[17]

During the first six years of his presidency, Roosevelt's administration unleashed major changes in the federal government.[18] The precise extent to which these changes represented a radical break with the past is a matter of some debate among scholars, but the fact that he created a massive number of new administrative agencies with far-reaching legal powers is not.[19] It is this latter fact that becomes immediately important to our account, since it gave rise to three interrelated political debates that culminated in the latter part of Roosevelt's second term. The first was whether the amalgam of new agencies—often initially justified as temporary and allowed to function independently in part (according to the White House itself) as a means of getting them off the ground quickly—should ultimately be abolished. The second was whether the president should have executive authority to reorganize the functions of the executive branch—including independent agencies and departmental sub-units. Eventually he gained that authority, and he used it to create a sprawling new agency called the Federal Security Agency. The third was whether the president could fire commissioners appointed to fixed terms, such as those who served in the FTC, the SEC (Securities and Exchange Commission), and the SSB. President Roosevelt craved such firing authority. But the Supreme Court proved hostile to this move.[20] This response gave the White House even greater reason to concoct new strategies, perhaps involving reorganization, to gain power over the independent agencies.

And that power often seemed well within Roosevelt's grasp. The president's popularity had attained commanding heights between 1933 and 1937. He was, however, not immune to conventional political pressures. During the early phase of his presidency, when the banking crisis and uncertainty about his own intentions were most pronounced, the new president compared the nation's economic problems to a foreign invasion.[21] As a consequence, he reasoned, the president would need to deploy powers associated with a national security emergency to address the problems afflicting the nation. By framing the emergency in these terms, the president seemed to be achieving two separate goals. He was emphasizing his administration's contrast to the previous one in recognizing the severity of the crisis. Simultaneously, he was promoting a favorable background political context for his legally questionable decision to invoke wartime statutory powers, such as those contained in the 1917 Trading with the Enemy Act,[22] to respond to the economic emergency.[23] The president's strategic efforts to blur the distinction between domestic and national security crises served as important political precursors to his subsequent decisions about how to organize the government's policy functions.[24] Those efforts would not be forgotten.

By mid-1938 the administration faced new political challenges. It had achieved major legislative changes, including passage of the Social Security Act and the Food, Drug, and Cosmetic Act of 1938. But the cohesiveness of the New Deal coalition was affected by lingering economic weakness and increasingly shrill public attacks from political opponents.[25] At first, some of the administration's apparent loss of political support in Congress probably reflected its boldness—fueled by the size of its victories in the 1936 elections—in seeking legislative proposals that might have been controversial even among moderate supporters of the New Deal. Such a pattern is consistent with passage of the Wagner Act and the Food, Drug, and Cosmetic Act, for example. Nonetheless, whether because of deliberate administration choices to press its political advantage, secular trends, or economic problems, the administration's public standing was deteriorating by 1938. There was a recession that began around mid-1937 at the latest.[26] The court-packing fight saturated the country with charges that Roosevelt was an aspiring dictator and polarized otherwise progressive civil libertarians against him.[27] It was perceived and reported on as a political failure in the president's relationship with Congress and an example of alleged presidential lust for power, lending credence to critics who painted the president as an aspiring dictator. By the time the first executive reorganization bill was voted on, even non-marginal Democratic legislators who voted for the Wagner Act were ignoring Roosevelt's entreaties and voting against the White House on reorganization.[28]

Political realities were reflected in Roosevelt's mixed record of success and failure. By the middle of his second term, the president had plainly succeeded in the broad outlines of his policy goals—creating transformative new policy and regulatory programs such as the SSB, the SEC, the

Tennessee Valley Authority, and the Works Progress Administration. Congress had just approved a potentially sweeping Food, Drug, and Cosmetic Act, expanding the government's power to regulate growing industries.[29] But as the cycle of the Roosevelt presidency unfolded, organized interests disagreeing with the administration over economic policy increasingly asserted themselves. Opposition also grew among the public and the elites in the South who frowned on the sharp expansion in federal power. The disaffected Southern Democrats, in turn, were joined in growing numbers by many wealthy Americans throughout the country who were opposed to Roosevelt's regulatory and social welfare policies.[30]

The political trends in public opinion and media coverage tended to affect legislators' willingness to support the president in swing districts. As public and media support weakened during the president's second term, he lost support in Congress. Changes in the composition of the legislature in absolute terms also weakened the extent of support the president had previously achieved in Congress.[31] The result of these changes was increasing frustration of the president's political agenda on Capitol Hill, most obviously demonstrated by the fate of the "court-packing" plan but also evident in the delay the White House faced in achieving broad powers to reorganize government agencies.[32]

Adding to White House concerns was the evolving direction of legal doctrine governing the president's relationship with the national government that he had vigorously fought to create. Since the 1920s, courts had increasingly taken up questions about the scope of executive power, complicating the prospects for full presidential control of the machinery of national policymaking.[33] In *Myers*, the Supreme Court recognized presidential primacy in controlling senior officials with core executive functions when it invalidated limitations on presidential firing powers and prohibited other forms of excessive congressional encroachment.[34] But this decision also acknowledged congressional power to shield inferior officials through civil service protections—beyond appearing to outlaw schemes requiring congressional assent to fire federal officials—and provided little guidance on how to define core executive functions.[35]

Given such ambiguity and the enormous congressional efforts to protect new agencies from direct presidential control, the subsequent legal showdown over executive power in *Humphrey's Executor* should have been entirely predictable. There, the Court upheld congressional power to prevent fixed-term commissioners of independent agencies such as the FTC from being forced to leave their jobs before their terms were up.[36] Without explicitly overruling *Myers*, the *Humphrey's Executor* Court sought to distinguish the present case on the basis of the FTC's status as an agency of mixed (executive and legislative) functions.[37] If *Myers* bequeathed a legacy of uncertainty about precisely what counted as core executive functions undertaken by senior officials, at a conceptual level, *Humphrey's Executor* left unresolved the matter of what exactly counted as sufficient mixing of functions. At a practical level, however, *Humphrey's Executor* left unchallenged congressional efforts to greatly complicate presidential control of the executive branch. And it was little consolation, surely, that lower courts at the time were accepting fairly broad readings of presidential statutory power to reorganize agencies. In *Istbrandtsen-Moller v. United States*,[38] for example, a district court found that statutory presidential reorganization authority extended not only to traditional executive bureaus but also to boards and commissions such as the U.S. Shipping Board, which straddled the divide between legislative and executive power.[39] But that power was subject to some congressional control and had in fact expired by the end of 1935.[40] This left the president facing an environment where a growing proportion of a swelling federal government involved difficult-to-control independent commissions, yet his own statutory power to shape the operation of that government through reorganization had expired at a time when his political fortunes were becoming more complicated.

The effect of the president's more difficult political and legal position was plainly apparent in the fight over executive reorganization. Previous law from the early 1930s created limited reorganization authority.[41] That law undoubtedly whetted Roosevelt's appetite for broader powers to reshape the architecture of an executive branch that had grown piecemeal through executive compromise with Congress. In 1938 the White House introduced a sprawling original bill modeled on the recommendations of the President's Committee on Administrative Management, commonly known as the Brownlow Committee. This body of scholars had conveniently elided distinctions between "efficiency" and presidential control.

The bill called for the creation of two cabinet departments—one of them a Department of Welfare that would have included all or much of what ended up in the FSA—and made no provision for a congressional veto. (For example, some action from both houses would have been required to stop a reorganization plan.) Nor did the original plan exempt independent regulatory agencies.[42] The resulting bill had two-house veto provisions for reorganization plans, exempted the independent agencies, and had authority that was set to expire after several years.[43]

Roosevelt intensely supported the plan. His introduction of the reorganization bill generated considerable fanfare among supporters in the House and Senate.[44] One academic observer later described the introduction of the bill as a study in masterful presidential strategy.[45] Highlighting the fact that Congress itself had chartered the commission that recommended the sweeping reorganization reforms, the president introduced a package that would have allowed him to reorganize executive branch agencies without the two-house veto provision that appeared in the watered-down 1939 bill. The earlier bill allowed for the creation of two cabinet departments—including a Department of Welfare that would include responsibility for federal pensions, social security, rural relief activities, and public health. Despite the concerns of some lawmakers, the bill made no provision for a congressional veto. Nor did it exempt independent regulatory agencies from being subjected to reorganization.[46]

Two further details about the reorganization fight are worth noting. First, after the introduction of the president's original bill (which was essentially the Brownlow Committee proposal), the legislative process produced a slew of amendments to the bill.[47] But the White House pushed back, impressing the legislative leadership with the importance of slowing down or blocking votes on changes that could result in a substantially weaker bill.[48] As a result, these amendments did not result in a compromise bill that could have simultaneously commanded support among winning legislative coalitions and the White House. Second, the White House and its top political staffers insisted that the president would not discuss specific reorganization plans, making it easier for opponents to dramatize the potential for "dictatorship" and harder for supporters to point to specific savings or "efficiency" gains that could be achieved through consolidation.[49]

But vigorous opposition soon emerged in both houses. The underlying logic of that opposition appears to reflect two mutually reinforcing dynamics that together contributed to the deteriorating prospects for Roosevelt's reorganization plan. One dynamic was about signaling and symbolism, suggesting that opposition to the reorganization plan swelled because it was simply the best issue for opponents to rally around.[50] Second, there was a more directly political story rooted in the prospect that reorganization had the potential to bestow upon Roosevelt significant powers that could change the amount and tenor of federal administrative activity. Both almost certainly played a role. The reorganization bill became a rallying point for opponents of the New Deal. A self-styled National Committee to Uphold Constitutional Government, fresh from its perceived victory during the court-packing fight, flooded the country with letters and surrogate speakers opposing the reorganization plan. After all, the White House had officially billed the court-packing plan as "judicial reorganization" legislation, and the network of businessmen, lawyers, and economic conservatives that had galvanized the fight over the court-packing issue saw an opening to allege that Roosevelt was now continuing his efforts to centralize dictatorial powers in the presidency.[51]

To complicate matters, the extent of the powers the president was requesting combined with the public attacks to prompt political defections even among legislators who were otherwise supportive of the administration. Later we will return to the full range of reasons why legislators had to limit the president's reorganization authority. At this point it is simply worth emphasizing that the opposition was not merely symbolic. Even when the New Deal coalition had been more prominent in the legislature, some of the administration's legislative victories had depended on lodging regulatory power in independent multi-member commissions rather than ordinary executive departments. Legislators were plainly concerned about the implications of the reorganization bill for both the recently created and the more long-standing independent regulatory commissions, including the FTC, the Interstate Commerce Commission, the NLRB, and the SEC.[52]

The president eagerly sought to revisit the legislative bargain giving these agencies broad statutory powers but also formal independence and a multi-member structure. By 1938 he had already made efforts to control these commissions through decisions to fire appointees with fixed terms, but the Supreme Court had thwarted him, finding that Congress could provide for fixed terms that would prevent the president from simply eliminating commissioners who disagreed with him.[53] How else could the White House get power over these agencies? The reorganization bill would do the trick: the SEC's authority could simply be placed under Treasury or Commerce, where loyal political appointees could reign. Congressional compromises creating new regulatory powers but yoking them to cumbersome structures could easily become undone.

Ever sensitive to interest-group pressures, legislators were also keenly aware that important constituencies ranging from veterans to unions to doctors believed they had something to lose from reorganization. Veterans were concerned that consolidation of the multi-member Civil Service Commission would erode the preference for hiring veterans for government jobs. Veterans also feared that the Veterans Administration would be consolidated into the proposed new Department of Welfare, disrupting the client-like relationship that had developed between veterans and their bureau.[54] The NAACP had been angling for the appointment of an African American to the Civil Service Commission and feared that this project would be thwarted by consolidation.[55] In effect, the opposition to executive reorganization was dispersed beyond the committed ideological opponents of the New Deal. Doctors sought to continue their dominance of the PHS and—curiously—preferred that it remain lodged deep inside the Treasury Department instead of forming the core of a new cabinet-level Welfare Department. Although senior Treasury officials were unlikely to view the work of the PHS as a priority, the more politically active doctors saw this as an advantage, since it allowed organized medical professionals to more easily dominate the work of the bureau.[56]

As opposition to the reorganization bill mounted, the White House sought to allay fears that the president would use reorganization to circumvent previous congressional compromises. White House allies supported amendments to the bill excluding some independent regulatory agencies from its coverage, imposing sunsets, and otherwise limiting its scope.[57] Nonetheless, by 1938, the ill-fated executive reorganization project had too many strikes against it. The most vigorous opponents of the

New Deal—working through citizens' committees outside the legislature and through conservative Republicans and Southern Democrats within it—tarred the reorganization bill by associating it with the court-packing plan.[58] Moderate New Deal supporters sensitive to interest group concerns were less inclined to be supportive of the president at a time when his public standing was visibly declining and when reorganization could dilute legislators' own power to structure political compromises through independent commissions.[59] Moderates who sought to make the bill more amenable politically by advancing amendments that exempted certain agencies or otherwise weakened the bill had to contend with opposition from the committed foes of the New Deal (who often voted strategically against the amendments) and with uncertain reactions from the White House (which occasionally sought to thwart the amendments, hoping to preserve a stronger bill).[60] And even the more vigorous White House supporters were occasionally miffed by the administration's less-than-adroit responses to criticism, which included sheepish press statements from the president denying any interest in "dictatorial" power and copious refusals to discuss the types of reorganization plans the president would pursue. The bill died.[61]

But the president was undaunted. Choosing to treat the demise of the 1938 bill as a temporary setback, he almost immediately instructed his aides to reopen negotiations on a more limited bill. In sharp contrast to their earlier strategy, White House negotiators now allowed the congressional leadership to take a major role in crafting the bill.[62] The civic organizations that had opposed reorganization seemed unconcerned about the lower-profile negotiations still unfolding, having declared victory and perhaps waiting for a different opportunity to weaken the administration. Meanwhile, some Democratic legislators who had scuttled the previous plan now supported it. The White House's nominal supporters in the second iteration may have been swayed by changes in the bill itself, which now included a two-house veto provision governing reorganization plans, exempted many independent agencies, and included sunset provisions.[63] Since most of the president's party still supported the substance of the federal government's new administrative and regulatory functions—even if they differed with the president about the power he should have to reorganize them—some legislators may have also sought to blunt conservative lawmakers' attacks on the allegedly sprawling and disorganized regulatory state that the New Deal had created.[64]

The resulting bill epitomized the exercise in compromise that the late New Deal had become. At long last, Roosevelt had reacquired executive powers over the very architecture of the federal state. He had gained the power to transfer, abolish, or modify existing agencies to reflect his goals, regardless of whether these involved short-term conflicts with congressional conservatives eager to dismember fragile New Deal bureaus or longer-term concerns about the legacy of his signature programs.[65] He could even abolish entire agencies without transferring their functions,[66] thereby exercising a sort of line-item veto power bound to increase presidential bargaining leverage,[67] as long as he returned the unspent appropriations to the Treasury for Congress to control.[68] The bill's design also contemplated reorganization plans that could result in major layoffs or functional changes in the work of agency employees,[69] thereby freeing up already appropriated resources to hire new officials more likely to be loyal to the White House.[70]

All of this came at a price, however. Deft navigation would be necessary for Roosevelt, the one-time Navy subcabinet official, to use these powers. Serious constraints were built into the new law.[71] The White House had to justify reorganization on the basis of financial savings or efficiency.[72] It had to report to Congress how much would be saved by each reorganization plan.[73] Virtually all independent agencies except the Social Security Board were off-limits, leaving in place statutory deals that had been blessed by the Supreme Court in *Humphrey's Executor* and that frustrated presidential efforts to control agencies directly.[74] Roosevelt was specifically barred from creating new cabinet agencies or abolishing existing ones.[75] No reorganization plan could explicitly change the purpose of appropriations (though who *controlled* the interpretation of that purpose within agencies could obviously change), shield agencies from existing litigation, preserve agencies that had already been legally subject to termination through statutory action, or create legal authority out of whole cloth for entirely novel government functions not vested in any existing agency (though existing legal authority could be transferred to new entities).[76] And there was the two-house veto:

reorganization plans had no effect until after sixty days had elapsed (during which Congress had to be in session). Before the sixty-day clock had run its course, a simple majority vote in both houses disapproving the reorganization plan invalidated its legal effect.[77] In short, despite Roosevelt's best efforts to avoid these limitations on his authority, the incremental authority he gained was sufficient to give him room to operate as both a legal and a political architect at a critical juncture. He would soon use it.

CREATION OF THE FSA:
"TO STRENGTHEN THE ARMS OF DEMOCRACY"[78]

Once passage of the Reorganization Act of 1939 appeared imminent, the small group of presidential advisors working on the new executive branch architecture shifted their attention from selling the legislature to finalizing what bureaus would move where. The president took a keen interest in the details of this process. Inside the White House, the president worked with a close-knit group of advisors to set reorganization priorities. The FSA was to be among the first agencies created, with the initial transfers of authority affecting the Social Security Board, Office of Education, Public Health Service, and a number of smaller and temporary New Deal legacy agencies. Only later did the president decree (perhaps wanting to dispel his opponents' concern that he was attempting to replicate the features of the defeated 1938 reorganization bill) that the FSA would be enlarged with the addition of the FDA.[79]

On April 25, 1939, just three weeks after the executive reorganization legislation passed, the White House issued an elaborate public announcement accompanying the first use of the president's authority from the act. The centerpiece of the announcement was the creation of a non-cabinet independent agency under a single administrator to manage health, education, and various aspects of "security" policy. Gone were references to welfare. In its stead, a "Federal Security Agency" was announced, centralizing power over the SSB (an independent agency), the PHS (from Treasury), the Office of Education (from Interior), the U.S. Employment Service (from Labor), and relief programs including the National Youth Administration (from the Works Progress Administration) and the Civilian Conservation Corps (another independent agency).[80] In keeping with the president's wishes, the transfer of the FDA (from Agriculture) was *not* announced but followed in 1940 in accordance with the administration's secret plans (see Table 3.1).[81] To run the FSA, the president recruited the ambitious Paul McNutt, a former law professor and governor of Indiana who was then completing a tour as the American colonial official in charge of the Philippines.[82]

It is telling that Roosevelt chose to feature "security" so prominently in the agency's name. While the term was broadly identified with pensions and unemployment benefits at the time,[83] "security" was also a fertile domain for legal and policy entrepreneurship. Even half a decade before the creation of the FSA, Roosevelt was already referring to "security" in relation to the administration's crime control initiatives, a domain of sharp, and

TABLE 3.1 *Selected Bureaus Transferred to the FSA by 1940*

Bureau	Budget (1940)	Previous Status	Key Functions (1940)
Social Security Board	$368 million	Independent Commission	Administering social insurance payments for older Americans; providing grants for states to develop pension and unemployment insurance schemes
Office of Education	$19.1 million	Bureau of the Interior Department	Allocating education assistance grants to states; developing vocational education programs; conducting and funding education-related research
U.S. Employment Service	$6.7 million	Bureau of the Labor Department	Providing employment placement and training services
Food and Drug Administration	$2.7 million	Bureau of the Agriculture Department	Ensuring the safety of most food products; regulating the pharmaceutical and cosmetics industries
Public Health Service	$29.2 million	Bureau of the Treasury Department	Conducting health research; providing public health services to combat infectious diseases; providing health services to communities that were economically marginalized (especially in rural areas) or affected by disasters; administering health-related grants to states

Sources: Division of Public Inquiries, *United States Government Manual, Winter 1943–1944*, 423–43; Federal Security Agency, *Organizational Charts and Budgets, FY 1952*

not entirely uncontroversial, federal expansion and policy entrepreneurship during the early New Deal.[84] He underscored security as a defining goal for a host of federal regulatory policies.[85] Early references to "security" policy in the Roosevelt administration also occasionally encompassed geostrategic national defense. Indeed, a survey of Roosevelt's public statements during his second term (the term in which the FSA was created) reveal nearly as many references to "security" that do not concern pensions or unemployment benefits as references that do.[86] The administration's description of its goals, moreover, appeared to reflect not only an exercise in public rhetoric but a politically significant willingness to reshape the federal bureaucracy and yoke bureaus together under a new set of legal parameters.

It is also telling that Roosevelt so vigorously prioritized bureaucratic changes in his lawmaking agenda. Aside from his expansion of the Executive Office of the President itself, the creation of the FSA was his most immediate political priority.[87] Though in some respects the administration already appears to have had a plan that resulted in the merger of agencies within the FSA, the political and legal context was also beginning to have some effect on how the plan was being crafted. The new reorganization law required a focus on thrift and efficiency, so Roosevelt's aides made at least a symbolic effort to play this up in their justification for the reorganization plan. But the other contextual factor shaping the reorganization foreshadowed one of Roosevelt's distinctive political innovations. In 1939 the possibility of a war that might affect the United States was no longer remote, even if the administration itself had yet to settle on a course for managing the associated foreign policy problems. Growing public concerns about national defense were also echoed in the legislature, where conservative Democrats and Republicans (even isolationist ones) often tended to support activities related to national defense.[88] In light of this, Roosevelt's plan emphasized the potential benefits to national security of creating a single agency to focus on health and economic security that could be more easily managed and more easily deployed to strengthen national defense.[89] As the president's reorganization message emphasized:

In these days of ruthless attempts to destroy democratic government, it is boldly asserted that democracies must always be weak in order to be democratic at all; and that, therefore, it will be easy to crush all free states out of existence. . . . We are not free if our administration is weak. But we are free if we know, and others know, that we are strong; that we can be tough as well as tender-hearted; and that what the American people decide to do can and will be done, capably and effectively, with the best national equipment that modern organizing ability can supply in a country where management and organization is so well understood in private affairs.[90]

If promoting the national defense in the face of external threats was the goal Roosevelt emphasized in the reorganization message, "efficiency" and accountability were to be the publicly asserted means of achieving that goal. Indeed, the president's effort to justify and create the FSA was inextricably bound up with the fight to pass a reorganization bill, which had culminated in a bill that forced the president to submit plans to Congress for approval. As a matter of statutory formalism, the primary goal of the plans, moreover, had to be cost savings.[91] Accordingly, much of Roosevelt's initial justification for the FSA focused on the potential savings and fiscal efficiency that could be achieved by consolidating agencies with conceptually related functions. This is amply borne out in the president's reorganization statement. Nonetheless, that statement deftly links the "economy" argument with two other ideas that are presented as being intimately connected to cost: the first is an "efficiency" rationale that essentially amounts to a thinly disguised justification for presidential control; the second is an assertion that the national security capacities of the United States depended on an effectively organized government. This latter point in the reorganization message is developed by reference to repressive dictatorships (presumably an allusion to Hitler) and resonates with the repeated efforts made almost immediately after the FSA's creation to emphasize its role in the war effort.[92]

The agency's creation received considerable media attention. Although some newspaper coverage in fact focused on the efficiencies that the agency merger would allegedly create, much of it discussed the merger in the larger context of the previous year's battle over reorganization.[93] This connection highlights how the reorganization process was understood to involve political stakes that would affect the relationship between the president and core regulatory and administrative functions of government. Indeed, at times the newspaper coverage acknowledged—in part because of Roosevelt's own rhetoric about the reorganization—that the changes would enhance the president's ability to control bureaucratic functions more directly.[94] Other observers, including the consistently anti-Roosevelt *Chicago Daily Tribune*, tried to forge a rhetorical boomerang by turning the president's own allusions to external threats against his reorganization plan:

A Nazi or Fascist could look at the three new agencies and their component parts and find something very familiar in them. This is the story of a totalitarian state. These authorities, administrations, and corporations now rearranged for more direct control by the chief executive are agencies by which the government pursues its program of mobilizing national activities under what the Germans call the Fuehrer.[95]

Despite such lingering opposition in some quarters and the previous year's spirited fight over reorganization, the president allayed the concerns of many of his critics. The centralizing structure of the FSA was decidedly incremental. It did not include the Veterans Administration, prisons, or responsibility for government employee pensions. Moderate legislators who had earlier opposed the reorganization were more inclined to support it. The agency was not cabinet level, giving those legislators further control over this dimension of reorganization in the future. And by consolidating disparate bureaus, the White House blunted Republicans' and Southern Democrats' arguments about the sprawling proliferation of smaller agencies. Bureaucrats occasionally offered spirited resistance. Sounding a note of alarm at the prospect of combining employment placement and social insurance services, the Labor Department all but predicted the collapse of the economy if its U.S. Employment Service was consolidated with the SSB under the FSA:

We are opposed to the proposed transference of the U.S. Employment Service to the Social Security Board on the following grounds. . . . An insurance dominated employment service would almost certainly lead to neglect of aggressive placement activities, which in turn would lead to increased demands upon insurance benefits. *The net result? A static, dying economic order.*[96]

Most officials, however, quickly fell into line. Some, particularly FDA officials who had chafed under an unsympathetic Agriculture Department, were quite favorably inclined toward the move. Nor did the president, generally skilled at quelling internal administration dissent, run into much opposition in his own administration. Though Harold Ickes's Interior Department was a "loser" in the reorganization process, the president considered the effort a priority, and even Ickes ultimately cooperated.[97]

The combination of the intense battle over reorganization and the newspaper coverage about the creation of the agency itself suggests that a substantial proportion of the nation's elites and its politically engaged public were aware of the FSA's creation.[98] Polls taken not long after the agency's creation suggest that Roosevelt's action met with considerable support, either because it was perceived as advancing the relatively anodyne efficiency goals he sought to emphasize (thrift appealed even to moderate Republicans) or because some constituents supported the health and public benefit programs that the FSA would administer and correctly perceived that the move would bode well for the political future of these programs. The most vociferous opponents were Republicans and a smattering of Southern Democrats who by this point were emphatically opposed to the president's agenda. These anti-Roosevelt partisans also repeatedly noted that the creation of the FSA was probably a move to make permanent a number of allegedly temporary programs.[99] Over time this proved to be partly true and partly false. Complex currents only partially anticipated by the Roosevelt administration were soon shaping the agency's trajectory.

CHAPTER 4

Just How Secure Are You at This Moment?

Growing and Elevating Federal Security

IN THE EVENTFUL YEARS that connected the twilight of Roosevelt's Presidency to Truman's, the FSA became more of a fixture in American life. Although the decade or so that followed the creation of the FSA was indeed a time of "considerable shifting," consistency also characterized the basic structure of the agency, including the four core agencies—the FDA, the SSB, the PHS, and the Office of Education—that accounted for the lion's share of the FSA's budget and regulatory responsibilities.[1] Some explicitly war-related functions, most notably the War Research Service, focused on biological weapons, and the Office of Community War Services, were eventually transferred or abolished.[2] Changes also affected employment-related functions, some of which were abolished or eventually transferred to Labor. Finally, President Truman centralized control over social security in 1947 by abolishing the SSB altogether and transferring its functions to the FSA administrator.[3]

The overall trajectory of the FSA during and after the war was one of sharp expansion. Most FSA bureaus experienced marked budget increases, growing administrative responsibilities, and continuity of their organizational lease on life.[4] The National Institutes of Health (NIH) (at the time known as the National Institute of Health)—a component of the PHS—acquired new funds and responsibilities for research related to national defense.[5] The SSB covered agricultural workers and domestic workers. The resources funneled to state education programs through the FSA's Office of Education skyrocketed.[6] In contrast, the Federal Loan Agency and the Federal Works Agency—the other two "superagencies" created when the FSA was forged— soon suffered declines in funding and both were eventually abolished.[7]

Some of the changes that occurred during the war years can be appreciated in the budgets of the FSA's four major administrative and policymaking bureaus. As Figure 4.1 shows, the FDA managed to retain its budget even during the war years. Both the Public Health Service and the Office of

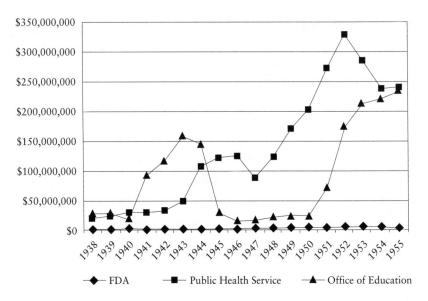

FIGURE 4.1 *Selected FSA Bureau Appropriations (Constant 1938 Dollars)*

Source: Budget of the United States (1938–1955 editions).

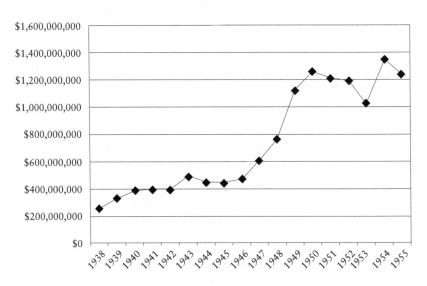

FIGURE 4.2 *Social Security Expenditures (Constant 1938 Dollars)*

Source: Budget of the United States (1938–1955 editions).

Education experienced dramatic increases during that time, with the Public Health Service increases coming later and becoming more permanent than those seen by the Office of Education. As Figure 4.2 shows, growth in appropriations for the sprawling social security apparatus—including grants for states to establish social insurance systems—continued to increase during much of the war, even while many other domestic agencies were forced to accept flat or declining budgets. Increases became even more pronounced for the Public Health Service and the Office of Education in the postwar period.[8]

Beginning in 1947 President Truman sought to use the recently renewed presidential reorganization authority to elevate the agency to cabinet status. The president's move may have had some symbolic purposes, but it was bound up with more practical political considerations. For one, Truman decided to make a major push to achieve national health insurance.[9] He may have believed the plan would be furthered by elevating its primary proponent—FSA administrator Oscar Ewing—to cabinet status.[10] Doing so would have generated additional (and, assuming that the plan to elevate the agency to cabinet status succeeded, probably favorable) news coverage and would have enhanced perceptions that the necessary federal administrative structure to administer national health insurance was already in place.[11] For another, the structural impact of turning an independent agency into a cabinet agency could be significant. In effect, doing so would have added yet another layer of political appointees (three assistant secretaries) to the mix of senior FSA officials, further increasing the administration's ability to direct how food and drug regulations were administered (something that the first HEW secretary, Oveta Hobby of the Eisenhower administration, soon realized would absorb a considerable amount of her time and effort), how benefit payments were issued, and how the agency's myriad other functions were carried out.[12] Despite the fact that Truman retained reorganization authority much like Roosevelt's, his efforts to elevate the FSA were thwarted by a legislative veto—the only such veto of one of his reorganization plans.[13]

Where Truman failed, President Eisenhower eventually succeeded. Shortly after his inauguration, he submitted a reorganization plan that sailed through congressional review and, by the middle of 1953, transformed the FSA into HEW.[14] In the process, the FSA again garnered considerable media attention, some of it—as with the newspaper article quoted below—chronicling the agency's staggering growth during and after the war years:

The reception in political and professional circles accorded new Administration proposals to raise the Federal Security Agency to Cabinet status indicates the great importance that has come to be attached to Federal welfare activities.

The agency that would, thus, attain full and responsible membership in the Administration family is one of the youngest in the Government. It mushroomed out of the New and Fair Deal eras. Moreover, in its days of fabulous growth, since its birth in 1939, it has embraced a number of old-line offices.

The organization of 38,000 employees . . . *collects and disburses billions of dollars in old age and survivors insurance. And it also enforces the Federal pure food and drug laws. It builds hospitals and operates research laboratories. It runs an institution for the mentally ill, and funnels public funds for a printing house to the blind.*[15]

Even more dramatic than changes in the agency as a whole were the evolving capacities of specific bureaus, perhaps most notably at the Public Health Service:

[The Public Health Service,] which came into the agency in 1939 with 6,200 employees and an annual appropriation of $24,692,000, has experienced phenomenal growth, even in a fast-expanding agency. Public Health today has a personnel of 15,170 and for 1953 has an appropriation of $283,452,000. It makes grants for hospitals ($134,700,000 this year), maintains laboratories, and directs such important research organizations as the National Cancer Institute and the National Health Institute.[16]

As with Roosevelt's own reorganization plan of 1938, the transformation of the FSA into a cabinet-level department proved to be something of a battle, which was given a measure of coverage in national newspapers. Truman's effort to create a cabinet-level security and welfare department failed initially amid opposition in the Republican-controlled Congress.[17] Part of the reason is likely to have been divided government. As David Lewis later speculates in his study of the politics of agency design, during periods of divided government, the legislature is skeptical of supporting a president's reorganization efforts.[18] Elevating the FSA at the time was particularly troubling because of its health-related functions and the identification of its administrator, Oscar Ewing, with efforts to achieve national health insurance—a goal that was particularly offensive to the congressional Republican leadership.[19]

Illustrating again how a president could use the structure of the FSA in the service of a legislative agenda, Truman ordered Ewing to deploy "all the resources within the FSA for vigorous and united action toward achieving public understanding of the need for a national health program."[20] The newspapers covered this.[21] They also covered Eisenhower's efforts to elevate the department in 1953—one of his first substantive actions as president—which was achieved with relatively little opposition.[22]

Between the end of the Roosevelt administration and the agency's attainment of cabinet status early in the Eisenhower administration, the FSA lived through the eventful years of the Truman administration. During this critical period, the agency navigated a transition through a postwar political and budgetary environment. Its staff played a major role in President Truman's "Fair Deal."[23] And FSA administrator Oscar Ewing, an ambitious New York lawyer eager to raise his profile, continued to promote the idea that security-related laws and policies should encompass both defense-related and domestic risk-reduction initiatives.[24] Each of these developments appears to have left its mark on the organization.

Although funding for some wartime education- and health-related programs dried up, the agency found itself awash in appropriations for health research and public health initiatives. Wartime programs in this domain appeared to whet congressional appetites for a large health research infrastructure.[25] Social security benefits payments also rose as wartime financing constraints began to ebb. As the agency grew, the White House forged a domestic agenda—Truman's "Fair Deal"—that involved further expansion of the FSA programs to include national health insurance and bestowal of cabinet status.[26]

The FSA also began playing a more explicit role in civil defense during the Truman years. Civil defense and security functions lay dormant in the United States for most of the period between the end of World War I and the beginning of World War II. Roosevelt formally convened efforts at civil preparedness within the White House in 1940 as American participation in the spreading conflict in Europe and Asia was becoming more likely.[27] Those functions remained lodged in the White House for much of the war. Although the initial interagency group that focused on civil defense did not specifically include the FSA, the FSA's history is in fact connected to civil defense activities in a number of ways. First, Roosevelt's creation of the FSA emphasized the need for preparedness and held up the agency as an example of it. In that statement and in subsequent speeches, his administration emphasized the link between domestic regulatory and welfare functions and national defense (both before and during the war itself). Second, the White House was in fact drawing on the new superagency for a number of functions related to civil defense preparedness, including military draft-related planning and the use of SSB resources for placing workers in defense-related industries.[28] Later, during the war itself, Roosevelt gave the FSA head a major role in overseeing certain manpower-related preparedness functions.[29] Third, despite the reluctance of civil defense head Fiorello LaGuardia (concurrently also serving as mayor of New York City) to focus on "sissy stuff,"[30] the formal civil defense preparedness effort was eventually forced to shift attention to the public health, education, and welfare aspects of civil defense. These pursuits related directly to the role the FSA was expected to play in emergencies.[31]

Administrator Oscar Ewing did not consider civil defense to be the only security priority within his mandate. When he became one of the administration's point men on national health insurance, he encountered an environment of intense social cleavages and political disagreements about domestic policy.[32] At least some of these tensions were tangled up with anxiety about the spread of communism and socialism.[33] While the American Medical Association (AMA) relentlessly sought to link national health insurance to socialism,[34] Ewing sought to respond with an even more pointed version of the Roosevelt-era penchant for melding domestic risk reduction and geostrategic national defense concerns into a single overarching appeal to the value of security. Writing in the auspiciously named *American Magazine* in 1949, Ewing celebrated the value of expanding FSA programs by deliberately framing security concerns in a manner that could apply interchangeably to risk regulation and national defense. "[S]ecurity measures," Ewing opined, "[are] simply an orderly way to take care of ourselves in times of distress—as well as keep us well—with everyone sharing the burden."[35] He continued:

Just how secure are you at this moment? If, tomorrow, you have an acute attack . . . could you foot the bill . . . ? If a child is born in your family, are you secure in the knowledge that he will receive the best attention the medical profession can offer—that he can have the education he may set his heart upon, perhaps a college degree? Suppose you lose your job, or become disabled. What sort of world would lie ahead for you? *These personal matters of security* are the direct concern of your Federal Security Agency, of which I happen to be the Administrator. . . . As I see it, security means a sure knowledge that we shall not want for the basic necessities of life, no matter what Fate may have in store. . . . With that sure knowledge, we can proceed to go about getting the things we want from life under the American system of free choice.[36]

"Free choice," Ewing's philosophy here implied, depended at least as much on remedying potential market failures as it did on allowing consumers to feel that they were making ostensibly unconstrained choices: "When . . . an American buys a can of food from a grocery-store shelf, he is so sure that the food is healthful, and that the contents are according to the label, he scarcely thinks about it. *I call this real security.*"[37] From these theoretical foundations, Ewing then offered an explicit response—again mixing geostrategic national defense concerns and risk-reduction rationales—to the AMA's charges about how the FSA was putting the United States on the road toward socialism:

Some people will tell you that these advances for the good of the general welfare are approaches toward Communism. The exact opposite is true. Security is the best defense we have against Communism. When a man is provided through democratic government with the basic securities which make it possible for him to get what he wants, to stand on his own two feet, independently, he will not listen to wild isms.[38]

Ewing's pointed advocacy drew the attention of the Republican majority in Congress, who took the kinetic administrator to task for excessive lobbying and travel. In one such matter, congressional investigators criticized Ewing for an elaborate trip he took to Europe with the apparent purpose of playing up Western Europe's success in building national health insurance arrangements.[39] In response, Ewing again played the security fugue, insisting:

For more than a year, the Federal Security agency had been working on plans for civilian defense, first at the request of the Department of Defense and later for the National Security Resources Board. We knew that in the United Kingdom the Ministry of Health and the Home Office had done a great deal of planning in this field; and the time had come when it was necessary for us to have face-to-face discussions on the subject. . . . Our talks covered plans for distribution of medical and related manpower as between civil and military activities in wartime; recruitment, training, and assignment of medical personnel for defense operations; organization of the nation for civil defense; and organization of other health-related services.[40]

These controversies did not stop Ewing's advocacy. Nonetheless, congressional pressure, coupled with the advent of the Korean War, kept the FSA from attaining cabinet status and made it marginally harder for the Truman administration to obtain statutory changes expanding health and welfare programs.[41] The controversies did not, however, diminish the importance of the agency's bureaus to the overall scope of federal activity—even if cabinet status was not obtained until the beginning of the Eisenhower administration.[42] Neither did they stop the FSA from remaining involved in explicitly defense-related activities, as discussed in more detail below.

BROADENING THE SCOPE OF "SECURITY"

Ewing's tendency to parry criticisms of the FSA by playing up the agency's role in national defense had some basis in what the agency actually did. Defense-related activities were a major constant of the FSA as it endured the war years and its responsibilities continued to swell. Increasingly, the FSA framed its essential purpose both to external constituencies and to internal employees in terms of national security. For instance, a newsletter to FDA employees during the war proclaimed, "Few . . . have better opportunities for service of value both to the armed forces and to the civilian population than those who guard the entrance to the alimentary canal."[43] While other domestic agencies occasionally assisted in the war effort, they generally did so by seconding resources or cooperating with temporary wartime coordinating bureaucracies.[44] Rarely did those agencies directly assume responsibility for national security–related efforts, nor did they (as the FDA did) brand entire regulatory programs as essential to national defense.

In contrast, at nearly every turn the FSA assumed responsibility connected to national security or framed its regulatory activities as essential to the same. Consider some examples from early in the war. The FSA's annual reports emphasized the war-related functions of bureaus such as the PHS, the Office of Education, and the SSB.[45] The frequently mentioned specific examples were then combined with overarching discussions of the war effort, the importance of national security, and the allegedly deep connections of both to the health- and welfare-related work of the FSA.[46] The SSB paid benefits to bereaved families of the military. Because the agency's mandate at the time included employment placement, the agency served as a conduit to funnel displaced (or otherwise willing) workers into war-related industries.[47] The Office of Education, its budget swelling during wartime, trained workers for war-related industrial occupations.[48] So did the National Youth Administration while it continued in existence as part of the FSA.[49] In Congress, the agency's staff constantly used national security arguments to ask for greater appropriations. The FDA relentlessly promoted its mission of "guarding the alimentary canal" and ensuring the flow of safe pharmaceutical products to the armed forces as essential national security functions.[50] The PHS, working through its NIH unit, devoted a growing share of its resources to defense-related research projects.[51] The FSA also created specialized war-related units through the FSA administrator's internal reorganization authority. These included the War Research Service to spearhead American biological weapons research[52] and the Office of Community War Services to provide health and related services to the military and engage in anti-prostitution enforcement near military bases.[53] Working with the War Relocation Authority, the FSA also played a crucial support role in the relocation of Japanese Americans by serving as a conduit for the provision of benefits and assisting in the placement of Japanese Americans in approved supervised occupations in the areas to which they were being relocated.[54] Together, these activities blurred the distinction between national security and the economic and social security that was initially associated with the bureaus of the FSA.[55]

Although the agency's defense-related activities had begun before the war and increased in the early phase of the conflict, the pace of these activities quickened as the conflict progressed. Together, McNutt and his assistants formed an agency-wide "Victory Council" to imbue the agency's employees with a sense of mission about the war effort and to obtain suggestions. Letters such as the following poured in:

A suggestion for saving hundreds of pounds of fat in the form of soap. Calgonite or Tri-sodium Phosphate compound can be used for washing glass-ware and other laboratory apparatus, and washing dishes in a pan instead of holding soap and glass-ware under faucet and allowing the cleanser to flow down the waste pipe before it is fully used. A few users of great quantities of soap: U.S. Public Health, Regional Laboratories, US Food & Drug Administration.[56]

As early as 1940, the FSA also became involved in developing a nation-wide system to register young men for a military draft. To do this the FSA leveraged its nationwide network of the SSB and U.S. Employment Service offices and its relationship with state employment services.[57] That same year, the FSA's Office of Education worked with the War Department to design a system of "individual record cards to be issued to students of vocational schools" so they could be more quickly placed in defense-related industries upon completion of their training.[58] A few months later, the president involved the FSA in an interagency committee to "study at this time the question of making some financial provision for the dependents of men in the military service."[59]

The new structure also served the needs of the political appointees chosen to run it. On occasion, McNutt and his assistants seemed to view the FSA as a national early-warning system for detecting trends among the civilian population that could eventually imperil some expanded version of "national security." Fearing that the simmering possibility of war would begin to siphon young men away from college and into the military, McNutt warned Roosevelt in 1940: "[A] large number of young people who had planned to enter college this September and many of those who attended college last year are intending to interrupt their education to find employment in industries essential to national defense, to enlist in the Army or Navy."[60] He recommended that Roosevelt "advise the young people of the country . . . to continue their education and assure them that they will be promptly advised if they are needed for other patriotic services."[61] White House records indicate that the president obliged, "urging college students to continue their education, as any other decision would be unfortunate. Must have intelligent citizens, scientists, engineers, and economists. Patriotic duty of all young people to continue the normal course of their education, unless and until they are called."[62]

This coterie of activities supporting traditional defense-related functions made the FSA stand out even among the larger milieu of domestic agencies that had been enlisted in the war effort. As the war progressed, these functions expanded to include biological weapons research. Such work was controversial even among military officials and Congress; the U.S. government had signed a treaty outlawing such research in 1925 (though the Senate had yet to ratify it).[63] Once the president was persuaded that the research should include both offensive and defensive applications, he decided that it should occur within the FSA. Funds would be made available from the president's emergency fund, which required no elaborate accounting to appropriations overseers.[64] The FSA boasted a comparatively small and loyal oversight staff[65] and less-developed relationships to congressional committees compared to the War Department. Moreover, its overt health-related mission provided what aides described as "political cover," allowing top university scientists across the country to receive the laundered White House funds without revealing the sensitive nature of their work. After conferring with the president, McNutt selected pharmaceutical mogul George Merck of Merck & Co. to run what became the newest bureau of the FSA, the War Research Service.[66] McNutt described the early stages of the project thus:

In accordance with our understanding, Mr. George W. Merck has assumed the duties as Director of the Branch of War Research in Chemistry on my staff [sic]. It is my understanding that following the letter which Secretary Stimson wrote you on April 29, 1942, concerning this whole program, you indicated that you would make available $200,000 out of our Special Emergency Fund for preliminary expenses. It is desirable now to establish the headquarters office of the organization in the Federal Security Agency. I therefore request that this $200,000 be made available for the purposes covered in this program to me as Federal Security Administrator and that an immediate transfer of $50,000 be effected for first steps in the program. After a conference with the staff of the Secretary of War, it appears desirable to request that this money be spent as part of the $25,000,000 in the proviso of the supplemental national defense appropriation Act for 1943. . . . It is understood, of course, that all appropriate records will be kept as part of the secret files of the Director and of the Federal Security Administrator.[67]

A further characteristic of the FSA's national security focus is evident in the extent to which the agency's leadership joined the White House in promoting its elastic conception of "security" during the length of the war and in subsequent years. The public message about the FSA from the White House and the agency's leadership was as ubiquitous as it was simple: "security" encompassed not only explicit war-related functions but also the agency's more conventional domestic and regulatory responsibilities such as food safety, nutrition education, and public health activities not concerning the military.[68]

Agency activities during the Truman administration amply demonstrated the persistence of defense-related roles and responsibilities well after World War II. Lured both by domestic political concerns associated with the Cold War and by the Korean War, Truman established an elaborate coterie of national security–related bureaucracies using statutory and executive authority. He set up a National Security Council and a National Security Resources Board.[69] The latter also included a Federal Civil Defense office that combined some of the functions now included in the Federal Emergency Management Agency (FEMA) and the Office of State and Local Coordination within DHS. Nonetheless, the FSA's explicit defense-related functions persisted. It played the preeminent role in health research and assessments relevant to outbreaks of communicable disease, germ warfare attacks, and preparedness of human military resources.[70] Despite the fact that other agencies were also involved in civil defense efforts, the FSA's role was pronounced. FSA-led functions are mentioned twenty-one separate times in the National Security Resources Board document describing agency missions critical to strengthening defense on the home front.[71] And FSA administrator Ewing, along with President Truman, continually framed the administration's domestic welfare and regulatory agenda as an element of a broader security policy to disrupt the spread of ostensibly subversive ideas.[72]

The picture thus emerging from this historical progression is one of an agency straddling the line between welfare and defense—an agency that proved valuable to Truman as well as Roosevelt. Also emerging is a picture of Roosevelt as a president who greatly valued the power to reorganize the bureaus that performed administrative and regulatory functions. Given his earlier proposals to Congress and where he first deployed his newly acquired reorganization authority, it seems that he was especially concerned with those functions involving the White House, public health, social welfare, education, and temporary relief programs that he had created earlier in the New Deal. What remains to be addressed are (1) precisely why Roosevelt believed he needed reorganization authority—which could be used to create a new agency—to accomplish his goals; (2) why the FSA blended domestic administrative and regulatory functions with national security ones; and (3) what the merger actually seems to have accomplished. The answers will emerge in part by placing the FSA in the context of theoretical approaches to law and bureaucracy and in part by closely scrutinizing the events that unfolded as Roosevelt's initial reorganization decision culminated some years later in a new cabinet-level super-department.

CHAPTER 5

Democracies Need Not Always Be Weak

More Control, and More to Control

That federal authority could be a double-edged sword was nowhere more clearly illustrated than in the evacuation of Japanese-Americans from the West Coast, a process facilitated by a number of New Deal welfare agencies. . . . The ease with which relief programs could serve the cause of relocation suggested that such a massive and efficient movement of people would have been immeasurably more difficult before the advent of the social service state.[1]

ON APRIL 26, 1939, readers of the nation's paper of daily record awoke to the following headline: *President Decrees Three Big Offices in Centralizing 21—Relief, Social Security and Lending Agencies Grouped in Reorganization Message—A Warning to Dictators—Democracies Need Not Always Be Weak, He Says, but Must Keep Tools Up to Date.*[2] Under the Reorganization Act of 1939, readers learned, the new Federal Security Agency would be born, along with two smaller agencies—as long as no house of Congress approved a resolution disfavoring the plan. While the immediate consequences of this move were clear enough to readers of the nation's newspapers that morning, what we have discovered here suggests that our theoretical tools to explain why and how politicians decide whether to create agencies such as the FSA are incomplete. In particular, such theories should more thoroughly address how structural changes allow politicians to simultaneously assert greater control over agencies, build their capacity, and reshape how political elites and the mass public understand a bureaucracy's mission.

By taking a closer look at the early history of the FSA, we begin in this chapter to provide support for those theoretical refinements. Its focus is on demonstrating how presidents can control the bureaucracy by *building* bureaucratic capacity and how they can enlarge support for regulatory and administrative activities by engineering bureaucracies to reshape public views and to bolster legislative coalitions. The payoff is not only in better understanding what happened with a major portion of the federal government housed at the FSA and its successor agencies, but also in elucidating how political actors more generally shape legal mandates through organizational choices that parallel and interact with their decisions about how to interpret statutes and legal doctrines.

EXECUTIVE CAPACITY AND PRESIDENTIAL
MOTIVATIONS: MORE CONTROL,
AND MORE TO CONTROL

Consider the stakes involved for Roosevelt and his advisors when it came to the future of the bureaus that were folded into the FSA. Unlike most other presidents before him or since, Roosevelt had previously served in a senior position within the executive bureaucracy. He arrived into that bureaucracy via a position as assistant secretary of the Navy in the State, War, and Navy Building, where he sat behind the same massive mahogany desk his cousin Theodore Roosevelt had occupied in the same position decades earlier.[3] He began learning firsthand of the political techniques lawmakers used to control bureaus.[4] He decried the formal legal independence of bureaus within the Navy Department, which allowed bureau chiefs to bypass the Navy Department and even the president in their dealings with Congress.[5] For an astute young assistant secretary, these constraints naturally led him to acquire a measure of human capital optimized for the task of strengthening control—even in a legally restrictive environment—over bureaus whose performance could so heavily impact his political future.[6]

Against the backdrop of these experiences, it should have been only too clear to Franklin Roosevelt, the president two decades later, how much the political context gave the White House a cluster of overlapping reasons to be concerned about the bureaucracy in general, and particularly about the fate of key regulatory and administrative bureaus with major new or politically important responsibilities (for example, the FDA, the PHS, the SSB, and the Office of Education). First, Roosevelt's insistence on reorganization authority, and his almost immediate use of that authority once he obtained it, reflects the challenges he faced in dealing with the increasing political controversy associated with the New Deal. Perhaps largely as a result of the president's own determination to wring maximal policymaking advantage from his 1936 electoral victory, the administration's allies in Congress had dwindled by 1938.[7] The Republicans had gained eighty seats in the legislature that year.[8] It was not inconceivable that the growing ranks of New Deal opponents would seek to block presidential efforts to carry out the new legal mandates—for which he had secured approval—by trying to assert legislative control over the bureaucracies. Opponents could impose administrative burdens on bureaus, seek subtle but significant technical changes in the underlying legislation that would limit the scope of regulatory powers, or restrict the budgets that funded agency operations.[9] Indeed, an increasingly threatening political environment should have led the White House to desire more political control of bureaus in the short term even if it eventually wanted those entities to become impervious to political manipulation by less sympathetic presidents.[10] In effect, the White House would have found itself in a stronger position to make use of scarce agency resources to serve a range of political goals (including, perhaps, growing the political autonomy of prized programs) if it had secured greater control over the bureaus in the short term, and realigned agency responsibilities to facilitate the bureaus' growth in the longer term. Whatever concerns Roosevelt or his staff may have had about how subsequent presidents might use greater authority over the bureaus would have been mitigated somewhat by the fact that nearly 50 percent of the president's second term remained. And even well before World War II, the notoriously optimistic Roosevelt had copiously declined to rule out a third term.[11]

The White House's rocky time expanding the Social Security program illustrates the stakes. By 1950, Social Security expanded to cover farm-related employment.[12] But before then, its advocates sustained a number of defeats in trying to move toward expansion. Even the SSB sometimes rejected opportunities for expansion. Early on, supporters of Social Security were among those who were cautious. Some urged that the focus should be on private, wage-earning employment to simplify administrative burdens on the agency at the time when it would be most vulnerable. The role of the SSB illustrates the stakes for Roosevelt in trying to assert greater control over the bureaucratic structures associated with his programs. At the same time, the link between bureaucratic capacity to supervise program administration and further expansion suggests that the president could have had incentives to expand the resources that could be made available to the SSB by subsuming it into a larger agency that could draw on the budgets and capacities of other agencies (and indeed, the Labor Department–related functions transferred into the FSA were in fact placed at the disposal of the SSB).[13]

With tighter control over administrative bureaus, the White House could also steer a growing stream of federal grants in a manner that could simultaneously fulfill their statutory purposes and cement the new Democratic coalition. Three of the bureaus administering some of the largest national grant programs at the time—the SSB, the PHS, and the Office of Education—were among those moved to the FSA.[14] By the second half of the 1930s, the federal government had increased resources and legal authority to provide grant funds to states and localities. Just four years before the FSA's creation, significant legislative changes further opened the spigot of federal grant money that would eventually be housed within the new superagency.[15] States received a growing amount of funds for public assistance, child and maternal health, unemployment compensation, child welfare, and (through the PHS) the provision of medical services in underserved areas.[16] Although the grants came with strings requiring the development of merit systems for staffing the new programs, the statutory enactments left the administration a measure of flexibility for directing *where* the funds were spent.[17] Indeed, some historians have suggested that the Roosevelt administration sought to direct funding to states that were politically supportive.[18] But with grant funds and bureaucracies expanding, the administration may have had a particular interest in increasing its capacity to monitor how grants were being administered and where funds were going. In addition, temporary relief entities such as the National Youth Administration were folded into the new agency. The president insisted through his advisors that "all projects of [the National Youth Administration] [ ] be presented to him for approval."[19]

Second, the often complex new mandates for which the administration had secured approval required growth in the bureaucracy. The functions mandated by the National Labor Relations Act, the Food, Drug, and Cosmetic Act, and the Social Security Act could not be carried out without an army of lawyers, clerks, supervisors, and analysts. As the bureaucracy grew, the president's own capacity to supervise and control how that bureaucracy executed the mandates remained limited.[20]

Third, even before the outbreak of the war, the White House sought to conduct certain projects in relative secrecy. The strong existing relationships—even back then—between legislators and some established departments, such as War and Navy, made this more difficult than it might have been at a new, subcabinet agency with fewer existing links to Congress and a leaner bureaucratic structure.[21]

Fourth, there is likely something to an account occasionally developed in the political science literature discussing how the president's connection to a national constituency likely makes him somewhat more interested in the extent to which the bureaucracy can achieve relatively widely held political goals.[22] Other things being equal, one should expect legislators to have a comparatively lesser interest in "efficiency" (as one might refer to the capacity of the bureaucracy to achieve widely held political goals) because only rarely are individual legislators sufficiently identified with government performance to make it worth their while to sacrifice jurisdiction-specific gains in exchange for benefits at the national level.[23] Hence, veterans' opposition to the creation of a Department of Welfare should be expected to sway a legislator in a district with a large concentration of veterans and no countervailing political pressures even if the performance of the federal government as a whole would be enhanced by the move.[24] Presidents, in contrast, face fewer "common pool" problems.[25]

ADDING A LAYER OF POLITICAL STAFF

As it forged the new FSA, the White House sought to achieve its objectives precisely along the lines of what the theory developed above would imply. The creation of the FSA established a new layer of political appointees loyal to the president, a new staff to oversee the bureaus' legal determinations, and a capacity to develop and advocate for legislative proposals that could cut across different agency functions at a time when the White House staff—even after the White House–related changes in reorganization—was tiny. All of these changes made it easier for the president to monitor policy developments, control how legal authority was deployed in the present, and control how proposals for future statutory and regulatory changes were developed.

The most immediate consequence of the FSA's creation is plain from comparing the *United States Government Manual* of 1940 or 1941 to that of 1938 or 1939.[26] The reorganization yielded for the White House the bounty of a new staff to monitor the activities of a bundle of government bureaus.[27] A job description for one of the junior analysts in what became Paul McNutt's office at FSA headquarters gives an inkling of what these appointees might accomplish:

[R]esponsibilities primarily along the following lines: (1) Maintaining current knowledge of all policies, programs, and procedures involved in the work of the United States Public Health Service, the Food and Drug Administration, the Health and Medical Committee of the Office of Defense Health and Welfare Services, and all other Governmental organizations whose activities bear upon health problems. (2) With respect to the Public Health Service this involves an understanding of various projects and programs and the objectives of such operations particularly in their non-technical aspects; with respect to the Food and Drug Administration this involves an acquaintanceship with the meaning and intent of various standards and policies, procedures with respect to legal actions, and the relation of specific cases to other work in the Food and Drug Administration.[28]

Such officials augmented what was, by twentieth-century standards, a paltry White House staff. They also expanded what even quite loyal staff at existing executive departments could accomplish in overseeing the bureaucracy. The challenge of departmental staff management was all the more acute if the department's (and the political staff's) reputation depended more heavily on performing core functions unrelated to those of the soon-to-be-transferred bureau. Thus, beyond the fact that the FSA added generally loyal supervisory staff, the concern of Treasury political appointees about the PHS was unlikely to ever approximate that of the FSA's appointees.[29] Nor was the president shy in using that new layer of staff for developing policy proposals that leveraged both the administrative expertise and the perceived competence of the FSA. For example, when Truman asked FSA administrator Oscar Ewing to use the agency to promote national health insurance, Ewing responded with an FSA-prepared report purporting to draw on the experience of the agency's full complement of bureaus to urge adoption of national health insurance legislation.[30]

Because the White House staff was small and other mechanisms of bureaucratic control (including partisan patronage politics) were fraying, the White House sought to add a contingent of political staff to facilitate the White House's monitoring and control of bureaus placed within the FSA. In effect, the creation of the FSA allowed the president to move agencies such as the FDA and the SSB, changing their structure to make them more amenable to oversight.

As Figure 5.1 indicates, the White House staff in the 1930s was minute compared to what it would be a few decades later. Meanwhile, the executive branch was expanding. Some of this expansion was among the military, but a substantial chunk of it was occurring among the ranks of civilian executive branch workers.[31] For instance, the SSB was an independent agency that lost its independence under the plan and did not regain it until the mid-1990s.[32] Because the goal of monitoring and controlling government functions depends in part on civilian staff, the White House sought to increase the size of that staff beginning in the late 1930s. But the Roosevelt administration also sought substitutes for the White House staff increases in the form of new layers of political appointees to oversee existing bureaus and in the form of initiatives limiting the formal legal insulation from presidential control of independent commissions such as the SSB.[33]

Along with the SSB, all the bureaus within the FSA would now report to the administrator and his senior staff. The agency head, moreover, would be vested with the legal authority to undertake all the agency's functions. Even with respect to the bureaus that were not previously independent as a matter of law, the officials associated with the new FSA structure represented a net increase in the number of staff available to monitor bureaus (compared to the status quo), with the significance of the staff accentuated by the fact that it would be dedicated to monitoring certain bureaus, such as the PHS, that had previously received relatively meager attention in their original bureaucratic homes.[34]

The difficulties associated with White House monitoring and control of the executive bureaucracy can be further appreciated by examining the percentage of federal executive branch employees working at the White House (Figure 5.2). As early as 1934, that ratio was falling and could be

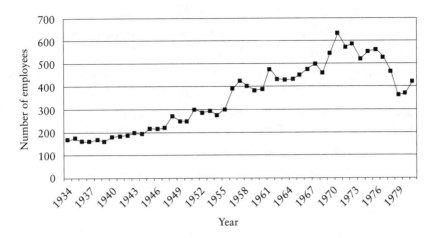

FIGURE 5.1 *White House Employees, 1934–1980*

Source: Based on data in Charles E. Walcott and Karen M. Hult, *White House Staff Size: Examples and Implications*, 29 Pres. Stud. Q. 638, 641–42 (1999).

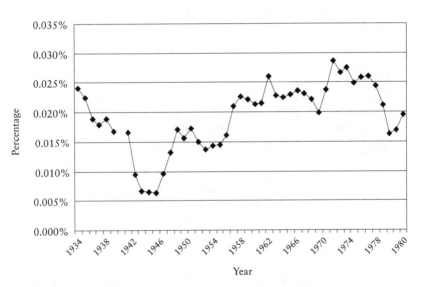

FIGURE 5.2 *Percentage of Civilian Executive Branch Employees Working at the White House, 1934–1980*

Sources: Based on author's calculations from data in Charles E. Walcott and Karen M. Hult, *White House Staff Size: Examples and Implications*, 29 Pres. Stud. Q. 638, 641–42 (1999). *U.S. Census Bureau, Statistical Abstract of the United States 2003* at 94 table HS-50.

anticipated to fall even further. Even if Roosevelt succeeded in gradually expanding the purview of the White House to include new federal employees temporarily loaned on detail from existing departments and the Bureau of the Budget, the task of overseeing bureaucratic activity was becoming ever more challenging for the White House. If legislators would continue restraining growth in White House staff, the White House could respond by changing the oversight structure that was directly responsible for the bureaus—both by increasing the number of politically loyal overseers and by reallocating legal authority over bureaucratic responsibilities and vesting it more clearly in higher-level officials.[35]

The consequences of the FSA's new position, allowing it to better monitor its bureaus, were not lost on participants at the time. The president had tremendous interest in "trying to find some method by which he and future presidents would be relieved of a certain amount of paper work and a certain amount of personal conferences" and believed that "this had been in great part accomplished through the Reorganization"—in part through the creation of the Federal Security Agency.[36] Along with this goal, the president's staff sought a "reduction in [the] number of independent agencies," such as the SSB, which had been designed by Congress to limit presidential control.[37] While public administration intellectuals such as Louis Brownlow credited reorganization for nearly every American wartime success, internal White House documents belie the administration's insistence that reorganization was meant to advance widely held social goals rather than presidential power.[38] Lest there be any doubt about the White House's *actual* goal of using efficiency to benefit the president, an internal White House memorandum setting forth the guiding principles for using the president's coveted reorganization powers provides further insight:

[A]s a guide to the timing of steps in reorganization the following is suggested: First, do those things which when done will *reduce the difficulties of the President in dealing with his multifarious duties and which will assist him in discharging his responsibilities as the chief administrator of the government.* Second, do *those things which when done will advantage the work of those administrative aides who have been chosen by the President to assist him in the discharge of his duties . . . whose responsibility to the people is through the President.* (These two purposes may be accomplished by (1) reduction of the number of independent agencies reporting directly to the President, and (2) better organization of the managerial arms of the President—budget, planning and personnel agencies). Third, *do those things which when done will advantage heads of departments in the discharge of their own* responsibilities. (This can be accomplished by bringing together scattered agencies dealing with the same functions so that the heads of departments may better plan and coordinate their work).[39]

Roosevelt, as the assistant secretary of the Navy, could have written a similar memorandum decades earlier and indeed did at the time exalt the notion of executive accountability functioning through cabinet (and sub-cabinet) officials reporting to the president.[40]

The nature of these goals as they map onto the competition *between* branches becomes even clearer in the next passage of the analysis, which is styled as a "historical note":

[D]uring the era of legislative encroachment on executive prerogative the President's assistants (cabinet officers et al.) have had *direct* access to Congressional committees denied to the President and often have unwittingly aided in the process of undermining Executive authority by making parochial trades with special interest committees in the Congress. A thorough reorganization will give the Congress the benefit of the considered and rounded knowledge and opinion of the whole Executive Branch rather than, as has been so often the case, the specialized opinion of a particular part of the administrative corps.

It is an interesting fact that few federal administrators have spoken to the members of the President's Committee on Administrative Management in terms of the *interest* of the President or the presidency or the Administration—but nearly always in terms of the immediate and particular interest of a department or a bureau as if it were satrapy.[41]

The analysis proved to be more than theory. It was, in fact, precisely the view articulated by subsequent FSA officials explaining their role in overseeing the agency's coterie of bureaus. Paying no regard to the complexities associated with statutory grants of authority to *subordinate* officials, Oscar Ewing was particularly explicit about his perceived duty to the White House when testifying before the House Select Committee on Lobbying Activities in 1950:

The department head must be regarded as an extension of the President's personality. He is expected to carry out any basic instructions which a President may provide for his guidance. . . . Furthermore, a department head is expected to provide a certain political point of view to departmental operations. He must be more than a mere channel of communication between the department and the President for vital matters on which the latter must make a decision. The department head should bring a political attitude to all departmental affairs. Such a political attitude is not to be defined in terms of a narrow partisanship. . . . Rather, a political attitude reflects prevailing beliefs on broad public issues, beliefs about the scope and magnitude of Government activities, about both the ends and means of government action.[42]

With the president's new political appointees more tightly controlling the FSA's bureaus, they assisted the White House in monitoring regulatory developments at the agencies, giving political speeches about the FSA's work across the country,[43] and developing new policy and legislative proposals that often, in turn, led to increased budgets.[44] Given the extent to which the reorganization changed the White House's capacity to control bureaus, it is surprising that some observers believe presidential control of the bureaucracy is a relatively recent development. Elena Kagan's magisterial account of presidential administration is an example.[45] Although Kagan acknowledges the significance of some battles over reorganization, such as the conflict over Roosevelt's 1938 reorganization plan,[46] she still describes the trajectory of presidential control by emphasizing the innovations of the Clinton administration.[47] These techniques, including taking credit for rulemaking and using the White House staff to monitor bureaucratic developments, surely enhanced presidential control at a time when the White House confronted a politically empowered and Republican-controlled Congress.[48] But presidential administration at the end of the twentieth century was in fact foreshadowed by the uses and consequences of organizational structure in the 1940s and 1950s.[49]

CHANGING THE ORGANIZATIONAL ENVIRONMENT
AFFECTING PRESIDENTIAL GOALS

New organizational structures altered the context of decision makers who wielded statutory authority. Even when the White House could not directly monitor what bureaus were doing, their work could be shaped by placing them in organizational environments more amenable to the missions that the administration supported. Recall that the AMA explicitly *wanted* the Public Health Service to remain at Treasury at one point; the bureaus were in agencies that made their work almost certainly peripheral (the Office of Education, in the Interior Department, faced the same situation).[50] The Agriculture secretary eventually made a halfhearted effort to keep the FDA in his department in 1940.[51] When the former Bureau of Chemistry was nonetheless transferred to the new health and security agency, the bureau's employees faced a new political equation. Agricultural interests lacked the same close relationship they had enjoyed with the Agriculture Department's leadership.[52]

The importance of shifting the organizational context was not lost on the White House. Facing daunting practical constraints when seeking policy results from government bureaus, administration officials understood themselves to be changing the agencies' political environment as a means of bolstering policy goals. Return to the internal White House analyses of the first reorganization plan, from 1938. Although they contain a brief reference to the rhetoric about "democracy" found in public statements about the plan, the analyses quickly define a specific version of democracy that emphasizes the importance of presidential control, the goal of strengthening functions considered critical by the White House, and—crucially—the value of changing the existing relationships among bureaus, interest groups, and Congress.[53] Even if changes at the top of the hierarchy did not guarantee that policies more aligned with the president's goals, at a minimum such shifts provided an opportunity that could be exploited to scramble and complicate the existing relationships of external organized interests, bureaus, and their legislative overseers.

Consider, for example, how a broad new agency mandate could be used to shroud the details of a sensitive, presidentially sanctioned project.

In Roosevelt's day, the creation of a new agency with a broad mandate for "security" allowed the president to take advantage of bureaucratic resources at his disposal for sensitive projects that commanded the president's attention and would have been more difficult to control or hide within established bureaucracies subject to significant monitoring from interest groups and Congress. For instance, the biological weapons research activity conducted by the FSA was by its nature politically sensitive and was paid for with White House funds. Placing it in the FSA was later described in a memorandum to the president as justified because of the need for political "cover."[54] As former War Research Service (WRS) director George Merck explained in a speech just a few years after the war:

In the fall of 1941, opinion in the United States regarding the value of Biological Warfare was by no means united. But common prudence dictated to those responsible for the nation's defense that they give serious consideration to the dangers of possible attack. . . . Starting as a project under the most extreme secrecy, the work was undertaken under the wing (and cloak) of the Federal Security Agency. Emerging from this "cover" (but not from secrecy) the Army, with the Navy collaborating, took over. Unique facilities were built by the Chemical Warfare Service and by the Navy for experimentation on pathogenic agents.[55]

Neither these divisions in opinion nor the fact that the U.S. government had signed a treaty against biological weapons stopped the White House from fomenting such research, however.[56] During the years when the WRS operated from the bowels of the FSA, the White House managed to funnel millions of dollars into secret—and highly controversial—biological and chemical weapons research. Eventually, once the work of the WRS had matured, political appointees at the War Department and the FSA agreed to recommend that the president transfer many of its functions to the War Department.[57] The 1944 joint memorandum moving many WRS functions to the War Department admits not only that the FSA was doing both offensive and defensive weapons research, but that these functions were initially placed at FSA for political cover.[58] The extent of Nazi atrocities in the interim period may have made it less politically important for the president to seek cover by the end of 1944 for such secret activities. Conversely, by then the organizational and research capacity of the War

Department had expanded substantially, making it potentially less important to keep these functions at the new FSA bureaucracy.[59]

Nonetheless, the FSA continued to engage in biological and chemical weapons research even after the transfer of the WRS to the War Department. And by the war's end, Merck proudly proclaimed that he considered the WRS's chief accomplishment to have been

[t]he development of methods and facilities for the mass production of pathogenic microorganisms and their products: First, the microorganisms selected for exhaustive investigation were made as virulent as possible, produced in specially developed culture media under optimum conditions for growth. . . . In this work it was necessary to determine how well various organisms of high disease-producing power could retain their virulence, and how long they would remain alive under different conditions of storage.[60]

Nor were the sensitive political functions of the FSA confined to the national defense sphere. Correspondence and newspaper articles suggest that Paul McNutt had almost unquenchable presidential aspirations at the time that Roosevelt put him in charge of the largest of the new agencies he created using his reorganization authority. McNutt's biography uncannily foreshadows that of another ambitious heartland governor who attained the White House a half century later: William Jefferson Clinton. Like the Arkansan Clinton, McNutt grew up in a heartland state, attended an Ivy League law school, began his career as a law professor, and continued it as a governor.[61] Also like Clinton, McNutt's gift of effortless articulation and his record as a moderate Democratic governor soon earned him a national following—and a few committed enemies eager to sabotage his presidential ambitions.[62]

Even before McNutt left for his Philippines post in 1937, it appears that "he was thinking of the Presidency in 1940."[63] By the summer of 1939, some columnists were suggesting that there were "'just two genuine, gilt-edge candidates for the Democratic Presidential nomination in 1940—President Roosevelt and his newly appointed Federal Security Administrator.'"[64] Yet the new agency gave the president a major new slot to deploy—large enough to entice his potential rival for the nomination while requiring sufficiently close collaboration and subjecting the new FSA administrator to enough supervision that it would allow the president to minimize McNutt's ability to act independently. The point was not lost on some observers in the press:

Despite his disclaimers, President Roosevelt cannot put a stop to the reading of political significance into the surprising appointment of Paul V. McNutt to head the new Federal Security Agency. . . . In most quarters, the feeling is growing that McNutt, no matter how canny he may have been in the past, was neatly taken in by the White House. He is, to veteran interpreters, right behind the eight ball. Outside the official circle, he could campaign freely, walking a tightrope if necessary, criticizing unpopular New Deal policies and Presidential actions. . . . It will be hard for him to come out next year with convincing statements that he did not approve of things which happened while he was in Mr. Roosevelt's good graces. If the President wants to deflate the McNutt boom, the appointment was a brilliant stroke. Coordinating the far-flung social ventures of the Federal government will be a man-sized job, with plenty of chances for error and bungling. . . . Of course, there still is the chance the White House wants to look him over at close range, with a view to making him the crown prince or the President's running mate on a third-term ticket. But this gamble seems exceedingly risky to individuals who have kept a constant watch on the political machinations of the Chief Executive and the palace clique. The consensus is that McNutt's ambition overreached itself.[65]

Such risks could hardly have escaped McNutt. But the former governor was nonetheless inveigled by the challenge of running the new super-department and encouraged to accept it by his friend General Douglas MacArthur.[66]

If the FSA proved useful in carrying out secret weapons development projects and co-opting the ambition of a potential rival, why would a president not have been able to achieve these goals *without* creating the FSA? Although the White House also supported military research at the War and Navy Departments, it anticipated some of the challenges presidents have faced repeatedly in the decades since: the military is both difficult to control and capable of severely damaging policies that prove controversial among the armed services.[67] Biological weapons research was controversial in the military. In contrast, the White House could benefit by creating an agency with a range of functions in order to provide a measure of cover that could facilitate certain defense-related work. While the agency was trumpeting its relevance to national security, it was not publicly announcing its role in offensive biological weapons research, allowing civilian scientists and the universities where they worked relative anonymity. New bureaucratic offices—not characterized by close relationships to existing legislative committees—could administer programs secretly by expending White House funds. Finally, perhaps the president could even benefit from having an additional high-level position to bestow on an ambitious individual such as McNutt, harnessing his ambition to the fate of the new agency and possibly transforming a potential political rival into a supporter without having to reshuffle his existing cabinet.

OVERCOMING CONGRESSIONAL HOSTILITY
AND RESHAPING THE BUREAUCRACY

Why did congressional majorities in 1939 allow Roosevelt to undertake a reorganization that enhanced his power when they had denied him such powers in 1938 and before? Recall that the Reorganization Act of 1939 was a *compromise* saddled with a two-house veto and a coterie of limits on presidential power over nearly all independent commissions[68]—perhaps one that the median legislator believed would yield somewhat less authority than the president actually exploited. Even supporters of the president had initially balked at giving FDR all the powers he had first sought in the 1938 reorganization bill, in part because critical organized interests—including veterans and doctors working through the AMA—strenuously objected to some aspects of the bill.[69]

In contrast, the new reorganization bill included sunset provisions, statutory limits on what reorganizations could be proposed, provisions for a two-house congressional veto, and reporting requirements facilitating legislative policing of reorganization plans.[70] The president was supposed to be limited to reorganizations that were justifiable on financial grounds, but he made something of a mockery of that statutory requirement. The final reorganization bill also preserved preexisting legislative compromises protecting independent commissions by exempting many of them from reorganization.[71]

Finally, some members of the legislative coalition supporting reorganization authority were almost certainly concerned about the fate of certain administrative or regulatory programs and may have been quite happy to have the president gain some authority to more effectively shield these from subsequent legislative encroachment. This last category of legislators, in particular, may have been reacting to new information revealed in the 1938 elections, where the New Deal coalition was further eroded by the arrival of eighty congressional Republicans. With the New Deal majority slipping away, legislators who might have preferred expansive regulation (subject to legislative control) may have opted for vesting greater power in the president, hoping that such power would be used to create the bureaucratic structures that would protect the agencies from subsequent encroachment by a more hostile Congress.[72]

Given that hostility, a key dimension of the FSA's trajectory reflects the president's strategy in the days leading up to World War II to use the agency's creation as a vehicle for asserting greater political control over bureaucratic functions. Although this goal was repeatedly camouflaged amid discussions of strengthening national security and promoting efficiency through reorganization, the control-related aspects of the reorganization were not lost on Congress or the press. Though it is understandable that newspaper accounts of the FSA's creation would emphasize presidential control as much as anodyne efficiency goals, it is worth recognizing that such efforts to enhance White House control do not necessarily culminate in an emaciated agency with little power to resist external political interference. On the contrary: in the FSA's case, the shorter-term policy goals pursued by the Roosevelt administration (and subsequently, the Truman administration) also coincided with the strategies that would enhance the agency's policymaking capacity—and even a measure of its bureaucratic autonomy—in the coming years.

While this account emphasizes the ways in which structural changes could further presidential control and objectives through the building of presidential capacity, it is not meant to suggest that the White House was devoid of congressional allies in this process. In at least some sense, legislative majorities ratified Roosevelt's initial choices by conferring on him a limited authority to reorganize the government and by not vetoing his initial changes. But even at the risk of unduly minimizing the legislature's crucial role, the building of bureaucratic capacity here still seems best understood as a vehicle for enhancing presidential control. The president had the preeminent role in forging the legislative coalition supporting reorganization and tracing the path of different bundles of legal responsibility across the government's elaborate preexisting jurisdictional lines.[73] The capacities engineered within the bureaucracy, including the capability to undertake sensitive projects using White House funds and the cadre of legal and political superiors foisted on bureaus, seem especially suited to serve presidential needs.[74]

Some might still insist on examining the FSA's history through a theoretical lens focused on congressional power. In that account, congressional majorities would be seen as achieving their goal of protecting domestic agencies at a time when war was growing increasingly likely and Roosevelt's political fortunes were declining. Even so, that story is one where the legislative majority sought to achieve goals by strengthening presidential power and where the end result was not a contribution to maintaining the status quo but the setting in motion of a process that further grew the resources available to the FSA's bureaus as well as their underlying legal powers.[75]

Occasionally, it seems, even a president competing for influence with Congress can persuade a majority of lawmakers to join him in supporting new executive authority. As Chapter 6 explains, whether that authority worked the way lawmakers expected it to is another matter entirely.

Crosscurrents or Greater Velocity

Shifting Functions, Justifications, and Capacity

WHEN FORMER INDIANA GOVERNOR Paul McNutt traded in his position as high commissioner to the Philippines for a domestic appointment as FSA administrator, he left a role as the president's personal representative in a rapidly changing region that posed strategic challenges to the United States. Yet ironically, McNutt's new responsibilities within the United States also involved him heavily in building relationships between the Roosevelt administration and external constituencies in a fast-evolving political environment. He did so as the leader of an agency whose very existence had the potential to reshape, in subtle but politically important ways, how the Roosevelt White House set priorities for a nation facing a coterie of domestic challenges and international threats.

In fact, another major implication of the FSA's existence emerges if we focus not only on how its creation affected the internal workings of the executive branch, but also on how it affected the external relationships of the administration. At some level, it may not seem remarkable to observe that the FSA's creation allowed the administration to engage in an epistemic process of "framing" policy priorities by emphasizing their role in achieving the widely desired goal of "security." While it is common for political and legal observers to talk about the impact of "framing" effects in law and policy, that term has multiple meanings. In addition, it is not obvious how or why *re*framing can change the political prospects for the implementation of a certain law.[1] But a closer look at the context surrounding the FSA in light of our previously articulated theory of organization showcases the potentially far-reaching implications of organization for the executive branch's relationships with political friends and foes.

The Roosevelt administration's determination to identify the FSA with the concept of security involves a different type of framing. One advantage of considering that "framing" process in a specific context is that it becomes possible to make more fine-grained observations of *how* the reorganization could have had an epistemic, or "framing," effect in several political settings. In particular, developments regarding the FSA suggest the importance of two specific mechanisms—identified earlier in our discussion of refining existing theories—through which the blurring of the security concept could enhance the FSA's prospects: one involves shaping the perceptions of the mass public about the meaning of security; the other involves the separate enlargement of legislative coalitions that support agency functions, accomplished by ambiguating the extent to which a vote for the FSA also constitutes a vote for national security or war-related efforts.

Both of these strategies depend heavily on demonstrating to legislators, organized interests, and the public at large that the legal mandates the FSA was implementing were inextricably connected to national defense and the war effort. Regardless of whether the Roosevelt administration wanted to enter the war at the time the FSA was created, the White House was increasingly cognizant of a foreign policy crisis that could further complicate its domestic political goals. As one historian observed, it was by March 15, 1939—just over a month before the reorganization creating the FSA was publicly proclaimed—that "foreign affairs achieved the absolute dominance over domestic affairs that they were destined ever after to retain in [Roosevelt's] mind."[2] The impending foreign policy problems made the president increasingly anticipate that the nation could find itself embroiled in war:

The experience was, for him, not dissimilar in some essentials to that of the spring of 1933 when, amid universal ruin and collapse, he had presided over the birth of the New Deal. . . . ("Never in my life have I seen things moving in the world with more cross currents or greater velocity" he wrote in a personal letter on March 25, 1939).[3]

Nor was the president alone, as some legislators increasingly favored repealing federal neutrality laws to facilitate American involvement in the European theater.[4]

The administration's goal of emphasizing the connection between the work of the FSA and national defense became easier to achieve because of the importance to the military of the new agency's activities. The FSA's functions not only contributed to an expansive conception of security that encompassed ordinary health, education, and public welfare activities, but also served ends specifically connected to domestic and international security in the conventional sense. These included a role in the relocation of interned Japanese Americans, technical assistance to law enforcement agencies engaged in police work against juvenile delinquents, the aforementioned research programs in biological weapons and related areas, an anti-prostitution enforcement program designed particularly to protect the armed forces, and the development of disaster assistance programs to be deployed in case of war-related attacks against civilians. In addition, the FSA emphasized the defense-related import of a host of other activities, ranging from vocational education to nutrition. Together, these presidentially driven choices afforded the administration an opportunity to affect how the public understood the concept of security and how legislators understood the payoffs of supporting the FSA as the nation prepared for war.[5]

SHAPING PUBLIC PERCEPTIONS AND THE MEANING OF "SECURITY"

Following the merger, FSA officials endeavored to present the public with information about the blending of national security and domestic administrative, regulatory, and social welfare functions. Speeches in 1939 and 1940, such as the following statement made by Paul McNutt to college students in Lakeland, Florida, set the stage for future appeals:

The formation of the Federal Security Agency, mobilizing as it does, the Government's technical facilities for coordinated action, represents a first stage in the campaign against insecurity and want, but the battle is not yet won. *Here, as elsewhere, in the conflict with the enemies of democracy, vigilance and courage are necessary at all times, for here, if not elsewhere, America cannot afford to wage a defensive war. We have assumed and must retain the offensive.*[6]

In television programs and live speeches, McNutt unrelentingly alluded to the "enemies of democracy" and the need to quicken the pace of efforts against "insecurity and want" so that the nation would better be able to face its adversaries.[7] So pointed was McNutt's war-focused rhetoric at a time when public and legislative opinion was still largely isolationist that the White House received correspondence criticizing "the jingoism of Paul McNutt over NBC last Saturday evening. He is doing his best to defeat the excellent leadership for peace you are so nobly exercising."[8] Yet the White House joined McNutt and his aides—particularly by mid-1940— in issuing statements linking national defense to "preparedness" on the home front. On June 12, in response to a request from Senator Claude Pepper for a message "on national defense," the president indicated to the National Convention of Townsend Clubs, meeting in St. Louis, that "we have mobilized our industrial resources to meet pressing conditions confronting us and assure[d them] that the Government has no intention of neglecting the other phase of preparedness, namely continued improvement of social, economic, and moral structures of American life."[9] Statements such as these echoed the content of the presidential reorganization message accompanying the executive order that created the FSA, thus reinforcing the president's message.

Over time, that message appears to have contributed in subtle but material ways to how the agency was perceived in the public sphere. In the process, the White House and Roosevelt administration officials used the creation of the FSA as part of an effort to shape public perceptions, particularly of the meaning of "security." They sought to broaden the scope of the term to place social, economic, and health-related security *on par with* traditional definitions of national security, and they sought to emphasize the interconnections between national security and security involving public health, economic, and social guarantees. There was by the time of the FSA's creation widespread familiarity with the Roosevelt administration's tendency to describe social and economic challenges as akin to war, and historians since then have widely acknowledged this pattern.[10] But the realignment of health, education, and security functions within the FSA, and the circumstances immediately following this realignment, show how government officials directly sought to blur the distinction between national, economic, and social security at the level of organizational structure and bureaucratic mandate. This dimension of the FSA's trajectory included efforts to justify the FSA's creation in terms of strengthening national capacity to counter brutal dictatorships, deployment of FSA resources to support the war effort, and public communications emphasizing the FSA's national defense role.[11]

The determination of the White House and the FSA's leadership to identify the new agency with national security and defense emerged almost immediately upon its creation. Less than one year after its creation, the agency issued a report chronicling its activities.[12] The report provides a revealing picture of the agency's aggressive focus on activities related to national security. The SSB, for example, had engendered a program to organize the massive movement of workers—some of whom were unemployed and others who sought more desirable jobs—toward defense-related industries.[13] The SSB had more than a thousand offices nationwide, a national system for keeping records of employees, and a mission that broadly encompassed the provision of assistance to individuals seeking work.[14] Increasingly, the SSB achieved its employment-related goals through grants to states, allowing it to graft the state bureaucracies onto its growing administrative structure.[15] These characteristics made the SSB a useful vehicle in lubricating the massive defense-related reallocation of labor that was already afoot by 1940. This is how one agency report to congressional staff put it:

[T]he Board's Bureau of Employment Security was directing, through the 1,500 local offices of the United States Employment Service, efforts to insure orderly redeployment of the existing labor supply and more effective placement of workers already employed. Procedures for obtaining more current information needed for recruiting workers through the local employment offices were also put into effect. In June 1940, $2,000,000 was appropriated for the use of the Social Security Board in providing special Federal assistance to, and supervision of, State employment services for the selection, testing, and placement of defense workers in occupations essential to national defense.[16]

While the SSB was busy funneling workers into defense-related industries and helping the states develop administrative systems to do the same, the rest of the FSA was also in the process of forging defense-related capacities. In contrast to the SSB, many of the other bureaus folded into the FSA lacked a dense, nationwide network of offices or a copious nationwide record-keeping system. Nonetheless, the fledgling new agency emphasized how its bureaus were aggressively contributing to the national defense:

In the last month of the fiscal year the Congress appropriated the sum of $15,000,000 for the vocational education of defense workers. The appropriation act provided that the program was to be carried out under plans submitted by agencies of the several States and approved by the Commissioner of Education. It was specified that the plans must include courses supplementary to employment in occupations essential to the national defense and pre-employment refresher courses for workers, selected from the public employment office registers, preparing for such occupations. The Office of Education immediately began to set in motion the machinery for carrying out the purposes of these appropriations.

At the same time, the Public Health Service was in consultation with the Council of National Defense for the purpose of formulating plans for advising the Council regarding the health and medical aspects of national defense and to coordinate health and medical activities affecting it. The Public Health Service was also laying the groundwork for a program allied to defense to promote the health and improve the physical fitness of out-of-school young people employed on projects administered by the National Youth Administration.

The National Institute of Health at the request of the Navy Department was also conducting studies of physiological problems connected with high altitude flying and rapid decompression. Both Army and Navy authorities were advised on standard immunization procedures for the military forces. Cooperation of the International Health Division of the Rockefeller Foundation was secured in the manufacture of 150,000 doses of yellow fever vaccine. Plans have been made for the continued production on a large scale of this vaccine at the Rocky Mountain Laboratory, Hamilton [Montana].[17]

These descriptions emphasize not only the speed with which the FSA's units sought to create a perception among the public of their roles in defense efforts, but also the extent to which the young agency had begun convincing Congress to appropriate resources to fund its defense-related activities. Over time, the perceptions the agency fomented in Congress contributed to the creation of a bureaucratic reality in which significant policy innovation increasingly blurred the distinctions between national security and social or economic security.[18]

The agency's own employees were still another audience for senior officials' emphasis on defense-related efforts. Periodically, the FSA administrator's office would convene conferences to review the agency's progress in defense-related pursuits. The Office of Community War Services (CWS), focused on providing health and welfare services to military and civilian individuals in areas surrounding military establishments, was the hub of these conferences. Documents such as the following conference agenda conveyed to employees one of the critical missions the FSA now prioritized:

For over three years, CWS has been concerned with the provision of adequate health, welfare, and related community services to the citizens of the Nation during the period of the war emergency—particularly in critical war production centers and in centers adjacent to military establishments. It is the purpose of this conference to review our past achievement, to analyze critically our present direction, and to plan together further accomplishment.[19]

The extent of the FSA's identification with war and national security left its mark in the long term. Eventually, some of the most explicitly militarized or national security–related functions of the FSA were shut down, including the quasi-military Civilian Conservation Corps, the War Research Service, the operations to facilitate relocation of Japanese Americans, and the Office of Community War Services. At the same time, a substantial cluster of defense-related research projects continued.[20] The Truman administration allowed George Merck to announce publicly the FSA's success in building for the country a viable biological weapons capacity. An article in the *New York Times* described the disclosures in May 1946:

While the physicists spoke on the bomb, a biologist, George W. Merck, of Merck & Co, pharmaceutical house, exemplified the peculiar duality of modern science by discussing more horrors to come in the field of biological sciences. In a review of work done in the field during the war, *Mr. Merck discussed American achievements both in the production of disease for large-scale use as a weapon and in defenses against enemy-sent disease.* Like all reports on this subject made to date, Mr. Merck's remarks were clothed in a security-forced vagueness. Discussing the matter of security, however, he assured his hearers that, should the needs of humanity call for release of any information so far withheld, the Army would at once release it. One of his more interesting revelations was the discovery by biologists of a new chemical agent on living plants. This agent, of which the identity was not revealed, may be spread on enemy farmlands. The enemy then cultivates and works his farm, and everything appears normal. Only when harvest time comes does he discover that his months of work have been—literally—fruitless. His garden and field crops have borne no fruit, for just before harvest time their roots have withered away and they cannot yield.[21]

Continuing agency involvement in defense-related activities dovetailed nicely with Eisenhower's choice when appointing the first secretary of HEW, the FSA's successor agency. Oveta Hobby was chosen for the post. Her principal experience before being entrusted with the mammoth cabinet agency was running the Women's Army Corps.[22] Even to this day, the commissioned corps of the Public Health Service retains a quasi-military organizational structure and wears correspondingly martial uniforms. The Centers for Disease Control retains the preeminent operational role in responding to deliberately promoted or natural outbreaks of infectious diseases, and the NIH continues to engage in substantial research activities funded by or related to military mandates.[23]

The administration's persistence in broadening the scope of security by discussing national defense suggests several realities. First, the administration emphasized the existence of another dimension to the political choices associated with FSA bureaus.[24] In response, some public constituencies already concerned about defense—like the editorial writers who shaped the public discourse—likely found themselves more drawn to supporting the bureaus than they otherwise would have been.[25] A few may even have found resonance in the idea that security was a concept that extended (if not seamlessly, then at least malleably) from strengthening military capacity to boosting the nation's resilience in the face of adversity. Whether that adversity came from economic dislocation or military disaster mattered less, in this conception, than whether the government had built the administrative capacity to assist citizens in responding to crises. Second, there were some voters who lacked—then as now—the sophistication, time, and political knowledge to form elaborate opinions about the proper scope of "security." For them, the determination of the administration and the FSA to identify the agency with national security efforts suggests something else. Perhaps the agency's identification with the symbols of national power sufficiently reinforced the administration's political rhetoric, translating into longer-term support of broad policy prescriptions. At a time when the administration was also seeking to broaden support for a potential U.S. role in the international conflict, Roosevelt probably also gained some political rewards by conveying a sense of urgency about looming international threats. Even progressives concerned with the erosion of New Deal programs could be reassured that budgetary and administrative initiatives to expand national defense would not necessarily erode New Deal goals.[26] As the war progressed and the agency's responsibilities grew, so too did the support these members of the mass public were willing to provide for the idea that the FSA's assortment of bureaus should become the newest cabinet-level department of the federal government.

While these dynamics help to explain the importance that the White House and the FSA officials assigned to promoting their conception of national security, one might question the precise connection between their framing strategy and the bureaucratic changes that wrought the FSA. Perhaps the White House could have argued that nutrition, physical education, social insurance, and medical research were essential to national security even without acquiring reorganization authority or using it to create the FSA. But the bureaucratic changes seem to have enhanced the administration's position in pursuing its distinctive security agenda. The creation of the agency generated considerable media attention, giving the administration a chance to ply its version of security. The FSA increased the bureaucratic capacity at the White House's disposal that could help make a case to the public that the FSA's programs were contributing to national defense as well as to the expansive conception of security that encompassed both war-related and domestic regulatory activity.[27] Paul McNutt, imbued with the singular authority of the "FSA administrator," traveled the country discussing his agency's role in promoting its particular brand of "national security."[28]

When he was *not* giving speeches, McNutt could join his aides in managing the bureaus' new relationships with constituencies *within* the government. Serving wartime and national security needs while expanding domestic functions required political engagement from top agency administrators who could curry favor with legislators, other federal government officials, and the mass public. This was unlikely to be available to the agencies that represented the federal government's health, social welfare, regulatory, and educational capacity if they had remained scattered throughout government. Treasury and Agriculture secretaries had more pressing demands than building up the FDA or the PHS. The dynamic that the White House faced therefore suggests that bureaucratic changes could make a difference, even if individual bureaus would have sought—on their own—to refocus some of their work on defense-related activities as the war approached. In contrast, fragmentation of health, social welfare, education, and regulatory capacity could have strengthened arguments for meeting wartime needs by developing exclusively military—or temporarily war-focused—programs. Such moves would have placed the future of many health and welfare initiatives in doubt after the war.

In some respects, the FSA was not alone. The efforts of its top officials to emphasize the centrality of its work for national defense represented an administration-wide move to stress the importance of defense as international conflict became more likely. Yet the rhetoric emanating from the FSA appears more pronounced than what was emerging from other agencies (with the occasional exception of the Agriculture Department, whose budget followed a similar trajectory to that of the FSA in some years). The FSA appears to have differed from other major domestic administrative and regulatory agencies such as the Department of Agriculture and the Department of the Interior, from which some of its major bureaus were drawn, and the sister agencies created by reorganization (the Federal Works Agency and the Federal Loan Agency) in *two* ways: by having a greater concentration of *actual* defense-related activities[29] and by repeatedly emphasizing how even the work it was performing that was *not* explicitly related to defense was nonetheless integral to a broad version of the concept of security. To take just one example, the FSA's summaries of its annual activities in the transition to war between 1940 and 1942 mentioned "war," "emergency," and "national defense" more often on average than did other major domestic agencies' summaries.[30] The agency's national security focus is starker still in the headings of some annual reports, which emphasize the bureaus' war-related activities and describe the agency's goal of providing "Security for America."[31] If anything, the tendency of the FSA administrator to promote an expansive conception of the security trope and specifically to link the FSA's work to national defense continued even more aggressively under the leadership of Oscar Ewing in the Truman administration.[32]

It should also be noted, however, that the precise implications of linking domestic administrative and regulatory programs to *security* depend heavily on whether the underlying concept of security is defined broadly or narrowly, which in turn depends considerably on presidential choices. Thus, while associating the domestic administrative and regulatory functions of the FSA with the concept of security appears to have enhanced their budgets and political support, a different scenario seems to have emerged with the creation of DHS. In that case, the president used a similar political opening to shift resources away from the "legacy" mandates of domestic and regulatory agencies rather than expanding them. In situations where actual bureaucratic discretion and statutory mandates give an administration some flexibility to use the new resources, one should expect the administration's political agenda to make a difference.[33]

ENLARGING LEGISLATIVE COALITIONS BY AMBIGUATING FUNCTIONS

Apart from shaping public perceptions directly, Roosevelt and his supporters had a lot to gain from emphasizing the connection between national defense and domestic policy initiatives that he favored. Southern Democrats and Republicans who were skeptical of the New Deal were often also quite negative about American participation in international conflicts. But there is some indication that these constituencies in fact favored a strong, vigorous military—both for domestic political reasons and (perhaps) for purposes of deterring international activity that could offend U.S. interests and provoke conflict.[34] By blurring the distinction between national defense and domestic regulatory efforts, Roosevelt could make it at least possible to galvanize new sources of support for his programs. At the same time, his focus on threats facing the United States when presenting his new superagency to the American public served the purpose of highlighting the relative immediacy of threats facing the nation, even as he also endeavored to convey how he was preparing the structures of government to respond effectively in the face of such threats.

Recall that diminished legislative coalitions were a challenge for FDR during the second phase of the New Deal. Politically, Roosevelt had pushed the envelope in passing expansive new legislation, resulting in the shedding of marginal coalition members. And political support could be adversely affected and further wane with continued defeats. Consider Social Security as an example. From its origins, the program was politically controversial. Though it was relatively popular among midwestern and northeastern urban constituencies, it was not universally supported.[35] In part as a compromise with Southerners, the administration settled for a program that entirely excluded the farm sector from coverage.[36] The importance of conservative Southern Democrats underscores Roosevelt's challenge in expanding constituencies for one of his signature domestic policy efforts. If at all possible, he would have welcomed the chance to build such support among Southerners, who were in a position to block the program's functions or future expansion.[37] Moreover, other things being equal, the outbreak of war was likely to erode support for domestic regulatory and administrative programs unconnected to the war effort.[38]

Finally, a nontrivial group of legislators, including prominent Southern Democrats and Republicans, were more inclined to support national security programs—though not necessarily active participation in international conflicts—than domestic regulatory, administrative, or social welfare programs.[39] Before 1939, a number of such lawmakers viewed military strength in a different light than New Deal programs. Spurred by editorials and growing constituent concerns about defense, lawmakers showed themselves to be increasingly willing to fund military activities. Even in light of lingering isolationist concern, in 1936 House and Senate leaders began ramping up military appropriations at the behest of the White House and the military.[40] Against the backdrop of lingering concerns about budget deficits, many lawmakers as early as 1937 were nonetheless "volunteering to help unbalance [the budget] still further by making the sky the limit in appropriations for new naval buildings."[41] Newspaper editorials openly exhorted Congress to prioritize "the need for a stronger air fleet,

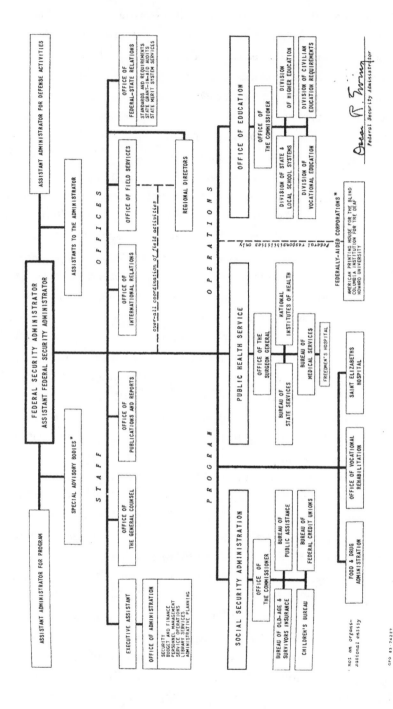

FEDERAL SECURITY AGENCY

FIGURE 6.1 *Organizational Chart of the Federal Security Agency, December 15, 1951*

Source: Federal Security Agency, Organizational Charts and Budgets

a larger navy," and national security at a time when "the Government is spending recklessly for numerous other purposes."[42] Prominent Southern Democrats and Republicans—blocs rarely supportive of the president's domestic agenda—nonetheless lauded the president's criticism of dictatorship and voiced approval for ratcheting up national defense expenditures.[43] Indeed, by 1939, lawmakers were more readily persuaded of the value in increasing their support for defense-related programs while considerable debate persisted about core New Deal programs.[44]

In a world where presidential supporters could exert some influence over budgets and public discussion of federal priorities, the asymmetry in legislative attitudes regarding defense and social welfare posed an opportunity as well as a challenge. Once again, the White House could use reorganization to secure greater support for the bureaucracies entrusted with legal responsibilities that the administration prioritized. By blending national security with health regulation and public benefits, the Roosevelt administration provided legislators who were eager to support national security functions but skeptical about domestic welfare and regulatory programs with a new reason to support bureaus within the FSA. This development was especially important in expanding the extent of political support for administrative bureaus that conservatives (especially Southern Democrats) would have otherwise been less interested in supporting.

Notice that the FSA's internal activities—not just the public justification of its functions—reflected strong connections to national defense. Biological weapons research was being conducted through the WRS. The SSB was providing special assistance to families impacted by the war. It was also assisting with placement of job seekers in war-related industries through its employment service. The FSA was training employees for war-related industries through the Office of Education. It was conducting antiprostitution enforcement through the PHS. Budget increases for the agency during the war years were substantial, and somewhat greater emphasis on war and defense is qualitatively apparent when comparing the FSA's *Annual Reports* to those of other major domestic agencies, including Interior and Agriculture, from which some of its bureaus were drawn.[45] And years after the war, the focus on defense continued. As Figure 6.1 indicates, the FSA organizational chart continued to show the presence of an assistant administrator for defense activities into the 1950s, with no comparable positions existing at Interior, Agriculture, or Treasury.

The Roosevelt administration clearly understood that lawmakers were among the most critical audience for the FSA's national security-related work. McNutt had his aides monitor congressional hearings that focused on defense research to ensure that legislators were aware of the FSA's work in areas such as improving the prospects for "high altitude military flights."[46] Even after the war, FSA staff prepared organizational charts for congressional staff explaining the enlarged scope of the FSA's defense-related activities:

The period of defense preparation and of actual war coincides with the time during which the Federal Security Agency was formed and has been developed. In this emergency because of the very nature of its functions—the safeguarding of health, the fostering of education, and the promotion of social and economic security—the Agency became the center around which numerous war activities were developed. At the very beginning of the Defense Program of 1940, the Federal Security Administrator was named Coordinator of the Office of Health, Welfare, and Related Defense Activities which was established by the Council of National Defense on November 28, 1940 for the coordination of all health, medical, welfare, nutrition, education, recreation and other related fields of activity affecting the national defense. . . . The Council established the Health and Medical Committee . . . to advise on health and medical aspects of national defense and to coordinate health and medical activities affecting national defense. With the approval of the President this Committee was transferred to the FSA on November 28, 1940. The Family Security Committee was established on February 12, 1941 to study the problem of maintaining the security of American homes in the face of wartime social and economic dislocations. The Committee on Social Protection was established on June 14, 1941 to render advice with respect to the social protection aspects of national defense.[47]

These changes were associated with rising budgets at many of the FSA's bureaus. Although the FSA's budget did not increase continuously throughout the war years (and even experienced some decreases during the later part of the war), the administration's strategy seems to have succeeded in sparing the FSA the more severe funding declines that afflicted some major domestic agencies.[48] Two things are notable about its funding trajectory. First, as Figure 6.2 indicates, in contrast to other major domestic agencies such as the Federal Works Agency, the FSA fared relatively well in the appropriations game. Even when compared to the massive Agriculture Department, the FSA's decline in funding from its wartime high was more limited, and growth in its appropriations after the war more rapid. Moreover, between 1940 and 1945 the FSA's four major permanent bureaus (those that remained with the agency for the long term—the PHS, the Office of Education, the SSB, and the FDA) saw their combined appropriations increase by approximately one-third in constant dollars. Among these bureaus, even sharper increases were apparent at the PHS, whose budget quintupled in constant dollars between 1940 and 1945.

Second, the declines in funding that the FSA experienced between its wartime highest funding levels and the year after the war were less than those of Agriculture and the Federal Works Agency. As Figure 6.2 demonstrates, the FSA's four principal bureaus saw steadily rising appropriations, with only slight declines in 1943 and 1944, which were followed by further increases. And some of the FSA's key bureaus—most notably

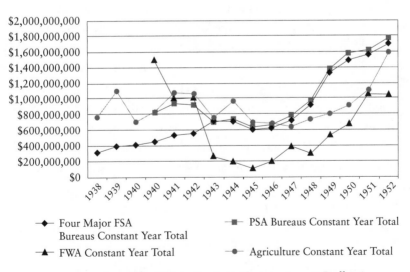

FIGURE 6.2 *The FSA in Context (Constant 1938 Dollars)*

Source: Budget of the United States, 1938–1953 (including two sets of figures for 1940, reflecting changes in the budget after the FSA was created).

the PHS—experienced pronounced and long-term increases in the rate of growth of appropriations and legal responsibilities. The declines in FSA funding were driven largely by the discontinuation of New Deal–era relief programs such as the Civilian Conservation Corps and the National Youth Administration.[49] These developments track the expanding responsibilities of the FSA's four core bureaus and suggest that the agency's leaders and allies successfully marshaled support for its work during and after the war.

It may seem at first as though the national defense–oriented work of the FSA merely reflected a broader change throughout the government. Even if this were the case, it would still be significant that Roosevelt, McNutt, and the rest of the administration sought so emphatically to include the FSA in the coterie of government agencies that could lay claim to importance in a time of war. The FSA's connection to national security issues appears to have been distinctive not only in the intensity of its public communications but also in the substance of its work. In contrast to other major domestic administrative agencies at the time, the FSA was directly involved in sophisticated weapons research (through the War Research Service).[50] In the early phase of the war and during the preparation for it, the FSA's administrator, the ambitious Paul McNutt, was the only official who was appointed coordinator of homeland security matters involving health, welfare, and "related activities" and also chairman of the War Manpower Commission while he continued to serve as FSA administrator.[51] Though all of the three agencies Roosevelt created using reorganization authority were justified publicly as essential to strengthening national capacity at a time of international instability, only the FSA's budget grew substantially during the war. And only the FSA was specifically structured—from its inception—to include a military liaison.[52] Finally, the defense-related focus of the FSA lingered well after the war. In sharp contrast to any other domestic administrative agency—whether cabinet or independent—only the FSA's structure included a high-level deputy in charge of defense-related programs.[53]

Why would organizational changes contribute to "rebranding" the agency? If it is true that injecting a substantial national defense ingredient into the mix of "security" bureaus could serve the president's goals, why did the White House wait to pursue this strategy until it could order a bureaucratic reorganization? The answers reveal still further ways in which bureaucratic structure can play an essential role in cementing public expectations about government's legal responsibilities.

Although the type of rebranding Roosevelt sought to pull off by melding domestic policy and national defense through an expansive "security" metaphor may not have been impossible without reorganization authority, it would have proven far more difficult. Imagine, for instance, how much more trying it would have been for FDR to discuss his expansive version of security during fireside chats if the agencies carrying out that work were scattered bits and pieces across the government (for example, the PHS at Treasury, the FDA at Agriculture, and the Office of Education at Interior). In effect, the reorganization delivered three things that redounded to the benefit of the rebranding. First, the administration gained a high-profile opportunity to *announce* changes and make a case to the nation about its conception of security. The newspaper coverage of the reorganization announcement was intense, and Roosevelt's "warning to dictators" when he reorganized was widely disseminated.[54] Second, the administration put in place a structure—consisting of appointees to oversee bureaus with the legal authority to control what they did—to better monitor bureau activities, anticipate threats, and coordinate actions to advance the "expansive" security message. Finally, the administration gained a staff whose job it was in part to promote what the bureaus were doing across the country, build alliances, and manage external relationships in a manner that promoted the desired conception of security.

CHANGING CAPACITY FOR AGENCY-DRIVEN POLICY INNOVATION

The sequence of events triggered by the formation of the FSA has a number of implications in vital areas such as the prospects for agency autonomy and congressional reorganization. Although the available evidence does not establish whether these effects were explicitly intended in the case of the FSA, they nonetheless demonstrate additional goals that politicians may pursue in the course of allocating bureaucratic jurisdictions over legal mandates.

Over time, as their budgets and personnel swelled within an agency focused on health and welfare, some of the FSA's bureaus appear to have acquired greater capacity for autonomous policy innovation. Neither the White House nor Congress lost its grip on the bureaus. Instead, both the rate and the significance of policy innovations emerging from the bureaus quickened compared to what could be observed when the bureaus were in their original bureaucratic environments. These characteristics were buoyed by developments in the bureaus' organizational culture, recruiting practices, and effectiveness in building external coalitions of support.[55]

The FSA bureaus' relative independence is apparent in the agency's policymaking record after the merger and in contrast to what the bureaus had achieved before the merger. Officials at the Office of Education developed plans for new vocational education initiatives. Leveraging the security-related focus at the White House, these officials promoted the new vocational programs among legislators and White House officials.[56] By 1943, the Office of Education's budget had more than quintupled from its prewar highs, dwarfing the budget of the entire Department of the Interior, from which the Office of Education had been transferred just four years earlier.[57] FSA and SSB employees took the lead in developing major changes to the scope of Social Security coverage during its existence; these changes had not been possible at the outset of the program and appeared to require the close collaboration of the FSA staff, the White House, and the SSB staff.[58] During the existence of the FSA, the NIH grew dramatically, and in a fashion that required promotion of health research and coordination with other agencies that would have been unlikely to materialize had the PHS been a small bureau of the Treasury Department.[59] After promoting these statutory changes, FSA bureaucrats then insisted to legislative staff that they would require larger appropriations to carry out the changes:

Due to enactment during the closing days of the second session, 79th Congress, of amendments to the Social Security Act, the Public Health Service Act, the Vocational Education Act, and other new legislation, it will be necessary to request additional appropriations to carry out the Federal Security Agency's programs for the fiscal year 1947.[60]

Throughout this time, the FSA administrator served as the senior government official in charge of administering health-related programs. Increasingly, during the Truman administration, the head of the FSA served as the president's primary spokesperson to promote national health insurance and used the resources of the FSA to make the case for it.[61] No official with such legitimacy and bureaucratic resources would have existed without the FSA. Conservative Southern Democrats and Republicans strongly opposed the elevation of the FSA to cabinet-level status because (according to historians of the period) they did not want to bestow additional status and authority on the FSA administrator.[62]

Even before its rise to cabinet status, the FSA already had a status and role that greatly facilitated the development of health, welfare, and related regulatory policies. By creating the FSA, the White House appears to have facilitated—wittingly or unwittingly—the evolution of the organizational cultures of the component bureaus. In particular, the reorganization signaled to employees of the bureaus that they were part of a larger agency whose core mission was more closely related to their own missions. It allowed these same bureaus to reap the prestige and resources associated with war-related and national security functions. The agency's political appointees emphasized civil service and merit appointments at lower levels[63] (something increasingly common across some but not all agencies of the federal government) and among grant recipients.[64] And the new overarching administrative structure provided bureaus with enhanced capacity for outreach, advocacy of agency positions with respect to other entities of government, and access to the White House. Together, these changes may have spurred some of the qualities that allowed the agency to gain a measure of autonomy in pursuing significant policy changes on Capitol Hill.[65]

As these changes took hold within and around the federal bureaucracy, the FSA's own administrators sought to trumpet the organization's new esprit to employees and the public. Discussing the management of his agency with congressional appropriators in early 1950, Administrator Oscar Ewing put it thus:

The movement toward a cohesive Agency has not resulted only from . . . administrative shifts; it has resulted in considerable measure from an increasing desire by the heads of all the units to work together to strengthen the Agency. Without such cooperation what progress we have made would have been extremely difficult, if not impossible.[66]

Bureaucratic autonomy has proven essential to many features of modern life mediated through legal and policy programs promoted by autonomous bureaucratic actors. Structural changes can and do presage such autonomy. To the extent that other political actors recognize this and have a stake in promoting such autonomy (or avoiding it), they will attempt to shape bureaucratic structures with an eye on the autonomy-related consequences. Thus, structural changes may prove fundamental to understanding the evolution of legal mandates.

LINKS BETWEEN EXECUTIVE AND LEGISLATIVE ORGANIZATION: USING AGENCY STRUCTURE TO SHAPE PRESSURE FOR LEGISLATIVE REORGANIZATION

The creation of the FSA provoked intense debate in Congress in part because of the potential that it would create pressure to change existing congressional jurisdiction among committees.[67] Eventually, the realignments in executive branch functions *did* lead a reluctant Congress to sharply reform existing committee jurisdictions.[68] In the short term, the reorganization plan that allowed the FSA to be created also led to the establishment of a reorganization committee in Congress. Although neither this committee nor the reorganization plan itself had the power to directly change the allocation of committee jurisdiction, both allowed for changes in the executive branch that had the potential to generate more conflicts among committees (for example, when a committee given primary jurisdiction over a newly reorganized agency might be in conflict with a committee retaining jurisdiction over a lower-level bureau).[69] In the longer term, the FSA and similar reorganizations created growing pressure for the legislature to reshape committee jurisdictions to account for the changes in the executive branch.[70] Eventually, during the 1940s, these pressures led to the most dramatic changes in congressional jurisdiction in modern history.[71] Congress also made decisive procedural changes that dramatically enhanced lawmakers' capacity to monitor the swelling bureaucracy that the executive had come to control more closely.[72]

These changes underscore how one important implication of bureaucratic structure is its effect on the probability of subsequent congressional reorganization. Even if such reorganization is resisted in the short term—as it largely has been in the years since the creation of the new DHS structure[73]—crucial factions in Congress may eventually find that the mismatch between executive reorganizations and the internal allocation of legislative power becomes all but impossible to ignore. Legislative entrepreneurs can use the disconnect between legislative and executive organization to agitate publicly for a different jurisdictional arrangement (as did Senator Joe Lieberman years later in the homeland security context[74]). The mismatch between legislative and executive organization can also make it harder for legislators to oversee bureaucratic activity when responsibility falls between the cracks of existing committee coverage. Even when this is not the case, the lack of fit between congressional and executive structure generates jurisdictional disputes that require resolution by committee chairs and the congressional leadership.[75] For all these reasons, when executive agencies are reorganized, legislators receive a lottery ticket that could yield gains or losses in the power of committees in which the members have a vested interest. The ex ante fight over bureaucratic structure becomes even more convoluted because the returns from that lottery are not distributed equally for legislators.[76]

While the executive-legislative nexus in reorganization helps explain why fights over structure can become so intense, it also reiterates questions about the prescriptive merits of such reorganizations. Leave aside the substantive problem of agreeing on the precise meaning of efficiency or effectiveness in the context of a government program with contested functions. Even assuming that it could be shown that centralization of functions was wiser relative to some defensible set of policy goals, there is a separate question regarding legislative power. Effective centralization depends to some extent on legislators' allowing that centralization to be meaningful. But when legislatures reorganize committee jurisdiction, it may not even be in a way that furthers the goals of a particular agency.[77] In the case of the FSA, Congress eventually did reorganize, and it tightly vested primary responsibility for the agency—and its future cabinet-level offspring—in a small number of committees. The larger lesson from the FSA story here is that bureaucratic reorganizations have the potential not only to affect the balance of power between the White House and Congress but also to reshape the allocation of power within Congress itself.

THE FSA'S TRAJECTORY AND ITS ORGANIZATIONAL
IMPLICATIONS: CONCLUDING THOUGHTS

The FSA's evolution into the Department of Health, Education, and Welfare and then the Department of Health and Human Services reflects decades of changes in jurisdiction and a revolving cadre of executive branch leaders. Although the agency's role in America became increasingly identified with the management of social risk and social insurance, it never entirely abandoned its heritage as an entity that bundled public health, human services, and more conventionally defined defense and emergency-response functions.

With the benefit of the framework developed earlier and the evidence reviewed in these last two chapters, we can revisit some of the lingering questions about this evolution: why Roosevelt forged the agency in the first place, why it mixed defense and ordinary domestic mandates, and what impact its creation may have wrought. The FSA's creation was a means of increasing presidential control and infusing defense-related missions into the agency as a way to enlarge the coalition supporting administrative and regulatory programs important to the Roosevelt administration. It is of course possible that legislative majorities simply liked the fact that the new agency would help protect the New Deal programs, though it remains remarkable that Roosevelt wrested reorganization authority from lawmakers.

But a more interesting picture emerges if we examine the situation dynamically. After Congress grudgingly gave the administration limited reorganization authority, the president pushed the envelope, making a mockery of the legal requirement that reorganizations be justified only on the basis of cost savings and administrative efficiency. He then gained a new layer of political appointees, abolished the Social Security Board's status as an independent agency, and created a new structure through which to fund sensitive presidential projects that he kept shielded from Congress (including political control of grant money and biological weapons research). Perhaps more crucially, he structured the agency to render ambiguous the precise boundary between national security and domestic administrative functions, thereby creating a means of giving reluctant legislative opponents (and even members of the public) a reason to reexamine what they might be "buying" by supporting the FSA. The result tended to make the agency prosper despite the undeniable New Deal lineage of certain programs.

In contrast, other domestic agencies encountered serious problems during the war years. Agriculture and Interior, both among the most sprawling and important executive departments, assumed some war-related responsibilities, as evidenced by the creation of bureaus such as the War Food Authority in Agriculture.[78] Nonetheless, their budgets stayed flat or fluctuated in comparison to the steady growth in the FSA's four major bureaus.[79] The Farm Security Administration, which provided assistance to farmers, also sought to market itself as a war agency protecting the food supply.[80] Its moves in this direction were complicated, however, by the fractured nature of farming programs split between that agency and the Agriculture Department, the bureau's lack of success in forging genuine ties to defense agencies (in contrast to the FSA), and the relatively narrow scope of its overall mission—thereby calling into question its efforts to persuade lawmakers or the public that its legal functions were critical to national security efforts.[81] In the end, skeptical lawmakers decimated many of Farm Security's most prominent programs and transferred its remaining functions to an even more narrowly focused bureau within the Agriculture Department.[82] Similarly, the narrowly focused Federal Works Agency, a second major agency born from Roosevelt's fateful reorganization in the spring of 1939, saw its own funding plummet amid waning interest in domestic affairs. Eventually the agency was abolished.[83] The FSA's broader mix of functions, explicit ties to defense agencies, and greater White House protection spared it such a fate, helping McNutt and other administrators find opportunities for agency growth during the war.

The creation of the FSA appears to have placed its bureaus on a safer path. Reorganization opened the door to growth in bureaucratic capacity and to reframing the purposes of the agency through incorporation of national security responsibilities, which in turn resulted in larger budgets and congressional acceptance of new legislation that expanded the agency's powers. Americans still experience political conflict over matters such as the proper federal role in managing health risks, regulating pharmaceutical products, improving education, and other functions once entrusted to the FSA. But the agency's eventual cabinet-level status, and the continuing growth of its resources and legal responsibilities, are in large measure a testament to the success of the Roosevelt administration in forging an executive branch structure to embody its ambitious conception of security.

CHAPTER 7

Maybe It's Time to Think Big

Creating DHS and Defining Homeland Security

WHEN ROOSEVELT BEGAN hatching the scheme to pry executive reorganization authority away from Congress and forge a new federal super-agency focused on social risk and public health, he could scarcely have foreseen certain distinctive features in that agency's trajectory. He may not have expected that the agency would need to wait well over a decade before it attained cabinet status, or that the intricate lines of its organizational charts would help shroud a White House–sanctioned biological weapons program. Perhaps he only dimly understood that defense-related health research would become such a boon for efforts to grow the organization. Yet in some respects the FSA's legacy is just as important as a general illustration of the outsized role agencies play in turning legal arrangements written on paper into powerful elements of social organization. Public bureaucracies decide where dams are built, whether nuclear power plants will add to energy production, how intelligence operations are conducted, who gets turned away at the border, and what environmental standards must be met. Politicians delegate authority by crafting legislative compromises, which lawyers and judges then seek to interpret. But bureaucratic agencies are often the entities that most directly wield the power to spend money, impose penalties, provide public services, and regulate individuals and organizations. Although legal scholars are consumed by normative debates concerning who *should* exercise such control, those debates are difficult to resolve or even follow in the abstract without some knowledge of the techniques used in the political process to control bureaucratic power over legal interpretations and over the execution of regulatory mandates.[1]

Consequently, a central question in public law concerns who exactly controls the bureaucracy's power to interpret and execute law. As with the imaginary lines that subdivide metropolitan areas into distinct jurisdictions, enormous practical significance flows from the legal rules allocating power among bureaucracies. Lurking behind the design of those rules can be a complex political story that is at least as much about securing control of agencies as it is about safeguarding the well-being of the public.

Yet as we have seen in earlier chapters, the creation or reorganization of bureaucratic units—such as the new Department of Homeland Security (DHS)—remains among the least-understood techniques for controlling bureaucracies.[2] We know that politicians may create or reorganize agencies for multiple reasons: to appear as if they are addressing a salient policy,[3] to please organized interests most likely to be directly impacted by the agencies,[4] to create procedures that bias agency policy in particular directions,[5] and (perhaps more occasionally) genuinely to address a major problem of public concern in a prescriptively defensible manner.[6] We know far less, however, about how these different potential motivations interact, how agency structure is affected by major crises such as the September 11 terrorist attacks, or why politicians allocate different chunks of legal responsibility to distinct bureaucratic units.[7]

These gaps are evident in the persistence of many unsolved puzzles about the largest government reorganization in half a century—the creation of DHS.[8] For instance, why did the president support the creation of DHS after initially opposing it? Why did the department become so vast, including in the reorganization a wide range of components with little or no responsibility for homeland security? We also understand little about whether the crisis enabled or forced politicians to forge a bureaucracy that actually enhanced the government's capacity to undertake security-related functions. Even as the creation and operation of DHS continues to inspire controversy, policymakers and scholars have yet to address these questions.[9] Nor have they been resolved in the wide-ranging criticisms leveled at DHS following the Katrina disaster, or in light of the national security threats the department was nominally designed to address.[10]

The colossal new DHS melded the functions of twenty-two previously existing agencies, from Treasury's Customs Service, to Agriculture's Plum Island Animal Disease Center, to the previously independent Federal Emergency Management Agency (FEMA). Upon its creation, the department gained regulatory authority over transportation security and matters as disparate as marine ecosystems and refugee admissions. Its ranks swelled with nearly a quarter of a million federal employees ranging from border inspectors to environmental compliance officers. Nothing of this scope had happened in the United States since the creation of the Department of Defense half a century earlier.[11]

Even for reorganizations of smaller scope than that of DHS or the Defense Department, the structural changes are unlikely to be solely symbolic, devoid of legal and policy consequences. Such an assumption ignores the aggressive infighting over structure among legislators, the executive branch, and organized interests.[12] Ignoring the significance of changes in bureaucratic structure also neglects the findings of work in political science and sociology,[13] and the legal doctrines vesting valuable discretion to interpret statutes in specific administrative agencies.[14] Yet we are only beginning to understand precisely how changes in structure shape the implementation of legal mandates, and how those changes would affect legislative bargaining over the contours of agencies such as DHS.

I address these questions by combining a detailed analysis of the legislative process creating DHS with a further exploration of the impact of bureaucratic structure on the execution of legal mandates. Our theoretical approach extends existing accounts of bureaucratic structure to address key features of the DHS case that also arise in other cases of bureaucratic change, especially the role of crises in loosening the constraints of organizational interests and the impact of senior legislators guarding their committee jurisdiction.[15] In the process, this account fills several gaps in the legal and political science literature concerning some matters, such as how reorganizations differ from familiar procedural techniques for controlling the bureaucracy, including environmental impact requirements or cost-benefit analyses; how reorganizations may be enacted despite their adverse impact on the performance of widely held goals; and how presidents, legislators, and organized interests sometimes bargain about bureaucratic structure in the shadow of an engaged, rather than disconnected, mass public.

As crises enlarge windows of opportunity for legislative action, policy changes in the area of concern—in this case, the domain that has come to be known as homeland security—can be driven by the efforts of politicians trying to affect regulatory and administrative activities in a different domain.

Changes in the nature and scope of security policy may powerfully affect other legal and policy domains, such as the Coast Guard's environmental regulatory functions or the application of immigration laws. Moreover, politicians use the occasion of legislation to force changes in other areas having little to do with the principal issue being addressed. For just one of many examples, consider the savings and loan crisis of the late twentieth century. In addressing the crisis, Congress allowed the magnitude of losses from savings and loans to rise by failing to produce legislation in 1986. The conflict stemmed from differences in which add-ons should be included in the legislation, such as housing benefits or unrelated features of bank regulation. Similarly, the major savings and loan bailout legislation in 1989 greatly increased the costs of dealing with that crisis by prescribing other benefits as part of the legislation, notably, housing and urban redevelopment.[16] While these themes are particularly relevant in the context of national and homeland security, they also hold important implications for the more-often-studied aspects of bureaucratic politics, affecting domains such as pharmaceutical and environmental regulation. In fact, politicians may endeavor to achieve policy- or control-related goals by strategically blurring distinctions between more-conventional security functions and broader domestic regulatory and service provision responsibilities within the same agency.

Against this theoretical backdrop, my account also yields answers to the DHS-specific questions. The president changed his mind about the reorganization in part because he did not want to be on the losing side of a major issue. But, more importantly, the administration appears to have supported reorganization on such a massive scale to further domestic policy priorities independent of homeland security. By moving a large set of agencies to the new department and giving them new homeland security responsibilities without the promise of additional budgets, the president all but forced these agencies to draw resources away from their legacy mandates. This outcome contrasts with the early history of the FSA.

Though such changes have unquestionably become part of the president's own legacy, fixing the precise extent to which he and his top advisors consciously schemed to weaken domestic legacy mandates without regard for a corresponding homeland security benefit must await the judgment of history. But this account does establish three crucial realities. First, the administration eventually pressed for the largest possible department despite the security-related risks of the merger identified by some of the administration's own aides. Second, many of the key players participating in or affected by the department's creation—including legislators and bureau employees—explicitly grasped how the merger threatened legacy mandates. Third, key features of the legislative progression that culminated in the creation of DHS—in particular, the president's pledge of revenue neutrality and the White House's willingness to consider including agencies such as the Nuclear Regulatory Commission and the Federal Aviation Administration (FAA)—make little sense without assuming that the White House harbored the goal of affecting the performance of legacy mandates, even if doing so failed to yield a corresponding security benefit. At a minimum, these realities suggest that the administration provided the fertile soil in which arguments supporting reorganization became deeply rooted—arguments that had glaring prescriptive problems yet happened to serve many of the White House's political objectives.

From a prescriptive point of view, the conclusions are sobering. This account shows how the merger often tended to adversely affect even those legal mandates that were plainly relevant to homeland security.[17] More generally, it explains how decisions about whether to create a new security agency, what scope and size to give it, and how to organize congressional jurisdiction over it are unlikely to have been driven primarily by meaningful prescriptive concerns. Yet such decisions are also unlikely to be merely *symbolic*. They can powerfully (and covertly) reshape how laws are implemented while making it more difficult for government to achieve broadly shared prescriptive goals. Marginal improvements depend on solving problems of legislative oversight, and on whether competent bureaucrats will succeed in forging autonomy and capacity in a world unlikely to support it. While these scenarios remain elusive, this account does not yield a blanket condemnation of bureaucracies created through high-profile reorganizations. Bureaucracies forged in crisis may not be inexorably doomed to fail in carrying out their legal responsibilities, and there may yet be reasons to defer to their legal interpretations. But it is worth highlighting the difficulties in averting such failure.

THE ORGANIZATIONAL EMERGENCE
OF HOMELAND SECURITY

The end of the Cold War dramatically affected debates about American security. By the middle of 2001, American policymakers had largely altered a national security argot once replete with references to a balance of power, containment, and mutually assured destruction. Instead the rhetoric of national security policymakers and analysts increasingly focused on terrorism, asymmetric warfare, and above all "homeland security."[18] Terrorists had struck several times during the previous eight years, most notably at the World Trade Center in 1993 and in Oklahoma City in 1995.[19] Numerous blue-ribbon commissions had called for heightened attention to the threat of terrorism.[20] In response, the new president-elect created a structure within the White House National Security Council (NSC) to coordinate matters involving terrorism, its prevention, and the nation's ability to prepare and respond to such attacks.[21] Unlike previous directives, the focus was primarily on attacks targeting the United States itself.[22]

The perceived need for coordination arose in part from the sprawling nature of modern government. Numerous bureaus were responsible for preventing, preparing for, and responding to man-made threats against the United States.[23] Homeland security encompassed aspects of the work of the Departments of State and Defense, as well as that of the NSC.[24] Rounding out the coterie of national security bureaucracies were agencies devoted to intelligence, criminal investigation, and prosecution. The Central Intelligence Agency (CIA) combined an explicit core function of intelligence gathering with its covert operations.[25] By 2001, it had multiple task forces working on terrorism-related issues. An elaborate group focused almost entirely on Osama bin Laden and al Qaeda.[26] Specialized intelligence entities, such as the National Security Agency (NSA), further complemented these activities by engaging in electronic eavesdropping outside the United States and gathering considerable signals intelligence. Homeland security and terrorism prevention were also considered the province of federal special agents and the law enforcement agencies for which they worked. As hearings in three Senate committees during the week of May 7, 2001, demonstrated, law enforcement agencies were routinely considered to be responsible for protecting the American public.[27] The

Federal Bureau of Investigation (FBI) commanded vast budgets and statutory responsibility, serving as the lead counterterrorism law enforcement agency.[28] Foreign attacks on American interests, such as the bombing of the USS *Cole* in Yemen, invariably led to the deployment of an FBI team.

Several other bureaus also performed missions relevant to homeland security. A host of specialized law enforcement agencies existed, such as the Immigration and Naturalization Service (INS) and the Drug Enforcement Administration (DEA). The INS served multiple inspection, detention, investigation, quasi-adjudication, and policy functions related to controlling the flow of people into the country. Customs had the similarly daunting task of preventing prohibited items, including drugs and explosives, from entering.[29] Within the U.S. Treasury Department, Customs was one of the largest bureaus in terms of budget, staff, and enforcement responsibilities. Like INS, it performed more than just investigative functions (e.g., tracking down money launderers, drug traffickers, and illicit brokers of technology subject to export controls). It also played a regulatory function. While INS regulated the entry of people, Customs controlled the vast flow of goods into (and, in theory, out of) the United States. The Secret Service investigated counterfeiting and fraud-related financial crimes as well as serving in its most visible role, protecting the president. In addition to collecting excise taxes, the Bureau of Alcohol, Tobacco, and Firearms had become a law enforcement agency focused on firearms and explosives, with a wealth of technical expertise on these subjects unrivaled elsewhere in the federal government.[30]

Transportation and coastal security were handled largely through a tangle of overlapping functions nominally overseen from within the Department of Transportation. The Federal Aviation Administration (FAA) looked after the security of the aviation infrastructure, imposing (among other things) mandates on airlines and airports requiring them to pay for employees to screen passengers and their luggage. The Coast Guard similarly shared with Customs responsibility for key aspects of port security. It also performed coastal search-and-rescue operations along with a multitude of safety, rate-setting, and environmental regulatory functions.[31]

Presumably, the work of these agencies could forestall a disaster that would have had to be handled by emergency response bureaucracies, which together formed the final pillar of homeland security—emergency response.[32] Of these, the Federal Emergency Management Agency (FEMA) was the most important. In addition to fielding emergency response teams and serving as a conduit for disaster relief money, FEMA also encompassed insurance programs to help mitigate the longer-term impact of various natural disasters.[33]

Three features characterized the homeland security status quo before the September 11 attacks. First, policymakers assumed homeland security bureaucracies to be capable of operating reasonably effectively even though they had largely separate reporting structures and bureaucratic identities. Though some legislators and independent commissions complained about the fragmentation of responsibility for security-related problems, legislators tolerated the decentralization of bureaucratic power over national and homeland security.[34] Second, the description of the agencies above demonstrates that virtually *every* bureaucratic unit that had a role to play in homeland security also had separate functions—such as INS's role in providing immigration services—that were different in scope and, therefore, potentially in conflict with security. Finally, enormous variation existed in the degree of coordination across relevant units. Some problems were undeniable, such as the relationship between the FBI and the CIA (and, for that matter, between the FBI and just about everyone else). But there were also apparent successes, as when federal officials foiled a plot to bomb traffic tunnels leading into New York City and some of its major landmarks.

The administration's initial response to the September 11 attacks focused on proposing substantive legal changes. Working groups at the Justice Department soon pulled together legislative proposals from preceding years to fashion an outline of what would become the USA PATRIOT Act (Patriot Act).[35] The White House supported federal agents' aggressive use of immigration and material witness authority to detain scores of people almost immediately following the attacks, and the president used his authority under the International Emergency Economic Powers Act (IEEPA) to block the assets of various individuals and organizations suspected of being tied to terrorists.[36]

The White House staff also oversaw the implementation of two noteworthy changes in organizational structure, though its approach to each

demonstrated a great deal of caution about major changes in the allocation of bureaucratic jurisdiction. On October 8, using existing statutory
authority, the president created the position of homeland security advisor
within the Executive Office of the President and appointed Pennsylvania
governor Tom Ridge to fill it. Ridge sought to build a structure around his
position to match the president's ambitious rhetoric that the new Office of
Homeland Security would "coordinate" policy by creating a Homeland Security Council, paralleling the structure of the National Security Council.[37]

An implicit presumption that underlay the creation of Ridge's office
concerned the value of coordinating separate agencies mixing homeland
security missions with other functions. White House officials presumed
a gap to exist not only in the provision of advice but also in the extent
of coordination among a great many agencies and bureaus.[38] These officials believed that success in the arena of homeland security depended
on enhancing such coordination.[39] Notice that in a context encompassing border patrol agents, disaster response specialists, counterterrorism
investigators, and cybersecurity specialists, the precise definition of "success" is not entirely straightforward. Gauging success is also complicated
because the absence of attacks does not prove success. Notwithstanding
these ambiguities, Ridge sought to provide that coordination, or at least
the trappings of it. But even delivering the image of greater coordination
to the public proved daunting. The national counterterrorism coordinator
structure set up at the NSC now had a mandate overlapping with that of
the new Homeland Security Office (HSO). There were no precedents for
how to resolve the potential jurisdictional conflicts, nor was it obvious
precisely what it meant for Ridge to coordinate, what his role would be
in a crisis, or whether the conflict between the NSC and the HSO would
prove a major impediment to the goal of coordination.[40]

Sensing disarray, some legislators proposed alternative structures. They
insisted that the new homeland security advisor should be subject to Senate confirmation and have statutory powers over budgets. Senator Bob
Graham, a Democrat from Florida, introduced a bill to transform Ridge's
entity into a new National Office for Combating Terrorism to achieve the
aforementioned purposes.[41] Other legislators went even further, reiterat-
ing occasional calls made earlier by selected legislators and blue-ribbon

commissions for the creation of a new cabinet-level department focused on domestic security.[42]

The president opposed these efforts. Instead, White House aides emphasized the advantages of the status quo. From October 2001 until at least March of 2002, the White House press secretary insisted that creating a cabinet department was unnecessary and possibly counterproductive.[43] Unfortunately for the White House, the performance of the new office during the anthrax attacks belied the president's argument that coordination had been sufficiently bolstered by the creation of Ridge's office. During the anthrax episode, some observers described Ridge's response as tentative and uncertain.[44] Despite the new homeland security advisor's declaration that he was in charge of the response, Health and Human Services Secretary Tommy Thompson (leading what was once the FSA) appeared to contradict Ridge. During this period, despite the absence of formal budget authority, Ridge pressed for, and helped the White House achieve, a $1.2 billion increase in the immigration enforcement budget.[45]

A second structural change took shape in response to discussions between Congress and a reluctant White House. These negotiations culminated in the creation of a new federal bureaucracy to consolidate responsibility for transportation security.[46] Upon its creation in 2002, the Transportation Security Agency (TSA) assumed complicated responsibilities over the security of the nation's transportation infrastructure.[47] The White House initially opposed the idea. The president preferred to forgo creating a new bureaucracy and to keep the screeners private. Whether that opposition was rooted in ideology or in concern for the organized interests likely to be affected, the administration later abandoned its reluctance and endorsed the idea. Some observers with access to the deliberations now report that the administration's acquiescence reflected not only mounting pressure from congressional Democrats but also the recognition that the mass public was unlikely to trust private screeners given their inability to prevent the hijackings.[48] The new law placed TSA within the Transportation Department. The new agency's creation was also accompanied by an initial dismemberment of the FAA's security capacity (provoking bitter opposition by some FAA employees),[49] lodging it elsewhere in the Transportation Department.

Whether TSA would even remain at the Transportation Department would soon become a matter of intense political debate. Well before September 11, a number of legislators and blue-ribbon commissions had called for consolidating some bureaus with a homeland security mandate in a cabinet-level agency.[50] Various plans on Capitol Hill focused on three functions: border security and enforcement, disaster response functions relevant to terrorist attacks, and policymaking activities to facilitate the prevention of attacks.[51] Following the attacks, Senator Joseph Lieberman, then serving as chair of the Senate Governmental Affairs Committee, re-introduced legislation to centralize certain government functions into a single homeland security department. While some Republican legislators, such as Arlen Specter, expressed some interest, the president did not. He believed that such consolidation would constitute a waste of time at best. On March 19, 2002, for instance, in response to a questioner who asked "[w]hy . . . the White House continue[s] to resist the idea of making the Office of Homeland Security a Cabinet-level department," Press Secretary Ari Fleischer insisted:

I'm not aware of a single proposal on Capitol Hill that would take every single one of those agencies [dealing with terrorism] out from their current missions and put them under Homeland Security. So even if you took half of them out and put them under a Cabinet level Office of Homeland Security, the White House would still need, in the President's estimation, an advisor on how to coordinate all that myriad of activities the federal government is involved in. So creating a Cabinet office doesn't solve the problem. You still will have agencies within the federal government that have to be coordinated.[52]

Several factors might have made the creation of a new department seem problematic from the president's perspective. The substantive benefits of a consolidation were unobvious, indeed, highly uncertain—a point to which we return below. Major changes were likely to provoke opposition from powerful legislators whose committees stood to lose some jurisdiction and from the interest groups they served.[53] Moreover, career officials and political appointees within the administration were likely to resist the transfer. Opposition among the bureaucracies could have proven politically costly to the president,[54] increasing the risk that reorganization would backfire and potentially exposing the administration to criticism in the press or on Capitol Hill.[55] Critics of previous reorganizations had, after all, pointed out that they had created such problems in the past.[56] Finally, to the extent that prescriptive concerns mattered at all (something we explore and question below), they might cut sharply *against* the sort of reorganization that might seem superficially appealing to the public. Reorganizations almost inevitably cost money and create friction among people and organizations scrambling to understand the consequences of the new hierarchy under which they must work. Moreover, reorganizations create new authority structures that typically engender friction, which hinders one of the main reasons for reorganization—namely, coordination.

Even in the midst of its crisis mode, White House aides may have appreciated certain risks inherent in taking responsibility for a massive reorganization. In the short run, there was a substantial chance that reorganization would actually decrease agencies' effectiveness in responding to security threats, at a time when the administration would have thought such threats would almost certainly persist or grow. Though little is known about the impact of reorganizations on bureaucratic performance, it is widely acknowledged that performance suffers at the outset.[57] One account of the frantic days following September 11 underscores the extent to which these prescriptive concerns, intermingled with an appreciation of the political costs, *were* on the White House radar screen even two days after the terrorist attack:

By Thursday, Abbot, Kuntz, and Libby [aides to Vice President Cheney] had concluded that the first thing the Bush administration should do would be *not* to reorganize all those agencies, but to hire a heavyweight to come work in the White House and *coordinate* them, much the way Condoleezza Rice, the National Security Advisor, coordinated the various agencies involved in foreign and defense policy. They could never get all the agencies with some role in domestic security into one department, they reasoned, because so many also did so many other, unrelated jobs. (FEMA, for example, administrates flood insurance in addition to coordinating the federal response to disasters.) The goal should be to coordinate whatever they did related to homeland security, rather than spend a lot of time and money dislodging them from their current departments.[58]

The White House emphatically followed that path. In the weeks following the attacks, aides insisted that Ridge's office fit the bill, coordinating both the sprawling federal security apparatus and the thousands of local police and fire departments, from Manhattan to Minnesota to Manhattan Beach, still scrambling to enhance security in their local jurisdictions.[59]

Despite the Democrats' control of the Senate, Congress broadly supported the president in the two months following the attack. The administration achieved rapid passage of the Patriot Act and a resolution authorizing the use of force abroad in response to the attacks. Even individual Democratic legislators seemed initially inclined to cooperate. Senator Graham, for example, agreed to the president's proposed legislation. The extent of congressional support contributed to an impression of considerable (if not frantic) policy change and implementation. The administration's burst of activity since September 11—including the Patriot Act, the creation of a large new transportation security bureaucracy, the private sector's thrust to crack a new homeland security market, state and local officials' regional exercises, the invasion of a Central Asian nation, and the forging of a new White House staff office—seemed to push the limits of what the nation's political machinery could digest in such a short time.

SHAPING A REORGANIZATION AND
STRIKING LEGISLATIVE BARGAINS

Legislators were not entirely passive participants in the policymaking process, however. Emboldened by White House reluctance and public opinion surveys, a score of legislators called for a new cabinet department focused on homeland security.[60] White House aides thus encountered a more complex political terrain. By late October 2001, Democrat Joseph Lieberman in the Senate and Republican Mac Thornberry in the House led what had begun as an unlikely (if not downright outlandish) crusade to merge agencies into a new super-bureaucracy that began to pick up support among both Republican and Democratic legislators.[61] The response from the White House through the rest of 2001 and early 2002 remained an emphatic "no."

But this negative response was not the last word from the White House. On June 6, President Bush unveiled his own proposal for the new Department of Homeland Security.[62] Hints that something was in the works had appeared beginning in April, when budget director Mitch Daniels publicly stated that the president could propose reforms at a later date.[63] What Daniels did not say was that the president had already set the process in motion. In late 2001 and early 2002, the president had several conversations with Ridge and Chief of Staff Andrew Card about the merits of creating a new department to administer homeland security.[64] Responding to congressional resistance to an earlier border consolidation plan, the president apparently noted that the plan "seems kind of small to me," and then added:

You know . . . maybe we should stop getting pecked to death like this. *Maybe it's time to think big.* When you do something piecemeal, all the interests here come at you one by one and kill you. Let's just make believe we are re-creating the government from scratch and map out what we'd put in a new homeland department and then maybe we'll go for it.[65]

By March, aides to Ridge, Card, and Daniels were holding secret meetings in an underground White House bunker.[66] Participants in the meetings now suggest that their deliberations were driven largely by prescriptive concerns about the organizational merits of consolidating various units. The group was also driven by concerns about what could be sold on Capitol Hill, as underscored by the fact that the initial small group soon expanded to include staff from the White House legislative affairs operation.

Although the small amount of information available regarding these early meetings makes it impossible to determine the participants' precise mix of concerns, the discussions soon yielded a rough picture of a department with two significant features. First, it would be significantly larger in scope and size than anything that had been proposed by the Democrats or previous independent commissions. "The PEOC [Presidential Emergency Operations Center] group," noted one commentator (referring to the underground bunker where White House aides were meeting to plan the new agency), "had now created a mega-agency that far exceeded Senator Lieberman's relatively modest proposal for a Department of Homeland Security, and they weren't finished."[67] The working group demonstrated a willingness to contemplate an even larger department by its inclination to consider moving the FBI, the FAA, and ATF into the Department (moves that were ultimately rejected) (Table 7.1). Precisely why the White House process contemplated and produced such a sprawling department is not immediately clear, a matter to which we will return. Second, the PEOC group intended the new department to serve as a showcase for the value of flexibility in presidential control of personnel. The goal of watering down civil service protections appealed to the president's aides, particularly Daniels.[68]

The thirty-five-page legislative proposal that emerged from the meetings of the "PEOC group" sought to establish four primary "directorates" at the core of the new department: border and transportation security, information analysis and critical infrastructure protection, science and technology, and preparedness and emergency response. It included provisions allowing the president to appoint more than half a dozen assistant secretaries without Senate confirmation, and sought to imbue the president with power to redistribute appropriations among several different agencies. It called on political appointees to rewrite civil service protections governing many of the agency's new employees and to replace them with a "flexible" system, presumably vesting greater power over career officials in the hands of political officials.[69]

The plan's starkest feature was its scope. It sought to move some twenty-two agencies into DHS, despite the fact that not all of their functions conformed to even the most expansive definition of homeland security. The marine environmental portions of the Coast Guard, for instance, were to be entirely absorbed by the department, as were the revenue collection and trade enforcement functions of the Customs Service, and the agricultural regulatory functions of the Animal and Plant Health Inspection Service (APHIS).[70]

In contrast, many previous proposals for the creation of a homeland security agency had contemplated more modest changes. For example, Republican Representative Mac Thornberry's pre–September 11 bill, introduced in March of that year, essentially contemplated moving FEMA, Customs, the Coast Guard, and border patrol to the new department.[71] Unlike the president's plan, agencies such as the Secret Service, APHIS, the investigative and regulatory functions of immigration authorities, health-related functions such as the national vaccine stockpile, and the Treasury's

TABLE 7.1 *Selected Agencies Considered for Transfer to DHS*

Bureau Considered for Transfer[a]	Responsibilities for "Homeland Security"[b]	Non–Homeland Security Responsibilities	Transferred?
Animal Plant and Health Inspection Service (Agriculture)	Capable of providing personnel for support of inspections at the border	Regulate movement of animals and plants into and out of the country	Yes (partially)
U.S. Secret Service (Treasury)	Protect top U.S. officials; provide security at high-profile public events	Investigate financial fraud ("wire" and "access device" fraud) and counterfeiting, anti-counterfeiting policy development	Yes
U.S. Coast Guard (Transportation)	Patrol U.S. territorial waters; capable of responding in emergencies; can deploy as part of the Navy in wartime/emergencies; interdict drugs	Marine safety enforcement (regulate ships and companies owning ships); set rates for use of marine facilities and waterways; set rules for use of drawbridges and similar facilities; enforce marine environmental regulations (oil and chemical spills, marine water pollution rules); search and rescue	Yes
INS[c] (Justice)	Screen entrants at the border (including potential terrorists); enforce internal immigration laws	Provide immigration services to the public	Yes
FEMA	Provide disaster relief and recovery services in response to terrorist attacks	Provide disaster relief and recovery services for natural disasters and major industrial accidents; flood insurance; nutrition assistance; mitigate natural disasters	Yes
U.S. Customs Service[c] (Treasury)	Inspections at the border (screening for explosives, WMD); interdict narcotics	Enforce tariff and trade-related tax law; write and enforce trade regulations, including those involving child or forced labor, environmental provisions, and strategic trade rules	Yes
Critical Infrastructure Assurance Office (Commerce)	Promote private sector activities to protect critical infrastructure from terrorist attacks	Encourage private sector activity to protect critical infrastructure from natural disasters	Yes

Bureau Considered for Transfer[a]	Responsibilities for "Homeland Security"[b]	Non–Homeland Security Responsibilities	Transferred?
National Infrastructure Protection Center (Justice)	Investigate, analyze, and respond to man-made threats to critical infrastructure	Minimal	Yes
Office of Domestic Preparedness (Justice)	Offer grants for domestic preparedness	Respond to disasters (including non-terrorism related disasters)	Yes
Bureau of Alcohol, Tobacco, and Firearms (Treasury)	Enforce explosives law (regulation and criminal investigation)	Collect excise taxes on alcohol, tobacco, firearms, and explosives; regulate firearms extensively (including access, sales, and licensing)	No (moved to Justice)
Federal Aviation Administration (Transportation)	Protect aviation security	Regulate air traffic and aviation safety	No
State Department Visa Processing Functions	Screen visa applications (including requests by potential terrorists)	Screen visa applications (including those requested by everyone else)	No (but included in President's plan)
Transportation Security Agency (Transportation)	Manage national airport screening system; non-aviation security responsibilities	Handle security involving threats other than terrorism	Yes
Nuclear Regulatory Commission	Reduce the vulnerability of nuclear power plants to terrorist attacks; safeguard nuclear materials used for civilian applications in the United States	Regulate nearly all aspects of civilian nuclear industry (including licensing of new nuclear reactors and civilian nuclear technologies); regulation of the ongoing use of nuclear technologies	No

Sources: Homeland Security Act of 2002, Pub. L. No. 107-296, 116 Stat. 2135 (2002) (codified as amended at 6 U.S.C § 101-557 (2006)) (listing agencies included in DHS); Brill, After, 447–49 (describing the White House PEOC group's deliberations); Office of Fed. Register, National Archives and Records Administration, United States Government Manual 2002–2003, at 107–353, 413–16 (2002) (describing agency functions); President's Plan (describing agencies the president sought to move into the new department); Memorandum on Critical Infrastructure Protection, Presidential Decision Directive/NSC-63 (May 22, 1998), http://www.fas.org/irp/offdocs/pdd/pdd-63.htm (describing formation of National Infrastructure Protection Center); Press Release, Department of Justice Office of Justice Programs, Attorney General Ashcroft Announces Nearly $10 Million for New York City to Fight Terrorism (Apr. 23, 2002); available at 2002 WL 663507 (describing responsibilities of Office of Domestic Preparedness).

[a] Displayed in **bold** if not slated for transfer before White House deliberations began

[b] Using administration's definition focused on terrorism and explicit man-made threats

[c] Separated into Bureau of Citizenship and Immigration Services (encompassing both Customs and INS criminal investigation functions) and a Bureau of Customs and Border Protection (encompassing both Customs and INS border enforcement and administration)

Federal Law Enforcement Training Center were left untouched.[72] The administration-supported reorganization's mixing of a wide range of legacy missions with new homeland security responsibilities raised the question of how the trade-offs were to be made across these missions.[73]

A flurry of activity followed the White House's June 7 announcement. The White House briefed cabinet members (many of whom were just learning about the plan at that point) and legislative leaders. The president's aides spoke to the media, and at 8 p.m. Eastern Time, the president spoke to the nation about the plan.[74] The elaborate rollout confirmed that the president and his staff were now not only joining the chorus of support for the reorganization but sought to lead the reorganization drive. The building blocks of the new proposal broke from past plans in the larger scope of agencies to be included and in the provisions weakening civil service rules. Despite these differences, publicly the plan was premised on the same logic that the alternatives were: the value of centralization.

The administration's decision to develop that plan did not unfold in a political vacuum. Several factors may have underscored to the White House that it would face rising costs by continuing its opposition to the creation of a new cabinet department. Its legislative affairs staff documented increasing support for consolidation among legislators.[75] Security issues continued to hold much of the public's attention, particularly given congressional hearings about the September 11 attacks and public debate about whether an independent commission would ultimately be created to investigate the attacks.[76] The White House opposed that commission too. White House officials may have anticipated risks from opposing a new department along with an independent commission heading into the midterm congressional elections. In addition, creating a new department may have had particularly strong political salience because of its appeal to latent, if potentially superficial, notions of effective governance.[77] But these developments fail to account for the choices the White House made regarding the size, scope, and prescriptive merits of the new department.

The president's June announcement found Congress still mired in divisions about the merits of creating a new department at all. Support remained vigorous among members of the Senate Governmental Affairs Committee, whose members had proposed renaming the committee "Homeland

Security and Governmental Affairs" and who almost certainly stood to gain prestige, power, and influence if their expectations were fulfilled and the new department fell under their jurisdiction. At the same time, a stubborn core of opposition persisted among lawmakers who had committee jurisdiction to lose, or who saw position-taking opportunities in opposing substantive civil service changes, earmarks, and liability protections in the president's proposal.

The depth of those divisions reflects the deeper institutional logic of a legislature that rewards members in large measure for what the public observes and what organized interests value. When lawmakers in the agriculture committees of the House and Senate jockey for jurisdictional advantage relative to committees focused on health when it comes to food safety, they are responding to a context that makes the food safety issue important to voters and groups representing economic or consumer interests. In analogous fashion, legislators deciding on the fate of the White House proposal to create a new domestic security agency divided into several groups: (a) those who sit on committees that oversee bureaucracies that would be moved to the new DHS (these members have something to lose from the reorganization); (b) those who sit on the committees likely to gain oversight power over the new DHS; and (c) all others, who might evaluate the details of legislative proposals on the basis of potentially desirable position-taking opportunities or specific provisions affecting their political goals. Although a significant consolidation of jurisdiction over homeland security funding into a single subcommittee within legislative appropriations committees was eventually achieved, this occurred years after the department was established and over substantial legislative opposition. Other aspects of homeland security policy (including power over legislative authorization) remain substantially decentralized.[78]

With a growing number of legislators joining the president in supporting the creation of a new department, there followed a period of intense bargaining. In the House, Speaker Dennis Hastert and the Republican leadership created a two-track process to evaluate the bill, christened the "Homeland Security Act" (HSA). More than a dozen committees with existing jurisdiction over various aspects of homeland security would mark up the bill, but their votes would be considered advisory in nature.

Meanwhile, Hastert would empanel a Select Committee on Homeland Security, which would include most of the chairs of existing committees with jurisdiction over homeland security, to make final decisions on the House version.[79]

Hastert's move was understandable. If the leadership had left the decision making solely to the existing standing committees with existing authority, they would likely oppose the major reorganization that the president was now publicly committed to support and that a growing chunk of the public appeared to support. Alternatively, if Hastert created his own handpicked committee, existing members and committees would likely be opposed to the result.

The markups revealed widespread concern among the committees regarding potential changes in their jurisdiction. For example, the House Judiciary Committee voted to transfer the Secret Service to the Justice Department, over which it had jurisdiction, instead of letting it go to the new department. The House committee with jurisdiction over transportation issues sought (like the one in the Senate) to prevent or delay moving the new Transportation Security Agency to the new department. And many legislators sought to limit the presidential powers in the new bill, such as those allowing the White House to appoint assistant secretaries without Senate confirmation.[80]

Although the first stage of advisory markups appears symbolic, since the Select Committee would have final say, the procedure resulting in these votes could also be understood as serving as a critical information-collecting device for party leaders who favored the reorganization. The House leadership appeared inclined to support the president's push for reorganization. Nonetheless, the membership was likely to be quite wary of a wholesale redistribution of power within the legislature, which was an almost inevitable consequence of the reorganization legislation. The markups thus allowed the committees to reveal which portions of the proposed changes were politically most costly to them and which were less so. The Select Committee could then take these committee actions into account in its decisions, either by incorporating the committees' changes or by searching for other means to assuage the committees' ostensible concerns. The Select Committee reported its version of the HSA

on July 19, 2002, on a straight 5–4 party-line vote. This legislation became the basis for the final bill, described below and passed by the full
house on July 26, 2002.[81]

Partisan divisions on the House Select Committee foreshadowed greater
conflict in the Senate, where Democrats controlled the chamber by a tiny
margin. Already, the president's June announcement had probably begun
to blunt the perception, which Senator Lieberman had intensely sought to
foster, that creating the new superagency was a Democratic initiative.
Lieberman now sought to recapture the initiative. In late July, the Senate
Governmental Affairs Committee approved a Lieberman-sponsored version
of the homeland security bill with civil service provisions more acceptable
to the Democrats and provisions transforming Ridge's existing office at
the White House into an Office of Counterterrorism with a director subject to Senate confirmation.[82] The Senate then received the House version
of the HSA, which gave the president, among other things, the power to
exempt parts of government from federal labor management relations
statutes.[83] Lieberman and his allies sought to substitute his new bill for
the House version. But Senator Phil Gramm filibustered cloture motions
to limit debate.[84] In the end, Senate Democrats were unable to pass a cloture motion to force a vote on their preferred version of the bill, which
would have triggered a House-Senate conference on the creation of the new
department. And they were unwilling to compromise on the civil service
provisions. Thus, when the midterm elections arrived, the Senate had not
agreed to support the president's and the House Republican leadership's
version of the HSA. Ironically, the Democrats were exposed to the charge
that they opposed the creation of a department that they had played such
a key role in forcing the president to accept.[85]

The elections brought further unwelcome news for the Democrats,
who lost the Senate and were dealt an even more lopsided minority in the
House. After a final attempt to strip provisions allowing the president to
suspend collective bargaining protections, the Democrats compromised
and allowed cloture to be invoked in the Senate by a vote of 83 to 16 on
November 19, 2002. The Senate then passed the House bill with minor
amendments that were approved in the House by voice vote, and the bill
was sent to the president on November 22, 2002.[86]

THE FINAL BILL

When the president declared victory three days later, he signed a bill that was far more detailed than what the White House had proposed. The details reflected protracted presidential bargaining with Congress. On the surface, the final bill established a department that was quite similar to what President Bush had proposed. Consistent with the president's proposal, the core functions of DHS were grouped into four directorates: Border and Transportation Security (including the bulk of the department's employees and resources), Intelligence and Infrastructure Protection (incorporating some of the smaller infrastructure protection offices absorbed from the Commerce Department's Critical Infrastructure Assurance Office and the FBI), Science and Technology (including the Homeland Security Advanced Research Projects Agency, or HSARPA, initially projected to administer a $500 million fund supporting innovative research and development projects), and Preparedness (primarily FEMA).[87] Not every agency that the White House working group considered placing within DHS ended up in the department,[88] but the sprawling agency had nonetheless come to encompass functions ranging from international child labor investigations to marine fuel leaks, and included nearly every entity that the president ultimately proposed to move into the new agency.

Despite the White House's relative success, the legislative bargaining process also introduced some important changes. The final Homeland Security Act contained nearly two hundred separate legislative provisions (with some stretching over half a dozen pages). In contrast, the president's original proposal contained fewer than fifty sparsely written provisions focusing primarily on the structure of the four aforementioned directorates. This disparity reflects complexities lurking beneath the surface of the HSA.

Unlike the original White House bill, for instance, the resulting HSA simultaneously included language explicitly emphasizing the importance of missions not explicitly linked to the Bush administration's initial, narrowly focused conception of homeland security along with the terrorism-focused language[89] and provisions establishing the secretary's power over the bureaus.[90] It could not have been lost on legislators that the first *three* of the department's six functions concerned terrorism. At the same time, lawmakers supplemented the blanket entreaty for the new department to "[e]nsure that the functions of the agencies and subdivisions within the Department that are not related directly to securing the homeland are not diminished or neglected except by an explicit Act of Congress" with additional agency-specific language.[91] In the case of the Coast Guard, legislators actually allowed some (ostensibly limited) diminution of non-homeland-security functions, but sought to monitor changes in its non-security regulatory and safety missions by requiring regular reports from the inspector general and the secretary.[92] The HSA also contained similarly detailed provisions governing a wide array of other agencies transferred to the new department, specifying (for example) that some revenue-collection regulatory functions of Customs would remain at Treasury[93] while the secretary of Homeland Security could administer others, and providing that FEMA should carry out an "all hazards" mission while simultaneously allowing the secretary the flexibility to refocus FEMA's actual operations.[94]

These provisions reflect the existence of legislative compromises amounting to contradictions. As lawmakers and executive officials pressing for the new agency scrambled to compromise with committee chairs and regional interests, they crafted a statute that simultaneously included language emphasizing the importance of legacy mandates while actually conferring greater authority on executive officials. The revenue provision does not allow Treasury to retain exclusive control over the revenue-related regulatory functions of Customs. Under the HSA, the secretary of the Treasury has the power to delegate these functions to the secretary of Homeland Security, and—where such delegation has not occurred—must consult with the secretary of Homeland Security on the performance of these functions. Thus, even if the secretary of the Treasury chose not to delegate any of these powers, the law allows Treasury to wield its tariff-related regulatory authority only in consultation with the Department of Homeland Security. The secretary of Homeland Security, moreover, retains considerable discretion to set enforcement priorities at Customs despite language in sections 413 and 417 placing limited restrictions on the secretary's ability to directly diminish or discontinue revenue-related functions. For example, while the secretary may not directly "reduce the staffing level, or reduce the resources attributable to" functions performed by Customs' dedicated revenue and trade staff, the secretary appears to retain authority to affect the priorities of the more than 20,000 employees under the Office of Field Operations that administer ports of entry, thereby changing the amount of information produced about potential revenue and trade violations.[95]

The resulting bill also denied to the White House many of the sweeping presidential powers contained in the original proposal. Despite Republican congressional majorities, the bill did not allow the White House to directly control the timing of agency transfers, to redistribute appropriations among different agencies, or to appoint assistant secretaries without Senate confirmation. The HSA also created a host of research institutes and centers of excellence with mandates to focus on exceedingly broad conceptions of homeland security (including, for example, one center focused on developing new prison-related technologies).[96] Over time these institutions would almost certainly serve as conduits for federal spending benefiting particular regions or industries.[97]

Finally, the legislation accomplished a proliferation of other goals, many of which were initially addressed in separate legislative proposals. For instance, although the Justice Department lost virtually all its immigration enforcement power when INS was transferred into the new department, it gained most of Treasury's Bureau of Alcohol, Tobacco, and Firearms.[98] Pilots gained a right to be armed.[99] Airlines obtained new insurance and financial protections,[100] and the department gained new regulatory powers to protect manufacturers of "anti-terrorism" technologies from liability.[101]

Together these features evince the importance of four recurring themes associated with the legislative bargaining process. First, although the new bill granted the secretary of Homeland Security sweeping powers of "direction, authority, and control" over the new department,[102] legislators recoiled from granting the president the sweeping powers he had requested to reallocate appropriations, appoint assistant secretaries without confirmation, and control the timing of agency transfers. Second, legislators showed predictable interest in creating conduits for the transfer of federal money to particular regions or industries—in short, pork barrel. Third, lawmakers used the fast-moving HSA to advance discrete legislative projects that allowed them to signal desirable positions to the public (as with the provision for arming pilots) or achieve major substantive policy goals sought by organized interests (such as the expansion in airline liability protections).

Fourth, even as they ultimately voted for legislation that transferred major agencies into a new bureaucracy, legislators insisted on asserting control over those agencies by including provisions governing how those agencies were supposed to discharge their missions. In particular, legislators showed some awareness that the department would—true to its name—emphasize homeland security over a plethora of legacy missions. In response, lawmakers made modest efforts to stress the continued importance of the agencies' myriad non-homeland-security responsibilities.[103]

Equally noteworthy is what the bill omitted—congressional organization. The HSA describes the "sense of Congress that each House . . . should review its committee structure in light of the reorganization of responsibilities within the executive branch by the establishment of the Department,"[104] but the bill requires no changes in structure. Thus, as tens of thousands of inspectors, agents, and government employees began a long journey toward their positions in DHS in late November 2002, the congressional oversight structure dealing with the department's components remained largely unchanged.[105]

Earlier the White House had sought to bolster its reorganization plan by arguing that too many congressional committees were involved in overseeing homeland security.[106] It now acquiesced to a status-quo-driven congressional oversight structure. Although the Senate's Homeland Security and Governmental Affairs Committee appears to have gained some degree of jurisdiction at the expense of other committees, the Senate's Appropriations, Judiciary, Armed Services, and Finance Committees (among others) all retain substantial homeland security oversight responsibilities. In the House even less centralization occurred in the legislative oversight structure. The relative preservation of the status quo in the House probably indicated the leadership's reaction to the repeated standing committee "advisory" markups seeking to limit the size and scope of the department. Although such votes had not succeeded in limiting the scope of the sprawling new department, little had changed with respect to congressional oversight as late as mid-2004:

In reality, jurisdiction [over DHS] in both chambers remains allocated to dozens of committees and subcommittees. From January to June 2004, DHS officials testified before 126 hearings, or about 1 1/2 per day of legislative session, not including briefings or other meetings. Secretary Ridge estimated that he has been called to appear before 80 different committees and subcommittees on the Hill.[107]

Potential problems with congressional oversight did little to dampen the political enthusiasm for the new department when it finally opened its doors in mid-2003. The president had switched from opposing the merger to fashioning—with legislative allies—a new homeland security agency larger than anything previously proposed. Neither the administration nor members of Congress involved in forging the department expressed much uncertainty about how well this sprawling arrangement would function. But history would soon extinguish any certainty about the legislation's merits.

CHAPTER 8

The Political Logic and Early Legacy of DHS

SURROUNDED BY a bipartisan cast of lawmakers, President Bush signed the Homeland Security Act in the East Room of the White House just fourteen months after the September 11 attacks. Although the legislative process that spawned the new agency was undeniably motivated by concerns about terrorist attacks, the president spoke of the department's goals in sweeping terms, explaining that the new agency would "focus the full resources of the American government on the safety of the American people."[1] Within months, senior officials implementing the new law had taken apart the nation's immigration and border enforcement responsibilities, shattering the long-lived Immigration and Naturalization Service (INS) and wresting the nation's first revenue-collecting agency, the U.S. Customs Service, away from the Treasury Department after two hundred years. Federal employees braced themselves for potentially far-reaching consequences.

Since November 2002, observers of immigration and border policy have sought to understand the consequences of the new agency. A new Citizenship and Immigration Services (CIS) agency was carved from the former INS to manage immigration services. Immigration and Customs Enforcement (ICE) merged customs and immigration investigative responsibilities, but cut off routine patrols of the border from much of the rest of law enforcement responsibilities involving borders and immigration. A reconstituted Bureau of Customs and Border Protection (CBP) consolidated immigration and customs inspections with border patrol responsibilities, but lacked capacity for even routine investigations. Critics and commentators have repeatedly raised concerns that the resulting organizational structure is far from optimal. One implication for DHS is that it renders the secretary and the deputy secretary the only decision makers in the chain of command who can resolve disagreements, generating long-festering stalemates. Immigration policy analysts note that the "flat organizational structure" means that DHS lacks an effective system to make high-level decisions and is "undermined by an absence of policy coordination across individual immigration agencies."[2] Separately, analysts at the Government Accountability Office (GAO) outlined a range of management and organizational challenges that arose from moving immigration and border functions within DHS.[3] Some officials noted that investigative and operational issues, including responsibility for internal affairs, led to constant bickering between CBP and ICE. In contrast, the previous structure allowed most such issues to be resolved within a single bureau.[4] Relatedly, there is tension as to whether it can be argued that the language in the Homeland Security Act of 2002 (HSA) has left the attorney general with concurrent authority over immigration law.[5] Selected operations have reportedly been hampered by the absence of communication and coordination between CBP and ICE. Further, CBP and ICE lack formal guidance for addressing some overlapping responsibilities.[6] Indeed, according to some observers, the creation of DHS resulted in immigration policy's being framed and treated as "almost solely a security issue," in the narrow sense of the term.[7] Observers have nonetheless also questioned the efficacy of even some security-focused border initiatives. Problems with the technically elaborate Secure Border Initiative to deploy more sophisticated remote sensing technology at the border, for example, appeared to receive little sustained attention from senior officials.[8]

Whatever else one believes about the future of U.S. immigration and border policy, these developments illustrate at least two broader challenges associated with the creation of DHS. First, organizational changes carry costs. Some are simply transition costs that reflect organizations' coming to terms with new bosses, rewiring their information technology infrastructure, and grappling with a newly emerging organizational culture. Previously routine activities such as the referral of a corruption investigation from one office to another become politically risky decisions that involve multiple bureaus. At the same time, longer-term costs can also arise, involving the trade-offs inherent in unifying some functions (such as inspections at the border) at the expense of fragmenting others (such as immigration enforcement). Perhaps some of these costs are worth bearing if sufficient security benefits result. But therein lies another potential cost, involving the tension between narrower conceptions of security-related priorities such as the disruption of terrorist mobility and broader formulations emphasizing far-reaching national priorities with more-abstract connections to security. Those priorities, for example, might encompass integration of immigrants into society and the consequent benefits to social harmony and even the nation's capacity for innovation. Even in an agency with far-reaching legal authority, if agency leaders choose to change the order of priorities to emphasize the disruption of terrorist mobility, costs may arise to the broader immigration-related missions of an agency.

Although much remains for us to learn about the fate of immigration and border policy at DHS, the changes already occurring call for a broader inquiry into the details of the most significant security-related federal organizational change in five decades. One issue to explore is whether, as with the FSA, the president drove most of the choices about the agency's structure, or whether instead Congress played a more assertive role in reshaping immigration jurisdiction and countless other areas under the purview of DHS. To better understand how those choices, in turn, affected tens of thousands of federal workers and millions of Americans, we can also explore further how particular agency functions fared in a world of scarce budgets and potentially drastic organizational changes. The discussion that follows provides additional support for the theoretical refinements about crisis and organizations introduced in Chapter 2 by exploring these issues. Along the way, we will gain more insight into why the Bush administration switched from opposing the creation of a new cabinet-level security agency to supporting it, and why the administration was comfortable proposing the creation of a far larger agency than previously proposed by lawmakers.

THE PROMINENCE OF CONGRESSIONAL ACTION
IN SHAPING EXECUTIVE BRANCH ORGANIZATION

The FSA bore the hallmarks of Franklin Roosevelt's compromise with lawmakers over reorganization authority and, specifically, illustrated the lack of executive power to create from whole cloth a cabinet-level agency. Still, the bulk of the new agency's features reflected plans hatched within the White House. While the executive branch unquestionably played a major role, congressional influence far outstripped the role played by lawmakers in 1939 with the FSA. The story of DHS is more complex. In fact, lawmakers' influence permeated nearly every aspect of the HSA legislation and the bureaucratic machinery it spawned. The administration's bill was short—fifty brief provisions in comparison with the congressional legislation, which included two hundred provisions—many of them in the convoluted legislative lexicon characteristically associated with lawmakers' desire to control the bureaucracy.[9] The difference between the president's proposal and the final congressional legislation reflects more than just filling in details and gaps; it reveals the effects of the congressional politics engineering the new bureaucracy to serve the interests of its members— that is, to conform with the political-bureaucratic system.

The early evolution of DHS soon turns out to embody some recurring themes emphasized in the earlier discussions of the origins of DHS (in Chapter 7) and the theoretical issues relevant to understanding public organizations (in Chapter 2): goal distortion and the tendency to create organizations that can distribute benefits to separate constituencies; multiple veto points forcing alterations in the legislation, intra-congressional committee jurisdictional issues; electoral goals of the majority party against the minority party; uncertainty about the reorganization; and the role of the crisis. Together, these themes add up to a set of policies that are not obviously designed to obtain the stated objective of homeland security.

Consider, for example, the impact of goal distortion as it plays out through the distributive tendency. Calculating the optimal allocation of funds is a complex task. As Robert Powell suggests, this calculation must take into account a wide range of characteristics, including: (1) estimations of risk, themselves subject to uncertainty, such as the differential risks associated with targets in high-profile cities, in places such as New York and Washington; (2) factors that reduce risk everywhere, such as increased border security; and (3) the notion that making one target far more secure makes the next most vulnerable target more attractive to strategic terrorists.[10]

Despite the difficulty with creating an optimal spending plan, nearly everyone agrees that the allocation of funds should be based on the factors noted above, especially assessments of differential risk. Yet, as noted in the theory, spending money according to the optimal factors often implies a high concentration of funds in particular districts, making these programs less popular in Congress. The congressional tendency is therefore to alter the criteria for spending in a way that spreads the money around, even at the expense of efficient pursuit of the legislation's goals. And this seems to be exactly what has happened.

DHS secretary Michael Chertoff's statements on January 4, 2006, provide evidence for this story. In response to sharp criticism, Chertoff made the astounding public announcement that thenceforth the department would base part of its homeland security grant allocation on risk factors (DHS could not allocate all the funds based on objective factors because the legislation required minimum-percentage spending in every state). Chertoff announced new rules about the distribution of such funds based on the risk of terrorist attack to thirty-five urban areas deemed especially vulnerable. Chertoff also stated that homeland security grants are "not party favors to be distributed as widely as possible," thereby suggesting that the previous approach to distributing grants amounted to such "party favors."[11] This admission acknowledged that the department had *not* based its assessments on risk factors prior to this time.[12]

Indeed, a wide range of commentators imply that some DHS spending may have degenerated into another source of congressional pork, especially through spending money in rural states with relatively low risks of terrorist attack.[13] While the port of New York and New Jersey is widely regarded as at the highest risk, it received only $6.6 million in FY 2005, about equal to Memphis and far behind Houston's $35.3 million.[14] The attempts to renew the Patriot Act in late 2005 reflect efforts in the House to place greater emphasis on risk factors and to lower the guaranteed minimum percentage going to each state from the prevailing 0.75 percent to 0.25 percent. The Senate, with its greater rural bias, beat back this plan so that the original law would prevail.[15] Similarly, an analysis of per capita homeland security grant spending for FY 2003 and FY 2004 indicates that in both years Wyoming—the best-funded state—received $35.30 and $37.74 per capita, respectively. New York State, on the other hand, received only $5.10 and $5.41 per capita in each of those two fiscal years.[16] The small-state bias seems rooted in legislators' distributive interests, filtered through institutions enhancing the political power of small states, rather than in meticulous analyses of why such funding should be allocated to Wyoming or similar states.

As the theory suggests, legislators' distribution of federal funds reflects a *common pool problem*: while all are better off from a homeland security program that fulfills its objectives, each is better off if his or her district gains a bigger share of the total. When all members seek greater funds for their districts, however, the consequences can be enormous. Members of Congress have greatly hindered DHS's ability to address the pressing problems of terrorism in America by prescribing constraints on spending that have little or nothing to do with homeland security and everything to do with their reelection prospects.

Another policy realm where legislators' parochial concerns seem paramount to conventionally-defined security concerns is the creation of the "Homeland Security Centers of Excellence." Each "HS-Center" received a grant of between $10 million and $18 million over a three- or five-year period to study topics ranging from network analysis to the economic consequences of terrorist attacks.[17] Instead of creating a mechanism for choosing center locations on the basis of defensible analytic criteria, the structure set up by the statute essentially dictated the location of the new centers. The department created six HS-Centers, located at the following universities: Johns Hopkins, the University of Southern California, Texas A&M, the University of Minnesota, the University of Maryland, and Michigan State. One would expect that these centers would be created in the districts of legislators facing a risk of losing committee jurisdiction as part of the transfer. It is telling that the statute happened to place the centers in geographic areas represented by at least one lawmaker who was in exactly that situation, a pattern that suggests the outlines of a potential logroll.[18] Although such a loss of committee authority is almost never welcome among legislators, funding for the new homeland security centers may have served as part of the political exchange to increase support for the legislation among members who faced the prospect of diminished committee power.

A third example of political bias in the distribution of funds concerns the new structures for the transfers of funds. After 2001, Congress slightly reduced funding for natural disaster grants and dramatically increased funding for counterterrorism grants.[19] One example of an explosion in grant funding can be seen with grant opportunities provided through what was once the Department of Justice's tiny Office of Domestic Preparedness. The office was transferred to DHS, and thereafter its grant-making abilities have grown exponentially. In FY 1998, the Office of Domestic Preparedness awarded $12 million through a single grant program. By FY 2003, the office was in charge of meting out funds in seven separate programs, with total funding for each ranging from $65 million to $1.5 billion.[20] Far from reluctant participants in this growth, legislative majorities voted to fund the grants well beyond what the president requested—adding more than $800 million to the president's request in this category for the FY 2004 budget.[21]

While the funding of preparedness and research has proven to be an important aspect of the new department's activity, the legislative process did more than simply inject distributive concerns into the architecture of DHS. It also diluted the extent to which lawmakers considered the prescriptive merits of reorganization, or reorganized the internal distribution of legislative committee jurisdiction to realize those benefits.

The frequently stated rationale for creating the massive department was coordination. Yet the prescriptive benefits of reorganization are highly uncertain. Centralization creates a far more massive organization, implying that organizational leaders have much greater difficulty mastering the various pieces. Department leaders' difficulties in managing FEMA and its natural disaster mission have made this plain, particularly in the aftermath of the Katrina disaster.[22] Centralization may also contribute to greater monopolization of functions within the government, yielding less competition among bureaus and dissipating the potential benefits of competition. Reorganization creates considerable uncertainty about future career paths for bureaucrats. Those whose futures have been downgraded or who face the most uncertainty are most likely to work less hard or leave the agency. This has also become evident in FEMA, as many of its former employees simply moved on.[23] Finally, substantial short-run costs arise from centralization as agencies undergo the transaction expenses of integrating personal, information, financial, management, and field systems. These problems raise serious questions—almost entirely neglected in the legislative process—about whether the massive centralization of DHS was worth pursuing.[24]

During most of the department's history, legislators also neglected the mismatch of congressional jurisdictions and bureaucratic centralization. Although the reorganization made massive changes in bureaucratic organization, Congress declined to engineer parallel changes in congressional oversight. The House Judiciary Committee is particularly illustrative of this point. Among the Judiciary Committee's many amendments, the committee voted to transfer only the law enforcement functions of INS to DHS, keeping the immigration functions at the Department of Justice (DOJ) and, obviously, under the purview of the committee. Besides retaining its oversight functions, the Judiciary Committee also voted to increase its responsibility by approving an amendment to transfer the Secret Service and the Federal Law Enforcement Training Center from Treasury to the DOJ.[25] The House leadership did create a special nine-member Select Committee on Homeland Security in July 2002 to screen the changes made by individual committees,[26] but House Speaker Dennis Hastert populated this panel largely with committee chairs who could protect their jurisdictions.[27] Legislators also showed significant resistance at the time the HSA was passed. President Bush reportedly made some early attempts to encourage Congress to solve the jurisdictional issue,[28] but legislators essentially ignored him.

The massive bureaucratic reorganization unaccompanied by any congressional reorganization implies that the structure of bureaucratic incentives induced by congressional oversight works against the effects of centralization. This problem raises another variant of the congressional common pool problem: though all members may have wanted to achieve improved homeland security coordination, they also sought to control a piece of the bureaucracy. By so doing, legislators could claim credit for steering policy in a highly salient domain,[29] and for steering funds in directions benefiting constituents. Many members of the relevant subcommittees have specialized in helping existing constituents of the agencies being moved to DHS. To the extent that coordination lowers the level of service that legislators can provide to their constituents, these members are likely to use their oversight jurisdiction to impede coordination.[30]

Because the creation of DHS made massive changes to the bureaucracy while leaving the existing structure of congressional jurisdictions in place, congressional incentives cut against the goals of centralization and coordination.[31] The piecemeal set of congressional jurisdictions reflected the old set of priorities; in particular, a set of agencies that did *not* coordinate. Much of the lack of coordination under the old system represents a set of diverse agencies serving diverse constituencies and overseen by a diverse set of subcommittees. Leaving the old congressional jurisdictions intact allows representatives of the old, uncoordinated system to pull their agencies away from the coordination-related goals of the new system and to continue to serve the interests of their old constituents. In addition, leaving the existing distribution of committee jurisdiction in place yields another problem interfering with the potential benefits of centralization: DHS's leaders must now report to all of the separate congressional committees, depleting the time they can devote to coordinating. In a less sprawling reorganization, such reporting demands might prove less problematic. Not so with DHS; during the first half of 2004, department officials were called to testify—on average—almost twenty times a month.[32]

Yet most of these prescriptive concerns—whether about the merits of centralization or about the need to overhaul congressional committee jurisdiction in order to capture the benefits of centralization—were cast aside. Instead, senior legislators from both parties maneuvered to preserve their committees' power. And the parties themselves competed in trying to take credit for an impending reorganization with growing public salience. In the process, Republicans contrasted themselves with the Democrats on several issues, notably the drug liability and civil service exemptions. In the debate just prior to the 2002 elections, several visible Democrats opposed these provisions. The Republican strategy seemed to work: those Democrats who opposed these provisions were painted as being against homeland security, and several key members, most notably Senator Max Cleland, lost their re-election bids.[33] In the weeks before the November 5, 2002, midterm congressional election, polling results reveal that the public viewed the president and the Republican Party as better at handling national security–related issues. A July 2002 CBS News/New York Times poll of registered voters found that 49 percent of respondents thought that the Republican Party would be "more likely to make the right decisions when it comes to dealing with terrorism," while only 22 percent believed the Democratic Party would do so.[34] These results suggest that voters responded to a successful effort by the president and the Republicans to project a favorable image of their handling of homeland security immediately before the midterm election. While these poll numbers may be explained by a variety of factors, it is difficult to discount the successfully-cultivated image of being tough with regard to national security issues as a most likely explanation for the shift in public opinion. According to a December 12, 2002, ABC News poll—taken about one month after the 2002 midterm elections—67 percent of respondents approved of the president's handling of homeland security.[35] These numbers suggest the president had succeeded in projecting an image of vigorous and favorable activity, encompassing the administration's role in creating TSA, the invasion of Afghanistan, and its ultimate decision to spearhead the creation of DHS.

THE INFLUENCE OF THE WHITE HOUSE ON THE ORGANIZATION OF HOMELAND SECURITY

As amply demonstrated by the trajectory of the FSA, the president and his White House advisors were also in a position to exert considerable influence over the creation of DHS. Even with a far more emboldened legislature—reflecting the intimate connection between the dramatic 9/11 attacks and the arguments for creating DHS—and despite the lack of the kind of reorganization authority that Roosevelt had pried loose from Congress, the White House played a critical role in shaping DHS. The White House's role in the reorganization showcases some of the trade-offs that the president and his advisors made when working with Congress to forge the new agency.

The administration charted a course that reflected strongly held policy goals as well as political constraints. Even where executive branch policymakers genuinely sought to achieve normatively defensible goals of enhancing federal capacity to manage threats posed by terrorism, a variety of political considerations almost certainly weighed on the president and his advisors in the tumultuous days leading up to the creation of DHS. Some observers place significant explanatory weight on the existence of what might be termed a "bandwagon" effect, in which the president's hand was forced by growing legislative interest in creating the new department. To the extent that some form of reorganization was likely to pass, the argument presumes, the president's public image was best served by being in favor of DHS rather than by opposing it and losing.[36] Moreover, perhaps the president also had an incentive to differentiate his plan from others so as to be able to claim credit for the reorganization.[37]

Although the bandwagon effect undoubtedly came into play—and may even explain the president's initial willingness to revisit the creation of the department—it cannot explain the details of the White House proposal, such as why the president's alternative plan was so massive. The president could have joined the bandwagon with a reorganization only modestly different from those already before Congress. He would almost certainly have heightened the possibility of its adoption by proposing a smaller reorganization devoid of features such as assistant secretary positions not subject to Senate confirmation that were designed to increase presidential influence.[38] Viewed from this perspective, a reorganization of comparatively larger scope and size may have posed more risk to the president's image as an effective leader. These factors raise the question of whether White House partisan and policy goals made the administration become such a fertile ground for arguments in favor of crafting the department in a particular way, even if the prescriptive costs were high.

To address this issue, we begin by examining another piece of the puzzle. Why did Bush, so fiscally profligate in general, insist that the DHS be "revenue neutral"? The stated rationale for the large DHS umbrella was that centralization and coordination would improve homeland security. Yet this rationale alone cannot explain why centralization went so far to include so many agencies (and parts of agencies) whose missions are so tangential to homeland security. As we have seen, the uncertainty about the effects of reorganization combined with the lack of congressional jurisdictional reorganization served to bring into question whether centralization would yield net benefits for homeland security. Given the Bush administration's initial misgivings about reorganization, it is clear that the administration understood these problems in advance, and they weighed against centralization.

Yet it is quite plausible that a major reason why DHS encompassed a massive reorganization is that such a path was broadly consistent with Bush Administration *domestic* policy interests that were largely independent of homeland security. Indeed, a major consequence of the new DHS structure—perhaps the most important consequence—concerns domestic policy, not homeland security. Legislators understood that the creation of a new department would inevitably have consequences for domestic policy. First, legislators were clearly concerned about what the department would mean for the important non-security duties with which the agencies in question were charged. Much of the early debate in Congress about the president's proposal focused on whether, for example, it was wise to transfer FEMA and the Coast Guard to DHS, given their domestic policy mandates. As noted above, the legislation addressed this directly.[39]

The HSA demonstrates the extent to which political actors recognized the domestic regulatory policy stakes of the creation of the department.[40] The committee report accompanying the legislation concludes:

[M]any agencies within the Department . . . perform important non-homeland security missions that Americans rely on every day. The Animal and Plant Health Inspection Service protects ecosystems from invasive species. The Federal Emergency Management Agency assists local communities to prepare for and respond to natural disasters. The U.S. Coast Guard performs essential maritime search and rescue, fisheries enforcement, marine safety, marine environmental protection, navigation assistance, and migrant interdiction functions. The Department of Homeland Security's Bureau of Citizenship and Immigration Services provides asylum for refugees and assists immigrants in becoming American citizens. The Customs Service protects and monitors foreign trade that is essential for a healthy American economy. The Secret Service monitors and protects against identity theft, counterfeiting, and other financial crimes.[41]

Nonetheless, the provisions in the bill also demonstrate how, despite these concerns, the explicit terms of legislative compromise creating DHS allow for a diminution in domestic regulatory activities. Put simply, the DHS provides a statutory and organizational framework that allowed Bush officials to divert a wide range of resources from agency legacy mandates to homeland security activities. Regardless of whether these activities have any impact on security, the administration had reason to value the diversion of resources out of the legacy mandates it found worthy of disapproval.

The potential to reshape legal implementation through reorganization can be further grasped by contrasting reorganization with strategies deployed by the Reagan administration. A major policy goal of President Ronald Reagan's was to reduce what many Republicans believed was a bloated federal government, which included a wide range of governmental programs that the Reagan administration did not value or believed to be outright harmful to the economy. Reagan was ideologically opposed to an elaborate regulatory state, which he disparagingly termed "big government." When he took office, he appointed a range of administrative heads who shared his views. Many sought to sabotage their agency's efforts, in part by simply stopping its efforts to enforce the law.[42]

This strategy failed. Constituencies benefiting from the regulations took the agencies to court in an attempt to get them to enforce the existing set of laws. The courts agreed and, absent agency proceedings that decided on a different enforcement strategy, forced them to continue administering the law as they had been doing. Anne Gorsuch's leadership of the EPA illustrates this failure. Her attempts to slash the agency's budget and her failure to uphold environmental laws led to her resignation.[43]

George W. Bush's goals were not the same as Reagan's, and he did not appear to share the full extent of Reagan's ideological commitment to the market.[44] Like Reagan, however, Bush believed a wide range of domestic programs should be outside the purview of the national government. The Reagan administration's experience nonetheless demonstrated that the strategy of direct sabotage, shirking, and neglect of the law was unlikely to work.

But, as we have seen, crises have a capacity to change the political equation. One such change—which may have initially seemed unrelated to the administration's regulatory and administrative agenda—involved the president's homeland security agenda. Even after the September 11 attacks, the president was reluctant to create a new homeland security cabinet agency. Despite the uncertain long-term benefits of centralizing homeland security and the high transition costs, Congress nonetheless accepted the reorganization because of their conventional common pool problems. In the president's case, his revealed preference of no reorganization eventually dissipated in the face of gathering congressional and public support for reorganization, and continuing protests from some aides seeking limited changes in the structure of land-border enforcement.

Once the White House recognized that avoiding reorganization altogether was not an option, the administration's strategy became decidedly more ambitious. Perhaps the September 11 attacks would provide the Bush administration with a unique opportunity to lead a policy that would achieve a range of domestic goals of which both key officials in the administration and many Republicans in the legislature approved. The president appeared to have come into office inclined to hold constant or even roll back federal regulatory controls.[45] The Coast Guard's extensive regulatory functions—including the protection of marine ecosystems, the regulation of marine safety, and setting requirements for the use of port facilities—were long unpopular with a number of business constituencies that could express concerns to Republicans, including cargo vessel operators,[46] the fishing industry,[47] tanker and oil companies,[48] and cruise lines.[49] Republicans also questioned certain FEMA functions that could be framed as essentially social welfare policies, including FEMA's role in food and shelter assistance, noncompetitive mitigation grants, and subsidized flood insurance.[50] As historian Douglas Brinkley has written, even just a few years after FEMA's creation, "the incoming Reagan administration saw the outfit as a feel-good liberal money drain, a cousin to HUD [Department of Housing and Urban Development] and HEW."[51]

The new strategy sought to bring a wide range of agencies with domestic programs under the umbrella of the DHS. Three separate components of the DHS umbrella could have furthered Bush's domestic policy goals: one legislative, one organizational, and one budgetary. The legislative component gave all the agencies moved to DHS new statutory responsibility that differed from their legacy mandates. Specifically, agencies brought under the umbrella were subject to a new law requiring them to act. In contrast to the agencies in the Reagan era, the agencies moved to DHS now faced a set of statutes with conflicting goals—their legacy mandates versus the new homeland security mandate. Indeed, even before the creation of DHS formalized the importance of the Coast Guard's new security priorities, the media began reporting how the agency had been forced to reorient its resources: "While only 1 percent of [the Coast Guard's] resources were dedicated to port security before Sept. 11, more than 50 percent of all coast guardsmen are now [in mid-2002] focused on homeland security."[52] As one longtime Coast Guard observer noted at the time, "[T]here wasn't a whole lot of capacity for [the Coast Guard] essentially to pick up this new mission without it impacting significantly on its traditional missions."[53]

Second, Bush's insistence that DHS be budget neutral forced the agencies to devote fewer resources to their legacy mandates, since resources that went to homeland security were not available for the legacy mandates. The more they spent on homeland security, the less they spent on their legacy mandates.

Third, placing these agencies within the DHS organizational framework served to further the diversion of resources. If an agency were left independent or in its former department, the agency (possibly in collaboration with its former department) would make the determination of the trade-off of how many resources to transfer from its legacy mandate to homeland security concerns. It could, for example, decide that 3 percent of its resources would be appropriate. Placing these agencies within DHS, however, empowered Bush administration officials to help make that trade-off. In particular, placing these agencies within DHS allowed departmental leaders leverage with which to force agencies to make a greater trade-off than they would otherwise have done—that is, to devote greater resources to homeland security than the agency would do on its own.

It is worth noting the paucity of defensible prescriptive arguments for creating such a vast department at the time, and for insisting that it be revenue neutral. Recall that early on, Bush advisors flatly opposed the creation of a new department,[54] and the president himself repeatedly claimed to be a critic of large bureaucracies.[55] Those within the White House seeking bureaucratic changes initially sought to merge Customs and INS within the Justice Department, and Homeland Security advisor Ridge reportedly decided it was best to "leave the Coast Guard out of it."[56] A larger proposal would likely exacerbate the legislative bargaining, transition, and internal management challenges associated with turning the legislative proposal into a new bureaucratic reality. And the administration's insistence on revenue neutrality proved a potential political liability—as both legislators and government auditors emphasized how the merger would not proceed effectively under revenue neutrality.[57] "More important than a precise cost of the transition," noted one GAO report directly contradicting White House claims, "is the recognition that there will be short-term transition costs."[58] Nonetheless, the creation of DHS, coupled with an insistence on revenue neutrality, appears to have allowed Bush to transfer resources out of agency legacy mandates into new homeland security concerns. Because it appears that the administration did not value these legacy mandates, Bush's combined statutory and bureaucratic approach made him better off even if the resources diverted from legacy mandates to homeland security activities produced *no* tangible homeland security benefits.

Legislators, too, recognized early on that DHS was, to some extent, a presidential power grab. Lawmakers therefore made efforts to rein in what they saw as an overextension of executive power. These attempts can be clearly demonstrated through a comparison of the president's initial bill proposal and the resulting HSA. Examples of how legislators refused to give the president the full authority he desired are repeatedly apparent. The final bill, for instance, did not give the White House the authority to appoint assistant secretaries without Senate confirmation, as was requested in the original proposal. Nor, as previously mentioned, was the president granted the right to control when agencies were transferred (section 802 in the proposal) or to control the allocation of funds from the transferred agencies to the secretary of DHS (section 803(c) in the proposal). Finally, Congress voted to include the establishment of the National Homeland Security Council within the Executive Office of the President—an agency that was not proposed for authorization in the president's plan.

In addition to the legislation's language, floor statements reveal legislators' weariness of conferring more power on the president. Senator Robert Byrd (D-W. Va.) said of the HSA in a floor statement to the Senate: "The President is clearly attempting to remove the limits on his power. I don't question his good intention. Maybe he doesn't understand what he is doing. But this is clearly an attempt to remove limits on the Executive's power."[59] This comment is representative of the deep distrust that some in Congress felt over what they perceived as a presidential grab for increased authority.

Legislators' efforts to limit increases in presidential power over the department indicate the extent to which the fight over DHS not only was about the appropriate degree of centralization that should govern homeland security policy, but also was concerned with the extent of direct presidential control over the regulatory, bureaucratic, and legal functions that would be vested in DHS. Although legislative responses limited how much power the president achieved through the HSA, its creation significantly enhanced the power of the executive. The new law allowed the president to select a cadre of political appointees to oversee twenty-two agencies lodged in a new bureaucracy with the daunting mission of protecting the homeland while continuing to carry out non-homeland-security missions. After a tense fight in Congress, the DHS civil service employees were also subject to more-flexible personnel rules, thereby allowing political appointees to control them more readily.

The umbrella structure had another organizational effect that also served the purpose of increasing executive power, or at least advancing broad executive priorities. When a bureau was placed within DHS, the department's hierarchy could make it clear that legacy mandates were no longer the agency's priority and that therefore bureaucrats specializing in those legacy mandates were less likely to be promoted into senior management. All this meant that these bureaucrats would be treated less well and would be more likely to leave.[60] At the very least, the DHS umbrella gave administration officials opposed to an agency's legacy mandate additional tools with which to demote the goal of preserving the bureaus' ability to perform their overall mandate.

As Bush administration aides met deep underground in the East Wing bunker to design the new department, their choices and the president's subsequent decisions raise two additional questions. First, if the administration's inclusion of regulatory agencies within DHS was partly motivated by a desire to control and curtail administrative and regulatory activity, why did some Democratic proposals also include large regulatory agencies such as the Coast Guard? Although Lieberman's proposal was nearly as large in scope as Bush's, the context and substance of their proposals differed in important ways. Lieberman was likely motivated by the prospect of grabbing power for the Senate Governmental Affairs Committee, in which he played a leading role. Moreover, recall that President Bush's proposal was not only larger in the end, but its development nearly resulted in the inclusion of even more regulatory agencies that were not included in Democratic proposals—such as the Nuclear Regulatory Commission and the Federal Aviation Administration. In addition, Bush's proposal featured elements expanding presidential power by weakening the civil service and allowing the appointment of assistant secretaries without Senate confirmation. Finally, as noted below, Bush's proposal was coupled with moves that essentially accepted budgetary restrictions on agencies, with the consequence of forcing agencies to substitute homeland security efforts for their legacy mandates.

A second question is why the department was not even larger. As with past reorganization efforts, the White House was likely to best achieve its goals by balancing the costs and benefits of marginal increases in the scope and size of the department. If increasing the size of a new superagency in charge of security had its benefits, so too did it carry a coterie of risks and costs. Legislative resistance from affected committees, for example, would be greater as more functions were placed in the department (the judiciary committees, in particular, may have objected far more strenuously if the primary department under their jurisdiction, the Justice Department, had lost the FBI or had not received ATF). There was a risk, too, that the relatively shrouded domestic policy consequences of the reorganization might become starkly apparent to some of the public and galvanize concern about issues such as marine safety or environmental protection. In some cases, resistance to transfer from bureaus with greater autonomy, such as the FBI, would have generated additional friction. Finally, earlier White House concerns about large-scale reorganization strongly suggest that the leadership of the administration understood that reorganizations carried operational risk. Accordingly, the White House may have been concerned about the possibility that even more massive reorganizations, implicating agencies such as the FBI, would adversely affect critical functions such as air traffic control (which was considered and ultimately rejected as a candidate for inclusion).

In the end, some observers may be tempted to conclude that the creation of DHS appears to represent a clever domestic political innovation, allowing Bush to attain goals in ways in which President Reagan failed to do. Reagan's direct attempt to circumvent or ignore domestic regulatory laws largely ended in disaster.[61] By giving the Bush administration new statutory and organizational tools, the DHS umbrella provided the legal means to divert considerable resources away from domestic legacy mandates. In the end, it is certainly possible to conclude that such consequences reflect a difference in administration priorities (placing counterterrorism above other missions) more than a deliberate effort to fully squelch the domestic service and regulatory missions of the affected bureaus. What the executive branch officials designing DHS would find it all but impossible to ignore, however, was the fact that the bureaus being placed under the new security agency that would soon occupy a former naval facility on Nebraska Avenue would confront considerable organizational consequences.

THE ROLE OF CRISIS: A REPRISE

As with the Roosevelt administration's efforts to reshape the executive branch, the presence of a far-reaching crisis or looming threat played a prominent role in the birth of DHS. Specifically, the crisis following the September 11 terrorist attacks had several predictable effects on the policymaking process concerning homeland security. First, it gave the president an issue from which he could launch a new phase of his theretofore lackluster presidency and shore up his rapidly declining public approval rating. The weekend before the September 11 attacks, President Bush received a job approval rating of 51 percent; by September 21, 2001, his job approval rating had skyrocketed to a record-breaking 90 percent, representing the largest public opinion rally ever experienced by a U.S. president.[62] But this popularity was relatively short-lived, as Bush's approval rating steadily dropped over the next eight months to a post–September 11 low of 70 percent immediately before the DHS announcement. Because of the sharp decline in presidential popularity, the White House must have felt pressure to produce additional terrorism-related policy; the Patriot Act, the creation of the TSA, the invasion of Afghanistan, and a spate of other executive actions were not enough. Bush therefore sought to take visible command of the policymaking and shepherded the various pieces of legislation through the process—legislation that had clearly become his and not that of the Congress. To do so, he had to provide a plan that differentiated his administration's proposal from those under discussion in Congress.

Perhaps the most important aspect of a crisis is that the attentive public demands quick action. Especially in a national security crisis, when the public feels vulnerable, fast and decisive action is needed to assure citizens that risks have been substantially lowered. Perhaps most tellingly, the public cares deeply about terrorism and homeland security issues. Even before September 11, Gallup reported that a significant proportion of Americans were concerned about being victims of a terrorist attack. In an April 2000 poll, Gallup found that 24 percent of respondents were either very or somewhat worried that they or someone in their family would be a victim of an Oklahoma City–style bombing.[63] In January of 2001, Gallup found that 47 percent of respondents reported that it was somewhat or very likely that terrorists or another country using nuclear weapons within the next ten years would attack the United States.[64]

The public's concern with national security increased over time[65] and coincided with growing support for reorganization. Although only limited public opinion polls are available regarding the creation of DHS, available data suggest that Americans generally supported the idea of a cabinet-level Department of Homeland Security even before the president's announcement.[66] Additionally, a January 31, 2002, poll found that 84 percent of respondents approved of Bush's request to spend $38 billion on homeland security.[67] After President Bush made the June 7, 2002, announcement in which he endorsed the creation of DHS, public opinion reflected a belief that DHS was a fundamentally good idea. In a typical poll, Gallup found that 72 percent of respondents approved of the creation of DHS.[68] The widespread popularity of reorganization suggests the potential position-taking benefit that politicians could achieve by supporting the creation of DHS.

As legislators and the president pursued the creation of the massive department, the public's inability to assess the intricacies of the plan had three separate effects on crisis policymaking. First, popular demand for action induced political officials to prefer quick action that was less well considered and well designed to slower action that was better considered and better designed. Second, the need to pass something quickly also allowed political officials to hide other initiatives with very different aims within the plans to address the crisis. Third, the demanding public, unable to analyze the implications of transition costs or organizational details, put legislators seeking better plans (or opposing the plans) at a political disadvantage. Opposition delays action, and if the public cannot appreciate the policy-specificity of the argument, those seeking to improve the process appear simply to be opponents. Again, this clearly occurred in the case of Max Cleland.[69] All three effects appear to have influenced homeland security policymaking.

BUDGET POLITICS AND LEGACY MANDATES

Budget-related evidence is consistent with the hypothesis that reorganization furthered domestic legal and policy goals that cut against legacy mandates. Recall that in his initial proposal to create the department, Bush repeatedly promised that DHS would be "revenue-neutral," meaning that the new department would not cost any more than the combined budgets of its component parts.[70] The Bush administration's projected budgets for the Department of Homeland Security in FY 2003 and FY 2004 held resources constant compared to the 2002 figures (including both actual and supplemental expenditures).[71] In some respects, this push for budget neutrality suggests that the administration was contemplating cutbacks in legacy mandates during the creation of DHS; by giving new homeland security mandates to the agencies transferred to DHS and by not giving those agencies any new funding to perform these mandates, the president forced resources out of legacy regulatory functions.

In succeeding years, departmental spending exceeded the Bush administration's initial projections.[72] But once we remove supplemental appropriations such as those funding the aftermath of disasters like Katrina, a different picture emerges. As Figure 8.1 indicates, overall discretionary funding for DHS remained relatively constant between 2003 and 2006, and the president's request for 2007 continued the pattern.[73] The key comparison in the figure is between total DHS funding (excluding supplementals) and DHS homeland security spending. Because the latter rises faster than the former, these numbers indicate that DHS spending on legacy mandates decreased.

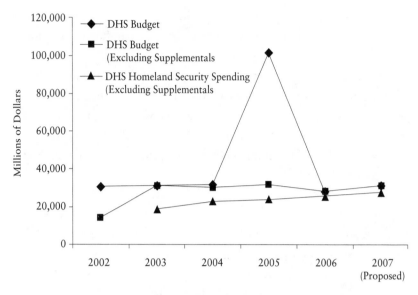

FIGURE 8.1 *DHS Budget Authority in Perspective*

Source: Calculations based on data from the Office of Management and Budget, *Budget of the United States Government* (fiscal years 2004–2007)

Although the budget for DHS and its components appears to have increased substantially, much of the increase occurred through a supplemental appropriation before the new department had been created, a figure that in large measure reflected disaster-related expenditures associated with the September 11 attacks, new grant programs, and the creation of the TSA.[74]

An even more telling picture emerges from the breakdown of appropriations flowing to DHS on the basis of whether or not the Office of Management and Budget considered an appropriation to be primarily related to homeland security.[75] Total DHS discretionary funds flowing to DHS remained essentially flat, but the dedicated homeland security resources within the department consistently rose. As Figure 8.2 shows, the proportion of resources flowing to functions most directly related to homeland security has increased from about 60 percent to roughly 90 percent during the life of the department. Admittedly, the appropriations designated as primarily homeland security–related almost certainly have the potential to provide a measure of non-security benefits.[76] It is revealing, however, that the White House directly identifies an increasingly dominant share of the department's resources with security-related missions.[77]

We can learn still more about budgetary developments by going beyond broad funding categories and examining patterns of individual bureaus. Some agencies that clearly encompass both traditional homeland security functions and domestic regulatory activities *did* experience budget increases.[78] But here, too, a different picture emerges from the details. Consider first the Coast Guard. Some of the budget increases for the Coast Guard cover a portion of long-anticipated infrastructure needs.[79] Despite the flow of some additional resources to the bureau, some legislators maintained that the agency did not receive adequate resources to carry out its new mandates. In a debate during the Coast Guard reauthorization process, Representative Howard Coble thought "that the Coast Guard leaders 'must have a magic wand' because he said they have seamlessly assumed a range of new responsibilities without corresponding increases in funding."[80] Moreover, individual appropriations accounts for the Coast Guard tell a story of shifting priorities. Just before and during the creation of DHS, several major Coast Guard programs experienced a sharp decline, most notably Marine Environmental Protection and Search and Rescue, both of which

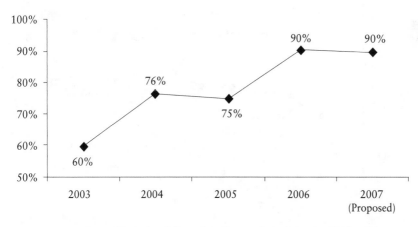

FIGURE 8.2 *Homeland Security–Focused Activity (as Defined by the Office of Management and Budget) as a Percentage of DHS Budget (Excluding Disaster Supplementals)*

Source: Calculations based on data from the Office of Management and Budget, *Budget of the United States Government* (fiscal years 2004–2007)

had been on a fairly strong upward budgetary trajectory since 1996.[81] On the other hand, as Figure 8.3 indicates, programs focused on security-related issues, such as Defense Readiness and Marine Safety and Security, experienced a dramatic increase in the same period, leaving a shrinking proportion of total Coast Guard outlays for domestic administrative and regulatory functions.

These budgetary changes took their toll on the Coast Guard's administrative and regulatory functions. Studies from the GAO confirm that Coast Guard programs suffered as a result of the new homeland security missions imposed on the agency by the transfer.[82] One report tracks the number of resource hours expended on each of the Coast Guard's programs over time, using the first quarter of 1998 as a baseline.[83] The general trend shows increasing reprioritization away from administrative and regulatory missions since the September 11 attacks, and particularly since passage of the HSA. For example, coastal security, which is the program that experienced the highest increase in resource hours, went from 2,400 resource hours in the first quarter of 1999 to 37,000 resource hours in the first quarter of 2003, more than a fifteen-fold increase.[84] Even where

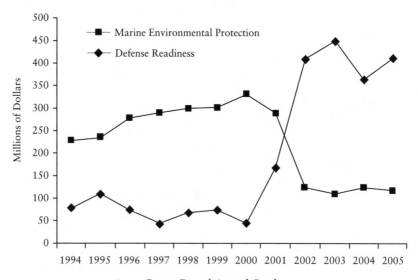

FIGURE 8.3 *Coast Guard Actual Outlays, 1994–2005*

Source: Data compiled from the Office of Management and Budget, *Appendix, Budget of the United States Government* (fiscal years 1996–2007)

such changes began before the Coast Guard's transfer, folding the bureau into the vast, terrorism-focused DHS bureaucracy almost certainly made it easier for these shifts in resources to be cemented into longer-term priorities. Placement of the entire bureau in DHS underscored the importance of the Coast Guard's counterterrorism functions, provided a new structure of national security–focused appointees to monitor the bureau's spending priorities, and weakened the prospect that congressional and departmental overseers more concerned about the bureau's domestic regulatory activities could have reversed the trend. Indeed, "for the foreseeable future," GAO investigators explicitly concluded that "the Coast Guard must absorb the cost of implementing a variety of newly mandated homeland security tasks by taking resources from ongoing activities."[85]

And the Coast Guard confronted these developments at a time when some important new regulatory initiatives, such as those implementing the International Convention for the Prevention of Pollution from Ships, which imposed new requirements for pollution prevention equipment,[86] were likely to demand additional enforcement resources. In other cases in the aftermath of its transfer to DHS, the Coast Guard postponed regulatory initiatives that had been in the works for years.[87]

Similar budgetary and priority-setting developments affected the administrative functions of FEMA, setting the stage for some of the events described in the opening pages of Chapter 1. FEMA's budget has two distinct components: responding to specific disasters, such as Katrina; and ("base") funding for FEMA's administrative capacity, mitigation grants, and discretionary disaster relief programs. The increase in FEMA's budget reflects both the core program budget and special appropriations for specific disasters such as the September 11 terrorist attacks that Congress and the president would find politically costly to ignore. In contrast, FEMA's ongoing administrative and discretionary functions, including activities such as oversight of disaster relief spending, flood insurance, and mitigation grants, may attract less public attention while inviting political controversy. As Figure 8.4 indicates, if we focus on FEMA's base budget, it becomes clear that FEMA's funding has remained essentially flat (or slightly declined) since the creation of DHS. By adding responsibilities and restricting FEMA's core resources, budgetary developments since the

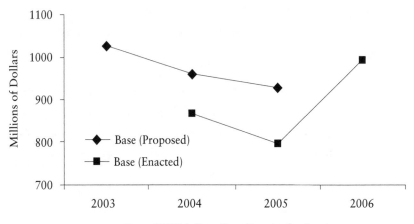

FIGURE 8.4 *FEMA Base Funding Authorization*

Source: Democratic Staff of H. Appropriations Comm., 109th Cong., *A Story of Neglect: A Review of FEMA and the Army Corps of Engineers in the Aftermath of Hurricane Katrina* (2005)

merger further strained FEMA's administrative capacities and its available resources for discretionary mitigation programs.[88] These constraints almost certainly diluted previous efforts from the agency's leadership to build capacity for natural disaster response and promote agency autonomy through enhanced connections to the president, Congress, governors, and disaster response professionals.[89]

The budgetary changes affecting the Coast Guard played out against the backdrop of larger shifts and pressing challenges at the agency. Notwithstanding its enormous size and vast responsibilities, the Coast Guard became something of a pawn after the September 11 attacks. Although the administration was initially reluctant to create a Department of Homeland Security, it eventually decided to proceed with such a venture in a manner that was all but guaranteed to pressure the Coast Guard to reduce its regulatory functions. Overcoming resistance from Congress to the idea of including the Coast Guard and reluctance from the president's own homeland security advisor, the administration placed the entire bureau in DHS.[90] The administration did not separate out the agency's regulatory policy or enforcement functions from its interdiction capabilities. Neither did it create within the new DHS a special office to ensure attention to environmental and safety functions within the Coast Guard or its sister bureaus, as it did to oversee narcotics enforcement and privacy issues. At the same time, new budgets only partially offset the burdens of the Coast Guard's growing security-related workload, and in some cases, policy-makers explicitly pursued cuts in budgets for regulatory enforcement that would have been more politically costly in normal circumstances. Regulatory performance has begun to shift in response. Consider each of these developments in turn.

For high-level officials in the new department, the task of overseeing the Coast Guard would proceed against the backdrop of the White House's narrow approach to defining homeland security. The administration construed homeland security primarily in terms of counterterrorism, thereby making it more difficult to protect legacy mandates merely by using homeland security rhetoric to describe long-standing missions.[91] And the possibility that organizational changes would diminish Coast Guard environmental and safety activities was not lost on members of Congress. "I am concerned," noted one lawmaker, echoing the reactions of others in both chambers, "about taking resources from traditional Coast Guard missions and diverting them to homeland defense."[92] In fact, the House committee overseeing the creation of the new department voted to keep the Coast Guard out of DHS. Across party lines, legislators cited concerns that folding the multifaceted bureau into the new super-department would erode its safety and environmental functions.[93] Government auditors echoed the legislators' concern about legacy mandates, concluding that the Coast Guard would face pressure to cut from existing resources absent dramatically higher financial resources.[94] In response, legislators added provisions to the Homeland Security Act in an attempt to limit the extent to which legacy functions might be eviscerated in the new department,[95] even though the overall statute still permits the department's leadership to refocus the agency's activities on defense and homeland security.

Within days of the September 11 attacks, the Coast Guard had been forced to assume new functions that placed further strain on the agency's already scarce resources. These responsibilities increased as the Coast Guard moved to DHS. Predictably enough, these changes made resource hours focused on homeland security–related activity at the Coast Guard (including domains such as defense readiness, port security, and interdiction) skyrocket 1200 percent by 2005 (compared to the pre–September 11 resource allocation).[96] Meanwhile, even before the move to DHS was completed, resource hours spent on legacy environmental and safety missions began to plummet, with hours spent on living marine resource protection falling by a third, hours spent on marine safety falling by 43 percent, and hours spent on marine environmental protection falling by 64 percent in the reporting period following the September 11 attacks.[97] These shifts dramatically illustrated the constraints under which the Coast Guard was laboring. They also underscore the extent to which Coast Guard legacy functions depended on substantial additional resources. The Coast Guard would likely continue being forced to cut back on environmental and safety regulation, moreover, by a succession of choices made by the administration with respect to the Coast Guard. These included, among others, adding responsibilities to an existing bureau rather than creating a new one, placing the entire bureau within DHS, and demanding such a high degree of security-related activity at the agency. After all, budgets interact with agency structure, management choices, and statutory priorities to affect government functions. Moreover, even before the September 11 attacks, the Coast Guard already faced substantial budgetary pressures to accomplish its full range of missions.[98]

The preceding changes in the Coast Guard's organizational context, missions, and budgets came at a time when the bureau's regulatory responsibilities for matters such as fisheries enforcement, ship safety, and environmental pollution remained substantial.[99] And in some cases, the Coast Guard's responsibilities in these domains are growing. The Coast Guard must now enforce a new regulatory requirement bringing the United States into compliance with treaty obligations under the International Convention for the Prevention of Pollution from Ships.[100] It must supervise a cruise industry that is growing dramatically.[101] Given these challenges, it may seem encouraging that the Coast Guard reported some slight increases in resource hours devoted to non-homeland-security missions around 2005,[102] and that some agency officials have also claimed relative success in meeting selected non-homeland-security performance goals in the years following the merger in spite of the budgetary changes noted above.[103] But there is less than meets the eye to both of these developments. First, although the Coast Guard's database for keeping track of how it uses its boats, cutters, and aircraft includes categories for recording the full range of non-homeland-security activity, it has provided information about resource hour increases in only a limited number of program areas, such as fisheries enforcement. And the increases do not erase the impact of the precipitous declines in activity registered earlier.[104] Moreover, non-homeland-security hours began declining again by 2007. Second, the Coast Guard's performance measures for non-homeland-security functions suffer from a number of problems. For instance, the Coast Guard currently measures its success in protecting living marine resources as a function of the "percent of fishermen in compliance with regulations."[105] Upon closer examination, it turns out that the bureau's measure focuses only on the proportion of compliance observed in vessels *boarded* by the Coast Guard.[106] Plainly, the Coast Guard could observe more compliance on the meager number of vessels it boards even if actual compliance is decreasing.[107] Similar problems afflict other regulatory performance measures.[108]

Meanwhile, the pace and focus of Coast Guard regulatory rulemaking activity—which combines with enforcement policy and resource allocation to shape overall regulatory activity—has also been shifting. While counts of regulatory rulemaking proceedings furnish an imperfect measure of life at the bureau, they do illustrate some apparent changes in agency activity and priorities. The average number of safety or environmental regulatory rules issued yearly by the Coast Guard dropped from about 3.8 in the last six years of the Clinton administration, to about 2.6 during the first two years of the Bush administration—before the Coast Guard was transferred to DHS—and then to approximately 2 per year during the four years the bureau has existed within DHS. Economically significant safety or environmental rules[109] were emerging from the bureau at the rate of about one a year during the last six years of the Clinton administration and the first two (pre-DHS) years of the Bush administration. Rules in this category issued during that period included, for example, limits on the release of harmful species in water ballast dumped into the Great Lakes, and requirements that shipping companies install tank pressure monitoring devices to reduce the danger of ruptured tanker vessels. In contrast, the Coast Guard has not issued a single economically significant safety or environmental rule since its transfer to DHS.[110] This slowdown appears to reflect the fact that major congressionally required Coast Guard environmental and safety rules have yet to be completed. For example, the Coast Guard postponed issuing comprehensive oil spill mitigation regulations designed to limit the extent and consequences of an *Exxon Valdez*–type oil spill. The rules were postponed, according to agency representatives, because of its "heavy workload guarding against terrorism in the post 9/11 era."[111]

THE BROADER CONSEQUENCES OF REORGANIZATION

The theoretical perspectives discussed earlier shed some light on the likely answers to the puzzles framed at the outset. Why is DHS so big, and why does it include so many agencies whose missions are only tangentially related to homeland security? Part of the answer is that Bush sought to take the lead in providing homeland security. But he, and his administration, also approached the creation of DHS in a manner consistent with its domestic policy goals. As we argued at the outset, the extent to which the creation of DHS was part of a deliberate plan to dilute and reassign domestic regulatory functions is still unclear. However, the fact remains that the Bush administration advocated the largest possible new department, despite warnings from within its own camps about the risks to security-related outcomes. Furthermore, given the wide-ranging array of bureaucracies that the administration considered for transfer, it is difficult to believe that one of the goals was *not* to affect legacy missions of the transferred agencies.

Requiring the transferred agencies to move under the homeland security umbrella had two separate, mutually supportive effects. First, the reorganization—especially with the stated goal of revenue neutrality—all but forced agencies to transfer resources formerly devoted to their legacy mandates to homeland security concerns. Second, the new organizational control allowed the administration to downplay the portions of the organization that remained focused on the legacy mandates, further disrupting the agency's ability to serve those mandates. The Bush administration seemed to value this transformation not necessarily because it improved homeland security but because it altered a variety of domestic programs.

Consider the final, related puzzle: why did Bush insist that this policy be budget neutral despite the fact that he was being so profligate in other areas? The answer may be that budget neutrality is a central tool in forcing agencies to change their operations so that they transfer resources out of their legacy mandates.

Another way to understand the dynamic of domestic regulatory impacts associated with the creation of DHS is to contrast it with an alternative approach for curbing administrative discretion. Suppose that instead of creating a massive new department, Congress had mandated that agencies undertake a "Homeland Security Impact Statement" (HSIS) in parallel with the Environmental Impact Statements (EIS) created in 1969. The HSIS would require agencies to study the impact of their proposed policies—and possibly also existing ones—on homeland security. As with an EIS, an HSIS would likely have had mixed implications. To be done seriously, it would take considerable effort. And, as with an EIS, the procedural nature of the exercise does not compel any policy changes. Moreover, this approach would not achieve Bush's domestic policy goals of forcing agencies to divert a considerable portion of resources and personnel from their legacy mandates.

Ironically, even shifting the focus away from legacy mandates does not guarantee the effectiveness of security policies. The distributive tendency has distorted DHS's spending priorities, moving away from high-risk targets to areas of significantly lower priority.[112] The legislature's failure to reorganize congressional oversight jurisdictions works to preserve the non-coordination status quo, directly hindering the goal of centralization and coordination. And partisan goals lead to some important consequences that are difficult simply to chalk up to the otherwise benign consequences of improved homeland security.

Regardless of the precise mix of political goals shaping the HSA, some of the problems afflicting its bureaus since the merger have become all too familiar. Indeed, the disastrous performance of DHS and FEMA in the aftermath of Hurricane Katrina in August 2005 is a natural consequence of a political process that played down transition costs and structural problems associated with the creation of DHS. Recall that the DHS merger accelerated a process through which FEMA's natural disaster and mitigation missions were eviscerated.[113] As the legacy missions were downgraded, many experienced workers left the agency.[114] Both a congressional committee and the White House issued reports detailing the mistakes made during the recovery efforts following the hurricane. The reports show how FEMA and DHS were unprepared for an emergency on the scale of Katrina. Both DHS and FEMA were indicted for "lack[ing] adequate trained and experienced staff."[115] The White House report suggests transferring certain disaster recovery responsibilities out of DHS, possibly by having the Department of Justice oversee law enforcement and HHS take over distributing aid to victims.[116] The congressional report goes beyond the conclusion that DHS and FEMA were unprepared. Its analysis highlights the problems resulting from a structure where layers of organization separated the White House from the operational command and technical advice most directly associated with the disaster response.[117] The report concludes that, had the structure worked better, the response to Katrina would have commenced several days earlier than it did.[118] An internal DHS Inspector General report also said as much.[119]

The storm and floods would have produced a crisis of major proportions under almost any circumstances. But the available evidence suggests that the structural problems associated with DHS—particularly early in the cycle of its existence—made things worse.[120] Even if one makes unrealistic assumptions about the potential coordination payoffs over time, the shortcomings in FEMA's and DHS's responses to Katrina are consistent with the existence of steep transition costs.

Nor was FEMA the only bureau to suffer challenges in the reorganization. Problems also arose in other units, such as TSA. The completion of its headquarters facility was delayed by the transfer to DHS.[121] Its internal structure was reorganized to remove federal air marshals from its jurisdiction.[122] The TSA's experience, like that of FEMA and other bureaus, demonstrated how the reorganization could trigger a variety of costs affecting the effective performance of legal mandates, including the need to adopt new technologies and internal bureaucratic procedures associated with a new department,[123] internal competition for control between bureau leaders and higher-level appointees,[124] and the burdens of adjusting to new management arrangements that altered the relationships among bureaus, other agencies, and the White House.[125] Border and immigration functions, too, reflected the costs of a new structure that also brought competing organizational priorities. Even if one views such management problems as temporary transition costs, they nevertheless raise the question of whether the potential efficiency from the creation of DHS made up for these costs.

THE CHALLENGES FACING DHS:
CONCLUDING OBSERVATIONS

Chapter 7 and this chapter used the evolution of homeland security policy after September 11 as a case study to analyze the allocation of legal authority within the bureaucracy, and the impact of bureaucratic structure on the implementation of legal mandates. Despite a large body of previous scholarship on bureaucracy and the implementation of legal mandates, such work has not yielded comprehensive theories linking the politics of bureaucratic structure to the behavior of the mass public in a crisis, inter- and intra-branch bargaining involving the legislature, and specific legal interpretations and policy outcomes straddling national security and more-conventional domestic policy issues. In part because of these gaps, existing explanations for the creation of the new Department of Homeland Security fail to provide adequate answers to crucial questions, such as why the president switched from opposition to support of the bureaucratic reorganization and why, after that initial resistance, the scope of his proposal was greater than that of past and existing proposals.

To address these specific questions, this analysis updates existing theories of the legislative process to encompass the following four premises: (1) Other things being equal, politicians and parties seek opportunities to control bureaucratic resources along with opportunities to signal positions that are appealing to the public. (2) The long-term marginal impact of a particular type of bureaucratic reorganization on the performance of complex legal mandates, such as promoting homeland security, is far less certain than politicians tend to acknowledge. Despite public perceptions to the contrary, centralization is no guarantee of enhanced performance. Nonetheless, changes in bureaucratic structure can have predictable statutory, organizational, and budgetary consequences by forcing bureaucracies to cut back on the performance of particular missions. (3) As the responses to drug scares, energy shortages, and the September 11 attacks demonstrate, a newly attentive public may favor structural changes even while they remain ignorant about the details. (4) Even *within* parties, legislators have divergent interests depending on their committee assignments and seniority. In terms of the debates covered in our theoretical survey in Chapter 2, these developments suggest a considerable degree of continuity between the fate of the most significant new security agency in half a century and the relatively familiar pattern of political competition and external influence shaping the organization of domestic regulatory and service-delivery agencies. And despite the considerable differences in the policy agendas of the Bush and Roosevelt administrations, we can see a measure of continuity, too, apparent in the administrations' response to crisis through organizational changes, and in the extent to which the blurring boundaries of the concept of national security opened up some strategic dilemmas and opportunities for the leadership of the executive branch.

None of these conclusions should be too controversial in light of the lessons gleaned from studying the department's early history. But taken together, they hold underappreciated implications for our understanding of the design and implementation of legal mandates. As individual legislators, the president, and political parties jockey for advantage, the political game tends to suppress important prescriptive concerns about the costs and benefits of centralization, the transition costs associated with reorganizations, and the fit between congressional and executive branch organization. Moreover, the combined effect of crises and uncertainty about the long-term impact of reorganization allows presidents to reshape administrative and regulatory policy and to assert greater control over bureaucratic discretion.

Hence, while the administration sold the new mix of bureaucratic structure, budgets, and statutory changes as a means of better responding to future crises, our evidence suggests that the administration exploited its legislative opening to enhance presidential control and reshape agencies' administrative discretion. It chose that course despite the risks—identified by the White House's own advisors—that doing so would adversely affect the performance of the security functions that justified the merger in the first place.[126] The president dismissed early consolidation efforts that seemed "kind of small to [him]," and directed his staff to "think big" as they forged a plan for the department.[127] In response, the secret group that made decisions about what to include in the president's proposal not only crafted a consolidation plan larger than anything legislators had proposed but seriously considered adding three more major regulatory agencies to DHS—the Nuclear Regulatory Commission, ATF, and the FAA. Despite the fact that many legislators anticipated the reorganization's adverse effect on legacy mandates, the HSA made statutory and organizational changes that allowed legacy regulatory and administrative functions to be compromised.[128] Republicans had a long record of wanting to control and limit the administrative activities of some agencies, such as FEMA and the Coast Guard, that were viewed as excessively intrusive or overly focused on social welfare policy. That goal was likely to be accomplished if the statutory and organizational changes made by the HSA were implemented in a revenue-constrained environment, as the president promised. And excluding supplemental appropriations, the administration proved surprisingly adept at keeping revenues flat for some core functions while shifting resources away from legacy mandates.

The aftershocks from the administration's decision to pursue reorganization have exacted a price. Key advisors within the Bush administration learned early on that creating the department risked making the problem of coordinating security worse. The concerns were not unfounded. Although my goal here is not primarily a normative assessment, we can now revisit—in light of this account—the question of whether the creation of DHS enhanced homeland security. Attributing marginal security-related effects to changes in organizational structure is difficult, and indeed the existence of uncertainty about this plays a role in our account. Might the uncertainty conceal a positive probability that the statutory choices made in creating the department could enhance the security of Americans at a time when many might be willing to trade off other government services in exchange for such improvements? We believe the answer is negative. The department's creation is almost certainly related to a net loss in the efficiencies associated with homeland security.

To see why, recall that virtually no serious observer questioned that the transition costs of creating the department would be pronounced—even if one accepted the administration's contention that the benefits would outweigh such costs.[129] The case for transition costs (defined as obstacles that would diminish the department's efficient output of security-related services for some discrete length of time) is fairly straightforward. Difficulties inherent in such a massive transition included the introduction of uncertainty regarding internal lines of authority, disruptions in established links between bureaucratic sub-units with one another and with the White House, a focus on setting up internal control structures rather than on performing the department's substantive mission, transfer of authority to a department that initially was almost entirely devoid of resources to monitor all the security-related functions of its new bureaus, a continuing fragmentation of legislative oversight authority, and a depletion of key staff so that they could serve on detail in the central department.[130] From a circumstantial perspective, the performance of the TSA during its time at DHS and of FEMA with Katrina is entirely consistent with the presence of long-term transition costs.[131] Indeed, the president's tremendous reluctance initially to create the department in part reflected these costs.[132]

The question, then, is whether the potential security benefits are high enough to offset the transition costs. These benefits may arise from two sources: (1) efficiency gains from coordination and centralization or (2) shifts in resources away from legacy mandates toward presumably more pressing security-related missions.[133] With respect to efficiency gains from coordination and centralization, we found the administration's theoretical case unconvincing.[134] It provided no reasonable explanation for why a single cabinet agency represented an improvement over the Homeland Security Council structure. No consideration is given in its public communications to the offsetting advantages of decentralization, which have been central to spurring aggressive antidrug enforcement and may play an important role in intelligence and policy innovation.[135] No discussion exists of the extent to which some agencies across cabinet departments have better coordination (such as ATF and FBI across the Treasury and Justice Departments) than other agencies within departments (such as the Navy and Army within Defense[136] or DEA and FBI within Justice).[137] And no attention is given to the reality that fragmentation actually persists because of the relative decentralization of congressional control.[138]

Moreover, a theoretically coherent prescriptive case for the department's creation would have been difficult for Congress to accept. If we examine the theoretical literature on organizations and bureaucracy,[139] the best case we could envision for the value of centralization is one that involves the value of either distinctive expertise at the top of the department or concentrated accountability in one official to permit trade-offs across (rather than within) bureaus. But neither of these benefits of centralization is consistent with the department's reality. It is difficult to accept that Ridge or Chertoff was simultaneously an expert in customs interdiction, disaster response, and technical cybersecurity. The resource-transfer goals could have been accomplished with congressional and presidential support of a White House–based Office of Homeland Security entailing fewer transition costs (which is, not coincidentally, what the president first chose to support).

This brings us to the difficult question of whether the security-related gains from the transfer of resources are sufficiently compelling to offset the transition costs. Such a prospect is unlikely. For one thing, homeland security threats may be plausibly viewed as encompassing natural disaster response functions, a position that the leadership of DHS has belatedly taken since Katrina and that accords with President William McKinley's nineteenth-century observation "I am more afraid of the West Indian Hurricane than I am of the entire Spanish Navy."[140] Yet natural disaster response appears to have suffered not only from the transition costs associated with the merger but from the administration's focus on statutory and administrative changes redirecting attention toward terrorism-related homeland security threats and away from natural disaster mitigation and response.[141] For another, it does not appear that the security problems that experts often cite as most pressing—involving efforts to secure weapons of mass destruction, strengthening public health and critical infrastructure, and enhancing response and recovery—have been meaningfully addressed by shifting resources within bureaus.[142] Finally, even if internal shifts in bureau resources (as opposed to additional resources) were essential in order to address the preceding problems, those benefits could have been partially or almost entirely captured without the creation of DHS.[143] Without the creation of DHS and its administrative oversight apparatus, however, the president would have been forced to be much more explicit about the bureau-level changes wrought by the HSA legislation.

To explain these developments, our account shows how three crucial variables affecting homeland security policy—whether to create a new department at all, its overall size and scope, and its congressional oversight structure—have been driven in specific directions by political rather than prescriptive considerations. Rare circumstances may create exceptions to this pattern displayed by DHS. In some policy domains, such as those involving benefit payments to retirees, results may be so easy to observe that electoral constraints force politicians to care about whether an agency is well organized to meet its stated goals. In other contexts, an agency whose leaders' agenda aligns with prescriptively attractive policies may find itself with a unique degree of autonomy, allowing it to leverage the mass public's reactions during a crisis. These observations also raise some questions about the canonical justifications—grounded in expertise and accountability through presidential control—for judicial deference to agency legal interpretations. Although these questions do not augur for rejection of those justifications altogether, they ought to prompt scholars and policymakers to reexamine the prescriptive merits of vesting discretion in agencies that are not effectively designed to carry out their alleged functions.

Years after DHS was created, policymakers would be reckless to seriously contemplate a complete reversal of the statutory changes that created the agency. Such a move would force Americans to incur more of the transition costs that have already depleted the nation's resources, and lose what benefits Americans have derived from an organization focused more emphatically on risks involving terrorism. Unquestionably, some changes in federal priorities should be expected following a major national security emergency. Nonetheless, a more defensible balance between conventional regulatory missions and narrowly defined security functions is likely to depend on the use of complementary techniques of institutional design and oversight. For example, several shorter-term changes could make a contribution to a principled balance. Congress should direct DHS to create an environmental protection and safety policy office staffed primarily with career officials within the agency, to focus attention on the environmental missions in the department. Although such an office does not guarantee that the department will honor its regulatory responsibilities, its existence can create an internal constituency for monitoring environmental performance and provide a unified point of contact within the agency for concerned legislative staff. The agency already has civil liberties, privacy, and counter-narcotics offices to play such a role in their respective domains.[144] In addition, enhanced regulatory review mechanisms—whether based in the DHS Inspector General's Office or elsewhere—should better monitor gaps in agency regulatory activity. Monitoring should encompass sanctions for failure to issue rules under statutes that require them or failure to adequately enforce the mandates that protect our marine resources, coastal areas, and clean water.

More generally, the incapacity of federal officials to effectively address broadly held concerns about security in the midst of a crisis is ironic. Principle and intuition would suggest that prescriptive concerns should be strongest during a crisis, particularly when the professed goal is to enhance the state's capacity to resolve broadly shared concerns. This analysis shows that it is otherwise in practice. In order for prescriptive concerns to prove significant, politicians must encounter or provide precisely the sort of counterweight that so rarely emerges in the political game over bureaucratic structure. Bureaucratic actors must forge a rare degree of autonomy and seek to use it in prescriptively attractive ways. A president must be willing to assume the political risk of forestalling popular legislative changes likely to exacerbate bureaucratic problems, even if doing so eliminates a means of exploiting a crisis to advance long-standing policy goals. Or an electorate must display an uncommon degree of sophistication, leading it to resist naive arguments about the benefits of some large reorganizations and to consider the benefits of more incremental changes. It should come as no surprise that history reveals such circumstances to be unusual. They are even less common in the midst of a crisis. But without them, a crisis bureaucracy is bound to be a bureaucracy in crisis.

CHAPTER 9

No Matter What Fate May Have in Store

Security and the Nation-State in a World of Economic Risk

DHS HOLDS NO MONOPOLY ON CRISIS. Even as President Truman's advisors worked to elevate the FSA to cabinet status, elsewhere in the White House the president and his staff confronted the domestic consequences of the worsening conflict in which the United States was embroiled in Korea. On April 8, 1952, President Truman signed an executive order that sought to seize control of a major chunk of American heavy industry—its steel mills. In *Youngstown Sheet & Tube v. Sawyer*,[1] the Supreme Court readily demonstrated just how fraught President Truman's dramatic action became. The nation's involvement in the Korean conflict was fueling substantial inflationary pressure, and union officials were convinced that the steel industry was achieving considerable profits at a time when workers' wages were flat or stagnating.[2] Because industrial power was America's defining military advantage, the president was not inclined to let a labor dispute erode this strategic asset. These circumstances help frame the conventional description of the dilemma in *Youngstown*, which turns on the executive's power to control the economy in the name of national security.

This depiction of the case, however, is hardly more than the tip of a vast iceberg. The larger context in which the *Youngstown* case arose involves a relationship between the economy and the concept of national security that neither side in the litigation—nor the Court—could afford to ignore. It was hardly lost on the Court that the logic of the government's argument spread far beyond the steel mills that were directly at issue in *Youngstown*. After all, steel is in some sense a means to the end of industrial strength, and the nation's strength is a function not just of material inputs to industry but also of the condition of its people: their health and wealth, their capacity to play productive roles in the economy, and even to believe that their country's security bears some meaningful relationship to their own. Just how, and how deeply, national security connects to individuals' ongoing sense of their own economic security, however, is rarely the subject of sustained attention.

The Roosevelt administration found in the concept of security a vehicle for engineering an expanded federal state. It did not, however, take the concept of security as a given. In light of their apparent success in reframing the work of what was supposed to be a "Department of Public Welfare," the administration's tactics illustrate two important points about the modern state. First, by the early twentieth century, citizens had come to expect the state to provide for their security. During the 1930s, many (though not all) uses of the term were commonly associated with social welfare programs designed to promote economic security. Many observers at the time might have understood a "security state" to imply not a government focused on deterring geostrategic military and terrorist threats but one endeavoring to cushion its citizens against economic and natural calamities.[3]

Yet, second, then as now—and in contrast to the Court's assumptions in cases such as *Curtiss-Wright*—the concept of security proves to some degree malleable, raising questions about the viability of approaches to legal interpretation that assume a tidy distinction between geostrategic national security and other types of safety and security. Although the term "security" was not unknown in military contexts at the time, the Roosevelt administration's strategy seemed premised on the idea that the concept could nonetheless comfortably encompass government activities that would benefit civilians and the military alike. As the Cold War picked up speed, the FSA gave birth to staples of modern government with defense and civilian applications such as an expanded National Institutes of Health and Centers for Disease Control.[4] The transformation of the term continued, to the point that the more salient association is with man-made violence and government officials actually question the extent to which FEMA's disaster relief responsibilities are appropriately understood to encompass "security."[5]

This chapter considers the roots of the interrelationship between the conventional geostrategic, military-related definition of national security (described simply as "national security" in this chapter) and the more malleable conception favored by Roosevelt in the late 1930s, encompassing defense as well as matters such as economic security and public health. Although this was decidedly not the vision prioritized in the early years of DHS, many of its components nonetheless retain jurisdiction over functions (ranging from flood insurance to civilian cybersecurity) that implicate the broader concerns with economic security that Roosevelt placed at the center of his own administration's organizational priorities. While much of the argument thus far underscores the strategic implications in law and politics of blurring distinctions among different types of security arguments, the focus here is on exploring some potentially deeper links between different conceptions of national security—links creating dilemmas for public organizations but perhaps explaining why politicians often appear to succeed when they frame security in broader terms.

In fact, economic security policy turns out to be entangled with the institutional, legal, economic, and political context of national security in a range of distinct domains. Economic security policy has implications for a nation's scarce resources, impacting the fiscal environment in ways that affect both short-term and long-term national security. Decisions about economic security shape a nation's social capital and institutional capacity—both of which have played a historically important role in the capacity of nations to impact their geostrategic environment. And the long-term viability of a nation-state—depending to some extent on citizens' loyalty and the capacity of interested parties to support coalitions that are consistent with a continued role for the state—is almost undeniably bound up to some extent with decisions about how to handle economic security.

Indeed, in a world where nation-states manage peacekeepers as well as public pension plans, policymakers face several important realities rooted in the nature of citizens, institutions, law, and politics. First, despite some observers' insistence to the contrary, defense-related and traditional national security policies heavily impact economic security policies, and vice versa.[6] Economic security policies can build the sort of human capital, institutional capacity, and commitment to national goals that can strengthen a state's ability to defend against external threats and its means of promoting peace and international security. Both domains fundamentally implicate the question of how the nation-state and its citizens manage the risks of an uncertain and rapidly evolving world.

Second, the politics of economic and national security are entangled in multiple ways. Poorly conceived economic security measures can have major fiscal effects constraining the resources available for more-conventional national security activities.[7] Politicians can deliberately blur the distinctions between the two domains, as when presidents created the Federal Security Agency (in the late 1930s) and the Department of Homeland Security more recently. Internal economic dislocation can exacerbate the risk of international conflicts. National security activities, moreover, can affect the demand for economic security measures such as veterans' benefits or broadened access to health insurance.

Finally, both economic and national security raise concerns about accountability and responsibility for the evolving nation-state, some of which involve the difficulty in imposing limits on the scope of legal authorities identified with national security. The steel seizure cases provide an excellent illustration of this difficulty. Ultimately, the relationship between economic and national security underscores the practical and organizational difficulties of segregating policymaking into separate domains, and raises persistent questions about a self-contained, narrow vision of geostrategic security that purports to minimize the significance of the public's economic and social condition.

COMMON ROOTS

As the Truman administration was litigating the steel-seizure cases, one of its senior officials—an ambitious New-York-City-lawyer-turned-federal-bureaucrat named Oscar Ewing—published a magazine article in a national publication. In the piece, Federal Security Agency administrator Ewing simultaneously made a case for his agency's expansion and for some of the core tenets of the Truman administration's "Fair Deal." As we earlier noted, Ewing, echoing themes that he was emphasizing in speeches across the country, made reference to "personal matters of security," by which he meant that citizens "shall not want for the basic necessities of life, no matter what Fate may have in store."[8]

Ewing's pitch was delivered at a time of great concern for national security, as the United States faced the challenges of the Korean War. By the 1950s, national security was generally understood to focus on geostrategic security.[9] So how was Ewing's emphasis on economic security (including access to health care) linked to national security? Ewing himself sometimes pointed out the role his agency was prepared to play in civil defense, and sought to stress the extent to which citizens ought to care about all the forms of security that could affect their lives.[10] As we have seen, he even responded forcefully to charges that his own agency, which was a focal point for the Truman administration's efforts to reform health insurance and administered other social insurance programs, was threatening the nation's economic system.[11]

While Ewing hinted at some of these potentially deeper connections between economic and national security, however, he did not explain or analyze the full range of them. Neither did the man who created the Federal Security Agency, Franklin Roosevelt. Roosevelt was all too willing to underscore the interdependence among different security spheres, but he too stopped well short of offering an explicit, analytically defensible explanation.

Any attempt to develop such an explanation of the interrelationship between economic and national security policy must begin by recognizing that both domains implicate the management of risk. Under almost any defensible account of individual motivation or social organization, policymakers should expect individuals, families, and communities to harbor profound concern about risks to their well-being—whether such risks involve acute health emergencies, disasters, or external attacks. Moreover, circumstances creating stress for the nation-state, such as natural disasters or the threat of external military coercion, imperil the state's capacity to manage risks and to create the conditions for citizens to build successful and fulfilling lives.

Indeed, the question of how a society manages risk—and what common bonds are forged by individuals in addressing uncertainty in economic and national security spheres—reflects profoundly on the nature of the nation-state itself. Charles Tilly's pathbreaking work chronicles the prominent importance of national capacity for fighting, and resisting the impact of, war in the development of the state.[12] The state's economic well-being cannot help but drive (or at least drastically impose limits on) a nation's capacity to defend itself and advance its version of its national interest. Early European states grew to a considerable degree around communities facing the possibility or the reality of fighting wars. These proto-states depended on their capacity to raise revenue and operate an administrative apparatus to maintain their war-fighting prowess. Forged in part with an eye toward fighting wars, few states were likely to have entirely rejected some of the links between the economic sphere and a nation's overall position relative to its neighbors.

As advanced industrialized countries emerged, individuals generally confronted an environment of increasingly complex public institutions and heightened individual expectations of personal and economic security—even as states continued to confront substantial threats to peace and to their own security. Because observers and policymakers rarely grasp the full extent and precise nature of the links public organizations must manage between economic security and national security, however, the discussion below elucidates some of these connections in greater detail.

Fiscal and Resource Interrelationships

Investments in both economic security and national security are constrained by a nation's overall resources. Resources devoted to one area may affect the level of resources available in the other realm. The argument that nations face a choice between "guns and butter" is perhaps the most pervasive conception of this trade-off.[13] This account is partially accurate. Choices about health care policy, social security, and other aspects of economic security clearly have an important impact on the resources available for national security.[14]

A key example involves health care. One of the fundamental elements of economic security, the cost of health care, exerts an outsized effect on the federal budget. Since 1970, Medicare and Medicaid spending has increased steadily from 1.7 percent of GDP in 1970 to approximately 5 percent in 2009.[15] Defense spending did not increase at this steady upward rate, declining from approximately 8 percent of GDP in 1970 to 4.7 percent in 2009.[16] As a partial response to the growing fiscal pressures created by rising health care costs, the Patient Protection and Affordable Care Act of 2010 is meant to stem this trend by curtailing rising health care expenditures. Before the bill's enactment, federal spending on the Medicare and Medicaid programs alone was projected to explode to 20 percent of gross domestic product by 2050, the same share of the economy as the entire 2007 federal budget consumed.[17] The 2010 legislation sought to curtail such growth with a combination of cost-saving reforms and reductions in Medicare payments.

Although some of these projected savings are contingent upon the policy choices of future Congresses and presidents, even partial success will free federal resources for national security.

The impact of health care policy on the fiscal resources available for broader national security goals is particularly severe—but not unique. U.S. infrastructure is vulnerable to both natural disaster and terrorist attack. A review by the American Society of Civil Engineers deemed a large portion of national infrastructure to be in need of significant repair.[18] State and local governments have failed to adequately plan for the risk that this vulnerable infrastructure will fail in the event of a terrorist attack or natural disaster. The Department of Homeland Security found that only 25 percent of state emergency operations plans and 10 percent of municipal plans were adequate in the face of a major terrorist attack or natural disaster.[19] Such exposure threatens the economic prospects of individuals, families, and communities at the same time that it imposes potentially heightened national security vulnerabilities.[20]

Vulnerable infrastructure threatens economic security by exposing property and services to risk. For instance, Hurricane Katrina destroyed fundamental elements of economic security in the Gulf Coast region such as shelter, food, clothing, and medical care. Katrina's impact on economic security also spread beyond the Gulf Coast region, disrupting the oil and chemical industries, harming the remainder of the U.S. economy. A future terrorist attack against vulnerable infrastructure could be equally economically disruptive.[21] As with Hurricane Katrina, a terrorist attack could damage core aspects of economic security such as shelter and medical care while also inflicting broader economic damage. For instance, extended closure of California's Port of Long Beach could impose billions of dollars in costs on a variety of industries. An attack on Chicago could disrupt 37 percent of total U.S. railway traffic,[22] and an attack on the New York City area could obviously greatly disrupt financial markets.[23] Such economic damage threatens to undermine the national ability to provide for citizens' economic security, and further underscores the fiscal connections between economic and national security policy.

The relationship between economic security and national security implicates more than the direct fiscal impact of spending on health care or infrastructure, however. The use of deficit spending to finance economic security obligations such as health care may risk undermining national security by creating fiscal burdens, financed to a considerable degree by foreign countries, that could limit this country's capacity to address future threats to peace and security. The U.S. government has recently run particularly pronounced deficits amounting to roughly 10 percent of GDP. Deficits of this size risk diminishing presidents' power and flexibility to deal with unexpected threats to peace and security, and may weaken the United States' global standing.[24]

Debt and defense may be difficult to disentangle. Although conventional economic assumptions suggest that countries holding U.S. Treasury bonds would seek to avoid creating instability that would reduce the value of their holdings, the public expression of concern by Chinese leaders regarding the safety of their Treasury bill investments on market activity suggested otherwise.[25] The incident forced President Obama to argue that the Chinese should hold confidence in U.S. investments: "And so I think that not just the Chinese government, but every investor, can have absolute confidence in the soundness of investments in the United States."[26] Similarly, statements from Chinese leaders regarding the need to reduce U.S. dollar holdings affected currency markets, highlighting the extent of Chinese influence.[27] The fact that the U.S. military planned an elaborate war game to study the threat posed by international economic interdependence on U.S. national security illustrates the seriousness of this potential challenge.[28]

Social Capital

Social capital has an important but subtle impact on national security. A nation that provides economic security to its citizens builds social capital, increasing its capacity for self-defense. Conversely, a nation that neglects economic security will fail to build social capital, undermining national security.

Even conventional national security considerations, such as the capacity of a nation's armed forces, readily demonstrate the fundamental role of social capital and public health—both of which are integral to a nation's economic security—in advancing national security interests. A nation that fails to provide economic security to its citizens will struggle to create and sustain strong armed forces. At the most basic level, a poor and unhealthy population will produce inadequate soldiers. Even nutrition constitutes a poignant example, as research by the U.S. military on nutrition for soldiers has shown that diet is critical for individual performance.[29] As a result, the U.S. military even established a "Committee on Military Nutrition Research" to determine the nutritional regime that would maximize soldier performance under different conditions—a step underscoring the intimate relationship between a society's level of food security and the condition of its armed forces.[30] A nation that fails to provide basic economic security to a broad base of its population will struggle to produce soldiers who can perform optimally under such difficult conditions.

Reading this lesson too narrowly carries its own risks. Certain nations, such as North Korea, have historically sought to provide economic security to their armed forces while the remainder of society struggles. A RAND Institute analysis noted that militaries sometimes reflect the difficulties of their host societies, reducing security.[31] Countries may be able to maintain a strong military in the short run by devoting resources to soldiers, but a society lacking broader social capital can ultimately struggle to generate the resources and innovation necessary to sustain this dichotomy and support the military.[32]

The importance of social capital for national defense has been recognized in the United States. For instance, former chairman of the Joint Chiefs of Staff General Hugh Shelton and former Navy secretary John Dalton founded a nonprofit agency to expand opportunities for early childhood education in order to increase the pool of individuals eligible for military service. Shelton and Dalton summarized their position by noting that "[t]he most important long-term investment we can make for a strong military is in the health and education of the American people."[33] This comment underscores the idea that a nation that fails to invest in social capital will see its relative military standing erode.

Education policy is another domain integral to economic security, and long recognized as relevant to national defense in the United States. National educational achievement greatly affects whether a country has the capacity to invest in and reap rewards from research and development.

By many accounts, the divergence in economic performance between East Asia and Latin America in the 1980s was increased by greater East Asian investment in education and research and development.[34] The Sputnik scare prompted Congress to pass the National Defense Education Act of 1958 and increased interest in science and technology. Warnings such as the Hart-Rudman Commission's admonition that "the inadequacies of our systems of research and education pose a greater threat to U.S. national security over the next quarter century than any potential conventional war that we might imagine"[35] received renewed attention. In response, policy initiatives explicitly sought to link education to national security.[36] This movement prompted important figures such as former House Speaker Newt Gingrich to note the importance of education to both economic and national security: "Investing in science (including math and science education) is the most important strategic investment we make in continued American leadership economically and militarily."[37]

An educated public will also produce individuals who are more capable of undertaking sophisticated analytical tasks and advanced technology, whether in military or civilian settings. The importance of this capability has almost certainly grown as advanced technology has become increasingly complex and increasingly central to military operations and strategy.[38] A military unable to attract educated soldiers will struggle to remain competitive and use such technology effectively. A report analyzing military recruitment in Pennsylvania found that 25 percent of young adults from ages seventeen to twenty-four were ineligible to serve because they lacked a high school diploma.[39] In a plea for better soldiers, a senior official of the U.S. armed forces highlighted the role of human capital: "The best aircraft, ships, and satellite-guided weapon systems are only as effective as the personnel the military can recruit to operate them."[40] This problem led the military to conclude that early childhood education is integral to national security.[41]

Institutional Capacity

Although the nation-state persists as perhaps the defining feature of international organization and domestic law, scholars consistently differ on how it should be defined. For Tilly, the state is an organization that controls the population, occupying a definite territory. Stephen Skowronek talks of an "integrated organization of institutions, procedures, and human talents," and Theda Skocpol describes the state in terms of a "set of administrative, policing, and military organizations."[42] These definitions unquestionably capture subtly different qualities associated with nations, and the differences are therefore relevant to the definition of national security. At their core, however, they all reference to some degree the idea of institutional capacity: a state's laws mean little without the organizations to honor them and to coax (or coerce) the public to do so. Institutional capacity is what lets nations and their citizens change the course of rivers to make deserts bloom, protect against crushing natural disasters, educate their children, and defend their cities. In Tilly's terms:

Low-capacity regimes offer a wider range of possibilities for opportunism. Whether democratic or undemocratic, they remain susceptible to unauthorized sequestering of resources by violent specialists as well as to seizure or damage of persons and property along the edges of authorized political claim making. . . . Especially vulnerable are low-capacity undemocratic regimes that combine portable resources of significant value on world markets with large diasporas . . . But low-capacity democratic regimes also invite both small-scale racketeering and forms of political struggle that facilitate private vengeance, pleasure seeking, and profit-taking.[43]

In effect, national security capabilities pivot heavily on nations' institutional capacity—and building such capacity is a core challenge of any nation that expects to provide for the broad security of its citizens.

While economic security policies depend to some extent on a core existing degree of institutional capacity,[44] the further strengthening of a nation's organizational infrastructure can be a major consequence of new economic security arrangements. Consider, for example, the early history of the Social Security program and its associated employment services elements during the Roosevelt administration. The program grew around the goal of providing social insurance. Over time, its infrastructure of records, offices, employees, and relationships with the public facilitated the expansion of the nation's social insurance program.[45] Fairly early in its history, however, that infrastructure also facilitated planning for and implementation of the military draft. Later, as World War II loomed larger, the employment placement services became a resource for placing Americans in war-related industries.[46]

State institutions used to collect revenue can also provide both economic security and national security. States require substantial revenue to wage war. In the United States, the federal government developed its revenue collection systems in response to the Civil War and World Wars I and II.[47] Revenue extraction was necessary for the government to build and maintain political institutions necessary to wage war and maintain sovereignty over its territory. Such systems were later used to collect revenue for social welfare programs necessary to provide economic security.

No doubt such examples partially reflect the complicated calculus involved in judging the normative legitimacy of national power. The national infrastructure necessary to provide people with access to social insurance and to future employment opportunities eventually helped ensure a steady supply of workers to war-related industries and facilitated a military draft. By the same token, the structures of domestic state power played a role in the historical episode of Japanese internment that now elicits widespread derision among Americans. In effect, a state's capacity to analyze, organize, regulate, and deploy its authority has dual roles in both economic and national security. As such, the institutional capacity that develops around robust economic security policies can facilitate coercion even as it also enables risk-spreading and the mitigation of otherwise potentially crippling natural and man-made disasters.

Longer-Term Support for (and Viability of) the Nation-State

By the middle of the twentieth century, much of Western Europe had embarked on an elaborate effort to create (or, in some cases, expand) the welfare state. In Britain, the creation of the National Health Service, providing the population with widespread access to health care, was emblematic of a larger trend.[48] Elsewhere in Europe, the long shadow of the Cold War coincided with renewed interest in forging the social safety nets and risk-spreading arrangements that might forestall greater domestic political conflict.[49] While these developments represented historical milestones in Europe, they also shed some light on two related dilemmas of any functioning nation-state that once more links its economic security policies to its larger national security agenda: how to give individuals and groups a stake in the continuing prosperity of the nation-state, and how to dampen the fervor and potential success of those who have the least to gain from an existing national arrangement. These dilemmas, moreover, recur in the history of nation-states and affect the extent of social capital, encompassing the propensity of individuals to associate with one another, to trust one another, and to engage in community activities.[50]

To understand whether states will eventually solve these dilemmas by building elaborate public organizations to help manage economic risks, it is important to acknowledge that not all states share precisely the same origin. Early European states diverged in key ways from the trajectory of an Ottoman Empire that depended far more on elaborate arrangements delegating power to local warlords.[51] Countries that have more recently emerged from colonial experiences often differ greatly from their predecessors. Where they converge is in the need to manage internal territory and populations in a world of scarce resources, and in the pressure they often experience (even in relatively secure times and regions) to leverage social, physical, and economic resources in order to provide for common defense. In at least some depictions of the state-formation process (particularly in Europe), it is the latter imperative that drives the former, and indeed that manifests itself as a core motivation for the territorial and legal scope of the state's authority in the first place.[52] States, after all, did not develop in a vacuum, and their continuing evolution reflects as much as it shapes individual human desires. People respond to their material circumstances and future prospects.[53] Individuals' capacity to act on their loyalty to the state (assuming it already exists) is hard to separate from their economic realities, unless we make unrealistic assumptions about individual desires or responses to incentives.

The contingent relationships between individuals, government, and the state underscore the fact that the nature and characteristics of nation-states are capable of evolving over time, though many individual states often reach a degree of stability and capacity that shapes a sense of timeless permanence. Legal and political arrangements between states and citizens evolve in a world where states thrive but also die.[54] The logic of the state depends on its capacity to create loyalty, provide incentives, and occasionally coerce. The capacity of the state to perform these functions, in turn, can falter when large proportions of the citizenry face severe, discontinuous economic and health-related risks—hence the recurring Cold War concerns, particularly in Europe, about the capacity of states to address the economic needs of their citizens.[55] Similarly, some scholars argue that states enhanced their social safety nets in response to growing public anxiety about their economic conditions in the midst of World War II.[56]

If recent history in many developed nations reflects a willingness to invest in creating social safety nets following the social dislocations of war and amid concerns about forestalling domestic political conflict, the rapid decolonization following World War II describes nearly the opposite. There, colonized territories made major sacrifices to fight the war, but confronted a pattern of economic insecurity and political disenfranchisement that was all the more difficult to reconcile with domestic aspirations given their role in the war. As Niall Ferguson puts it: "No one should ever underestimate the role played by the Empire—not just the familiar stalwart fellows from the dominions but the ordinary, loyal Indians, West Indians and Africans too—in defeating the Axis powers."[57] In short order, such unity became increasingly difficult to defend. Colonial populations had been continually exposed to a degree of economic insecurity and political marginalization that laid bare the profound practical and prescriptive limitations of colonial arrangements.[58] In contrast, within the United Kingdom and other former colonial powers, the experience of shared sacrifice turned attention to the creation of legal and financial arrangements providing greater economic security to their national populations.

These national populations understand the significance of their membership in the larger political community through a process almost inevitably shaped by economic security policies. The privileges and responsibilities associated with citizenship—or lawful presence in a particular jurisdiction—help define how a society views itself and its underlying goals. Courts sometimes understandably allude to the state's role providing the means of reducing risk when framing an individual's responsibility to society. There is a certain normative logic in passing along to individual members of society some of the reduced risk that their own participation in economic or national security activities helps to facilitate. The prescriptive power of a nation's example and its broader policy agenda is also difficult to divorce from the well-being of its citizens. For instance, concentrated poverty and inequality potentially undermine both a country's overall economic position and its capacity to leverage so-called "soft" power.[59]

Even leaving aside the more prescriptively oriented considerations, the only way to posit a world where economic security plays no role in encouraging people to take the state seriously is to make drastically unrealistic assumptions about the individuals who populate society. The people from whom soldiers, police, teachers, doctors, farmers, and lawyers are drawn would need to be stripped of much of their sensitivity to their economic conditions. Political leaders would have to be too naive or inhibited to respond to the potential political payoffs of mobilizing individuals adversely affected by a state that placed demands on them without accounting for their needs or dignitary interests. As Kirshner puts it:

[I]ncreasing inequality and social conflict will restrict the state's capability to pursue optimal foreign policies due to the hyper-politicization of fiscal policy. Concerning future power, inequality may reduce economic growth. While it was traditionally assumed that a widening and narrowing of inequality was natural over the course of economic development . . . , less attention was given to the role of distribution as an independent variable in explaining economic growth. Although it is reasonable to assume that very high levels of equality would yield an incentive structure that could contribute to slower growth, high levels of inequality can also produce such disincentives.[60]

History also suggests how the relationship between economic security policies and a nation's more conventional security challenges can cut in the opposite direction. Major national security crises can result in major turning points in the trajectory of a state's economic security policies. The United States, for example, created its first large-scale pension system for Civil War veterans.[61] Similarly, the GI Bill, a key driver of economic security, was enacted in the wake of World War II.

Scholars have yet to fully elucidate the precise dynamics through which national security threats (or efforts to face them) prompt the development of such shared national solidarity. National security crises may affect the salience of concerns that reach beyond individual interest, priming people to assign greater value to what some political scientists have labeled "sociotropic" concerns.[62] In a different vein, Narizny reviews case studies involving security expenditures in the United Kingdom, France, and the United States and finds left-leaning governments generally more willing to support the progressive taxation and public sector economic intervention associated with major rearmament programs.[63] Once achieved, the demand for economic expenditures benefiting large segments of the public—characteristics reflected in some social insurance measures as much as in national defense spending—may persist after political coalitions necessary to fight wars have overcome difficulties forging internal alliances.[64] Separately, the strains of war may forge greater interest in policies that reduce social divisions following the exertions of a national security emergency. Regardless of the precise theoretical mechanisms at work, it is far from unusual for states emerging from national security crises to face historical turning points in the development of more robust social institutions to help their citizens manage economic risks.[65]

IMPLICATIONS OF THE RELATIONSHIP

Whether the focus is on historical turning points involving major changes in domestic policy such as the postwar period in the United Kingdom or the Johnson administration in the United States, or on periods of relative policy stability similar to those the United States experienced during the 1990s, the relationship between economic security and national security has significant implications for modern states and their citizens. These become more readily apparent when discussion of national security pivots from a static focus on variables such as current force levels and postures to consider instead the implications of incentive structures, social cohesion, and national capacity in ensuring society's security and well-being.[66]

First, policymakers should think about risk across the conventional categories of economic and national security, because conceptually, economic and national security risks interact. A major natural or man-made disaster on the scale of the 9/11 attacks, for instance, can leave Americans uniquely vulnerable to further attacks coming immediately after the disaster—particularly if the initial response is inadequate. The Katrina disaster not only taxed the nation and arguably made it more vulnerable to certain national security threats at the time, but also disrupted the economic circumstances of hundreds of thousands of people. Accordingly, evaluating disaster response and mitigation policy would implicate considerations of economic security as well as national security. Resource constraints arising because of unjustified military spending or poorly conceived mandatory spending programs can deplete available capacity for more carefully designed economic security initiatives, and national security emergencies can also accelerate interest in economic security and related measures that may be helpful to mobilizing the country for war. National security emergencies can develop a shared sense of solidarity and otherwise increase support for expanded economic security policies. Meanwhile, greater economic risk can make it more difficult for countries to build the domestic support and capacity necessary to protect national security. Indeed, countries with major domestic needs may feel pressure to cut national security spending.[67]

Second, the politics of economic and national security are closely intertwined. The public can expect new economic security policies such as veterans' benefits to follow national security crises, as occurred in the United States after World War II. In addition, the close interrelationship between economic and national security may give politicians and members of civil society a persistent reason to make public appeals further blurring the distinctions between economic and national security policy. As World War II loomed, Roosevelt emphasized the importance of an agency reorganization to bolster economic security—by creating the FSA—as having direct and indirect benefits for national security. The Obama administration's first national security strategy, meanwhile, repeatedly emphasizes the national security implications of education policy, immigration, and responsible stewardship of the federal deficits.[68]

A darker consequence of the entanglement between economic and national security involves, according to some scholars, the potential for internal economic dislocation to exacerbate the risk of international conflict. Governments facing hard times may engage in military activity to displace attention from domestic economic circumstances that are politically costly.[69] The leaders of nations experiencing economic dislocation may also be drawn to Keynesian fiscal initiatives involving military spending, and both leaders and the public may ascribe heightened stakes to conflicts involving international economic opportunity.[70]

Third, policy problems involving economic and national security raise important issues of both accountability and responsibility. When citizens, civil society groups, and even policymakers navigate those challenges, they must contend with the two-edged quality of state capacity. On one hand, the organization and efficiency of public agencies can help remedy collective action problems, promote public safety, and manage economic risk. On the other hand, those same characteristics may also facilitate certain damaging uses of public authority, such as Japanese internment, upon which history ultimately casts a harsh light.[71] If the American experience is any guide, societies must also confront the persistent difficulty of segregating national security and domestic policy domains. Some legal disputes, such as the executive power cases *United States v. Curtiss-Wright Export Corp.* and the steel-seizure case, plainly implicate domestic policy even as the rationale motivating presidential action originated with concern about foreign relations and defense. Such cases can affect baseline assumptions about state power that may be relevant in the domestic context, even as some cases involving domestic statutes seemingly far afield from national security may influence developments in counterterrorism or national defense.[72] Ultimately, regardless of whether a legal or policy dispute involves surveillance or social security benefits, both contexts implicate questions of discretion, due process, and the potential for arbitrariness. These questions arise repeatedly in agency field offices, legislatures, courtrooms, and public discourse. They have the potential to impact the state's legitimacy as citizens evaluate whether their government is delivering a sufficient measure of security without imposing unreasonable economic, practical, or bureaucratic burdens on society.

SECURITY AND STATE CAPACITY:
LARGER IMPLICATIONS

In retrospect, the determination on the part of FSA and administration officials to convey their views to the public showcases the overlapping terms of the rhetorically powerful yet fundamentally contestable concept of "security," which politicians can deploy strategically to advance a host of domestic and international goals. For example, the agency's trajectory suggests that the term can implicate health and welfare services providing personal social and economic security. Perhaps the term also evokes the notion that the provision of health and welfare services can help forestall domestic unrest and more radical political change (the critique of revisionist New Deal historians).[73] The work of the FSA can also be understood to have a sort of externality effect on national security, as traditionally understood: war adjustment services, education for war production, biological weapons research, and facilitating the movement of interned Japanese Americans. Finally, the most ambitious conception of security is one that the Roosevelt administration seemed occasionally bent on promoting, though history reveals that it never entirely succeeded: security as an all-encompassing freedom from fear and want—whether the source of the problems is domestic insurrection, external aggression, disease, or economic deprivation. One of the many eloquent public statements in support of this particularly expansive version of the "security" concept is found in the second annual report of the FSA:

The security of America has always rested upon a foundation of cooperative effort. From our earliest days when struggling colonies on the seaboard faced the ever-present threats of famine, cold, and hostile tribes; from the days of the Revolution when all the colonies banded together to assure their economic survival; down through the years to more recent times when the Nation's only enemies were internal ones—mass joblessness, poverty, and suffering—Americans have come together, jointly to consider and solve their mutual problems.

The active role assumed by the Federal Government in the last decade in helping the individual to find security is as natural and inevitable in the American scheme of things as early barn-raisings and corn-huskings. In early years, cooperative effort to assure individual security was possible on a voluntary scale, but gradually the changes in economy and the amazing growth of this Nation geographically and numerically have made government action necessary—first, by local units and, as time went on, by larger and ever-larger governmental units until the Federal Government entered the picture. But today, as in colonial days, collective action provides only the foundation and the opportunity for each man to build his own security.[74]

If the story of the FSA shows that such a conception did not take permanent root in American law and politics (given today's more rigid separation between national security and economic security, for example), it also shows that politicians saw it as a coherent concept worth advancing with the public. And even today, this "thick" version of security finds resonance in the concerns of international organizations, advocates, and governance reformers with "human security" as an alternative to narrowly tailored conceptions of physical security.[75]

The reality of external conflict was an important change in the FSA's context. Impending war made it easier for the administration to blur the distinction between physical security and the more expansive variation on the theme. War made it far simpler for McNutt and his subordinates, in countless conferences and public speeches, to demonstrate how public health infrastructures, placement services for job seekers, and education grants could serve the war effort. This aspect of the account should not be surprising. It fits with the notion, associated most strongly with Charles Tilly, that "war makes the state."[76] The threat of war helped make the FSA, which spawned the modern federal bureaucracies that powerfully affect major aspects of our lives today.

But the implications of the FSA for the analysis of "security" go beyond the notion that war can spur state-building. As it happens, the FSA's relentless campaign to yoke its mission to national security proved to be more than a public relations effort. The campaign was, in some sense, providing an apt description of certain realities of the FSA's day-to-day activity. Some examples: the work of the Public Health Service in limiting disease and providing services to civilians, the military, and those civilians who would eventually join the armed forces; the role of physical education programs in preparing youths to join the armed forces; the role of the FDA in assuring a safe food supply and pharmaceutical products to both the public and the military; and the agency's role in training individuals for service in war-related industries and then placing them there.[77]

Although Roosevelt's expansive security ideas may have had a darker side, there is nothing inherently strained about the Roosevelt administration's elastic rendering of the "security" mantle. It seems at least as plausible that the FSA's amalgam of administrative and regulatory activity would contribute to a compelling definition of safety and security as it is to expect that the projection of naval force abroad would contribute to security. An internal White House memorandum summarized a letter from M. S. Robertson, an official of the National Education Association (and admittedly someone with a vested interest):

Wrote to the president re reports to the effect that secret agencies are working among the negro population in the South, urging the negroes to show their sympathies to the enemies of the US because of discriminations which exist in the South against negroes. . . . Asks that the President place his influence behind legislative efforts to solve these problems.[78]

Choosing to leave aside questions about the factual plausibility of Robertson's concern about subversives among African Americans, the president's response suggested at least an appreciation of the ultimate stakes involved in the performance of administrative and regulatory programs he had so aggressively sought to better control. The internal White House memorandum summarizing the correspondence notes:

The President replied June 4, saying he is in complete sympathy with efforts in the south or elsewhere in the country to improve educational opportunities for all children and to equalize educational facilities among all groups in our population. He said it is his belief that we have made and are making great social progress, and that he recognizes the importance of adult education in solving the problems Mr. Robertson mentions, and hopes everything possible may be done, in keeping with our defense efforts, to assure the full cooperation of everyone in the present crisis.[79]

Perhaps the president's response was simply a political sop. History has shown, however, that politicians—whether democrats or dictators—disregard the essential insight of the past at their peril.[80] If war makes the state, it is also true that bureaucratic capacity allowing the state to regulate, to protect critical infrastructures, and to quell the raw edge of political dissent through redistribution programs plays a central role in nearly any plausible account of national defense.

Indeed, the current concerns with homeland security have increasingly come to encompass infrastructures and public health mechanisms easily framed by some lawmakers or scholarly observers as critical to national life. Although the creation of a Department of Homeland Security appears to have fomented cuts in domestic regulatory mandates, such a development does not necessarily signal the demise of "security" as an organizing principle for promoting domestic regulatory and administrative activity. It is worth noting that both the rhetoric and the underlying substantive concerns advanced by some observers and policy entrepreneurs in the homeland security arena bear more than a passing resemblance to the FSA's mandates more than six decades ago. Their basic message is as simple as it is reminiscent of McNutt's and Roosevelt's speeches: a narrow focus on violent, man-made, geostrategic threats is a poor recipe for security, and even when the focus remains on those more conventional threats to national defense, success depends heavily on the nation's human and regulatory infrastructure.[81] In the national experience with the FSA, policy entrepreneurs may find hints about the viability of political coalitions supporting the development of bureaucratic capacity to achieve a blend of regulatory, redistributive, and more conventionally understood geostrategic national security goals.

Yet amid such underlying complexity associated with defining the nation-state's core responsibility to its citizens, only the barest hint seems to register in the emerging domain of legal practice and scholarship now defined as "national security law." Instead, that domain is primarily defined by attention to surveillance and investigation,[82] coercive authority to detain or use force,[83] and presidential power over emergencies or foreign affairs.[84] These topics are unquestionably important, but they leave aside certain areas that national security scholars and practitioners take for granted at their peril.

The more immediate question raised by the idea of national security relates to the politics of security, discussed above. Instead of assuming an unusual degree of insularity and consensus in the security sphere, we might ask instead: what individuals or interests *actually* secure control of bureaucracies with complex, overlapping international security and domestic regulatory functions? The new institutional architecture defining FSA not only advanced Roosevelt's own brand of security as a rationale for legal change, but also left the White House in a stronger position to control a major spigot of federal grants and align the bureaus' priorities with those of the administration.[85] Similarly, the impact of creating DHS decades later advanced the Bush administration's own version of a (counterterrorism-focused) security agenda[86] but also recast the statutory authority governing the immense department's bureaus and left the secretary of DHS with greater power over them.[87] The creation of the Department of Energy[88] and the passage of the Goldwater-Nichols Department of Defense Reorganization Act of 1996[89] also showcase how statutory changes putatively designed to achieve sensible prescriptive goals in national security inevitably operate to reallocate control over central functions of the nation-state as well.

CONCLUDING OBSERVATIONS

Americans confront substantial challenges to their national security in the early twenty-first century, including nuclear proliferation, potential terrorist attacks, and the need to protect the nation's public and private cyber infrastructure.[90] These threats rightly claim considerable attention because of their potential to disrupt so much of what citizens hold dear. Yet a country's economic security policies, and not just its more conventional security policies addressing matters such as military procurement or the size of the nation's armed forces, play a role in addressing these challenges and in advancing the nation's overall national security. As with accounts persuasively questioning the notion of a simple trade-off between freedom and national security, here too the realm of national security is itself dependent on citizens, institutions, laws, and political strategies reacting to background policies involving economic security.

This view contrasts with the position that national security policy is easily separable from domestic policy, and it also differs from the positions of those who posit one-dimensional trade-offs between guns or butter. Instead, our account provides a more complex picture. Economic security policies, whether they embody a new social insurance initiative or a de facto social decision to ignore rising health care costs—give rise to fiscal effects on the resources that are available for supporting national security policies. Economic security policies also impact human and social capital, thereby affecting the performance of the armed forces, the productivity of the labor force, and a society's capacity for innovation. The institutional structures designed to advance economic security policies can affect the capacity of the nation-state in a manner that supports robust national security activities. The infrastructure of the Social Security system, for example, helped to staff war-related industries. Finally, the long-term support for and viability of the nation-state is likely to be affected by economic security policy, as citizens adjust their expectations of their common responsibilities and individual circumstances in response to measures that help them manage economic uncertainty.

Although he did not map out the full extent of the common roots between economic and national security, Franklin Roosevelt readily alluded to these connections when he described domestic policies as "the arms of democracy" in announcing a powerful new Federal Security Agency to simultaneously improve the nation's economic security while strengthening the nation's capacity to fight dictatorships.[91] To neglect these links is to ignore the ways in which our nation's geostrategic capacity and resilience can be strengthened, the ways in which a public facing economic insecurity can fuel the conflicts that gave rise to the *Youngstown* case, and the ways in which politicians navigate their environment.

The deeper issue concerns the longer-term impact of security from risks—whether external or economic—on individual and social well-being. Societies care about national security (conventionally understood) because of the sharp discontinuities in peace and prosperity that wars and attacks can force them to confront. But as Oscar Ewing's words resonate well into a twenty-first century where millions of Americans face growing economic uncertainty, it is also worth remembering that people make enormous sacrifices to protect their nation because of what they think it represents, and its role as a bulwark against economic insecurity is no small measure of what many nations promise their citizens.

CHAPTER 10

An Organizational Gloss on
Separation of Powers

A COMMON THEME runs through battles over executive reorganization in the 1930s, cabinet-level status for the FSA under Oscar Ewing in the 1940s, and the shape of DHS in the early twenty-first century. In each of these conflicts, the players came to realize that choices about agency architecture inevitably affected the relationship between bureaus carrying out legal responsibilities and sources of external pressure such as the White House, lawmakers, or civil society organizations. Questions about agency architecture—whether legal authority is wielded by a single administrator or a fragmented board, how easy or difficult it is to fire a senior agency official, what essential missions an agency prioritizes—therefore also inevitably affect the president's power to control the legal machinery of the regulatory state. The Supreme Court recognized as much at least as early as *Myers*.[1] The Court's analysis turned on the intimate connection between the ease with which a president could control an agency and the overall balance of powers among branches.[2] In effect, the Court laid out why questions of agency architecture were likely to remain preeminent separation-of-powers concerns across the decades.

By understanding episodes of structural choice such as the evolution of the FSA and DHS, we can better understand the context for separation-of-powers disputes, including how structural changes shape the ultimate impact of judicial doctrines that police relations between Congress and the executive branch. In the course of this brief foray into separation of powers, we may also gain some insight into why courts in recent years have often been drawn to more functional approaches to the issue. These approaches often pivot on assessing the practical consequences of particular legislative or executive actions in particular situations that reflect evolving institutional realities affecting the ability of presidents to control the bureaucracy over time.

SEPARATION OF POWERS AND THE PROCESS
OF "SECURING" PRESIDENTIAL CONTROL

Americans live in a country where public power is fragmented vertically between a federal government and multiple states, and horizontally across distinct branches of government. The story of how we govern security is thus a story of federal and state officials planning civil defense operations and scientists at the Centers for Disease Control concerned about bioterrorism, but it is also a story of committee chairs and ranking members, legislative aides, and judges trying to make sense of densely written statutes like the Homeland Security Act. In this milieu, the jurisprudence of separation of powers has taken shape over many decades to become one important framework in which judges, executive branch officials, and even citizens work through problems involving the concentration of public power in particular institutions. Yet because important security functions ranging from counterterrorism to food safety often depend on the existence of agencies capable of rapidly deploying authority to prevent a problem, achieving the goals of separation-of-powers doctrine often comes at a cost. Because of those costs and the continuing process of historical evolution, the application of broad separation-of-powers principles to specific situations such as those involving the president's power to control a specific decision of a subordinate executive official often generates intense debate.

Any sensible effort to navigate such debate must begin by acknowledging some realities about the organization of power in the American system. Presidents juggle a bewildering array of separate yet complementary roles during the years they occupy the White House: "Commander in Chief, primary proposer of legislation and chief lobbyist, top executive in the executive branch, guardian of the economy, negotiator with other nations, head of state, party leader, and moral leader."[3] In undertaking these functions, presidents exercise considerable power over the bureaucracy. They appoint hundreds of senior officials to oversee complicated agencies. They tussle with Congress over authority for government to take on new functions, and appeal to citizens in an effort to control the public agenda. Such appeals affect not only the president's success in enacting legislation but also the chief executive's capacity to control what happens in the bureaucracy by changing the calculus of agency managers or lawmakers who are themselves competing for control of the bureaucracy.

We have seen time and again how, in the course of their efforts to control the bureaucracy, presidents and their advisors use organizational changes to advance their agendas. To some extent, courts understand the importance of agency organization. The understanding is even reflected in the jurisprudence that governs the standing necessary to bring federal lawsuits—a domain in which courts screen out claims that do not involve a tangible injury to a specific party pursuing the case. In *American Federation of Government Employees v. Pierce*, for example, the D.C. Circuit held that a lawmaker had standing to challenge the agency reorganization initiated by the secretary of the Housing and Urban Development Agency (HUD), based on his membership in the House Appropriations Committee.[4] The legislation funding HUD prohibited reorganizations that lacked consultation with the Appropriations Committee. Accordingly, the Court found that the secretary's reorganization of HUD effectively deprived the senator of his "specific statutory right to participate in the legislative process."[5] Some observers would readily question whether the statutory arrangement giving the House Appropriations Committee a special role in HUD-related reorganization should be valid in light of the Supreme Court's broad invalidation of legislative vetoes in *Immigration and Naturalization Service v. Chadha.*[6] The D.C. Circuit's decision nonetheless demonstrates the willingness of courts to recognize the practical significance of reorganization even when it does not involve changes in the substance of rights or agency responsibilities.

If the structure of government has an impact on hierarchy, information flows, and the rights of certain officials to make decisions affecting public organizations, it is also true that that impact occurs against the backdrop of legal doctrines that many citizens, lawmakers, and executive branch officials appear to treat as important. One such doctrinal issue implicates a presidential control that is rarely addressed by political scientists yet remains profoundly relevant to governing security—both in the sense of defining its scope and in the sense of securing control over the process of government. What precisely is the extent of a president's authority to legally control the bureaucracy, and how do the various tools of de facto control of the presidency (such as the White House staff) fit into that legal framework?

In fact, what lawyers have come to describe as the pragmatic, functional separation-of-powers approach to analyzing doctrinal problems in this domain almost inevitably involves regulating the power of different political actors over agency structure and decision making. As at least some courts and policymakers have realized, many problems in separation-of-powers doctrine involve questions about the amount of actual control a president can exercise over the bureaucracy.[7] By the time of *Sierra Club v. Costle*,[8] for example, courts routinely approached separation-of-powers questions by trying to calibrate precisely the extent of presidential power over internal agency matters.[9] In *Costle*, the D.C. Circuit simultaneously acknowledged the value of judicial oversight of the president-agency relationship and recognized that such oversight could also adversely impact the bureaucracy.[10] Indeed, right after *Humphrey's Executor* the stage was already set for the rise of a more functionalist paradigm in separation-of-powers law. With its decision in *Humphrey's Executor*, the Court both denied the White House a major instrument of control and ratified legislative experimentation with structures insulated from presidential control (for example, independent commissions).[11]

The White House responded to such constraints by making a determined effort to gain the executive reorganization authority that eventually led to the creation of the FSA. Despite the difficulties created by court decisions such as *Humphrey's Executor*, the swelling size of the federal government relative to the size of the White House staff, and basic problems with obtaining information across government, greater presidential success in achieving structural goals is likely to be associated with greater power to affect what federal bureaus actually do. Indeed, presidents' relative successes in achieving structural goals such as the creation of the FSA or DHS further blur a distinction—quite central to some otherwise cogent accounts of separation of powers—between presidential "oversight" and "directive authority."[12] True, directive authority implies that the president holds a special power to legally compel a decision from a subordinate, whereas oversight implies a power to force consultation and the production of information—something short of a specific decision. But in the absence of such explicit "directive" authority, presidential power to reorganize who holds directive authority within organizations (as Roosevelt did when he placed the SSB inside the FSA), to appoint loyal political supervisors to bureaus, and to control the flow of information to and from bureaus can limit the significance of formal distinctions between "oversight" and "directive authority."

Even if some subordinate executive branch officials let their responses to presidential requests turn on the distinction between oversight and directive authority, it is far from obvious that all or even most employees would be so passionately invested in the distinction. Structural changes can therefore help a president limit the significance of formal distinctions between oversight and directive authority. Accordingly, because separation-of-powers doctrine makes sense only if it encompasses some limits on presidential power and since structural arrangements are a key determinant of such power, courts should (other things being equal) prudently but closely scrutinize structural changes pursued by the White House. In fact, courts genuinely concerned with policing the extent of executive power will be left with little choice but to scrutinize the extent of structural power that the president *in fact* has been able to accrue, rather than merely relying on a formal examination of whether the president has made claims of authority that improperly violate the distinction between oversight and directive authority.[13]

The recent case of *Free Enterprise v. Public Company Accounting Oversight Board* showcases at least some of the distinctions that could emerge between an approach focused primarily on straightforward bright-line rules—explicitly prohibiting certain types of agency structures in every situation—and one that takes on the burdens and benefits of greater attention to context. Although the Court majority certainly leaves in place a doctrinal scheme that can accommodate attention to context, it describes in bright-line terms what the majority takes to be a fatal defect of the structure created by the statute. The problem, in a nutshell, is the existence of an independent agency board whose members are already quite insulated from the presidential threat of removal, which is then responsible for overseeing a subordinate board with important functions whose members are also removable only for narrowly specified reasons. The result is that the

Accounting Board consists of senior officials subject to relatively limited formal supervision by the Securities and Exchange Commission. That entity, in turn, is itself subject to far less direct presidential control than, say, the Department of Homeland Security or the Department of Health and Human Services—where presidents enjoy a broadly accepted role in setting these executive departments' overall policy agencies and senior agency officials serve at the pleasure of the president.

The bulk of the Court's analysis involves interpreting the significance of the relatively strict formal limits on the president's ability to fire members of the Accounting Board. While some passages of the majority opinion suggest lingering concern with independent agencies such as the SEC, the issue of immediate concern for the Court is the implausibility of assuming that the president could indirectly control the Accounting Board through the formal influence that the SEC could wield over the Accounting Board's members. Curiously, the majority considers the historical evolution of independent agencies and presidential power over them, but only for the limited purpose of establishing that presidents are widely understood to have limited power over independent agencies—even if the relevant statutes could in principle be read to yield more power than commonly acknowledged for the president to control independent agency appointees. In contrast, Justice Breyer's dissent delves more deeply into the subtle and far-reaching measures that presidents could use to control agencies, including the multi-member independent agencies most similar to the SEC. At the same time, Justice Breyer takes pains to document the existence of other examples of organizational arrangements involving so-called "double insulation," with at least two lawyers of "for cause" removal restrictions between the president and a senior official.

In considering how much the majority's reasoning in *Free Enterprise* extends to other cases, there is room for judges and lawyers to argue over the merits of simpler, rule-like decisions. A jurisprudential approach closer to Justice Breyer's, however, would allow legal decision makers to assess the permissible extent of legal control for the president at least partly in light of the amount of practical control the president has actually achieved. In a close case where conventional interpretive methods give out, some observers might even be inclined to consider the permissible extent of presidential control on the basis of how much independence an agency has actually achieved. They might, for example, permit the president a slightly greater measure of control where the agency has otherwise fortified legal and reputational structures permitting relatively independent operations.

The majority opinion in *Free Enterprise* thus aspires to establish more-stringent bright-line rules than the dissent when it comes to the regulation of agency structure. Still, the Court stops well short of reversing the long-standing trend toward more practical, functional decision making by courts in separation-of-powers disputes.[14] Judges may be drawn to considering the practical circumstances in part because of the changing nature of the executive branch itself, and the evolving techniques used by officials to compete for power over government agencies. Recall the Roosevelt White House's strong concerns about the trends in congressional and judicial action limiting what the administration considered the president's proper relationship to the bureaucracy, and the subsequent reorganization efforts to redress the balance. Once President Roosevelt installed the first FSA administrator, he proceeded to engage in frequent contact with the official nominally charged with overseeing some of the president's most prized initiatives. In effect, the president's relationship with the FSA after reorganization shows how key practices sometimes treated as legal innovations—such as close White House and agency collaboration in the development of regulatory rules, presidential claims of credit for agency initiatives, and efforts to build alliances with career staff—have a longer history than is commonly supposed.[15] Roosevelt doggedly sought reorganization authority at a time when the federal government was growing massively. The political stakes in controlling new regulatory bureaucracies were high, and the ratio of White House employees to total federal employees was declining. With Congress and the Supreme Court blocking the methods Roosevelt had earlier sought to use (control over appointments and the expansion of the White House staff),[16] the administration turned to structure as a powerful substitute. Having fashioned a new arrangement at the FSA, the White House used a mix of techniques including approval and announcements of grants (which Roosevelt instructed FSA administrator McNutt to clear with the White House), setting regulatory priorities (which White House staff monitored with bureau personnel at the SSB and the FDA), and controlling the flow of bureaucratic and financial resources (which the White House staff did through its new Bureau of the Budget).[17]

The now long-standing presidential move to control structure, plainly apparent in the late 1930s—and running through the entire history of the FSA and its transformation into the Department of Health and Human Services—is consistent with a nuanced and complicated, if realistic, view of separation of powers as a set of standards rather than rules. In that view, the branches are necessarily entangled because they are codependent. Sensibly—perhaps inevitably—the Supreme Court has recognized structural issues as being so central to the overall architecture of the federal state that it required power sharing.[18] Facing these doctrinal trends, the president pushed back in two ways amply illustrated by the story of the FSA: by grabbing as much power over structure as possible (something that required compromise with the legislature) and by insisting that "security" required structural reform (for example, to strengthen the performance of bureaus with missions relating to security and to enhance the nation's geostrategic security against external threats). The pattern continues through the twenty-first century, with the Bush administration's insistence on security as the fundamental rationale for re-forging a massive chunk of the federal government into DHS—with power over domains ranging from re-importation to refugees—while simultaneously proposing a sharp expansion of presidential power over the agency's myriad bureaus.[19]

Because presidents enjoy residual power over the difficult-to-observe details of quotidian executive branch management, austere restrictions of presidential power over structure (going beyond restrictions on powers arguably peripheral to core executive branch functions such as those at issue in *Humphrey's Executor* and those in traditional cabinet-level departments) can be hard to achieve—and if achieved, they might prove damaging to the president's ability to function as expected. On the other hand, blocking Congress from participation in this key domain is a plain recipe for staggering imbalance. Arguments could be made that too much branch blurring can complicate accountability (for example, the public assignment of responsibility) in a world of information-poor, cognitively constrained voters.[20] But absent convincing arguments in this regard, power over structure should be properly subject to sharing by branches that have learned, over time, to treat structure as a powerful tool to shape implementation of current law, future agency trajectories, and public expectations of what government does. In effect, blocking the sharing of power over structure inevitably disrupts an arrangement of separated powers.

The continuing competition over control of structure in the wake of the Court's decision to split power over bureaucratic structure sheds a different light on the presidentially inclined arguments of the Brownlow Committee. In particular, the efficiency rationales offered by the Brownlow Committee, promoted by Roosevelt and then offered again by the Hoover Commission during the Truman administration, were consistently under-theorized, even as they probably reflected the reality of presidential competition for control in a system of separated powers.[21] The efficiency rationales did not take into account the elements of separation-of-powers jurisprudence designed to complicate rather than facilitate policymaking. They did not consider the transition costs. They did not take into account the potential benefits of decentralization.[22] And in part perhaps because of such limitations in the technocratic arguments for organizational restructuring, key players understood at least some of the highly political stakes in reorganization—this is why both Truman and Roosevelt ran into so much political trouble when they pursued it. These observations raise a number of questions, of course, but they should lead us to be skeptical of claims by proponents of the unitary executive thesis that reorganization efforts support their claims of broad historical acknowledgment of the need for substantial executive power relative to Congress.[23]

SEPARATION-OF-POWERS DOCTRINE
AS AN IMPERFECT CONSTRAINT

Across the disparate decades that link diverse presidential administrations, the existence of separation-of-powers doctrine leaves the White House with certain dilemmas. Presidents tend to gain strong political and policy advantages by more tightly controlling public organizations. That goal can often be served by changing the organization of the executive branch to suit the demands of a president's policy agenda. We might therefore expect many administrations to assert that their power to faithfully execute the laws under Article II allows them to reorganize essentially at will, or to achieve much the same result by formally declaring control over all subordinates' decisions within the executive branch.

What we observe instead is a more nuanced process, where chief executives protect broad presidential prerogatives but stop well short of claiming absolute control over the structure of, or of decision making within, the executive branch. Even as scholars debate the precise extent of the power that any executive subordinate has to resist presidential decisions, administrations aggressively interpret statutes to avoid exclusive reliance on broad arguments about executive power. Moreover, the administrations of Franklin Roosevelt and George W. Bush reveal a keen appreciation of the complementarity between organizational structure and presidential control, a phenomenon broadly reflected in presidencies since at least the early twentieth century—even if they do so perhaps more acutely than the typical administration. Away from the glare of the higher-profile intellectual and legal arguments over presidential power, much of the real action governing the president's influence over the bureaucracy thus plays out in more prosaic efforts to alter the tools of bureaucratic statecraft. In addition to presidential efforts to grow or change the staff of the Executive Office of the President, administrations repeatedly seek statutory reorganization authority.[24]

It is telling that executive branch efforts to wrest reorganization authority from lawmakers have tended to acknowledge a fundamental role for Congress. Cabinet officials have some measure of power to routinely decide how to assign responsibilities among subordinates (particularly where lawmakers have not explicitly disallowed particular transfers).[25] Yet presidents as diverse as Franklin Roosevelt and George W. Bush have singularly avoided arguments ascribing inherent reorganization powers to the presidency.

Thus the intriguing reconciliation of American separation-of-powers jurisprudence with the realities of organizational control in the executive branch occurs on two levels. At a formal level, separation-of-powers doctrine seems to impose genuine constraints on presidents and their administrations. When major reorganizations happen, they occur in no small measure because lawmakers decide to support them, or at least to confer on the president the power to pursue them. Even when presidents are vigorously pursuing a relatively popular agenda, as with the execution of counterterrorism policies relating to the Bush administration in the years following the September 11 attacks, separation-of-powers principles implemented in court decisions often force the executive to compromise.[26] The fact that these constraints matter, of course, is less a testament to the inherent power of general phrases written on parchment than to the fact that political actors and citizens at large value some of these constraints even when they interfere with their shorter-term advantage.

On another level, however, legal doctrines aspiring to govern presidential relationships with subordinate officials or even independent agencies unavoidably play out in an institutional context that evolves organically. The Executive Office of the President occupies several large office blocks, including every inch of an ornate Second Empire–style building that was once one of the largest office buildings in the world and housed three entire cabinet agencies. With a larger staff, deployed and managed according to more-developed historical precedents, presidents can accomplish more even if their formal ability to command a subordinate to interpret the law in a particular fashion is often open to question. The evolution of presidential tools to control the execution of policy appears to evolve organically in response to presidential strategies such as Roosevelt's effort to acquire reorganization authority, exogenous shocks such as the September 11 attacks that eventually prompted the Bush administration to take a major role in reshaping executive branch organization through the creation of DHS, and developments in the technology of social organization such as the emergence and implementation of increasingly sophisticated techniques of budget management and regulatory analysis. In short, Roosevelt's actual power to secure control of governance with a larger White House staff and more political appointees running reorganized bureaus was greater than before he achieved his long-desired reforms. Conversely, a weakened president facing congressional encroachment into organizational domains that traditionally reflected considerable deference (such as the organization of the White House staff within the Executive Office of the President) could still be viewed by some reasonable observers as remaining within the bounds of appropriate presidential power if she tries to undertake some agency organizational changes at the outer limit of her statutory authority.

This somewhat contingent approach to policing presidential power would certainly not counsel exclusive reliance on contemporaneous historical occurrences. In keeping with jurisprudential trends regarding functionalism in separation of powers, the idea is simply to take account of how much power the president has actually achieved over agencies in the aggregate and to consider the resulting insights at the margin. Standards certainly have some drawbacks, but ignoring the realities of presidential control could risk the relevance of separation-of-powers doctrine in a world of pervasive competition to govern security.

One Supreme Objective for the Future

> The wartime experiences of this Agency, which form so large a part of its back-
> ground as a unified Agency to date, demonstrated the practicability and clarified the
> validity of wholesome cooperation and intelligent integration of the several security
> programs. The challenge facing the Federal Security Agency as it enters fiscal 1947,
> its first year in a peacetime world, is: Can the unstinting efforts so freely joined to
> help assure victory in a world at war be mobilized to help assure to the people of
> the United States a fuller life in a world at peace?[1]

THE GAUNT-FACED Franklin Roosevelt who delivered the State of the Union on January 11, 1944, appeared wearier than the confident new president who had cautioned the nation that the only thing to fear was "fear itself." Even as the war raged on in Europe and Asia, Roosevelt seemed intent on pivoting toward domestic concerns by focusing on matters such as employment and housing.[2] Declaring that the political rights enshrined in the Constitution were necessary but not sufficient "to assure us equality in the pursuit of happiness," Roosevelt sketched out a vision emphasizing the importance of access to employment with a living wage, the role of education in social advancement, and the priority that should be accorded to housing, health care access, and pensions.[3] Far from asserting a dramatic new development, Roosevelt sounded a consistent theme that echoed his message to the public on the eve of the FSA's creation well before the United States had even entered World War II. Deftly weaving together the allies' determination "to bring about the defeat of our enemies at the earliest possible time" with his vision for the country's future, Roosevelt again described his administration's lodestar in terms of managing risks:

> The one supreme objective for the future, which we discussed for each Nation
> individually, and for all the United Nations, can be summed up in one word:
> Security. And that means not only physical security which provide[s] safety from

attacks by aggressors. It means also economic security, social security, moral security, in a family of Nations.[4]

Roosevelt's speech indeed reflected a rhetorical effort to paint starkly on a larger canvas, thereby conveying his vision to the millions of civilian war workers "standing four-square behind our sailors and soldiers."[5] What some historical observers of the so-called Second Bill of Rights speech have failed to appreciate, however, is the extent to which Roosevelt had already moved, half a decade earlier, to align the organizational structure of the executive branch with the themes of his speech. By aligning his overarching vision for the country and the structure of government, moreover, Roosevelt and his advisors were engaged in the consummate process of leveraging the feedback relationships between the articulation of political goals and organizational capacities to shape the trajectory of a nation-state.

To witness another compelling example of the relationship between security priorities and organizational structure, we can travel forward in time less than six decades. On June 7, 2002, President George W. Bush announced a major initiative reshaping the architecture of the federal government to promote greater security for the American people.[6] DHS was the result. Unmistakable parallels link that initiative to Roosevelt's creation of the FSA sixty-three years before DHS opened its doors. Like Roosevelt, President Bush faced a national electorate growing increasingly concerned about international threats. The early twenty-first-century White House, like its predecessor in the 1930s, harbored an ambitious domestic policy agenda that would be affected by the reorganization. Both administrations faced hostility over their accumulation of presidential power,[7] and nonetheless sought to use reorganization to enhance their control over how laws are implemented in a sprawling regulatory state. Both ultimately succeeded in achieving their respective reorganizations.

Where the two administrations differed sharply was in how they defined the concept of security that the newly strengthened legal architecture of government was supposed to serve. In Bush's case, the reference to security implicated primarily the management of risks from terrorism or geostrategic threats, a narrowly focused mandate sharply conflicting with the broader missions of transferred bureaus and helping to create conditions that made

DHS perennially troubled.[8] When Hurricane Katrina struck the Gulf Coast roughly three years after DHS was created, the storm killed nearly two thousand people and caused more than $100 billion of damage.[9] The slow response from federal authorities, including DHS and FEMA, added to the hurricane's severe toll. As New Orleans slowly emerged from a flood of toxic waters, the Bush administration faced awkward questions not only about the structure of DHS (placing FEMA firmly under the purview of the Homeland Security secretary), but also about whether it had defined security too narrowly to assign natural disasters the priority they deserved.

Franklin Roosevelt's administration went in a different direction. For President Roosevelt and his advisors, the term "security" was meant to evoke a flexible conception of risk reduction that spread—like the FSA's jurisdiction eventually did—across the now-segregated domains of public health regulation, social welfare policy, and national defense. Against that backdrop, early FSA officials managed to create an environment supporting their bureaus' legal functions and adding to their resources rather than one calling for drastic reforms in agency priorities amid sharp resource constraints.[10] Even after Roosevelt's death, FSA administrator Oscar Ewing continued articulating the same notion of security as "a sure knowledge that we shall not want for the basic necessities of life, no matter what Fate may have in store,"[11] one that eerily parallels the views of some observers who criticize DHS for not being more steadily focused on the full range of risks facing Americans today.[12] What exactly it means to govern security remains a foundational question defining the law's evolution. But despite some unique features of the FSA, the larger picture often reflects a considerable degree of continuity across the legal and organizational landscape of the last century.

CROSS-CUTTING THEMES:
EXECUTIVE ORGANIZATION, SECURITY, AND
THE POLITICS OF LEGAL IMPLEMENTATION

The stories I have told about the dramas surrounding the evolution of the FSA and DHS are interesting in their own right, because they tell us something about the times during which these agencies were forged and the people whose careers and reputations were risked to create new structures within government. But those stories matter most in this book because they help us understand certain cross-cutting themes about law, security, and organizations that affect millions of people. Sometimes these insights emerge from carefully tracing the sequence of steps through which a far-reaching political idea became a functioning security agency with offices across the country or even the planet. We have gained perspective, too, from comparisons—implicating not only the FSA and DHS, but other agencies and bureaus—and from primary sources shedding light on what policymakers were thinking when they made their decisions. Together these materials have already given us some insight into the remarkable parallels and differences between Franklin Roosevelt and George W. Bush. Bush and Roosevelt presented in some respects eerie similarities in seeking power to reshape the executive branch and having a robust view of presidential power. Both placed security at the center of their respective presidencies and sought to re-forge the executive branch to respond to that priority; but each administration pursued a distinct conception of security that was also reflected in the new agencies it created to implement the federal government's legal responsibilities.

Our close analysis of the choices made in those administrations regarding security agencies develops the basic insight that governing security implicates two deeply entangled problems: how the executive branch defines security, and how policymakers compete to secure control over public organizations. In the course of exploring how these problems are entangled, we have also dealt with several other themes with implications for scholars, lawyers, and policymakers: the flexible scope of the security concept in law and politics, the complexities affecting the role of public organizations—including security agencies—within the executive branch, the dependence of public law and separation of powers on organizational realities affecting who actually controls major public agencies, and the often underappreciated incrementalism of the Roosevelt administration. Consider each of these in turn.

Although Paul McNutt, the first FSA administrator, served in high federal office roughly six decades before another former governor, Tom Ridge, became the first Homeland Security secretary, in some respects they operated in similar legal and political environments. They might both have concluded, for example, that the supremely challenging assignments they were handed involved the task of turning paper legal goals into organizational routines and operations. In the course of managing their organizations during the inevitably disorganized and trying days of their early existence, each former governor faced a world with the following characteristic: from DHS to immigration to economic policy and foreign affairs, time and again the ultimate impact of public law depends on who secures governing control of the nation-state's bureaucracy, and (in turn) on how organization is used to define the contested concept of the nation's security.

In the growth of the FSA and the birth of DHS, we can see how these dynamics are interrelated.[13] On the one hand, major actors in controlling public law—including key lawmakers, the White House, and courts—assign exceedingly high importance to the question of who controls the national bureaucracy. In the short run, control of the organizations that carry out legal functions translates into control over the interpretation and implementation of law. Organizational control of the bureaucracy shapes the architecture of public law in the longer run, because bureaucracies shape the legislative agenda, impact public perceptions, and develop degrees of autonomy or particular cultures affecting how legal powers are actually used.

On the other hand, political actors expend considerable effort to define *what* security means, whether the question is the relationship between health and national defense, the role of natural disaster response in national strategy, or the precise significance of immigration policy to some conception of security. Indeed, concerns about the nation's security drove not only the watershed reorganizations of the FSA and DHS, but also the creation of the Departments of Defense and Energy, and other agencies. With the FSA and DHS, such reorganization efforts are difficult to explain without considering policymakers' interests in securing control of the bureaucratic entities that carried out government functions while also, at the margin, affecting public perceptions of government activity.

These dynamics arise in part because organizational changes appear capable of exerting a more powerful influence than previously realized on the law's evolution. In the case of the FSA, reorganization helped a cluster of health research, human services, and education agencies to envision a common purpose and expand their bureaucratic mandate during a politically risky time. They set in motion the growth of much of the modern federal government, helping fragile administrative and regulatory bureaucracies develop coalitions of political supporters and distinct organizational cultures—qualities that would have been difficult to forge had these entities remained stuck as marginal bureaus in departments with discordant overarching missions (for example, PHS in Treasury, or the Office of Education in Interior) or as lone bureaus bereft of an organizational structure implying a larger project or purpose. These changes matter because agency capacity is a critical variable determining whether the FSA's new legal responsibility for public health research, for example, manages to create a far-reaching network of scientific investigation for civilian and military uses or a far more limited effort to please narrow political constituencies.

Politics can, of course, shatter an agency's capacity to implement the law effectively, but so can it bolster agency capacity. Agencies shaped by political pressures and reorganizations can perform effectively or ineffectively, depending on the context and political agendas—and this pattern exists within and beyond the somewhat malleable domain of security. In the case of DHS, even the early history of the new cabinet agency suggests that organizational choices can have substantive implications for matters such as the allocation of scarce immigration opportunities and decisions about how to reconstruct devastated communities. If it is true that the reorganization of security agencies can create greater capacity over time, the experience of DHS and its bureaus showcases how structural difficulties and funding problems limit the law's significance for citizens and communities. The challenges faced by DHS, moreover, underscore a degree of underappreciated continuity between domestic agencies and those with more-conventional security missions: both face a political environment replete with lawmakers and organized interests capable of imposing costs on agency officials and civil servants.

Yet organizations are not only creatures of politics; they are also actors within the political process. As the Roosevelt administration brought the FSA to life, the organizational structure embodied in the new agency further provided these bureaus with a mechanism for political and legal advocacy, facilitating relations with Congress, coordinating bureaus' activities, and allowing for the development of new legal interpretations and policy proposals. Nearly every major change in American regulatory policy that followed the New Deal during the twentieth century—from Social Security expansion and Medicare, to the original clean air regulatory framework, to the modern infrastructure for pharmaceutical, food, and consumer products regulation—initially involved the FSA or its successor agency. Had Roosevelt failed to create a bureaucratic mechanism for proposing, advocating, and implementing these policies, such initiatives would almost certainly have faced a less hospitable political environment. By the same token, opponents of national health insurance pointedly opposed the FSA's elevation to cabinet status while insisting that such a change would strengthen Truman's bureaucratic resources for pursuing the goal of broadening health care coverage.[14]

As a complement to the changes in the hierarchical machinery of the federal bureaucracy wrought by the creation of the FSA and DHS, agency architecture can help reshape the public imagination about the concept of security—thereby illustrating the flexible scope of this concept. Specifically, the agency's legal architecture emphasized how education and public health research could promote war production and civil defense. It was a rhetorical dynamic emphasized at every turn by both the FSA's leadership and the White House. The reorganization also helped the White House nurture, protect, and control some of its most prized administrative and regulatory programs at a time when the administration's political capital was on the wane, critics were pointing to the panoply of disaggregated independent agencies as a reason to shrink government, and White House staff resources to monitor and control administrative developments were almost nonexistent. These developments did not ensure that all subsequent legal and political battles on behalf of the FSA's subcomponents were won. On the other hand, the events surrounding the creation and evolution of the FSA left their mark in terms of the connection between defense and health in modern government bureaucracies and the relative centralization of regulatory power in just a few entities that indelibly shape American life.

That centralization process yields two final, broader implications for public law. First, because of the elevated stakes involved in organizing agencies, separation-of-powers disputes will continue to turn on how lawmakers and the White House split the power to structure (and restructure) the bureaucracy. Messy as the modern separation-of-powers doctrine has become,[15] with its functional concerns over branch aggrandizement and its basic acknowledgment of shared power in a host of domains, finding an alternative may be exceedingly difficult. Nor is the concept of security (and the closely related concept of what implicates foreign affairs) a particularly useful or self-contained route to resolving legal disputes. Crisp rules are elusive here, and neither history nor the basic logic of the relevant law supports the unitary executive theories rejected in *Humphrey's Executor*. If accepted, such theories would run the risk of leaving the president with enough power to achieve through practical control of the bureaucracy anything that she could not achieve through direct, ostensibly legally binding instructions that contradicted statutory commands. In the end, structural control over hiring, firing, budgets, and regulatory power works as a substitute and a complement for formal legal power achieved through interpretations of traditional separation-of-powers doctrine. For both lawmakers and executive branch officials, the dispute over organizational structure and control is a preeminent setting for conflict over separation of powers. It is precisely this story that the Roosevelt administration's reaction to *Humphrey's Executor* ultimately tells.

Second, the fight over security's multiple strands sheds light on lingering questions about the role of incrementalism in achieving legal and social change. Conceptual questions about the scope of security ran together with practical choices about how—and how rapidly—to alter existing legal arrangements. The answers to these questions at the FSA's origin emphasize the unique and sometimes discontinuous impact of political strategy. An incremental approach to building a "Department of Public Welfare" was not what Roosevelt first envisioned when he sought to secure greater control of the nation's bureaucracy. Reluctantly, he was forced to consider more carefully the nature of congressional opposition. But then, the mechanics through which the Social Security program had been turned into legislation half a decade earlier were themselves an excruciating exercise in compromise. Making deals with House and Senate tax-writing committees, the administration had simultaneously limited the program's scope and expanded its base of support among moderate and even conservative lawmakers on Capitol Hill. Much the same was true of the security-related reorganization that engendered the FSA. Had the Roosevelt administration succeeded in obtaining the sweeping reorganization powers it sought under the original bill, the president would almost certainly have proposed more—and more far-reaching—reorganization plans.

All these themes emerge from an account that illustrates time and again the extraordinary impact of public organizations on the lives of citizens, markets, and entire societies. Most of the people who come into contact with these agencies will naturally be more concerned about how civil servants speed or hinder their flight across the country, whether their food is safe, or whether federal officials are keeping them safe from terrorist attacks while at least endeavoring to safeguard their privacy. But lurking in the background we have repeatedly encountered a larger issue, one that is all the more important because it so often remains elusive. It concerns how advanced industrialized nation-states change and what they might become. This inquiry ties together much of the terrain that the book covers—from the relationship between public law and organizations, to the development of agencies in an environment of political competition, to the extent of "security" that a nation explicitly or implicitly promises its citizens. The hidden origins of the FSA and DHS emerge precisely at the intersection between large historical processes of social change and the familiar pressures of political competition that the law only ever partially succeeds in curbing. The United States, like nation-states across the planet, continues to evolve accordingly: with changing citizen conceptions of how to balance concerns about economic or security risks with skepticism of concentrated power in public organizations; transnational flows of people, money, licit and illicit products, and ideas; allocation of official or quasi-official functions to private entities; and evolving regional communities reflecting cross-border migration.

These trends will raise intriguing questions about the psychological dynamics that can strengthen or fray citizens' ties to their evolving nations, but they will also reprise some of the very dilemmas that Americans faced in the New Deal and in the post–September 11 era. In some countries, national crises could starkly demonstrate the consequences of limited state capacity to help citizens through difficult or risky historical periods. The erosion of state capacity in some regions could even coincide with laws and powerful organizations built around exceedingly narrow definitions of national security, with conventional geostrategic or counterterrorism concerns that are not placed in the larger web of a country's health, disaster relief, education, or economic priorities. In contrast, other states may engage in strategies that find rich echoes in the history of the FSA, involving efforts to enlarge coalitions of support for more robust state organizational capacity in furtherance of the kind of far-reaching risk regulation that was at the core of Roosevelt's vision of national security. Governing security means grappling with precisely these scenarios in a world of scarce resources and painful trade-offs.

CODA: THE NATION'S DILEMMA

Every few years, a new president walks into the same Oval Office from which Franklin Roosevelt called on the nation to prepare for war and George W. Bush announced a Department of Homeland Security more than six decades later. When a new presidential administration plans its priorities, one ineluctable dilemma will connect the new chief executive to her predecessors: how to set the administration's security priorities for the country. Whether the country faces a nuclear safety emergency, a pandemic, or an unexpected military entanglement in Central Asia will unquestionably drive part of the decision. But to presume that external events mechanically account for the resulting set of security priorities is to cast aside what we've learned from seeing presidential administrations build organizations and interpret laws in order to map historical realities onto viable policies.

Accordingly, as new political appointees take the case to the nation, we might imagine one somewhat stylized approach that pivots on defining security in the narrowest possible terms relating to geostrategic priorities and counterterrorism. The country's military capacity would be included in that frame, but not necessarily its ability to educate soldiers or reduce the risks of deadly pandemics. For the millions of Americans whose lives are affected in these debates, that narrower frame has some advantages. Some will look favorably on the narrower frame because it implicates more explicit trade-offs tending to favor priorities such as weapons acquisition and non-proliferation over disaster relief or food safety. Given the relationship between organizational priorities and public law that we have chronicled, the narrower frame may appear to favor leaving more market transactions to regulation by the common law. It also leans, on balance, in the direction of circumscribing at least the idea of expansive presidential power as it applies in the domestic sphere—because a bright line is presupposed by the administration in question and some members of the public between ordinary domestic issues and the more putatively serious national security and foreign policy domains.

But the simplicity purchased thus also comes at a cost. Defense, counterterrorism, and geostrategic capacity are rarely if ever independent of domestic concerns such as education, public health, or immigrant integration. To pretend otherwise can have serious practical consequences for organizational priorities, as in the early days of DHS. Far from being a new insight, this approach is at the heart of the FSA's story and Roosevelt's legacy. If the price attached is a far less clean idea of precisely where the more muscular extent of presidential power ends, it is worth recalling the limits in any event of doctrinal efforts to circumscribe security and foreign policy from domestic pursuits. And even if tougher legal and policy dilemmas are implicit in this broader, more complicated approach, what is gained is in part the very recognition of the inherent complexity of governing security as nation-states evolve, and seek to shape an uncertain environment of strategic risks and possibilities themselves.

As states confront a changing world in addressing these challenges, the domestic context will all but inevitably transform even the most high-minded questions into political puzzles that will often seem to depend on pieces that are perpetually mismatched or missing. Those puzzles were very much in evidence when President Roosevelt sought to decide how to reshape the executive branch. And there is something distinctive about Roosevelt's moves and the sprawling agency they produced. Although the concept of security may be inherently capable of encompassing a broad range of policies associated with social well-being and national strength, it was the Roosevelt administration's determined reaction—even in the face of congressional defeat—that transformed that broad concept into a viable bureaucratic structure. Frustrated though Roosevelt was at the time, the legislative backlash may have coaxed him in a direction that minimized opposition to the new agency at the moment when it was most vulnerable.

By settling for limited reorganization powers, the Roosevelt administration likely placed the FSA's bureaus in a more viable long-term position, one that combined incremental growth with a politically valuable blend of national security and domestic policy rationales. With the evolution of the FSA thus set in motion, Roosevelt demonstrated yet again the irony of how politics, to be commanded, must be obeyed.

In the end, though, Roosevelt's logic in designing the FSA obeyed more than simply the political logic of an administration seeking to achieve greater presidential control following adverse court decisions. Instead the president's goals reflected a particular vision of security against risk that remains relevant to the challenges facing DHS and the American public in the early twenty-first century. Notwithstanding frequent assumptions to the contrary, neither easily applied legal tests nor conceptual ideas can entirely separate security policy from the rest of the government's work. In fact, "security" and domestic regulation have become inextricably intertwined. Homeland security—even narrowly defined to encompass threats from terrorism or international conflict—depends crucially on decisions of agencies such as the Nuclear Regulatory Commission,[16] or the Federal Emergency Management Agency. Homeland security is also defined, and benefits and burdens distributed accordingly, through rulemaking proceedings governing the security of chemical facilities. A single attack against one such facility could risk the lives and health of thousands.[17] Security decisions of paramount importance also lurk elsewhere in the interstices of the regulatory state, in choices to rely largely on voluntary private-sector actions to secure a vulnerable cyber-infrastructure as critical to domestic public health and safety as it is to the country's capacity to advance its geostrategic interests abroad.

Moreover, just as American security may ultimately depend on regulatory policy, so too does the quality of Americans' health and safety protections depend on security policy. In this light, the story of DHS is painted on a far larger canvas than even the vastness of the agency would suggest: a canvas where domestic regulatory policy is increasingly affected by budgetary, statutory, and bureaucratic developments involving homeland security. Indeed, the nation's experience with major domestic challenges, including Hurricane Katrina, offers a cautionary note to anyone determined to exclude natural disasters, serious health emergencies, and infrastructure failures from the scope of discussions about security. Just as consequences arise from the organizational structure of major executive agencies, so too are lives shaped by how policymakers use the structure of executive agencies and their agenda-setting powers to define security. Americans cannot respond intelligently to these consequences if they are blind to them.

Notes

1. World Health Organization, Statement by Dr. Keiji Kukuda.

2. GAO, *Influenza Pandemic*.

3. Portions of this book are based on research published in earlier form as *"Securing" the Nation: Law, Politics, and Organization at the Federal Security Agency, 1939–1953*, 76 U. Chi. L. Rev. 587 (2009). In addition, some of the ideas developed in Chapters 7 and 8 draw on *Crisis Bureaucracy: Homeland Security and the Political Design of Legal Mandates*, 59 Stan. L. Rev. 673 (2006) (with Dara Cohen and Barry Weingast); and Chapter 9 draws on some of the ideas presented in "The Arms of Democracy: The Legacy of Economic Security Policy," in *Shared Responsibility, Shared Risk: Governments, Markets, and Social Policy in the Twenty-First Century*, ed. Jacob Hacker and Ann O'Leary, 55–74. I am grateful for permission from the relevant publishers, and for superb research assistance from Mindy Jeng, Shivan Sarin, Andy Parker, Britt Grant, Mrinal Menon, and Connor Raso.

1. See TPM Hurricane Katrina Timeline 1–6 (Sept. 20, 2005)(hereinafter TPM Timeline).

2. See generally Brinkley, *The Great Deluge*.

3. See TPM Timeline.

4. Wombell, *Army Support*, 45.

5. *Id.*

6. *Id.*

7. *Id.*

8. *Id.*

9. See TPM Timeline, 1–2.

10. *Id.*

11. *Id.*

12. Sullivan, *FEMA Official Says Agency Heads Ignored Warnings* ("FEMA failed to organize the massive mobilization of National Guard troops and evacuation buses needed for a quick and effective relief response when Katrina struck"); Hsu, *Chertoff*.

13. See TPM Timeline, 2.

14. *New Orleans 80 Percent Flooded*.

15. Haygood and Tyson, *It Was As If All of Us Were Pronounced Dead*.

16. *Id.*

17. *Id.*

18. *Id.*

19. *Id.*

20. *Id.*

21. *Tulane Maritime Law Center Newsletter* ("About half of Tulane's campus flooded, from Claiborne Avenue to Freret Street").

22. Homeland Security Act of 2002, 2229–33.

23. *Ex-FEMA Chief Deflects Blame for Katrina Response.*

24. See TPM Timeline, 2.

25. *Id.*

26. *Ex-FEMA Chief Deflects Blame.*

27. See TPM Timeline, 2.

28. *Id.*, 3.

29. Burton and Hicks, *Hurricane Katrina.*

30. Schneider, *Administrative Breakdowns*, 515 (internal citation omitted).

31. *Id.*

32. *Id.*

33. *Id.*

34. Select Bipartisan Comm., *Failure of Initiative*, 135.

35. *Id.*

36. S. Rep. No. 109-322, at 559 (2006).

37. See Kennedy, *Freedom from Fear*, 257 (explaining that Roosevelt's idea was to provide "present relief, future stability, and permanent security").

38. See Roosevelt, *Message of the President* (stating that the purpose of the FSA is to "promote social and economic security, educational opportunity and the health of the citizens of the Nation").

39. 295 U.S. 602 (1935).

40. *Id.* at 629–30.

41. 272 U.S. 52 (1926).

42. *Id.* at 175–77 (holding that the president can fire the postmaster general at his discretion even though the Congress passed a statute requiring the president to get the consent of the Senate to fire him).

43. See Derthick, *Agency Under Stress*, 20–21 ("Congress chose to make the [new SSB] independent of any executive department").

44. See Mansfield, *Federal Executive Reorganization*, 337 (describing Roosevelt's frustration); Davis, *FDR*, 19 (noting that, after Roosevelt's election to a second term, "the subject uppermost in his mind on this third morning of the new year was . . . governmental reorganization").

45. The term "legal mandate," used interchangeably with "legal responsibility," refers to legal rules or standards implemented by an agency (for example, through particular regulations, enforcement strategies, or allocation of responsibilities among bureaucracies).

46. For prominent work focusing on the near-inevitable production of ineffectiveness and failure through changes in formal organization, see Terry M. Moe, *Politics and the Theory of Organization*, 126. For an example of scholarship on the considerable extent to which legislative and bureaucratic changes may be explained by focusing on position-taking benefits, see Mayhew, *Congress*, 147–51. For work emphasizing the spontaneous development of routines and the diffusion of ideas as an explanation for bureaucratic organization, see Strang and Meyer, *Institutional Conditions*, 506.

47. The most extensive existing scholarly commentary on the FSA appears to be in Rufus Miles, *The Department of Health, Education, and Welfare* (18–24), about five pages long and containing virtually no analysis of White House motives for the reorganization, bureaus' budgets, or news coverage of the department. Perhaps influenced by the putative scope of his project's focus on the Department of Health, Education, and Welfare (HEW) as opposed to its predecessor agency, Miles stresses the expectations of those who participated

in the FSA's elevation to cabinet status, rather than those who forged the FSA. See, for example, *id.*, 3 ("When HEW first came into being as a Cabinet department in 1953, it did not occur to any of its many midwives that it would grow so rapidly"). A leading history of the Public Health Service (PHS) dismisses the significance of the FSA by citing Miles, and then proceeds to explain the important changes the PHS experienced during the war period without considering how the bureau would have fared if it had remained at the Department of the Treasury. See Mullan, *Plagues and Politics*, 111–16. Mullan also furnishes reason to question his contention about the relative insignificance of the merger by noting that it changed the PHS's relationship to the SSB. *Id.*, 110.

48. See Roosevelt, *Message of the President.*

49. See Miles, *Department of Health, Education, and Welfare*, 18–24.

50. *Id.*

51. For the text of the president's announcement, see Roosevelt, *Message of the President* (explaining that the total overhead of the agencies involved in the reorganization was $235 million). See also *Budget of the United States, 1980* (OMB 1979); Miles, *Department of Health, Education, and Welfare*, 3 (discussing HEW's budget in relation to those of other countries).

52. See Thomas, *Some Social Aspects of Japanese-American Demography*, 474; *Alien Enemies and Japanese-Americans*, 1324.

53. See letter from George W. Merck, Director, War Research Service to Lt. Col. Chester W. Goble, State Director, Selective Service System (May 1, 1944), National Archives, War Research Service Files, Entry 5A, Box 12.

54. *United States Government Manual, September 1941*, 364–86 (describing the activities of the FSA); Federal Security Agency, *Services of the Federal Security Agency*, 4, 8, 10–11, 16 (reviewing the role of the FSA in the executive branch). The treaty the United States had signed outlawing such work was *The Geneva Protocol for the Prohibition of the Use in War of Asphyxiating, Poisonous, or Other Gases, and of Bacterial Methods of Warfare* (hereafter *Geneva Protocol*). Although the United States had not ratified the treaty at the time, its signature would have presumably been understood to be a commitment not to frustrate the purposes of the treaty. See Swaine, *Unsigning*, 2061–62.

55. Surprisingly, the massive body of literature on the history of the American state during and after the New Deal all but ignores the FSA. The same is true for the somewhat smaller yet still substantial literature on regulatory governance before the 1946 passage of the Administrative Procedure Act. But the FSA's trajectory can be reconstructed from White House records, legislative documents, budget reports, and the agency's own files.

56. The President's Committee on Administrative Management, commonly known as the Brownlow Committee, provided a prescriptive, public administration justification but did not explain why the president would expend the resources he did to implement parts of that vision. See generally Fesler, *The Brownlow Committee Fifty Years Later*. With respect to the supervision of transferred bureaus by political supporters, bureaus such as Education and the PHS—in contrast to the SSB—were not independent commissions that might have triggered obvious concerns about political control. They were instead bureaus in departments overseen by White House loyalists such as Harold Ickes and Henry Morgenthau, Jr. See Polenberg, *Reorganizing Roosevelt's Government*, 82; Belair, *President Decrees Three Big Offices in Centralizing 21*, 18. It is also unusual for a president to transfer agencies from traditional executive departments—generally considered to be more tightly under presidential control—to an independent agency such as the early FSA. See Lewis, *Presidents and the Politics of Agency Design*, 143–44. Regarding the efficiency-focused rationales for reorga-

nization, see Polenberg, *Reorganizing Roosevelt's Government*, 3–5. Interestingly enough, Polenberg also reports that Roosevelt privately disparaged efficiency rationales for reorganization (even as he was willing to publicly espouse them); see *id.*, 8, 33–34. In one of the few scholarly references that are relevant to the subject, political scientist James Q. Wilson downplays the importance of the creation of HEW and concentrates more on the behavior of its component bureaus. But he does nothing to investigate the potential significance of the time those bureaus spent within the FSA, or the broader legacy of that agency. Wilson dismisses the significance of the creation of HEW in 1953. See Wilson, *Bureaucracy*, 267–68 ("[A]ssembling a variety of agencies together into a Department of Health, Education, and Welfare made little difference: the component bureaus, each with its distinctive culture, professional outlook, and congressional supporters, continued for the most part to operate independently of each other and of HEW's central leadership"). But he fails to address the potential significance of the creation of the FSA a decade and a half before, and even his account of the relative insignificance of HEW's creation is difficult to reconcile with the degree of conflict over this change and the internal administrative implications of elevating the FSA to cabinet status.

57. See Chapter 7 (discussing the Bush administration's narrow definition of "security" and the resulting domestic policy implications). See also Homeland Security Council, *National Strategy for Homeland Security* (defining homeland security as "a concerted national effort to prevent terrorist attacks within the United States, reduce America's vulnerability to terrorism, and minimize the damage and recover from attacks that do occur").

CHAPTER 2

1. *Nat'l Comm'n on Terrorist Attacks upon the U.S., The 9/11 Commission Report*, 326–27 [hereinafter *Commission Report*].

2. Eskridge and Ferejohn, *A Republic of Statutes*.

3. See McNeil, *Understanding Organizational Power*, 75–78 (discussing the application of Weber's theories to understanding why agencies are a vehicle for implementing rules and standards).

4. See *Dalton v. Specter*, 511 U.S. 462, 464–65 (1994) (discussing the legislative structures developed to manage the closure of military bases).

5. See Rothenberg, *Regulation, Organizations, and Politics*.

6. See Dahl, *The Federal Regulation of Waste from Cruise Ships in U.S. Waters*, 613.

7. *Id.*

8. See *Cruise Ships Sail Into Political Arena*, 5.

9. See Cohen, Cuéllar, and Weingast, *Crisis Bureaucracy*, 726. See also Dahl, *The Federal Regulation of Waste from Cruise Ships in U.S. Waters*, 613.

10. See Abrams, *Tauzin Slams Coast Guard Rules*.

11. See, for example, Durant, *Hazardous Waste, Regulatory Reform, and the Reagan Revolution*.

12. See *Motor Vehicle Mfrs. Ass'n v. State Farm Mut. Auto. Ins.*, 463 U.S. 29 (1983).

13. See Golden, *Exit, Voice, Loyalty, and Neglect*.

14. See generally Croley, *White House Review of Agency Rulemaking*, 827–28.

15. See *Chevron, U.S.A., Inc. v. Nat'l Res. Def. Council, Inc.*, 467 U.S. 837 (1984).

16. See Scalia, *Deference to Administrative Interpretations of Law*, 518.

17. See *State Farm*, 463 U.S. at 59 (Rehnquist, J., dissenting).

18. See *Microsoft Allies Urge Congress to Cut Antitrust Unit's Budget*.

19. See Cuéllar, *"Securing" the Bureaucracy*.

20. One of the major responsibilities of the Bureau of Alcohol, Tobacco, Firearms, and Explosives (previously Alcohol, Tobacco, and Firearms, or ATF) is to regulate the nation's federally licensed firearms dealers to limit the lucrative transfers of firearms from such dealers to individuals engaged in criminal activity or other prohibited purchasers. See Department of the Treasury, Bureau of Alcohol, Tobacco, and Firearms, *Commerce in Firearms in the United States*. While the number of Federal Firearms Licenses (FFLs) grew from 152,232 in 1973 to 250,833 in 1994 (*id.*, A-21), the number of agents stayed nearly flat from 1973 to 1994 (1,622 to 1,884), and the number of inspectors fell from 826 to 800 (*id.*, B-13). The rate of compliance inspections on FFLs fell from a high of 54.7 percent in 1969 to 4.8 percent in 1998 (*id.*, A-21). The decline took place as the ATF assumed the responsibility of tracing firearms from crime scenes (*id.*, A-25) and while it was being increasingly pressured to assign its agents to assist with federal prosecutions targeting firearms use connected to state and local offenses. See Richman, *"Project Exile" and the Allocation of Federal Law Enforcement Authority*.

21. See Mayhew, *Congress* (discussing how legislatures may enact regulatory acts and create regulatory agencies for "symbolic" value).

22. See Kagan, *Presidential Administration*, 2257–59 (noting the legislative vetoes and "fire alarm" monitoring systems that Congress has built into agency statutes); Cohen, Cuéllar, and Weingast, *Crisis Bureaucracy* (arguing that legislative allocation of agency authority is often not designed to achieve stated goals).

23. Regarding organizational culture and routines, see, for example, Perrow, *Complex Organizations*.

24. See generally Wood and Waterman, *The Dynamics of Political Control of the Bureaucracy*. For an insightful treatment of delegation dynamics, see Epstein and O'Halloran, *Delegating Powers*, 55–59.

25. See Cohen, Cuéllar, and Weingast, *Crisis Bureaucracy*, 739 (discussing the ambiguous prescriptive benefits of the Bush administration's reorganization of DHS).

26. See Wilson, *Bureaucracy*, 185–86 (explaining how the Defense Department represented a compromise among the Army, Navy, and Air Force regarding their degree of organizational autonomy).

27. See Walcott and Hult, *Governing the White House* (discussing the transaction costs associated with reorganization); Wilson, *Bureaucracy*, 11–12 (suggesting the futility or perversity of some reorganizations).

28. Wilson, *Bureaucracy*, 267–68 (asserting that the component bureaus of HEW "continued for the most part to operate independently" and contrasting this result with the removal of the Air Force from within the Army).

29. See, for example, Weber, *Economy and Society*, 1:225 (discussing the formal rationality of the bureaucracy and the impact of bureaucratic structure on the organization of social life); Giddens, *Capitalism and Modern Social Theory* (discussing Marx's deployment of economic determinism).

30. See Posen, *The Sources of Military Doctrine*, 34–35.

31. See Moe, *Politics and the Theory of Organization*, 125–26 (suggesting that a "winning group" in politics might choose to place formal limits on the abilities of a new agency out of fear that in the future the agency could otherwise act against the group's interest). See also Weingast, *Caught in the Middle*, 334–38 (describing how the political compromises necessary to get agreement by Congress and the executive branch create a "flawed system").

32. See Strang and Meyer, *Institutional Conditions for Diffusion*, 491 (arguing that institutionalized conceptions of formal organization can spread rapidly because the standardized categories and rules they use provide a "recipe" for adopters). See also Lovata, *Behavioral*

Theories Relating to the Design of Information Systems, 147–48 (discussing behavioral, nonrational bases for the structure of bureaucratic mechanisms to manage information).

33. See Cohen, Cuéllar, and Weingast, *Crisis Bureaucracy*, 727 (quoting a longtime Coast Guard observer who noted that the Coast Guard had to curtail its traditional regulatory activities in order to take on its new security-related mission).

34. See *id.*, 748 (questioning Carter's stated reason for creating the Department of Energy and arguing that his true purpose was to shift oil price regulation and nuclear weapons research from independent agencies to the White House).

35. See Zegart, *Flawed by Design* (discussing the Joint Chiefs of Staff); Walcott and Hult, *Governing the White House*, 12–13 (describing how structure can influence the conduct of overtly political tasks); Moe, *Politics and the Theory of Organization*, 123 (arguing that political institutions, which result from structural choices, are "means of legal coercion and redistribution" and therefore the choice of structure can make some groups better or worse off); Bach, *The Machinery and Politics of Monetary Policy-making* (discussing the relative political consensus surrounding the Federal Reserve).

36. See Zegart, *Flawed by Design*, 26 (arguing that legislators face substantial information problems when determining the success or dysfunction of foreign policy agencies).

37. Compare Strang and Meyer, *Institutional Conditions for Diffusion*, 499 (stating that new nation-states adopt organizational forms that have already been designed and legitimated by others), with Wilson, *Bureaucracy*, 295–97 (contrasting rules-oriented bureaucrats in the United States with Western European regulators who have more discretion over how to apply regulations).

38. See Vizzard, *In the Cross Fire*, 27–28. See also Richman, *Federal Criminal Law, Congressional Delegation, and Enforcement Discretion*, 796–97.

39. On Hoover and the FBI, see Theoharis, *The FBI and American Democracy* (describing how, despite the attorney general's order barring investigation of individuals' political beliefs, Hoover expanded political investigations and encouraged citizens to become "confidential informants").

40. With respect to political influence on the Federal Reserve, see Chang, *Appointing Central Bankers*, 66–71. Political control of the NLRB is analyzed in Terry M. Moe, *Control and Feedback in Economic Regulation*, 1108 (finding that half of the variance in NLRB decisions can be explained by political conditions, economic conditions, and NLRB staff filtering of caseloads, but that over time the NLRB's decisions equally favor labor and business).

41. See Acemoglu, *Why Not a Political Coase Theorem?*, 633–48 (showing how application of the political Coase theorem is limited by the fact that contracts between citizens and the state are, by definition, not enforceable, and suggesting that the use of incentive-related promises can sometimes overcome this issue).

42. With respect to the expansive readings of institutional sociology and social psychology, see Granovetter and Tilly, *Inequality and Labor Processes*, 205 (reporting that large, bureaucratic private firms experience the same bifurcation between private and organization goals seen in government bureaucracies); Selznick, *An Approach to a Theory of Bureaucracy*, 50–51 (developing an analytical model of bureaucracy where conflicts between the goals of individual bureaucrats and the formal goals of the organization create a new, informal structure).

43. Lewis, *Presidents and the Politics of Agency Design*, 92–97.

44. See *Chevron U.S.A. Inc. v. NRDC*, 467 U.S. 837, 842–43 (1984).

45. *Id.*

46. Compare *Budget of the United States* (1935) (showing a total budget for the two

agencies of slightly more than $1.5 million), with *Budget of the United States* (1950) (growing to $1.3 billion, with almost $5 million of this total appropriated for the FDA and the remainder appropriated for the Social Security Administration). See also Derthick, *Policymaking for Social Security*, 272–73 (discussing the growth in social security expenditures during this period); Gilbert, *The United States Food and Drug Administration* (chronicling the agency's growth in the decades after World War II).

47. See Swain, *The Rise of a Research Empire*, 1236.

48. See Ewing, *Conservation in Terms of Our Human Resources*, 23 (speech presented at the Utica Sesquicentennial, Utica, New York, July 3, 1948); available at Harry S. Truman Presidential Library, Papers of Oscar R. Ewing, Federal Security Agency, Speeches and Articles, 1948–1949, Box 38:

Today, in terms of military and productive strength, we are the greatest nation on earth. . . . We are strong. Yes. But we must maintain our vigor. And above all we must conserve both our natural and our *human* resources. For in the last analysis it is from the land and the people that a nation derives its real strength.

See also Polenberg, *War and Society*, 84–86 (discussing how the Farm Security Administration's defenders sought to avoid budget cuts by positioning it as a "'first-line war agency' that would 'help in meeting the food needs of wartime America'").

49. See Wilson, *Bureaucracy*, 268. See also Lewis, *Presidents and the Politics of Agency Design*, 70–87 (discussing why presidents would want to use structural changes to undo congressionally imposed constraints on presidential control).

50. See *United States Government Manual, 2007–2008*, 223, 288 (describing the work of the Agency for Toxic Substances and Disease Registry and the division of labor between OSHA and HHS on chemical exposure limits for workers).

51. See Cohen, Cuéllar, and Weingast, *Crisis Bureaucracy*, 713 (discussing divided control of occupational safety policy); Cuéllar, *The Tenuous Relationship* (discussing the consequences of the fragmentation of control in the anti-criminal finance system among prosecutors, regulators, and investigators).

52. As noted earlier, legal mandates are often too ambiguous and subject to contested interpretations to yield a consensus idea about what counts as "effectiveness" from a prescriptive perspective. Disagreement about goals thus makes it difficult to fix—conceptually—what it means for an agency to be structured in a prescriptively effective manner. Even when there is relative political consensus about underlying goals, we have limited existing knowledge of how changes in bureaucratic structure actually affect the implementation of legal mandates.

53. See Wilson, *Bureaucracy*, 90–91.

54. *Id.*, 91.

55. In their classic account of organizational behavior, for example, the behaviorally oriented social scientists Richard M. Cyert and James G. March (*A Behavioral Theory of the Firm*) cover a range of concepts relevant to their now-classic behavioral theory, including "expectations," "goals," and "information," but fail even to mention "organizational culture."

56. Wilson, *Bureaucracy*, 92.

57. See, for example, Harris, *Organizational Culture and Individual Sensemaking* (using psychological schema to explain the persistence of organizational culture); Arce, *Taking Corporate Culture Seriously* (providing a game-theoretic account).

58. Gwynne, *Empire of the Summer Moon*, 161.

59. See Pinter, *One Step Forward, Two Steps Back on U.S. Floodplains*, 208 (discussing the consensus supporting the Dutch levee system and its oversight structure). See also Skow-

ronek, *Building a New American State*, 145–48 (describing how railroad bankruptcies and destabilizing rate wars spurred Congress to create the Interstate Commerce Commission).

60. See Polenberg, *Reorganizing Roosevelt's Government*, 7 (stating that Roosevelt believed that the true purpose of reorganization was to make the administration "more responsive to the national interest"); Walcott and Hult, *Governing the White House*, 18 (proposing that the emergence of a White House staff can be viewed as a response to mounting demands on the president to formulate domestic policy and monitor executive branch agencies).

61. See Cohen, Cuéllar, and Weingast, *Crisis Bureaucracy*, 739–41 (arguing that structural problems related to the reorganization of FEMA into DHS turned Hurricane Katrina into an especially large crisis).

62. See Carpenter, *The Forging of Bureaucratic Autonomy*, 30–33 (discussing techniques that bureaucracies use to foment relative political independence); Carpenter, *Adaptive Signal Processing*, 288–89 (discussing how new layers of bureaucracy blunt the impact of legislative strategies to control the bureaucracy); Wright, *The Political Economy of New Deal Spending*, 30–31 (discussing econometric studies of the allocation of grant funds during the Roosevelt administration).

63. See Cohen, Cuéllar, and Weingast, *Crisis Bureaucracy*, 684–86 (describing public demand for increased security and how it eventually led to the creation of DHS); Wilson, *Bureaucracy*, 130 (discussing politicians' different reasons for supporting organizational changes); Jones and Strahan, *The Effect of Energy Politics*, 158–59 (discussing the creation of the Energy Department).

64. See Schlesinger and Lau, *The Meaning and Measure of Policy Metaphors*, 613–14 (developing a model of reasoning by policy metaphor); Burnell and Reeve, *Persuasion as a Political Concept*, 394–400 (discussing how attitude change occurs as the result of new information or symbolic imagery).

65. See Ting, *A Theory of Jurisdictional Assignments in Bureaucracies*, 365–67 (describing how politicians face difficulties when they consider restricting funding for an agency that performs both functions that they value and those that they do not value as much).

66. See generally Reeves, *President Nixon*, 604–5. The "Saturday Night Massacre" firings were not specifically a change in agency structure but rather an effort to use a pre-existing structure and to test the limits of the president's ability to control that structure.

67. See Cohen, Cuéllar, and Weingast, *Crisis Bureaucracy*, 708–9.

68. See Fearon, *Signaling Versus the Balance of Power and Interests*, 236, 252.

69. See *Massachusetts v. EPA*, 549 U.S. 497, 521–23 (2007).

70. See Gold and Talley, *Exxon CEO Advocates Emissions Tax*.

71. See Fletcher and Fears, *Bush Pushes Guest-Worker Program*.

72. Consider Morrow, *How Could Trade Affect Conflict?*, 484; Fearon, *Signaling Versus the Balance of Power and Interests*, 258.

73. This trade-off describes Franklin Roosevelt's situation in the years immediately before the entry of the United States into World War II, particularly as he navigated a period of transition from insisting that American forces would not participate in the European war to underscoring the dangers of that war to the interests of the United States. See Heinrichs, *Threshold of War*, 83–85 (describing the considerations that went into Roosevelt's May 27, 1941, speech on the strategic threats facing the United States).

74. Zegart, *Flawed by Design*.

75. *Id.*, 22–23.

76. *Id.*, 39.

77. *Id.*, 27, 39.

78. *Id.*, 38.
79. *Id.*, 28.
80. *Id.*, 39.
81. *Id.*
82. *Id.*, 44.

83. See Lewis, *Presidents and the Politics of Agency Design*, 110–15 (describing Congress's influence on Department of Energy reforms taken in response to allegations of espionage at Los Alamos National Laboratory).

84. See Carpenter, *The Forging of Bureaucratic Autonomy*, 366 (describing how the FDA's prompt action generated substantial public goodwill for the agency and, as a result, Congress expanded the agency's powers).

85. See generally Shull, *The Fourth Branch*.

CHAPTER 3

1. Regarding Roosevelt's political difficulties by the end of the 1930s, see Francis, *President's Influence Is Slipping as Solons Labor*, A5. Published at precisely the time Roosevelt was contemplating his reorganization plans, the article notes:

In the last month particularly rebuffs for Mr. Roosevelt have been frequent and irritating. The spirit of revolt is spreading steadily. Aware they can defy the administration with impunity, increasing numbers of Democrats are balking at New Deal proposals. Such a tendency was responsible for defeat of the Florida ship canal bill and of the plan to subsidize cotton exports; it was the factor behind the boost in flood-control funds and the rebellion against the Wage-Hour Act amendments.

This perception was widely shared among press observers and politicians at the time, as well as subsequent scholarly observers. See William E. Leuchtenburg, *Franklin D. Roosevelt and the New Deal*, 252. These difficulties are probably better explained by the administration's strategic decisions to obtain greater policy successes by shedding marginal coalition members than by secular declines in Roosevelt's popularity or political acuity. See Sundquist, *Dynamics of the Party System*, 199–214 (discussing evidence that Roosevelt accepted a "measurable" loss of conservative rural Democrats to the Republican ranks as a result of his New Deal policies). With respect to the first puzzle, it is worth noting that the Brownlow Committee provided a prescriptive, public-administration justification but did not explain why the president would expend the resources he did to implement parts of that vision.

2. See Polenberg, *Reorganizing Roosevelt's Government*, 146–55 (discussing Roosevelt's declining popularity and how it was hurting his ability to implement his reorganization plans).

3. Cuéllar, *"Securing" the Nation*, 686–94.

4. See Leuchtenburg, *Franklin D. Roosevelt and the New Deal*, 231–40, 275.

5. See Polenberg, *Reorganizing Roosevelt's Government*, 55 (discussing growing efforts by anti–New Deal organizations to capitalize on the administration's political vulnerability and perceived presidential overreaching during the reorganization fight). Polenberg notes:

On a Sunday morning in March 1938 a farmer in Muscatine, Iowa, received several special delivery letters. Sent by Frank Gannett's National Committee to Uphold Constitutional Government, they contained broadsides blasting the Reorganization bill as a "colossal snatch . . . for Presidential power," as a scheme to clamp "one man rule upon a free people."

6. *Id.*, 55–56 (discussing how opposition grew when FDR proposed enlarging the size of the Supreme Court).

7. See Miles, *The Department of Health, Education, and Welfare*, 20 ("Even though HEW's official birth did not occur until 1953, when FSA's name was changed and its head

became a Cabinet officer, [the formation of the FSA] was the real beginning of the Department of Health, Education, and Welfare").

8. Regarding previous fights to centralize functions in a health and welfare ministry, see Skocpol, *Protecting Soldiers and Mothers*, 304:

In the end, various bills . . . to establish a new national Department of Public Health, were deflected or defeated in Congress between 1908 and World War I. The nation was left with a consolidated Public Health Service, but without an omnibus health agency. Since the reformers had hoped that a new federal agency would stimulate and coordinate state and local health efforts and lay the evidentiary basis for new programs, the failure of the statebuilding effort certainly weakened the plausibility of the . . . campaign during 1916–1920 for public health insurance in the United States.

9. See Miles, *Department of Health, Education, and Welfare*, 25–28.

10. See Carpenter, *England's New Ministry of Health*, 662 (discussing Parliament's new act, which took control of health away from local government and put it in a ministry).

11. *Id.*, 664.

12. See Cuéllar, *"Securing" the Nation*, 620–37.

13. *Id.*, 630–37.

14. See *Food and Drug Administration v. Brown & Williamson Tobacco Corp.*, 529 U.S. 120, 161 (2000) (resolving whether the FDA had jurisdiction over tobacco); *Isbrandtsen-Moller Co. v. United States*, 14 F. Supp. 407, 412–13 (S.D.N.Y. 1936) (dismissing a complaint to prevent the president from abolishing the Shipping Board Bureau and transferring its power to the Department of Commerce), affirmed, 300 U.S. 139, 149 (1937).

15. See Cohen, Cuéllar, and Weingast, *Crisis Bureaucracy*, 699 (discussing the lack of congressional reorganization).

16. Cuéllar, *"Securing" the Nation*, 637–55.

17. See *id.*, 600–614, 630–37, for a discussion of this historical trajectory.

18. See Leuchtenburg, *Franklin D. Roosevelt and the New Deal*, 335:

By the end of the Roosevelt years, few questioned the right of the government to pay the farmer millions in subsidies not to grow crops, to enter plants to conduct union elections, to regulate business enterprises from utility companies to airlines, or even to compete directly with business by generating and distributing hydroelectric power.

See also McCubbins, Noll, and Weingast, *The Political Origins of the Administrative Procedure Act*, 190–91 (analyzing how expansion in federal power exacerbated efforts to control the bureaucracy).

19. For different perspectives on the extent to which the New Deal represented a "sharp break" from the previous legal regime, compare Ackerman, *Constitutional Politics/Constitutional Law* (describing the New Deal as one of the "great constitutional transformations"), with Landis, *Fate, Responsibility, and "Natural" Disaster Relief*, 259–61 (questioning Ackerman's and other scholars' view of the New Deal by arguing that it followed precedents in disaster relief situations).

20. President Roosevelt's efforts to fire independent commissioners spawned *Humphrey's Executor*, 295 U.S. 264.

21. See Alter, *The Defining Moment*, 3 (explaining that the greatest applause during Roosevelt's first inaugural speech came when he asked for powers to combat the emergency as if it were a "foreign foe").

22. Trading with the Enemy Act, Pub. L. No. 65-91, 40 Stat. 411 (1917), codified in various sections of 50 U.S.C. App.

23. See Dam, *From the Gold Clause Cases to the Gold Commission*, 510 (discussing

Roosevelt's early use of the Trading with the Enemy Act to prohibit banks from paying out or exporting gold coin or bullion).

24. See Leuchtenburg, *The FDR Years*, 59–65 ("In carrying the legislation of the First Hundred Days into effect, Roosevelt took full advantage of the receptivity of the country to wartime appeals").

25. See Leuchtenburg, *Franklin D. Roosevelt and the New Deal*, 253–73, 277 (describing the slow economic recovery in 1938).

26. *Id.*, 244–46.

27. See Polenberg, *Reorganizing Roosevelt's Government*, 55–56.

28. *Id.*, vii ("In April 1938 more than one hundred Democratic congressmen deserted President Roosevelt to defeat the [first] Executive Reorganization bill by a vote of 204 to 196"). Regarding Roosevelt's declining political fortunes, see Leuchtenburg, *Franklin D. Roosevelt and the New Deal*, 271 (discussing GOP gains in 1938); Francis, *President's Influence Is Slipping as Solons Labor* (describing Roosevelt's political influence as "ebbing"); Sundquist, *Dynamics of the Party System*, 200–201 (discussing the shedding of marginal coalition members). For a theoretical perspective on when leaders such as Roosevelt might prefer to shed marginal coalition members and when they might opt to maintain the largest possible winning coalition, see Weingast, *Reflections on Distributive Politics and Universalism*, 324 (comparing universal or near-unanimous coalitions with the reality of divisive political parties).

29. See generally Cavers, *The Food, Drug, and Cosmetic Act of 1938*.

30. See Polenberg, *Reorganizing Roosevelt's Government*, 56–58 (discussing wealthy supporters, including newspaper publisher Frank Gannett and New York lawyer Amos Pinchot, of civil society movements opposing the New Deal); *id.*, 64 (discussing Southern Democrats' opposition to Roosevelt's plans). Regarding the significance of the Food, Drug, and Cosmetic Act, see generally Gilbert, *The United States Food and Drug Administration*.

31. Polenberg, *Reorganizing Roosevelt's Government*, 146–61.

32. Regarding the impact of presidential popularity on legislative behavior, see Rivers and Rose, *Passing the President's Program*, 194–95. With respect to how this played out in the New Deal context, see Polenberg, *Reorganizing Roosevelt's Government*, 146–61 (detailing how Roosevelt's influence in Congress diminished as his popularity did in the late 1930s); Riddick, *American Government and Politics*, 303–4 (summarizing that Roosevelt vetoed 107 bills that year as Congress increased its opposition to his policies); Francis, *President's Influence Is Slipping as Solons Labor* (describing Roosevelt's decreasing influence as even Democrats began denying New Deal proposals).

33. See Oppenheimer, *The Supreme Court and Administrative Law*, 1–2 (acknowledging increases in how contentious the issues of executive power became in litigation between the 1920s and the 1930s).

34. 272 U.S. at 175–76.

35. See Kagan, *Presidential Administration*, 2322 (discussing the extent to which *Myers* left unresolved matters that were taken up in *Humphrey's Executor*).

36. *Humphrey's Executor*, 295 U.S. at 624–26.

37. *Id.* at 629 (noting that officials outside of the executive branch need to be "free from control or coercive influence").

38. 14 F. Supp. 407 (S.D.N.Y. 1936).

39. *Id.* at 412–13.

40. See Polenberg, *Reorganizing Roosevelt's Government*, 8.

41. See Executive Department Reorganization Act of June 30, 1932, Pub. L. No. 72-212, 47 Stat. 413, amended by 47 Stat. 1517 (1933). The act allowed the president to trans-

fer agencies and their legal responsibilities to different departments, subject to a one-house legislative veto in most circumstances. But soon after passing the law in 1932, congressional leaders passed an amendment limiting the validity of any reorganization plans after two years unless otherwise provided by Congress.

42. See generally 83 Cong. Rec. S 2497 (Feb. 28, 1938).

43. Compare Executive Reorganization Act, S 3331, 75th Cong., 3d Sess. (1938) (containing more ambitious policies but rejected by the House), with Reorganization Act of 1939, Pub. L. No. 76-19, 53 Stat 561 (containing less ambitious policies, including a two-house veto).

44. See Polenberg, *Reorganizing Roosevelt's Government*, 188.

45. *Id.*

46. For a discussion of the principled rationales the president sought to deploy to bolster the case for reorganization, see Short, *Adjusting the Departmental System*, 50–52 (describing the various suggestions for reorganization from the Brookings Institution, hired by the Senate, and the president's committee). Regarding the president's masterful performance, see Polenberg, *Reorganizing Roosevelt's Government*, 188 (elaborating on the success of Roosevelt in reorganizing the government even with earlier failure).

47. Polenberg, *Reorganizing Roosevelt's Government*, 185–88.

48. See Louis Brownlow, *A General View*, 105.

49. See Polenberg, *Reorganizing Roosevelt's Government*, 150–54 (describing the public's growing disapproval of the reorganization plan).

50. See generally Banks and Sobel, *Equilibrium Selection in Signaling Games* (explaining game theoretic accounts of signaling).

51. See Polenberg, *Reorganizing Roosevelt's Government*, 50–66.

52. *Id.*, 90–93. See also *Committee Set Up on Reorganization* (describing the appointment of a special House committee to handle the reorganization plan and summarizing a policy statement by the U.S. Chamber of Commerce expressing concern that independent commissions might cease to be independent if they were placed under executive control).

53. See *Humphrey's Executor*, 295 U.S. at 629–30.

54. See Polenberg, *Reorganizing Roosevelt's Government*, 80–81.

55. *Id.*, 83–84.

56. *Id.*, 81–83; Mansfield, *Federal Executive Reorganization*, 333–34.

57. See Polenberg, *Reorganizing Roosevelt's Government*, 164–66.

58. See Leuchtenburg, *Franklin D. Roosevelt and the New Deal*, 277 (asserting that the organizations that had opposed Roosevelt's court-packing plan "stamped reorganization as yet another attempt . . . to subvert democratic institutions").

59. See Polenberg, *Reorganizing Roosevelt's Government*, 167 (describing how some of Roosevelt's supporters in the House voted against the bill because they could not obtain formal exemptions for their "pet agencies").

60. Leuchtenburg, *Franklin D. Roosevelt and the New Deal*, 278.

61. *Id.*, 277–80 (discussing the fear of Roosevelt's despotism and the eventual death of the 1938 bill).

62. See Polenberg, *Reorganizing Roosevelt's Government*, 181–88.

63. *Id.*, 185.

64. See Teton, *Reorganization Revisited*, 583–84 (detailing how the New Deal–inspired Chandler Act authorized the SEC to intervene in bankruptcy proceedings before a judge and to render advisory opinions on reorganization plans); Rosenberg, *Reorganization Yesterday, Today, Tomorrow*, 131 (arguing that federal regulation or reorganization is unsurprising given the growth of state regulation over other areas of the economy).

65. See Reorganization Act of 1939 § 4, 53 Stat. at 562; 3 U.S.C. § 45a (1946); 31 U.S.C. § 2 (1941); 5 U.S.C. §§ 133–133r, 133t (1941).

66. *Id.* § 9, 53 Stat. at 563 (requiring that all appropriations not expended when an agency function is abolished be "impounded and returned to the Treasury").

67. Consider *Clinton v. New York*, 524 U.S. 417 (1998) (concluding that the line-item veto unduly and problematically enhanced executive power).

68. See Reorganization Act of 1939 § 4(d)(3), 53 Stat. at 562.

69. *Id.* § 10, 53 Stat. at 563.

70. The White House would have to argue that the funds for new employees were being expended for the same broad purpose that Congress had already approved through the appropriations process. But the bill's creation of presidential authority to allocate legal powers across bureaucratic entities (including new ones), coupled with its clear authority to lay off employees, implied some ability to reallocate funds to pay for new officials overseeing the work of newly reorganized bureaus.

71. See Polenberg, *Reorganizing Roosevelt's Government*, 185 (describing how the 1939 act authorized the president only to suggest plans of reorganization subject to a veto by a majority of both houses and to appoint six administrative assistants); Millett and Rogers, *The Legislative Veto and the Reorganization Act of 1939*, 177–78 (suggesting that the two-house veto in the 1939 act strikes a "new balance" between the executive and legislative branches over the organization of federal agencies).

72. Reorganization Act of 1939 § 1(a), 53 Stat. at 561 (circumscribing the president's reorganization authority to plans that achieve five efficiency-related purposes).

73. *Id.* § 4(e), 53 Stat. at 562.

74. *Id.* § 3(b), 53 Stat at 561.

75. *Id.* § 3(a), 53 Stat at 561.

76. *Id.* § 3(d)–(f), 53 Stat at 562.

77. *Id.* § 5, 53 Stat. at 562–63.

78. Roosevelt, *Message of the President*, 246 ("These measures have all had only one supreme purpose—to make democracy work—to strengthen the arms of democracy in peace or war and to ensure the solid blessings of free government to our people in increasing measure").

79. The procession of bureaus and functions added to the agency is described in the organizational charts the FSA prepared for congressional staff. See Federal Security Agency, *Organizational Charts and Budgets, FY 1952* (1952), National Archives, Organizational Charts, Federal Security Agency, Entry 9, Box 2 (chronicling the development of the FSA and prominently emphasizing its wartime activities).

80. See Miles, *The Department of Health, Education, and Welfare*, 19 (discussing use of the term "security" and how it was considered more acceptable to Vice President John Garner, and noting that it foreshadowed key structural decisions that affected the trajectory of the agency as a result of its involvement in defense-related pursuits). Regarding the structure of the agency itself, see *United States Government Manual, Fall 1942*, 581. With respect to the reorganization, see Roosevelt, *Message of the President*, 251–54.

81. See *Proposed Interdepartmental Transfers* (by department) (Apr. 14, 1939); available at Franklin D. Roosevelt Presidential Library, President's Committee on Administrative Management, Correspondence and Papers, Reorganization (1939), folder on Interdepartmental Transfers, Box 24 (summarizing efforts to transfer the Food and Drug Administration and noting responses).

82. Regarding McNutt's appointment, see Blake, *Paul V. McNutt: Portrait of a Hoosier Statesman*, 227–28.

83. See, for example, Miles, *The Department of Health, Education, and Welfare*, 18–19.

84. See Cuéllar, Review of *The Political Economies of Criminal Justice*, 960 (discussing Roosevelt's determination to forge crime control into a politically salient issue), reviewing Jonathan Simon, *Governing Through Crime: How the War on Crime Transformed American Democracy and Created a Culture of Fear* (Oxford 2007).

85. For example, in 1937 Roosevelt routinely made references to "security of property and the maintenance of order," "economic security," and "work security" as well as "international security," and the "security of the nation." Roosevelt discussed security in the ensuing years in the context of economic policy, crime control, and national defense. See American Presidency Project, *Results of Keyword Search for "Security" Between 1937 and 1945*; available at http://www.presidency.ucsb.edu/ws/index.php; accessed Apr. 14, 2009).

86. *Id.*

87. Polenberg, *Reorganizing Roosevelt's Government*, 6.

88. Polenberg, *War and Society*, 76–77 (indicating growing public concern about national defense, and a willingness of at least some otherwise conservative members of the legislature to support defense-related activities).

89. See Heinrichs, *Threshold of War*, 3–12. With respect to the use of the term "security," see Miles, *The Department of Health, Education, and Welfare*, 19.

90. Roosevelt, *Message of the President*, 245–46 (introducing the reorganization plan to Congress).

91. Reorganization Act of 1939 § 1(a), 53 Stat. at 561.

92. See Polenberg, *Reorganizing Roosevelt's Government*, 194–95 (discussing FDR's view that there is a strong relation between weak governments and dictatorships). See also Belair, *President Decrees Three Big Offices in Centralizing 21* (characterizing Roosevelt's message regarding the reorganization plan as "[a]pparently anticipating" scheduled remarks by Hitler).

93. See Belair, *President Decrees Three Big Offices in Centralizing 21* (describing how Congress voiced little opposition to Roosevelt's plan, in part because certain sections of it had been "so thoroughly discounted . . . and so well established" that little reason remained to engage in a public fight).

94. See, for example, Manly, *President Puts U.S. Agencies in 3 Supergroups* (diagramming the divisions and agencies, "some of them previously independent," that Roosevelt planned to make "responsible only to him"). The news coverage of the FSA's creation combined with the fact that polling organizations at the time were asking the public about the agency also indicates the relative degree of attention levied on the president's structural choices.

95. *Our Autocratic State*, 15.

96. U.S. Department of Labor, *Memorandum on Proposal to Transfer the US Employment Service to the Social Security Board* (1939); available at Franklin D. Roosevelt Presidential Library, Correspondence and Papers of the President's Committee on Administrative Management, Correspondence and Papers: Reorganization, Reorganization Plan I Folder, Box 24 (emphasis added) (establishing how agency opposition to reorganization created a nontrivial political cost).

97. Miles, *The Department of Health, Education, and Welfare*, 18–21; Polenberg, *Reorganizing Roosevelt's Government*, 188.

98. For an example of press opposition, see *Our Autocratic State*.

99. Manly, *President Puts U.S. Agencies in 3 Supergroups*, 2 (relaying objections to Roosevelt's plan by Rep. John Taber, ranking minority member of the House Appropriations Committee).

CHAPTER 4

1. See *United States Government Manual, October 1939*, 224–45; *United States Government Manual, Fall 1940*, 547; *United States Government Manual, September 1941*, 614; *United States Government Manual, Fall 1942*, 581; *United States Government Manual, Winter 1943–1944*, 420–21; *United States Government Manual, 1945*, 417–19; Federal Security Agency, *First Annual Report of the Federal Security Administrator*, 1–3; Federal Security Agency, *Second Annual Report*, 2–3; Federal Security Agency, *Annual Reports, for the Fiscal Years 1941–1942, 1942–1943*, v–vi; Federal Security Agency, *Annual Report, for the Fiscal Year 1944*, iii.

2. See *United States Government Manual, 1946*, 585; Federal Security Agency, *Annual Report, for the Fiscal Year 1945*, 518–21.

3. See Miles, *The Department of Health, Education, and Welfare*, 22 (discussing how this change was in keeping with the original recommendations of the Brownlow Committee).

4. Regarding changes in the responsibilities of FSA units, see, for example, Dean, *FDA at War*, 472–74.

5. See Swain, *The Rise of a Research Empire*, 1234–36 (discussing how the National Institute of Health increased its budget from $707,000 in 1940 to more than $60 million in 1951).

6. See Miles, *The Department of Health, Education, and Welfare*, 21–24 (summarizing the expansion of the Office of Education's responsibilities and later Truman's reorganization plan for the FSA).

7. Regarding dissolved agencies, see *United States Government Manual, 2001–2002*, 596–652 (2001). See also *Agency Absorbs 8 Bureaus but Boosts Payroll* (describing the transfer of agencies from the abolished Federal Works Agency to the new General Services Agency); Lawrence, *President Merges Housing Agencies*, 24 (discussing Roosevelt's abolition of the Federal Loan Agency and the transfer of its functions to a National Housing Agency and to the Commerce Department); Polenberg, *Reorganizing Roosevelt's Government*, 187 (referring to a Roosevelt administrative associate who wanted the reorganization plan to be "extensive and sweeping"). Regarding the legislature's role, see Morrow, *Congressional Committees*, 14–35. Regarding organized interests, see Polenberg, *War and Society*, 91–92; Francis, *President's Influence Is Slipping as Solons Labor*.

8. See U.S. Census Bureau, *Statistical Abstract of the United States*, 495, table 776. Agency figures were obtained from the 1935 through 1955 editions of the annual *Budget of the United States*.

9. See Miles, *The Department of Health, Education, and Welfare*, 23.

10. *Id.* (noting that as a result of Truman's "ill-starred effort," Ewing became the "chief scapegoat" for vocal critics of the national health insurance plan).

11. *Id.*, 28–29 (describing how Eisenhower's successful transformation of the FSA into the cabinet-level Department of Health, Education, and Welfare brought about this exact media effect).

12. *Id.*, 30 (detailing how the supposedly low-level regulatory responsibilities of HEW, the successor to the FSA, ended up occupying the attention of the department secretary).

13. *Id.*, 23–24 (identifying opposition to national health insurance as the reason why Truman was not able to elevate the FSA to cabinet status); Walz, *Welfare Agency Has Grown Fast* (reporting that Truman's proposal to elevate the FSA to cabinet status drew criticism from those who feared "the infiltration of politics" into medicine and education).

14. See Miles, *The Department of Health, Education, and Welfare*, 25.

15. Walz, *Welfare Agency Has Grown Fast* (emphasis added).

16. *Id.* Inflation-adjusted figures confirm the staggering growth at PHS, as do more scholarly accounts of the growth of the agency's research capacity through the creation of the National Cancer Institute and the modern National Institutes of Health. See, for example, Swain, *The Rise of a Research Empire.*

17. Miles, *Truman Undecided, May Again Ask Agency Bill*, 18 (reporting that a coalition of Republicans and Southern Democrats handed Truman "one of his severest setbacks of the session" when they disapproved of his plan to create a cabinet-level agency).

18. Lewis, *Presidents and the Politics of Agency Design*, 123–27 (providing empirical research to support his claim).

19. See Miles, *The Department of Health, Education, and Welfare*, 168.

20. Quadagno, *One Nation, Uninsured*, 30.

21. See, for example, *Truman Seeks Rise in Nation's Health*, 21 (describing Truman's request that Ewing study "feasible goals" to improve the health of Americans).

22. See, for example, Leviero, *Eisenhower Offers Plan to Give FSA Status in Cabinet.*

23. Consider President Harry S. Truman, *State of the Union Address*, 6 ("Our domestic programs are the foundation of our foreign policy. The world today looks to us for leadership because we have so largely realized, within our borders, those benefits of democracy for which most of the peoples of the world are yearning").

24. See generally Fuchs, *Oral history interview with Oscar R. Ewing.*

25. See Swain, *The Rise of a Research Empire*, 1235–36 (discussing the expansion of the National Institutes of Health in the postwar years).

26. See Fuchs, *Oral history interview with Oscar R. Ewing*, 6–27 (providing a behind-the-scenes look at Truman's abortive attempt to create a national health insurance program). See also Quadagno, *One Nation, Uninsured*, 27 (explaining that health care was a special concern of Truman's because "[a]s a county judge, Truman had 'been troubled by seeing so many sick people unable to get the care they need . . . because they had no money'"), quoting Truman, *Memoirs*, 2:19.

27. See Kerr, *Civil Defense in the U.S.*, 13 (suggesting that the isolationist sentiment that led Americans to ignore civil defense during the interwar period began to recede with the outbreak of war in Europe and the May 1940 proclamation of a state of emergency).

28. Federal Security Agency, *First Annual Report of the Federal Security Administrator*, 7–8 (highlighting the FSA's major defense programs: (1) selection and placement of defense workers and (2) vocational training for defense workers).

29. See Federal Security Agency, *Annual Report, for the Fiscal Year 1944*, ix (estimating that 1.5 million professional and technical workers were enrolled in college-level training for war industries, which was "particularly significant . . . in view of the rapidly developing advances in mechanized warfare").

30. Kerr, *Civil Defense in the U.S.*, 17 (explaining how LaGuardia placed a major emphasis on the "protection aspects" of civil defense and downplayed programs such as physical fitness, welfare, nutrition, child care, housing, and consumer advice).

31. See National Security Resources Board, *Materials for Use in NSRB Program Development* (identifying the general orders that provided the NSRB with its authority). The FSA and its bureaus are mentioned twenty-one times as integral to national defense–related functions. Some of its key roles include providing inventory of health manpower resources, providing estimates of wartime needs for health manpower, planning for the distribution and safety of food during wartime, administering a communicable disease control program, and assessing health needs following civilian wartime disasters.

32. See Poen, *Harry S. Truman Versus the Medical Lobby*, 140–41 (discussing how the

creation of the National Health Service in Great Britain and Truman's push for a national health insurance plan domestically led to unprecedented public interest in national health insurance, including critical coverage by newsweeklies and radio talk shows).

33. *Id.*, 141 n.2 (listing articles linking Truman's plan to "socialized medicine").

34. *Id.*, 140–41, 148.

35. Ewing, *More Security for You, Am. Mag.* 1, 2 (Jan. 1949), Harry S. Truman Presidential Library, Papers of Oscar R. Ewing, Federal Security Agency, Speeches and Articles, 1948–1949, Box 38.

36. *Id.*, 1 (emphasis added).

37. *Id.*, 3 (emphasis added) (arguing that this "security" is a result of the vigilance of the Food and Drug Administration).

38. *Id.*, 4 (presenting the "security" enhancements provided by welfare policy as a bulwark against Communism).

39. See Statement of Oscar R. Ewing, Federal Security Administrator, aboard SS *La-Guardia* (Jan. 17, 1950) (concluding that while Western European states "abhor communism," they realize that to stop it they must protect their citizens from "penniless old age, unemployment, disability, and disease").

40. Statement of Oscar R. Ewing, Federal Security Administrator, before the House Select Committee to Investigate Lobbying Activities (July 28, 1950) (responding to congressional accusations that the trip was designed to circumvent limits on lobbying by emphasizing the civil defense work of the FSA).

41. See Quadagno, *One Nation, Uninsured,* 30–32 (describing the Republicans' "aggressive probe" into Truman's efforts to expand the welfare state and their successful efforts to paint Truman's supporters as associates of known Communists).

42. See Leviero, *Eisenhower Offers Plan to Give FSA Cabinet Status.* With a Republican Congress, Eisenhower achieved cabinet status for the agency with almost no opposition.

43. Linton, *Federal Facts and Fancies,* 191 (encouraging the efforts of FDA employees to assist the war effort during World War II).

44. See, for example, *United States Government Manual, Winter 1943–1944,* 102–4 (explaining the responsibilities of the War Manpower Commission and listing the domestic agencies that had been ordered to cooperate with it).

45. See, for example, Federal Security Agency, *Annual Reports, for the Fiscal Years 1941–1942, 1942–1943,* v (highlighting the emergency measures taken by the FSA to "meet wartime threats to [the] foundations [of democracy]").

46. Regarding the connection between war and the growth of the state generally, see Tilly, *European Revolutions,* 31–32 (aphoristically developing the idea that war makes the state). Tilly's account suggests that Roosevelt's strategy for mixing references to national and economic security was not without precedent, but it does not entirely explain the political or legal consequences of the reorganization itself.

47. See Federal Security Agency, *Annual Reports, for the Fiscal Years 1941–1942, 1942–1943,* 40.

48. *Id.*, 18.

49. *Id.*, 50–53.

50. Dean, *FDA at War,* 472–74.

51. Federal Security Agency, *Annual Reports, for the Fiscal Years 1941–1942, 1942–1943,* 8 (listing, among research requested by the Army and Navy, efforts to procure more plasma, vaccines for various tropical diseases, military aviation, and nutrition).

52. See letter from George W. Merck, Director, War Research Service, to Lt. Col. Ches-

ter W. Goble, State Director, Selective Service System (May 1, 1944), National Archives, War Research Service Files, Entry 5A, Box 12, for an explanation of the secret status of the War Research Service.

53. Federal Security Agency, *Annual Reports, for the Fiscal Years 1941–1942, 1942–1943*, 58 (describing the Office of Community War Services as "a correlating center for health and welfare activities both within the [FSA] and in other . . . organizations").

54. Regarding the FSA's role in relocating Japanese Americans, see Thomas, *Some Social Aspects of Japanese-American Demography*, 474; *Alien Enemies and Japanese-Americans*. The FSA's role in the saga of Japanese American relocation and internment underscores not only the agency's considerable defense-related functions but also the darker, potentially coercive dimension of an expansive federal capacity. See Polenberg, *War and Society*, 83. Nonetheless, it should be noted that the FSA's role in the internment episode overall was limited compared to that of entities such as the War Relocation Authority. Indeed, the fact that the FSA was not more heavily involved in the program may reflect the Roosevelt administration's reluctance to assign a publicly controversial task to a relatively young agency harboring some of the administrative functions that were of greatest concern to the president. For a discussion of the administration's difficulty in finding a suitable bureaucratic unit to handle internment, see Kashima, *Judgment Without Trial*, 33–34.

55. See Federal Security Agency, *First Annual Report of the Federal Security Administrator*, 7 (describing the FSA's cooperation with the Advisory Commission to the Council of National Defense); Federal Security Agency, *Second Annual Report*, 14 (discussing tensions between defense emergencies and "the drive toward [domestic] security"); Federal Security Agency, *Annual Reports, for the Fiscal Years 1941–1942, 1942–1943*, 1 (explaining how the FSA's activities changed between 1941 and 1943 in line with the "rapidly changing conditions" created by World War II); Federal Security Agency, *Annual Report, for the Fiscal Year 1944*, vii (arguing that concepts and organizations developed during wartime should be retained and expanded during peacetime). See also Dean, *FDA at War*, 470–72 (discussing the FDA's changing responsibilities as the United States mobilized for war); Swain, *The Rise of a Research Empire*, 1235 (discussing the research activities of the PHS and NIH during wartime); Memorandum from Charles P. Taft to Paul V. McNutt, *Admiral McIntire's Testimony Before the Subcommittee of the Committee on Appropriations* (July 15, 1941) (criticizing a Navy admiral's failure to acknowledge to Congress that the National Institute of Health was engaged in experiments to improve high-altitude military flights).

56. FSA-WMC Victory Council, *Meeting Agenda for July 17, 1945*.

57. See Memorandum from Federal Security Agency, Social Security Board, Bureau of Employment Security, to All State Employment Security Agencies (Oct. 18, 1940).

58. See letter from J. M. Studebaker, Commissioner, Office of Education, to Paul V. McNutt, Administrator, Federal Security Agency, Re: War Department and Office of Education Record Cards Report (Feb. 12, 1940); available at National Archives, Federal Security Agency, Classification File, Entry 1, Folder 26, Box 21.

59. Internal White House Memorandum, *Summary of Discussion with Director, Bureau of the Budget* (circa Sept. 30, 1940, original correspondence Sept. 1, 1940 (emphasizing the role of social assistance in strengthening the war effort by providing for families of those in the armed forces).

60. Internal White House Memorandum, *Summary of Correspondence from Paul V. McNutt, Administrator, Federal Security Administration* [sic] (circa Aug. 14, 1940, original correspondence July 30, 1940) (seeking Roosevelt's help in making public statements emphasizing how higher education contributes to national defense).

61. *Id.*

62. *Id.* (paraphrasing Roosevelt's Aug. 14, 1940, reply).

63. See *Geneva Protocol.*

64. See Federal Security Agency, *Annual Reports, for the Fiscal Years 1941–1942, 1942–1943*, 1 (explaining that the president had delegated to the FSA responsibility for administering $5.9 million of the fund).

65. Consider *United States Government Manual, Fall 1942*, 581 (displaying an organizational chart indicating that the office of the FSA administrator had a wide degree of autonomy).

66. See letter from Paul V. McNutt to President Roosevelt (Sept. 4, 1942); available at Franklin D. Roosevelt Presidential Library, Federal Security Agency, 1942(1945 Folder, Official File 3700.

67. *Id.* See also letter from George W. Merck, Director, War Research Service, to Lt. Col. Chester W. Goble, State Director, Selective Service System (May 1, 1944); available at National Archives, War Research Service Files, Entry 5A, Box 12. There, Merck explains to a military official the basic outline of the program in order to arrange for a deferment for scientists working on the weapons projects administered by the FSA:

There has been established in the Office of the Administrator of the Federal Security Agency, by verbal Presidential directive, a unit known as the War Research Service. All activities relating to the work of the War Research Service have been classified by the Secretary of War as SECRET. The work is largely research and is carried out in collaboration with a small selected group of highly specialized scientists in universities throughout the country working under Federal Security Agency contracts.

68. See, for example, Memorandum from President Roosevelt to the Federal Security Administrator, U.S. Naval Communications Service (Mar. 28, 1941) (with attachments approving preparations for a public conference emphasizing the connection between nutrition and national defense); available at Franklin D. Roosevelt Presidential Library, President's Secretary's Files, Federal Security Agency, Box 134.

69. See *United States Government Manual, 1948*, 575 (displaying an organization chart that locates the National Security Council and the National Security Resources Board within the Executive Office of the President); Kerr, *Civil Defense in the U.S.*, 27–30 (discussing the Federal Civil Defense Act of 1950 and the creation of the Federal Civil Defense Administration).

70. See National Archives and Records Service, General Services Administration, *United States Government Organization Manual, 1950–1951*, 336.

71. See National Security Resources Board, *Materials for Use in NSRB Program Development: Preliminary Draft* (listing the key national defense–related roles of the FSA).

72. See, for example, Truman, *State of the Union Address*, 6 (presenting to Congress key elements of the Fair Deal).

CHAPTER 5

1. Polenberg, *War and Society*, 83.

2. Belair, *President Decrees Three Big Offices in Centralizing* 21.

3. See Smith, *FDR*, 101.

4. *Id.*, 102–3 (explaining that congressional opposition prevented the Navy Department from reorganizing its inefficient "quasi-independent bureaus" that had been designed in the "age of sail").

5. *Id.*, 103.

6. *Id.* (quoting Roosevelt as saying, "I get my fingers into just about everything and there's no law against it").

7. Some secular decline in political support is possible, but the decision to shed marginal members and reorient the Democratic Party toward the Northeast and activist government was probably more important. See Polenberg, *Reorganizing Roosevelt's Government*, 183–84 (describing Roosevelt's decision to "purge" the Democratic Party of conservatives); McCubbins, Noll, and Weingast ("McNollgast"), *The Political Origins of the Administrative Procedure Act*, 190–91 (explaining how, at the time of the Roosevelt administration and in succeeding years, civil rights issues split the Democratic Party into a New Deal wing and a Southern element that formed coalitions with Republicans).

8. See Polenberg, *Reorganizing Roosevelt's Government*, 184 (noting that despite Republican gains in Congress, the Reorganization Bill of 1939 passed "with little difficulty").

9. See Sundquist, *Dynamics of the Party System*, 215 (discussing the growing political power of opponents to the New Deal).

10. The existing literature on "policy insulation" seems to ignore the possibility that politicians' desire to create ultimate, long-term autonomy in bureaus might lead them to desire *more*, not *less* control in the short term to establish the conditions that increase the probability of bureau autonomy in the longer run (among others, these would likely include a constituency of public supporters, a more favorable portfolio of missions, actual or perceived technical competence, and a preferred position in the interagency process). Because short-term control could actually strengthen longer-term autonomy, politicians would face a host of interesting strategic problems in seeking to calibrate the timing of control. In a democratic system involving a measure of uncertainty over *who* will wield control in the long run, policymakers might ideally seek to secure enough control to shape the architecture of public programs in the long term without allowing the residual amount of control they secure to be used by subsequent politicians desirous of reengineering the federal bureaucracy.

11. See Smith, *FDR*, 411 (describing how FDR "encouraged and exploited" speculation that he might run for a third term, and suggesting that in all likelihood he had not made up his mind).

12. See Derthick, *Policymaking for Social Security*, 264.

13. *Id.*, 263–64.

14. See Polenberg, *Reorganizing Roosevelt's Government*, 82, and Cuéllar, *"Securing" the Nation*, 593 n.15, 621 n.126.

15. See Leuchtenburg, *Franklin D. Roosevelt and the New Deal*, 132.

16. *Id.*

17. See Miles, *The Department of Health, Education, and Welfare*, 15 (discussing the range of grant programs transferred to the FSA and the requirement for the state-level merit systems that contributed to the unraveling of patronage-based control of relief funds).

18. See Wright, *The Political Economy of New Deal Spending*, 38 (suggesting that "Roosevelt might well have lost the election" without the support of those who received federal employment as a result of his policies).

19. See Internal White House Memorandum (Aug. 11, 1939); available at Franklin D. Roosevelt Presidential Library, Federal Security Agency, 1939 Folder, Official File 3700. See also Miles, *The Department of Health, Education, and Welfare*, 15 (discussing the range of grant programs transferred to the FSA and the requirement for the state-level merit systems that contributed to the unraveling of patronage-based control of administrative activity). For analyses of the political rationales affecting the allocation of grant funds, see Wallis,

Employment, Politics, and Economic Recovery During the Great Depression, 519 (arguing that Wright's model overstated the impact of politics and that New Deal administrators targeted spending at states with lower employment levels); Wright, *The Political Economy of New Deal Spending*, 33 (finding that a political model of New Deal spending explains between 59 and 80 percent of the variance in per capita spending from 1933 to 1940).

20. See Jackson, *Food and Drug Legislation in the New Deal*, 192 (describing the legal burden that the Food, Drug, and Cosmetic Act's judicial review provisions placed on the FDA); Dean, *FDA at War*, 458–59 (showing the growth in FDA appropriations and staffing after enactment of the Food, Drug, and Cosmetic Act).

21. See Zegart, *Flawed by Design*, 70–71.

22. See, for example, *id.*, 16.

23. See Cohen, Cuéllar, and Weingast, *Crisis Bureaucracy*, 706–7.

24. See Polenberg, *Reorganizing Roosevelt's Government*, 80–81 (describing how veterans' organizations, through "a steady salvo of letters to Washington," were able to force Roosevelt to promise not to transfer the Veterans Administration).

25. See Cohen, Cuéllar, and Weingast, *Crisis Bureaucracy*, 706–7; Zegart, *Flawed by Design*, 16 (discussing presidential incentives for enhanced functioning of bureaucratic activities that are likely to be valued by national political constituencies). But see generally Nzelibe, *The Fable of the Nationalist President and the Parochial Congress* (questioning the presumption that presidents have unwavering incentives to focus on nationwide policy concerns while Congress focuses on parochial concerns). While Nzelibe may be right that some plausible scenarios involve presidential parochialism and congressional concern with nationwide policy implications, the White House is still likely to care about broad public opinion more than the relevant lawmakers (such as the median lawmaker, the leadership of relevant committees serving as vetogates, or the pivotal lawmaker in an enacting coalition). First, lawmakers delegate some measure of authority to committees that can be made up of preference outliers. See, for example, Londregan and Snyder, *Comparing Committee and Floor Preferences*, 168 (finding that one-third of committees in the House of Representatives from 1951 to 1984 were preference outliers when compared to the entire House). Thus, the members of the House Judiciary Subcommittee on Immigration are likely to come from districts that care more about immigration policy than the typical lawmaker does. Second, the White House's ability to command attention from the general public more easily than even the most powerful lawmakers is likely to make support from the mass electorate a more realistic counterweight to concentrated regional, sectoral, or economic interests in presidential deliberations. Third, even controlling for scale and acknowledging some presidential focus on competitive states with large concentrations of electoral votes, the relevant constituencies for the president tend to be more diverse (with a greater mix of offsetting concentrated interests) than those of the typical legislative jurisdiction.

26. See Cuéllar, *"Securing" the Nation*, 621 n.126 for an overview of the changes in the *United States Government Manual* during this time period.

27. See Walcott and Hult, *Governing the White House*, 101.

28. Federal Security Agency, *Employment Position Classification Sheet* (circa 1943).

29. See Polenberg, *Reorganizing Roosevelt's Government*, 81–82.

30. See Quadagno, *One Nation, Uninsured*, 30 (recounting how after Ewing convened a National Health Assembly, which did not endorse national health care, he released his own analysis that did).

31. See U.S. Census Bureau, *Statistical Abstract of the United States 2003: Mini-Historical*

Statistics 94, table HS-50 (detailing year-by-year executive branch employment numbers from 1901 through 2002, for the Department of Defense, civilian agencies, and the Post Office).

32. See 42 U.S.C. § 901.

33. See Walcott and Hult, *Governing the White House*, 101 (explaining how Roosevelt used the administrative assistant posts provided for by the Reorganization Act of 1939 to create new oversight mechanisms of executive branch agencies). See also Dickinson, *Bitter Harvest*, 112–13 (characterizing Roosevelt's administrative response to the growth in government programs as "a small White House Office supported by a vastly expanded institutional staff"). For a discussion of Roosevelt's initiatives to limit the SSB, see Cuéllar, *"Securing" the Nation*, 600–614.

34. See Federal Security Agency, *Organizational Charts FY 1952* (presenting the lines of reporting and authority within the FSA).

35. See Walcott and Hult, *Governing the White House*, 78–79 (providing a summary of Roosevelt's efforts to create an executive branch composed largely of New Dealers).

36. Internal White House Memorandum, *Summary of Correspondence from Dr. H. A. Morgan, Chairman of the Board, Tennessee Valley Authority* (Sept. 23, 1939) (indicating Roosevelt's interest in relieving pressure arising from the scarcity of time and staff); available at Franklin D. Roosevelt Presidential Library, Federal Security Agency, 1939 Folder, Official File 3700.

37. *White House Memorandum on Administrative Organization: General Recommendations* (1939); available at Franklin D. Roosevelt Presidential Library, Papers of John Winant, Box 157.

38. An article published in 1944 provides one of several examples of Louis Brownlow's continuing campaign to promote the wisdom of the reorganization with which he was so intimately involved:

In our own country the administrative success has been the greatest of all. . . . There were the indignant protests of those who believed that if this were not changed, or if that were not done, or if t'other were not stopped, the war was lost. Military men saw too much civilian interference, civilians too much military control. Industrialists feared the coddling of labor; labor feared the coddling of industry; farmers feared they were being neglected; and everybody else had his fears, too. Experts in every specialty wrung their hands as they saw their particular prescriptions seemingly tampered with by amateurs. Nobody was satisfied. Yet, despite all this (maybe because of all this), the success was achieved.

Brownlow, *Reconversion of the Federal Administrative Machinery from War to Peace*, 309. Brownlow also argued that the reorganization plan that led to the creation of the FSA would make it easier to "reconvert" federal activities to peacetime challenges after the war. *Id.*, 313.

39. Internal White House Memorandum, *Reorganization* (Apr. 16, 1939) (emphasis added).

40. See Smith, *FDR*, 102 n.13 (quoting the assistant secretary of the Navy seeking reforms to make bureau chiefs more directly responsible to the central Department of the Navy bureaucracy).

41. Internal White House Memorandum, *Reorganization* (emphasis added).

42. Official Verbatim Transcript of Statement of Oscar Ewing Before the House Select Committee on Lobbying Activities (Bureau of National Affairs, July 28, 1950) (responding to questions from lawmakers about the relationship between a senior federal agency administrator and the president).

43. Telegram from Stephen Early, Secretary to the President, to the Honorable Paul McNutt, Federal Security Administrator (Oct. 10, 1939); available at Franklin D. Roosevelt

Presidential Library, Federal Security Agency, 1939 Folder, Official File 3700 (relaying to McNutt an invitation from the governor of Nebraska to give a political advocacy speech).

44. See Bureau of the Budget Staff, *Recommendations for Interdepartmental Transfer* (Apr. 24, 1939) (recommending the transfer of certain independent agencies into the White House reporting structure); available at Franklin D. Roosevelt Presidential Library, President's Committee on Administrative Management, Correspondence and Papers, Reorganization (1939), Folder on Interdepartmental Transfer, Box 24. See also Internal White House Memorandum, *Other Reorganization Proposals*, circa Apr. 1939); available at Franklin D. Roosevelt Presidential Library, President's Committee on Administrative Management, Correspondence and Papers, Reorganization (1939), Folder on Interdepartmental Transfer, Box 24 (indicating the president's decision to have some agencies transferred after the FSA's first year of operations).

45. See generally Kagan, *Presidential Administration*.

46. *Id.*, 2274–75.

47. *Id.*, 2284–303.

48. *Id.*, 2311–15.

49. *Id.*, 2274 (discussing the "incipient efforts" of Roosevelt and Truman to exercise control over the federal bureaucracy).

50. See Polenberg, *Reorganizing Roosevelt's Government*, 82.

51. See Jackson, *Food and Drug Legislation in the New Deal*, 181–82 (describing a letter written to the president by Agriculture Secretary Wallace in which he stated that he would recommend veto of the reorganization plan if it was not amended).

52. See Polenberg, *Reorganizing Roosevelt's Government*, 82; Dean, *FDA at War*, 456.

53. See Internal White House Memorandum, *Reorganization*.

54. Letter from George B. Merck to Paul V. McNutt, Federal Security Administrator (Apr. 11, 1944); available at National Archives, War Research Service Files, Entry 5A, Box 11.

55. Merck, *Speech on the Implications of Biological Warfare*, 3–4 (May 17, 1946).

56. See *Geneva Protocol* for a discussion of the relevant treaty commitments.

57. See letter from George B. Merck (recognizing that McNutt, as FSA administrator, "must be considering some decision" as to what elements of the biological warfare program should be transferred to the War Department).

58. *Id.* (noting Merck's understanding that the War Research Service was placed in the FSA "at first primarily as a political cover for [biological weapons] activities").

59. *Id.*

60. Merck, *Speech on the Implications of Biological Warfare*, 3–4.

61. See Blake, *Paul V. McNutt*, xi–xii.

62. *Id.*, 227–92 (discussing the efforts of McNutt's enemies, most notably Postmaster General Farley, to derail McNutt's chances for the presidential or vice presidential nomination).

63. *Id.*, 173 (explaining how McNutt's presidential aspirations influenced his decision to accept the appointment as high commissioner of the Philippines).

64. *Id.*, 238, quoting Kidney, *Hoosiers in Washington*.

65. *Has the Wily Mr. McNutt of Indiana Been "Taken In" by Wilier Mr. Roosevelt?*

66. See Blake, *Paul V. McNutt*, 230 (relating how MacArthur told McNutt that the position would improve McNutt's position with the New Dealers yet maintain the "support of those who recognize the conservative caution of [McNutt's] liberalism"). Despite the aforementioned risks, from McNutt's perspective the FSA post may nonetheless have appeared as a fine perch from which to mount a presidential campaign if Roosevelt chose not to run. If the president did choose to pursue a third term, McNutt seemed to think that

the FSA would be a suitable vehicle for his work while furnishing him a chance to compete for the vice presidency.

67. See Luban, *On the Commander in Chief Power*, 534–35 (discussing various examples of military leaders inserting themselves into political or policy debates that would traditionally be decided by the commander in chief or Congress).

68. See Cuéllar, *"Securing" the Nation*, 610–13 nn.82–103 for a discussion of the changes in reorganization legislative proposals between 1938 and 1939.

69. *Id.*, 610–11 nn.82–87.

70. *Id.*, 613 nn.98–103.

71. *Id.*, 613 n.100.

72. See Polenberg, *Reorganizing Roosevelt's Government*, 186. See also Leuchtenburg, *Franklin D. Roosevelt and the New Deal*, 271–74 (describing how the 1938 elections strengthened a "Republican-conservative Democratic coalition" that began "aggressively to dismantle the New Deal").

73. See Internal White House Memorandum, *Other Reorganization Proposals* (explaining that Roosevelt's "[p]encil notes indicate . . . action" on the proposals presented by the Bureau of the Budget Staff).

74. See Bureau of the Budget Staff, *Recommendations for Interdepartmental Transfers* (identifying, by cabinet agency, bureaus for Roosevelt to transfer).

75. Given these details, the burden should be on those emphasizing congressional dominance or shared responsibility to further document the extent to which the legislature anticipated and stage-managed a process that seems now, even upon close inspection, to have been centrally forged by a White House that sought and gained sufficient legislative support for its own goals. For an interesting discussion emphasizing the centrality of the legislative role, see Weingast, *Bureaucratic Discretion or Congressional Control?* 771–74 (1983).

CHAPTER 6

1. Some discussions of framing effects involve perceptions of utility associated with gains and losses, and they have been extensively analyzed in the context of individual decision making. Myriad articles discuss framing effects in the cognitive, prospect-theory sense. The seminal work is Daniel Kahneman and Amos Tversky, *Prospect Theory: An Analysis of Decisions Under Risk* (developing a model for how people use "reference points" to make decisions and how a shift in this reference point can influence behavior). Other versions of the idea focus on the introduction of new dimensions of political competition to complicate, disrupt, and potentially realign existing coalitions. See Riker, *The Art of Political Manipulation*, 10–17 (discussing the effect of introducing new configurations into political battles).

2. Davis, *FDR*, 423 (explaining that Hitler's invasion of the Czech Republic in violation of the Munich Agreement was a watershed event in Roosevelt's mind).

3. *Id.*, 429.

4. *Id.*, 427 (discussing Senator Key Pittman's abortive introduction of a "neutrality bill" that responded to Roosevelt's concerns regarding Hitler's actions).

5. See Cuéllar, *"Securing" the Nation*, 630–37 for greater detail on the FSA's war-related programs.

6. Address by the Honorable Paul V. McNutt, Federal Security Administrator, to Congress on Education for Democracy, Florida Southern College, Lakeland, Fla., 3 (Nov. 12, 1939, available at Franklin D. Roosevelt Presidential Library, Papers of Richard V. Gilbert, Speeches on the Federal Security Agency by Paul V. McNutt, Box 18, emphasis added) (stressing the analogy between ordinary war and the domestic fight against "insecurity and want").

7. See, for example, *id.*

8. Letter from Franklin P. Cole, Minister of Williston Congregational Church, to President Roosevelt (Jan. 13, 1940); available at Franklin D. Roosevelt Presidential Library, Federal Security Agency, 1940 Folder, Official File 3700 (protesting McNutt's emphasis on the need for war-related preparation and the work of the FSA in promoting this).

9. Internal White House Memorandum, *Summary of Correspondence from Lowell Mellett* (circa June 12, 1940, original correspondence June 5, 1940; available at Franklin D. Roosevelt Presidential Library, Federal Security Agency, 1940 Folder, Official File 3700) (paraphrasing the president's message to a civil society event, and demonstrating McNutt's involvement in helping to craft a message from the president emphasizing the role of the FSA in defense).

10. Regarding Roosevelt's analogies to war, see Leuchtenburg, *The FDR Years*, 46–54 (showing just how deeply the theme of war was enmeshed in FDR's 1932 presidential campaign).

11. With respect to the FSA's priorities, see Federal Security Agency, *First Annual Report of the Federal Security Administrator*, 7; Federal Security Agency, *Second Annual Report*, 1; Federal Security Agency, *Annual Reports for the Fiscal Years 1941–1942, 1942–1943*, v–vi; Federal Security Agency, *Annual Report for the Fiscal Year 1944*; Federal Security Agency, *Annual Report of the Federal Security Agency for the Fiscal Year 1945*, 1–10, 184–88, 464–66; Federal Security Agency, *Annual Report of the Federal Security Agency, for the Fiscal Year 1946*, 72.

12. See Federal Security Agency, *First Annual Report of the Federal Security Administrator*, 7.

13. *Id.*, 50.

14. *Id.*, 44–47.

15. *Id.*, 47.

16. *Id.*, 7.

17. *Id.*, 7–8 (detailing the rapid expansion of the FSA's war-related institutional capacity).

18. See Cuéllar, *"Securing" the Nation*, 630–37.

19. Federal Security Agency, Community War Services, Agenda and Folder of Reference Material, Conference of Regional Directors and Assistant Regional Directors (Feb. 12, 1944) available at National Archives, Watson Miller Archive, Federal Security Agency, Community War Services Folder, Entry 10, Box 1, 1.

20. See *United States Government Manual 2001–2002*, 597–652 (listing these agencies in an appendix titled "Federal Executive Agencies Terminated, Transferred, or Changed in Name Subsequent to March 4, 1933").

21. NY Times (May 18, 1946); available at National Archives, War Research Service Files, Entry 5A, Box 12 (reporting on Merck's speech at the Westinghouse symposium in Pittsburgh revealing the FSA's wartime biological warfare research program).

22. See Miles, *The Department of Health, Education, and Welfare*, 25–26.

23. Mullan, *Plagues and Politics*, 207.

24. See Miles, *The Department of Health, Education, and Welfare*, 18. See also Chong and Druckman, *Framing Public Opinion in Competitive Democracies*, 638 (analyzing how public opinion in a democracy is affected when "elites" organize their proposals around particular frames of reference).

25. Chong and Druckman, *Framing Public Opinion in Competitive Democracies*, 651.

26. See Polenberg, *War and Society*, 73.

27. See Cuéllar, *"Securing" the Nation*, 600–614, 677–78 nn.330–33.

28. See *id.*, 677–78 nn.330–33 for more on Paul McNutt's travel and lobbying. See

also Paul V. McNutt, "Using Our Heads," 73 (unpublished book manuscript, Apr. 4, 1940) (referring to social security as part of "national security").

29. For detail regarding the FSA's defense-related activities, see, for example, *United States Government Manual, Fall 1942*, 390–92 (presenting organizational charts of the individual agencies and listing war-related bureaus).

30. Distinctions in the type of war-related rhetoric in the agencies' annual reports are apparent from how the reports discuss individual bureau activities, as well as the frequency with which report summaries (providing an overview of agency activities) mention war or national defense. Though all of these agencies were pervasively emphasizing war-related activity by 1943, the FSA's particular interest in these matters is apparent in its more aggressive use of defense-related rhetoric between 1940 and 1942. In fact, the incidence of the terms "war," "conflict," and "defense" per page in the FSA *Annual Report*'s summary was nearly 0.5 in 1940, just under 0.2 in 1941, and about 0.33 in 1942. By comparison, the figures for the Federal Works Agency were 0.25, 0.1, and 0.12 respectively, and were far lower for Interior and Agriculture. See generally Federal Security Agency, *First Annual Report of the Federal Security Administrator*; Federal Security Agency, *Second Annual Report*; Federal Security Agency, *Annual Reports, for the Fiscal Years 1941–1942, 1942–1943*.

31. See Federal Security Agency, *Second Annual Report*, 1. See also Cuéllar, *"Securing" the Nation*, 630–37.

32. See Cuéllar, *"Securing" the Nation*, 620–30.

33. Even when such flexibility is limited, presidential efforts to bolster an agency's standing may in some circumstances benefit from involving an agency in more politically salient activity. Consider, for example, the Roosevelt administration's efforts to persuade the public through public conferences and presidential statements that nutrition and physical education were components of defense and security. See, for example, Cuéllar, *"Securing" the Nation*, 635 n.193. In contrast, the Bush administration sought to persuade legislators and the public that regulatory agencies such as U.S. Customs and the U.S. Coast Guard needed to play a greater role in providing a distinctly narrow conception of national and homeland security—involving primarily protection against terrorist attacks—and that this function *contrasted* with the agencies' legacy mandates. See Cohen, Cuéllar, and Weingast, *Crisis Bureaucracy*, 725–28.

34. See Heinrichs, *Threshold of War*, 11–12.

35. See Derthick, *Policymaking for Social Security*, 134.

36. *Id.*, 263–64. See also Katznelson, *When Affirmative Action Was White*, 22–23, 43–44, 47–48 (pointing out that "the South's [congressional] representatives built ramparts within . . . the New Deal and the Fair Deal to safeguard the region's social organization," in part by excluding "categories of work in which blacks were heavily overrepresented, notably farmworkers and maids").

37. See Derthick, *Policymaking for Social Security*, 296–97 (noting that Roosevelt endorsed disability legislation in his 1942 budget message but did not pursue it due to legislative opposition); Katznelson, *When Affirmative Action Was White*, 22 (explaining that Southerners accomplished their legislative goal of excluding African Americans from Social Security "by making the most of their disproportionate numbers on committees, by their close acquaintance with legislative rules and procedures, and by exploiting the gap between the intensity of their feeling and the relative indifference of their fellow members of Congress").

38. See Polenberg, *War and Society*, 74 (discussing how preparations for defense absorbed the time and energy of a growing number of government officials).

39. See Leuchtenburg, *Franklin D. Roosevelt and the New Deal*, 300 (pointing out

examples of how Congress was aggressively supporting a defense buildup by the middle of 1940). Southern Democrats were increasingly opposed to Roosevelt's social welfare and regulatory agenda. See Polenberg, *War and Society*, 86 (quoting Southern Democrats who believed that some New Deal agencies were controlled by "social gainers, do-gooders, bleeding-hearts and long-hairs . . . [with] screwball ideas"). Yet they were viewed as inclined toward internationalism and concern about national defense in the period immediately before World War II. See DeConde, *The South and Isolationism*, 333; Dabney, *The South Looks Abroad*, 172–74, 177; Jewell, *Evaluating the Decline of Southern Internationalism Through Senatorial Roll Call Votes*, 646 (comparing Southern Democratic senators, who voted in support of Roosevelt's internationally focused fiscal programs 92 percent of the time, with Democratic senators as a whole, who supported these same programs 85 percent of the time).

40. See *House Military Bill Sets Peak for Peace Time* (summarizing a $389 million appropriations bill).

41. *The American Navy*.

42. Editorial, *To Safeguard Defense*.

43. See, for example, *Congress Divided on the Message* (referencing Southern Democratic senators' praise of the president's focus on international security problems); Albright, *Arms to Get Right of Way in Congress* (referencing Republican senators' support of the president's defense-related recommendations). See also Patterson, *A Conservative Coalition Forms in Congress*, 768 n.39 (noting how Southern Democrats overwhelmingly supported the president in a "key vote" in 1939 to "revise the neutrality law").

44. Summarizing an emerging consensus within official Washington, the *New York Times* reported:

The totalitarian states . . . lead the world in immensity of preparations and in volume of expenditures for war, but the United States, slow to "strain every nerve" in the international race for armaments, has speeded up all her preparations recently and the last session of Congress started her on her way toward one of the greatest peace-time national defense outlays in her history.

Baldwin, *Fourteen Billion Dollars a Year*.

45. For an overview of the FSA's defense-related activities, see Cuéllar, *"Securing" the Nation*, 620–30. For a description of the president and the FSA's strategy for using the WRS, see *id.*, 635 n.192.

46. See *id.*, 630–37. See also Memorandum from Charles P. Taft to Paul V. McNutt (criticizing a Navy admiral's failure to acknowledge to Congress that the National Institute of Health was engaged in experiments to improve high-altitude military flights).

47. Federal Security Agency, *Organizational Charts and Budgets, FY 1952*, 1–2 (emphasizing the FSA's wartime activities).

48. Budget information is based on the author's analysis of *Budget of the United States* from 1939 to 1954.

49. See *Budget of the United States, Historical Tables, 1945–1955*. See also Cuéllar, *"Securing" the Nation*, 598–630. Analysis of inflation-adjusted changes in appropriations percentages confirm the significance of these appropriations changes over the long term. Note also that total FSA appropriations and those of the preeminent four bureaus eventually converged almost entirely.

50. See Cuéllar, *"Securing" the Nation*, 634–35 nn.188–92.

51. See Blake, *Paul V. McNutt*, 294–95 (stating that McNutt's service at the FSA, the War Manpower Commission, the War Production Board, and the Economic Stabilization Board gave him a "unique vantage point").

52. See letter from Louis Johnson, Assistant Secretary of War, to Rudolph Forster, the White House (Aug. 17, 1939).

53. *Federal Security Organizational Chart* (Jan. 1, 1953) (showing that the FSA had an "Assistant Administrator for Defense Activities" in 1953 when it was on the verge of becoming the Department of Health, Education, and Welfare).

54. See Cuéllar, *"Securing" the Nation*, 655 n.251 for a description of media coverage.

55. See Carpenter, *Forging of Bureaucratic Autonomy*, 14 (proposing that bureaucratic autonomy, and therefore policy entrepreneurship, requires a bureaucracy to develop unique organizational capacities and build political legitimacy through multiple networks and coalitions).

56. See Cuéllar, *"Securing" the Nation*, 633 n.183.

57. See *id.*, 691–92 nn.371–73.

58. Consider Memorandum to the President from the Administrator, Federal Security Agency (Sept. 18, 1940) (demonstrating cooperation between the FSA and the White House on crafting economic security policy).

59. See Swain, *The Rise of a Research Empire* (estimating that between the creation of the Research Grants Office in the NIH in 1946 and December 1947, the NIH had awarded almost $12 million in grants to external researchers).

60. Federal Security Agency, *Organizational Charts and Budgets, FY 1946*.

61. See Quadagno, *One Nation, Uninsured*, 35.

62. See Miles, *The Department of Health, Education, and Welfare*, 23–24 (suggesting that "considerable separatist inclination on the part of some components of the FSA" combined with opposition to Truman's national health insurance plan doomed both of Truman's attempts to promote the FSA). See also Miles, *Truman Undecided*, 18 (describing how a "coalition of Republicans and Southern Democratic Senators" gave Truman "one of his severest setbacks of the session" by voting against his plan to create a new welfare department).

63. See Derthick, *Policymaking for Social Security*, 28 (noting that the chairman of the SSB wanted to hire the best people in the country).

64. See Swain, *The Rise of a Research Empire*, 1236 (stating the NIH's grant program objective "to encourage the development and to further the training of competent young researchers").

65. See Carpenter, *The Forging of Bureaucratic Autonomy*, 14–33 (discussing the factors that make it possible for agencies to enhance their autonomy).

66. See Hearings on Federal Security Agency Appropriations for 1951 Before the Subcommittee of the House Committee on Appropriations, 81st Cong., 2d Sess. 663 (1950) (testimony of Oscar E. Ewing, Federal Security Administrator).

67. See Morrow, *Congressional Committees*, 241–45 (explaining that government reform proposals may be opposed by congressional committee members "who want to preserve the status quo for personal [and] political reasons").

68. *Id.*, 9 (stating that the Legislative Reorganization Act of 1946 reorganized committees in Congress to match organizational changes in the executive branch).

69. *Id.*, 20–22.

70. *Id.*, 52 (stating that the Legislative Reorganization Act of 1946 provided each committee with an independent research staff to "counter the evolving specialization of the executive branch").

71. Morrow, *Congressional Committees*, 20 (noting how the 1946 reorganization of Congress reduced the number of standing committees in the House and Senate by more than 50 percent).

72. See McCubbins, Noll, and Weingast ("McNollgast"), *Structure and Process, Politics and Policy*, 441–42 (discussing how legislators can use administrative procedures to prevent agencies from carrying out a "fait accompli" that the legislators then find difficult to reverse).

73. See Cohen, Cuéllar, and Weingast, *Crisis Bureaucracy* (noting that the DHS reorganization bill did not address congressional committees and that as late as mid-2004 congressional oversight had yet to change).

74. *Id.*, 690, 695 (describing how Senator Lieberman introduced and aggressively pushed for the reorganization legislation that eventually created DHS).

75. *Id.*, 693–94 (recounting how Speaker of the House Dennis Hastert had to empanel a new committee to move the reorganization legislation forward).

76. *Id.*, 693 (pointing out that the initial congressional supporters of the DHS reorganization were those who "almost certainly stood to gain prestige, power, and influence").

77. *Id.*, 710 (arguing that there is always a large amount of uncertainty about the prescriptive benefits of a reorganization).

78. See *United States Government Manual, Winter 1943–1944*, 317–18, 324, 348–49.

79. See Cuéllar, *"Securing" the Nation*, 620–30.

80. See Polenberg, *War and Society*, 85 ("The agency claimed that by helping marginal farmers purchase land and equipment it boosted crop production").

81. *Id.*, 85–86.

82. *Id.*, 86.

83. See Cuéllar, "'Securing' the Nation," 620–30.

CHAPTER 7

1. For just a few thought-provoking examples of this sprawling genre, see Bressman, *How* Mead *Has Muddled Judicial Review of Agency Action*; Merrill and Hickman, *Chevron's Domain*; Molot, *Reexamining* Marbury *in the Administrative State*; Scalia, *Judicial Deference to Administrative Interpretations of Law*; Sunstein, *Beyond* Marbury: *The Executive's Power to Say What the Law Is*.

2. See, for example, Hult, *Agency Merger and Bureaucratic Redesign* ("Despite the popularity of reorganization, the jury deciding its impact is still out—and is sharply divided").

3. See Arnold, *The Logic of Congressional Action*; Kingdon, *Agendas, Alternatives, and Public Policies*.

4. See Moe and Wilson, *Presidents and the Politics of Structure*, 7–11; Weingast, *Regulation, Reregulation, and Deregulation*, 151.

5. McCubbins, Noll, and Weingast, *Administrative Procedures as Instruments of Political Control*, 254.

6. Zegart, *Flawed by Design*, 140–48 (discussing how the structure of the Joint Staff, through the Goldwater-Nichols reforms, was engineered to be more functional than it had been before).

7. See, for example, Lewis, *Presidents and the Politics of Agency Design* (emphasizing the extent of uncertainty regarding why presidents choose specific designs for agencies and reorganization plans); Wilson, *Bureaucracy*, 264 (discussing the difficulty in assessing the range of motivations for specific reorganization plans because "presidents have taken to reorganizations the way overweight people take to fad diets").

8. Regarding the size and scope of the reorganization that resulted in DHS, see Kettl, *Overview*, 1: "[A]t its inception on March 1, 2003, the DHS brought together twenty-two federal agencies and more than 170,000 employees—the largest restructuring since the creation of the Department of Defense [in 1947]."

9. For a cogent account of the creation of DHS that nonetheless fails to address the questions mentioned in the text, see Kettl, *System Under Stress*. Although Kettl notes that the president shifted his position regarding the creation of DHS, he does not address why the president proposed such a massive reorganization. Nor is his explanation of the president's change in position, which focuses on events such as the testimony of FBI whistleblower Colleen Rowley, entirely convincing (because the president changed positions on the creation of DHS well before Rowley's congressional testimony). *Id.*, 48.

10. For criticisms involving the response of DHS and its bureaus to Katrina, see, for example, Brinkley, *The Great Deluge*, 227–78. For criticisms of DHS, see, for example, Hsu, *DHS Terror Research Agency Struggling*; Lipton and Wald, *Focused on 9/11, U.S. Is Seen to Lag on New Threats*. See also Cohen, Cuéllar, and Weingast, *Crisis Bureaucracy*, 738–43 nn.223–36.

11. See Kettl, *Overview*, 1; see also Cohen, Cuéllar, and Weingast, *Crisis Bureaucracy*, 480–88.

12. See Polenberg, *Reorganizing Roosevelt's Government*; Szanton, *Federal Reorganization*; Zegart, *Flawed by Design*, 140–48. In a related vein, scholars of race, property, education, and economic geography would naturally question the analogous assumption that changes in geographic lines of territorial jurisdiction—where one city or county ends and another begins—are of little consequence. For an insightful discussion of the path-dependent social impact of territorial subdivisions, see Ford, *Law's Territory*.

13. Regarding the impact of structure on organizational culture, see Kreps, *Corporate Culture and Economic Theory*, 109–10; Perrow, *Complex Organizations* (1986). More generally, see Terry M. Moe, *Political Structure of Agencies*. For a review of the political science and political economy literature on the political implications of bureaucratic changes, see Weingast, *Caught in the Middle*, 312.

14. See Mashaw, *Norms, Practices, and the Paradox of Deference*.

15. Existing work in political science, and particularly in the field of positive political theory, provides important insights into how political officials use various ex ante and ex post techniques to control bureaucratic policy implementation, and, in particular, how they use bureaucratic structure to serve their political goals. There is a wide-ranging literature on this topic in political science and, more recently, in positive political theory and the law. See Cohen, Cuéllar, and Weingast, *Crisis Bureaucracy*, 700 n.109.

16. See Romer and Weingast, *Political Foundations of the Thrift Debacle*.

17. See Cohen, Cuéllar, and Weingast, *Crisis Bureaucracy*, 738–43. My claim is not that DHS is entirely dysfunctional, or that it is responsible for the full extent of the disaster following the flooding in New Orleans that resulted from Hurricane Katrina. Instead I contend that the prescriptive case for the creation of DHS is unpersuasive, that its creation entailed transition costs of uncertain duration and extent (a fact recognized even by many of its proponents), and that a plausible case can be made that specific difficulties—such those faced by the TSA or FEMA during and after the Katrina crisis—were exacerbated by the creation of DHS. Regarding the background degree of expert uncertainty permeating analyses of the policy implications of particular legal and policy changes, see Tetlock, *Expert Political Judgment*.

18. The term was generally taken to refer to the security of the American homeland, its infrastructure, and its population from a full range of man-made threats. See U.S. Commission on National Security in the 21st Century, *Seeking a National Strategy*, 13–15 (describing homeland defense as a preeminent security goal); *First Annual Report to the President and the Congress of the Advisory Panel to Assess Domestic Response Capabilities for Terrorism Involving Weapons of Mass Destruction*, 7 (discussing funding for "domestic prepared-

ness and homeland defense"). The reports of these high-level blue-ribbon panels contrast sharply with the prevailing rhetoric describing U.S. national security challenges from just a few years earlier. See, for example, Office of the Secretary of Defense, U.S. Department of Defense, *Quadrennial Defense Review* (failing to emphasize terrorism or homeland security as preeminent security challenges).

19. *Commission Report*, 71–82.

20. See Zegart, *September 11 and the Adaptation Failure of U.S. Intelligence Agencies*, 85.

21. *Id.*, 100–102.

22. *Id.*

23. See generally *id.*; *United States Government Manual: 2000–2001* (describing separate law enforcement, national security, and disaster relief missions for different government agencies). The identification of "homeland security" primarily with terrorism and similar man-made threats is derived from the Bush administration's own budget analyses. See, for example, Office of Management and Budget, *Budget of the United States Government, Fiscal Year 2003*, 23 ("To develop the homeland security budget, the Office of Homeland Security . . . identified those activities *that are focused on combating and protecting against terrorism and occur within the United States and its territories*" [emphasis added]). By using this definition, we do not mean to imply that it is a reasonable one. Indeed, as indicated by the discussion on Hurricane Katrina in Cohen, Cuéllar, and Weingast, *Crisis Bureaucracy*, 738–43, and this account of the prescriptive merits of the department's creation, there are considerable grounds for questioning the exclusion of major natural disasters from the definition of homeland security.

24. See *Commission Report*, 93–102.

25. *Id.*, 88–91.

26. See Clarke, *Against All Enemies*, 167–71; see also Wright, *The Looming Tower*, 3 (describing the existence of CIA and FBI offices "tracking the activities of . . . Osama bin Laden, whose name had arisen as the master financier of terror").

27. The Senate Armed Services, Appropriations, and Intelligence Committees held hearings analyzing the work of the approximately forty different agencies responsible for combating domestic terrorism. See, for example, *Terrorism and U.S. Government Capabilities*, 6–7 (statement of Paul H. O'Neill, Secretary of the Treasury).

28. *Commission Report*, 74, 82 ("For countering terrorism, the dominant agency under Justice is the Federal Bureau of Investigation. . . . [T]he FBI and the Justice Department . . . took on the lead role in addressing terrorism because they were asked to do so").

29. Customs was also responsible for trade-related revenue collection and the implementation of hundreds of legal mandates related to trade regulation. See U.S. General Accounting Office, *Customs Service*.

30. See *Commission Report*, 82 ("The [Bureau of Alcohol, Tobacco, and Firearms] laboratories and analysis were critical").

31. See *United States Government Manual, 2000–2001*, 308–35.

32. *Id.*

33. See Wamsley and Schroeder, *Escalating in a Quagmire*, 238–39. These efforts complement those of state and local responders who are likely to nearly always be the first on the scene in response to a terrorist attack. See Wise and Nader, *Organizing the Federal System for Homeland Security*, 46.

34. *House Speaker Forms Terrorism Panel*, 197.

35. Uniting and Strengthening America by Providing Appropriate Tools Required to Intercept and Obstruct Terrorism Act (USA PATRIOT Act) of 2001, Pub. L. No. 107-56, 115 Stat. 272 (codified in scattered sections of the U.S.C.). So eager was the department to

craft the new bill that Attorney General Ashcroft discussed it on Sunday morning talk shows even before the chairman of the House Judiciary Committee or the White House Counsel's Office had any copies of the proposal. See Brill, *After*, 73–74.

36. Brill, *After*, at 148.

37. See generally *id.*, 54 (noting how presidential advisors characterized their agenda as "*not* to reorganize all those agencies, but to hire a heavyweight to come work in the White House and *coordinate* them"); Kettl, *System Under Stress*; Ridge, *U.S. Is More Secure* (describing homeland security measures and their progress).

38. For a discussion of the potential benefits and costs of centralized control, see Cohen, Cuéllar, and Weingast, *Crisis Bureaucracy*, 700–714. For an interesting exploration of those benefits and costs in the context of intelligence agencies, see O'Connell, *The Architecture of Smart Intelligence*.

39. See generally Department of Homeland Security, *Performance and Accountability Report: Fiscal Year 2005*, 123–32.

40. See Brill, *After*, 54 ("[T]hat coordinating would be a lot harder than it sounded"); Kettl, *System Under Stress*, 49–56.

41. S. 1449, 107th Cong. § 1 (2001).

42. See Mitchell, *A Nation Challenged*.

43. Ari Fleischer, White House Press Secretary, Press Briefing (Oct. 2, 2001); transcript available at http://www.whitehouse.gov/news/releases/2001/10/20011002-11.html.

44. See Sutton, *Biodefense*.

45. The Coast Guard also received a funding increase of $282 million in 2002. Thessin, *Recent Developments*, 518 n.39; see also Cohen, Cuéllar, and Weingast, *Crisis Bureaucracy*, 714–43 (discussing the pressures interfering with continued performance of the Coast Guard's legacy missions following the creation of the Department of Homeland Security).

46. See Haynes, *Seeing Around Corners*, 375–76.

47. See Kettl, *System Under Stress*, 80.

48. See Brill, *After*, 166 (noting "widespread media reports and public disgust about the low quality of the airport screening force"); Clarke, *Against All Enemies*, 245; Kettl, *System Under Stress*, 46–47.

49. See Brill, *After*, 506 (discussing how new TSA managers perceived attacks on their agency as coming from "staff people at the FAA, who were bitterly jealous that TSA even existed").

50. See Zegart, *September 11 and the Adaptation Failure of U.S. Intelligence Agencies*, 85–87.

51. See Kettl, *System Under Stress*.

52. Ari Fleischer, White House Press Secretary, Press Briefing (Mar. 19, 2002); transcript available at http://www.whitehouse.gov/news/releases/2002/03/20020319-7.html.

53. Note that if this had been a genuine concern, it might still have been possible for the president to negotiate some agreement with the legislators in question.

54. See interview with Jimmy Gurulé, Professor of Law, Notre Dame Law School, in Stanford, Cal. (Apr. 20, 2004).

55. As an example of how presidents might suffer such criticism from subordinates, consider Richard Clarke's account of the challenges the White House faced in achieving covert action from reluctant bureaucracies:

Whether it was catching war criminals in Yugoslavia or terrorists in Africa and the Middle East, it was the same story. The White House wanted action. The senior military did not and made it almost impossible for the President to overcome their objections. When in 1993 the White House had leaned on the military to snatch Aideed in Somalia, they had bobbled the operation and blamed the White House in off-the-record conversations with reporters and Congressmen. What White House advisor would want a repeat of that?

Clarke, *Against All Enemies*, 145.

56. See, for example, Caraley, *The Politics of Military Unification*, 213–44 (1966); Szanton, *Federal Reorganization*; Wilson, *Bureaucracy*, 264–68.

57. See, for example, Balogh et al., *Making Democracy Work*.

58. Brill, *After*, 54. The extent to which the president's aides summarily concluded that social insurance functions were unrelated to domestic security is consistent with the administration's narrow identification of homeland security with terrorism. See Cohen, Cuéllar, and Weingast, *Crisis Bureaucracy*, 681 n.24. Such a position contrasts with the approach taken by the Roosevelt administration during the 1940s, in which public officials relentlessly sought to link social insurance, public health, education, and regulatory programs to the goal of "security" and national defense. See Cohen, Cuéllar, and Weingast, *Crisis Bureaucracy*, 746–48 nn.250–55.

59. See Brill, *After*, 54–55 (describing the negative reaction of Vice President Cheney's aides to the prospect of creating a new department).

60. See Cohen, Cuéllar, and Weingast, *Crisis Bureaucracy*, 714–22.

61. Haynes, *Seeing Around Corners*, 374–75.

62. See Flynn, *America the Vulnerable*, 139; see also Brill, *After*, 485–87.

63. See Brill, *After*, 416.

64. *Id.*, 397; Haynes, *Seeing Around Corners*, 372–78.

65. Brill, *After*, 397 (emphasis added).

66. *Id.*, 377–402.

67. *Id.*, 449.

68. *Id.*; Haynes, *Seeing Around Corners*, 379–80.

69. See White House, *Proposed Homeland Security Act of 2002* (June 2002) [hereinafter *President's Plan*].

70. See Lehrer, *The Homeland Security Bureaucracy*, 77–78. How FEMA is classified depends, of course, on the extent to which one views responses to accidental and natural disasters as a component of homeland security. Doing so is certainly plausible. Below I note how some of the prescriptive problems associated with the creation of the new department may involve the adverse impact of focusing on a particular type of man-made security problem (terrorism) to the neglect of others.

71. See H.R. 4660, 107th Cong. § 102 (2002).

72. See H.R. 1158, 107th Cong. (2001).

73. Note how the relevance of this question can be understood in at least two ways: either the legislation itself allows for some flexibility or, as a practical matter, it allows for department executives to retain some discretion. On the other hand, political pressures would be quite likely to encourage a DHS executive to focus on terrorism because that is the issue that would be most likely to be used to judge her. Cf. Wilson, *Bureaucracy*, 197 (explaining that an executive is judged on the appearance of success, including popularity).

74. See Brill, *After*, 486.

75. See Clarke, *Against All Enemies*, 250.

76. See *Commission Report*, 273–74, 540 n.94.

77. Some bureaucratic reforms may be easier to explain to the public, regardless of whether they are in fact more likely to deliver desired behaviors from the bureaucracy. Cf.

Kuklinski and Quirk, *Reconsidering the Rational Public*, 153 (suggesting that the difficulty of interpreting information, given the heuristics used by individuals to make sense of the political world, shapes opinion formation).

78. *Id.*; Lehrer, *The Homeland Security Bureaucracy*, 82–83 (discussing budgeting and shifting of resources among agencies). See Doyle, *HS Jurisdictional Split in Senate Seen as Maritime Industry Headache* (noting that while homeland security appropriations subcommittees already exist in both houses, "less than half of the duties performed by the DHS will come under the new Homeland Security and Governmental Affairs [authorization] Committee"); see also Cohen, Cuéllar, and Weingast, *Crisis Bureaucracy*, 714–22 (reviewing the extent of opposition to reorganization among more senior legislators). For an insightful account of the extent of congressional opposition to a previous presidential reorganization effort that threatened the internal allocation of legislative jurisdiction, see Polenberg, *Reorganizing Roosevelt's Government*.

79. See *Bush Security Plan Seeks Boost in Power*; *No Quick Homeland Security Fix*.

80. See, for example, Staff of H. Armed Servs. Comm., 107th Cong., *Summary of En Bloc Manager's Amendment to H.R. 5005* (illustrating the House Armed Services Committee protecting its jurisdiction); H. Comm. on the Judiciary, 107th Cong., *Views and Recommendations on H.R. 5005* (2002), 5; available at http://judiciary.house.gov/Legacy/homeland071502.pdf (discussing the House Judiciary Committee's efforts to transfer the Secret Service to the Justice Department); Staff of H. Comm. on Energy and Commerce, 107th Cong., *The Recommendations of the Committee on Energy and Commerce to the Select Committee on Homeland Security Concerning H.R. 5005*, 11 (chronicling the House Energy and Commerce Committee's efforts to stop the transfer of functions involving nuclear stockpile security and related matters from the Energy Department); Press Release, House Comm. on Transp. and Infrastructure, *U.S. House Transportation Committee Leadership's Testimony Before the Select Committee on Homeland Security* (July 17, 2002) (showing the House Transportation Committee seeking to delay the transfer of TSA). The provision for presidential appointment of assistant secretaries included in the original draft of the Homeland Security Act that the White House issued was not present in the final Homeland Security Act.

81. See Wolfensberger, *Congress and Policymaking in an Age of Terrorism*, 343; 58 Cong. Q. Almanac Plus 7-5 (2002).

82. S. 2452, 107th Cong. (2002).

83. H.R. 5005, 107th Cong. (2002); see also *Cong. Q. Wkly.*, July 27, 2002, at 2028.

84. Republicans emphasized that presidential waiver authority to modify the operation of collective bargaining agreements already existed for other departments, and that if anything, a president should have expanded authority to impact the implementation of collective action agreements in the homeland security context. See 148 Cong. Rec. H5804 (daily ed. July 26, 2002).

85. See Clarke, *Against All Enemies*, 249–51.

86. With respect to civil service provisions, the law gave the president most of what he sought, including the power to abrogate, for a period of up to five years, many civil service protections for key DHS employees. Homeland Security Act of 2002, § 841(a)(2), 116 Stat. 2135, 2229–33. The law allows the secretary, in conjunction with the director of the Office of Personnel Management, to prescribe a "human resources management system" for the department, waiving civil service provisions governing compensation, evaluation, reward, and punishment of employees. *Id.* § 841.

87. *President's Plan*, § 103.

88. See Table 1, Cohen, Cuéllar, and Weingast, *Crisis Bureaucracy*, 756.

89. Homeland Security Act § 101(b)(1)(E).

90. *Id.* § 102.

91. *Id.* § 101(b)(1)(E).

92. *Id.* § 888(f).

93. *Id.* § 412.

94. *Id.* § 507.

95. *Id.* § 412(b)(1).

96. *Id.* §§ 231–35, 312–13.

97. The extent to which legislators across parties collaborated in restraining White House efforts to expand the scope of presidential power illustrates the potential willingness of legislators to prioritize institutional prerogatives (which can translate into policymaking power and electoral advantage) despite partisan differences. For a contrary perspective playing down the possibility of cross-party institutional interests, see Levinson and Pildes, *Separation of Parties, Not Powers.*

98. Homeland Security Act §§ 451–56, 1111–15.

99. *Id.* § 1402.

100. *Id.* §§ 1201–03.

101. *Id.* §§ 862–65; see also Levinson and Pildes, *Separation of Parties, Not Powers.*

102. Homeland Security Act, § 102(a)(2). Although the secretary of Homeland Security was empowered to delegate many such powers to subordinates, the HSA had the effect of preempting all preexisting delegations from officials such as the transportation secretary to heads of bureaus such as the Coast Guard. See, for example, 33 C.F.R. § 1.01–70 (1998) (delegating the secretary of Transportation's authority under CERCLA, the Federal Water Pollution Control Act, and the Oil Pollution Act of 1990 to inferior Coast Guard officials).

103. See, for example, Homeland Security Act § 101(b)(1)(E).

104. *Id.* § 1503.

105. See Kettl, *System Under Stress*, 42–43 (discussing the importance of congressional oversight structures); see also *Balancing Civil Liberties and National Security Needs* (testimony of Mary A. Fetchet, Founding Director, Voices of September 11th) ("In the current structure most congressional committees have some jurisdiction over homeland security, making the current system prone to turf battles and inertia. . . . [E]veryone is in charge so no one is in charge"); *Balancing Civil Liberties and National Security Needs: Hearing Before the Subcomm. on Nat'l Security, Emerging Threats, and Int'l Rel. of the H. Comm. on H. Gov't Reform*, 109th Cong. 4 (2006); Gillman, *Quelling Qualms on Security* (discussing House committees' reluctance to yield turf to the newly permanent Homeland Security Committee).

106. See Bush, *The Department of Homeland Security*, 1, 7 fig. 3.

107. Susman, *Congressional Oversight of Homeland Security*, 3.

CHAPTER 8

1. White House, Office of the Press Secretary, *Remarks by the President at the Signing of H.R. 5005, the Homeland Security Act of 2002* (Nov. 25, 2002).

2. Migration Policy Institute, *DHS and Immigration*, 94.

3. US GAO, *Major Management Challenges and Program Risks: Department of Homeland Security*, 1.

4. Murray, Giovagnoli, Packer, and Waslin, *Second Annual DHS Progress Report*, 7, 37.

5. CRS Report, Immigration-Related Detention. The Ninth Circuit in *Armentero v. Immigration and Naturalization Service*, for example, appeared to struggle with determining who should be the correct respondent in a habeas petition filed by an INS detainee.

6. Migration Policy Institute, *DHS and Immigration*, 94.

7. US GAO, *Secure Border Initiative*, 86.

8. Hsu, *Work to Cease on "Virtual Fence" Along US-Mexico Border*.

9. See, for example, Homeland Security Act, 2249–50 (regarding the importance of preserving the Coast Guard's non–homeland security responsibilities).

10. See Powell, *Defending Against Terrorist Attacks with Limited Resources*.

11. Eggen, *D.C. May Benefit as DHS Bases Grants on Risk*.

12. *Better Late than Never*.

13. *The Congress from Nowhere; Failing on Homeland Security; Risky Funding*.

14. *Failing on Homeland Security*.

15. See Roberts, *Shifting Priorities*, 443–44.

16. *Id.*, 444–45.

17. U.S. Dep't of Homeland Sec., Homeland Security Centers of Excellence.

18. See Table 7.1.

19. Roberts, *Shifting Priorities*, 439–40.

20. See *House Appropriators Add $1 Billion to Homeland Security Request*.

21. *Id.* ("Other allocations include $4.4 billion for the Office of Domestic Preparedness, Firefighters and Emergency Management, an $888 million increase above the administration's request").

22. See Select Bipartisan Comm., *Failure of Initiative*, 3 (2006) ("DHS was not prepared to respond to the catastrophic effects of Hurricane Katrina," and "DHS . . . had varying degrees of unfamiliarity with [its] roles and responsibilities under the National Response Plan and National Incident Management System").

23. Elliston, *Disaster in the Making* ("Within FEMA, the shift away from mitigation programs is so pronounced that many longtime specialists in the field have quit. In fact, disaster professionals are leaving many parts of FEMA in droves").

24. See generally Lewis, *Presidents and Politics of Agency Design*, 141–45. Regarding the application of this insight to intelligence issues, see generally O'Connell, *The Architecture of Smart Intelligence*.

25. A similar pattern of efforts to protect or enhance committee jurisdiction may be observed in the markups of other committees. For example, the House Science Committee voted to strike the ability of the DHS secretary to carry out civilian human health research through the Department of Health and Human Services, essentially voting to maintain the Science Committee's jurisdiction over such programs. Finally, the House Transportation Committee, chaired by Representative Don Young (R-Ala.), one of the most outspoken critics of jurisdictional reorganization, voted to halt the transfer of the Coast Guard from the Department of Transportation to DHS and to retain FEMA as an independent agency. Moreover, these concerns were quite well founded. The transfer of agencies to DHS meant that some bureaucracies were losing huge proportions of their funding and facing a decrease in their security-related missions. These changes affected not only the agencies themselves but also their allies in Congress. As the Treasury *Budget in Brief* for FY 2004 states:

The transfer of the Federal Law Enforcement Training Center, United States Customs Service, United States Secret Service, a majority of the Bureau of Alcohol, Tobacco and Firearms, Counter-Terrorism Fund and Inter-Agency Crime and Drug Enforcement accounts represents *nearly 90 percent of Treasury's law enforcement mission* and almost *a third of Treasury's total FY 2003 budget* [emphasis added].

Office of Performance Budgeting, U.S. Dep't of Treasury, *The Budget in Brief: FY 2004*, VI.

26. Preston and Crabtree, *Hill Confronts Reorganization Turf Battles Erupt Over New Dept.*; see also *Bag Screening May Be Delayed.*

27. Epstein, *Homeland Security in Hot Seat; Top 4 in Bush's Cabinet Try to Head Off Partisan Turf Wars.*

28. Adetunji, *Bush Warns of Homeland Security Turf Battles Ahead.*

29. See generally Fiorina, *Congress: Keystone of the Washington Establishment*; Mayhew, *Congress.*

30. For a discussion of a similar strategic problem arising in the context of closing military bases, see *Dalton v. Specter*, 511 U.S. 462 (1994).

31. Fiorina makes this point more generally; see *Congressional Control of the Bureaucracy*, 332, 335.

32. See Susman, *Congressional Oversight of Homeland Security*, 3.

33. Regarding the strategy, see Clarke, *Against All Enemies*, 250 ("Those who opposed the legislation, the Administration's supporters implied, were unpatriotic"). Regarding its effects, see, for example, Kraushaar, *Veteran Operatives* ("Now-Sen. Saxby Chambliss, R-Ga., scored political points for attacking Cleland's opposition to the bill creating the Homeland Security Department because it lacked protections for the union rights of employees"); Kemper, *Loyalty to Bush Helps Georgian Rise.* Kemper notes:

In his 2002 race against Democratic Sen. Max Cleland, Chambliss ran a television ad juxtaposing images of Osama bin Laden, Saddam Hussein and Cleland, who lost both legs and an arm in the Vietnam War.

The ad attacked Cleland's vote against Bush's version of a bill to create the Department of Homeland Security. Cleland said he supported forming the department, but wanted workers to have civil service protections. The administration said the department, because of its sensitive nature, should not be encumbered by such labor rules.

34. Survey by CBS News/N.Y. Times (July 13–16, 2002); available at iPOLL Databank, Roper Center for Public Opinion Research, University of Connecticut, http://www.ropercenter.uconn.edu/ipoll.html. The same organizations found that in October 2002, 52 percent of respondents thought that the Republican Party would be "more likely to make the right decisions when it comes to dealing with terrorism," as compared to only 20 percent who believed the Democratic Party would do so. Survey by CBS News/N.Y. Times (Oct. 27–31, 2002); available at iPOLL Databank, Roper Center for Public Opinion Research, University of Connecticut, http://www.ropercenter.uconn.edu/ipoll.html. Other polling organizations revealed similar patterns. In an October 2002 poll, 49 percent of respondents thought that the Republican Party would do a better job dealing with the war on terrorism, while only 13 percent thought the Democrats would and 27 percent thought that both would do about the same. Survey by NBC News/Wall St. J./Hart & Teeter Research Cos. (Oct. 18–21, 2002); available at iPOLL Databank, Roper Center for Public Opinion Research, University of Connecticut, http://www.ropercenter.uconn.edu/ipoll.html.

35. Survey by ABC News/Wash. Post (Dec. 12–15, 2002); available at iPOLL Databank, Roper Center for Public Opinion Research, University of Connecticut, http://www.ropercenter.uconn.edu/ipoll.html.

36. For a cogent review of the somewhat contradictory evidence providing limited support for modest bandwagon effects, see Richard Nadeau et al., *New Evidence About the Existence of a Bandwagon Effect in the Opinion Formation Process.* For analyses of the evolution of homeland security policy claiming the impact of a bandwagon effect, see Clarke, *Against All Enemies*, 250–51; Kettl, *Overview*, 13, 23.

37. Elliott, Ackerman, and Millian detail a similar political competition between Senator Edmund Muskie (D-Me.) and President Richard Nixon in the formation of the first major environmental protection legislation. See Elliott et al., *Toward a Theory of Statutory Evolution*, 326–29.

38. A related contention focuses on the president's need to reinforce the public's perceptions of his leadership abilities, a goal that could be furthered if he was perceived as guiding the nation's new legislative effort. See Kettl, *Overview*. This factor may have also affected the president's actions, but it too fails to explain the massive size of the reorganization. Demonstrating presidential leadership qualities depends on achieving legislative victory; in contrast, presidents with grand proposals resulting in conspicuous legislative failure hardly convey the dynamic leadership qualities that they presumably seek to project.

39. The HSA ultimately included a provision in Title I of the act that explicitly requires DHS to respect the non-terrorism-related functions of the so-called legacy missions of the transferred agencies; Homeland Security Act of 2002, Pub. L. No. 107–296, § 101(b)(1) (E), 116 Stat. 2135, 2142. Perhaps more strikingly, the HSA provisions governing the Coast Guard reiterate the importance of respecting the non-homeland-security-oriented Coast Guard missions and impose monitoring requirements on its work, but still allowing the secretary to make some reductions on non-homeland-security work. See *id.* § 888.

40. See Homeland Security Act of 2002, § 888, 116 Stat. 2135, 2249–50 (referring to HSA provisions imposing monitoring requirements on the Coast Guard).

41. S. Rep. No. 108-115, 1–2 (2003). A bipartisan group of legislators successfully incorporated into the HSA a bill titled the Non-Homeland Security Mission Performance Act of 2003, S. 910, 108th Cong., creating multiple layers of reporting requirements that could assist legislators in monitoring the performance of DHS in the non-homeland-security areas. Nonetheless, the new law formally changed all the component agencies' missions to emphasize the homeland security function, and the secretary and his subordinates retained considerable de jure and de facto discretion to change agency priorities.

42. See, for example, Durant, *Hazardous Waste, Regulatory Reform, and the Reagan Revolution* (analyzing how legislative responses diluted the impact of White House intervention seeking to limit the regulatory reach of environmental protection policies); Golden, *Exit, Voice, Loyalty, and Neglect* (discussing techniques of bureaucratic resistance to presidential deregulatory efforts during the Reagan administration used by career civil servants at the Civil Rights Division of the Department of Justice and the National Highway Traffic Safety Administration).

43. See Ringquist, *Political Control and Policy Impact in EPA's Office of Water Quality* (discussing EPA administrator Anne Gorsuch's persistent efforts to limit regulatory enforcement and the limited but material effect of those efforts on the EPA's Office of Water Quality).

44. Indeed, Bush's commitment to social policy goals implied that he believed the government should pursue a wide range of other goals.

45. See McGinley, *Gore, Bush Would Lead Regulatory Army in Different Directions*.

46. See, for example, *Congress Signs Off on Record Tax Bill* ("Owners of commercial vessels, except fishing boats, would for the first time be charged fees by the Coast Guard for inspections, licenses for pilots and other seamen, and other services. *The fees will be determined by the Coast Guard*") (emphasis added); Wilner, *User Charges Proposed* (describing congressional Republicans' resistance to Clinton administration efforts to use Coast Guard regulatory and revenue authority for harbor deepening and environmental enforcement). The article describes congressional Republican concern with proposed Coast Guard activities thus:

Already, House Coast Guard and Marine Transportation Subcommittee Chairman Wayne Gilchrest, R. Md., has said the administration's intent to tax cargo-vessel operators almost $1 billion to fund coastal, Great Lakes and St. Lawrence Seaway harbor deepening and maintenance dredging, is "dead-on-arrival." Also under attack is a proposed vessel fee to fund Coast Guard navigation and other safety assistance activities.

47. Boren, *Coast Guard Report Is Making Waves for Miller*. Describing the consequences of a Washington State Republican congressman's efforts to delay enforcement of Coast Guard safety rules on a fisheries corporation, the article notes: "The sinking of a fish-processing trawler in calm waters off Alaska a year ago is creating a stormy sea for Congressman John Miller's pursuit of a U.S. Senate seat in 1992." The families of some of the nine crewmen who died last March when the *Aleutian Enterprise* sank recently have accused the Seattle Republican of causing those deaths by interfering in the Coast Guard's efforts to enforce marine safety rules on factory trawlers. *Id.*

48. Blumenthal, *Oil Tanker Restrictions in Sound Will Remain* ("A provision that would have lifted the 28-year-old [Coast Guard] restrictions on oil tanker traffic in Puget Sound will be dropped from a new energy bill, Washington state lawmakers said Thursday. The decision by *Republican sponsors of the bill* came after a lobbying effort by three of the state's House members") (emphasis added).

49. *Cruise Ships Sail Into Political Arena; The Industry Donated $262,925 to Candidates and Parties This Year, a Florida Paper Reports.* The report noted that cruise line companies have been "targeted as potential sources of tax dollars and criticized for dumping waste. To keep their tropical-dream business afloat, the luxury liners have gotten into the political game," and that "the chief responsibility for regulating the industries' environmental practices rests with the U.S. Coast Guard." *Id.* It also indicated that the industry appeared to generate $605 million in wages in Florida alone, and that the Republican Party took "the largest amount" of contributions from cruise lines. *Id.* In the story Florida Republican House member Tom Feeney also stated that "[t]he cruise industry probably learned that when they weren't super active in the political process . . . someone almost took their head off. I think they've decided they have to be active." *Id.*

50. See, for example, Mason and Masterson, *Houston Delegates at Odds* ("Bentsen went around [House Majority Whip Tom] DeLay and took a tough public stance against a GOP plan to slash FEMA's disaster assistance"); Walsh, *House Panel Strips Millions from FEMA Budget; Vitter Supports Cuts to Disaster Relief* ("Despite warnings that it could slow emergency response to future flood and hurricane victims, House Republicans have stripped $389 million in disaster relief money from the budget as part of an effort to keep federal spending in check").

51. Brinkley, *The Great Deluge*, 247.

52. James, *A Line in the Water*.

53. *Id.*

54. See Cohen, Cuéllar, and Weingast, *Crisis Bureaucracy*, 680–700.

55. See generally George W. Bush, *Renewing America's Purpose* (describing his goal of eviscerating the layers of bureaucracy between citizen and decision maker).

56. Brill, *After*, 397.

57. See, for example, US GAO, *Homeland Security: Management Challenges Facing Federal Leadership*, 44–45; Press Release, Office of Senator Joseph Lieberman, *Lieberman Warns Against Short-Changing Homeland Security* (Dec. 20, 2002).

58. US GAO, *Homeland Security: Management Challenges Facing Federal Leadership*, 45.

59. 148 Cong. Rec. S8046 (2002).

60. See, for example, Cillizza, *Bills Scold Executive Branch* ("Homeland Security has had two secretaries and three deputy secretaries in its brief existence. More than 40 percent of high-level staff positions are currently vacant"); Edmonson, *DHS Moving Ahead After Port Worker ID Delays* ("[E]mployee turnover at all levels in Homeland Security was a factor in delaying the program"); Keane, *Brain Drain Pains DHS*, 13 ("More turnover rattled the Department of Homeland Security"); *Homeland Security Struggles with "Extraordinary" Turnover*; Hsu, *Weaknesses in Nation's Emergency Preparedness Exposed Yet Again by Katrina* ("Personnel turnover, constantly changing priorities and split responsibilities among federal agencies . . . sap the nation's ability").

61. See Cohen, Cuéllar, and Weingast, *Crisis Bureaucracy*, 724–25 nn.175–76 (discussing the limits of President Reagan's capacity to dilute regulatory enforcement).

62. Newport, *The American Public Reacts.*

63. *Terrorist Attacks: Public Opinion from April 1995–January 2001.*

64. *Id.*

65. In the weeks following the attacks, as might be expected, the number of respondents concerned about terrorism increased, with 58 percent of respondents reporting that they were somewhat or very worried that they or someone in their family would be a victim of a terrorist attack. Saad, *Personal Impact on Americans' Lives.*

66. In a Time/CNN/Harris poll in late September 2001, 56 percent of respondents believed that the Office of Homeland Security would make the country safer.

67. Survey by L.A. Times (Jan. 31–Feb. 3, 2002); available at iPOLL Databank, Roper Center for Public Opinion Research, University of Connecticut, http://www.ropercenter.uconn.edu/ipoll.html.

68. Newport, *Americans Approve of Proposed Department of Homeland Security.*

69. Cohen, Cuéllar, and Weingast, *Crisis Bureaucracy*, 720 n.166. This aspect of the DHS suggests the impact of voters' knowledge and sophistication, and not just the salience of the underlying issue, on the allocation of legal responsibilities across bureaucracies. Cf. Lau and Redlawsk, *Advantages and Disadvantages of Cognitive Heuristics in Political Decision Making* (noting that the use of cognitive shortcuts or heuristics *increases* the probability of a correct vote by political experts but *decreases* the probability of a correct vote by novices). But see Lupia and McCubbins, *The Institutional Foundations of Political Competence* (arguing that low-information rationality and political competence are possible through heuristics and institutions allowing citizens to interpret complex information). There is little doubt that voters with limited knowledge can often make reasonable choices by analyzing the behavior of organized interests (and by drawing on perceptions about the relationship of their own views to those of the relevant organized interests). But voters' relative ignorance about the intricacies of legislative proposals may be especially likely to affect political circumstances during crises, where policy changes may happen more rapidly, and in circumstances where prominent organized interests (such as the NRA or the ACLU) do not take an explicit position. Both of those conditions were present when the HSA was under consideration.

70. *Looking for Fiscal Patriots* ("Bush's proposed Department of Homeland Security would be revenue neutral, the president's aides insist"); *Take Time on Homeland Plan* ("Mr. Bush says his proposal will be revenue-neutral").

71. The DHS's Discretionary Budget Authority, including actual and supplemental expenditures, was $31,051 million in FY 2002; U.S. Dep't of Homeland Security, *The Budget for Fiscal Year 2004*, 445. The Bush administration's projections for FY 2003 and FY 2004 were $27,884 million and $29,185 million, respectively. *Id.*

72. Office of Management and Budget, *Historical Tables, Budget of the United States Government, Fiscal Year 2007*, 113 (showing that the homeland security discretionary budget in 2003 equaled $30,759 million and in 2004 equaled $30,344 million).

73. *Id.*

74. See Office of Management and Budget, *Analytical Perspectives, Budget of the United States Government, Fiscal Year 2004*, 610 (showing supplemental appropriations as proportion of total resources provided for DHS bureaus in 2002).

75. Office of Management and Budget, *Analytical Perspectives, Budget of the United States Government, Fiscal Year 2007*, 19–34; Office of Management and Budget, *Analytical Perspectives, Budget of the United States Government, Fiscal Year 2006*, 37–52; Office of Management and Budget, *Analytical Perspectives, Budget of the United States Government, Fiscal Year 2005*, 25–39.

76. As best we can tell, OMB's definition of "homeland security" seems to focus on the protection of the American national territory, and its population and infrastructure, from man-made threats. See Cohen, Cuéllar, and Weingast, *Crisis Bureaucracy*, 680–700, for examples of other sources that have defined the term in a similar fashion.

77. Even if the resources of departments and bureaus were growing overall, changes in the proportion of resources dedicated to a particular mission would alter internal and external perceptions of a bureau's mission, the allocation of time and attention of its leadership, and its relationships to external constituencies. Cf. Rothenberg, *Regulation, Organizations, and Politics* (describing how the ICC's priorities, internal culture, and relationships with external interests shifted as the proportion of economic activity it regulated increasingly involved trucking instead of rail transportation).

78. See Figure 8.1.

79. O'Hanlon et al., *Protecting the American Homeland*, xix (noting that new Coast Guard funds "are doing little more than addressing previous shortfalls" and amount to "hardly a change commensurate with the new responsibilities of this agency").

80. Hunter, *House Adopts Revision to Coast Guard Reauthorization*.

81. See Office of Management and Budget, Public Budget Database, Budget Authority (providing account-level detail for budget authority from 1976 through 2007). Indeed, the fact that some limited declines in environmental enforcement outlays began during the Bush administration but before the creation of DHS was considered by Congress only underscores the extent to which the Bush administration assigned lower priorities to regulatory enforcement within the bureau compared to the previous administration.

82. See, for example, *Coast Guard's Move to the Department of Homeland Security: Hearing Before the Subcomm. on Coast Guard and Maritime Transp., of the H. Comm. on Transp. and Infrastructure*, 108th Cong. (2003) (statement of JayEtta Z. Hecker, Director Physical Infrastructure, U.S. Gen. Accounting Office); available at http://www.gao.gov/new.items/d03594t.pdf.

83. *Id.*

84. *Id.*

85. *Id.*, 3, 14.

86. See Pollution Prevention Equipment, 70 Fed. Reg. 67,066 (proposed Nov. 3, 2005) (to be codified at 46 C.F.R. pt. 162).

87. See, e.g., Draft Programmatic Environmental Impact Statement for Vessel and Facility Response Plans for Oil: 2003 Removal Equipment Requirements and Alternative Technology Revisions; Reopening Comment Period, 70 Fed. Reg. 45,409 (Aug. 5, 2005).

88. See Democratic Staff of H. Appropriations Comm., 109th Cong., A Story of Ne-

glect: A Review of FEMA and the Army Corps of Engineers in the Aftermath of Hurricane Katrina (2005); available at http://www.house.gov/appropriations_democrats/pdf/A-Story-of-Neglect.pdf. Although these figures were evidently compiled by Democratic committee staff, former FEMA director Michael Brown and the DHS inspector general identified the same trend. See *Failure of Initiative*, 155–56. The report indicates:

Brown claimed that FEMA's operational budget baseline (for non–Stafford Act disaster funding) had been permanently reduced by 14.8 percent since joining DHS in 2003. In addition to the permanent baseline reduction, he claimed FEMA lost $80 million and $90 million in fiscal years 2003 and 2004 respectively from its operating budget. Brown argued that these budget reductions were preventing FEMA officials from maintaining adequate levels of trained and ready staff.

Id.; see also Office of Inspector Gen., Dep't of Homeland Sec., *A Performance Review of FEMA's Disaster Management Activities in Response to Hurricane Katrina*, 111–12.

89. Roberts, *The Master of Disaster as Bureaucratic Entrepreneur*.

90. See Cohen, Cuéllar, and Weingast, *Crisis Bureaucracy*, 728.

91. *Id.*, 681 n.24.

92. See Office of Senator Kerry, *Senator Kerry on the Coast Guard Commandment*, speech, March 19, 2002.

93. See Klamper, *Congress Set for Tug-of-War Over Coast Guard Jurisdiction*. Even in other countries that have reason to view coast guard bureaus as an important national defense resource, the bureau is ordinarily treated as a stand-alone agency or placed within ministries focused on marine and fisheries issues.

94. See *Coast Guard: Comprehensive Blueprint Needed to Balance and Monitor Resource Use and Measure Performance for All Missions* (statement of JayEtta Z. Hecker, Director, Physical Infrastructure, General Accounting Office, GAO-03-544T [March 12, 2003]).

95. See Homeland Security Act.

96. See Blumenthal, *Old Fleet Asked to Fill New Mission*.

97. See Office of Sen. Murray, *New Coast Guard Report Shows Decline in Traditional Missions, May 1, 2003*, 1–2. These figures measure declines in the absolute number of resource hours (comparing the reporting period of April 2002–March 2003 with the previous reporting period) dedicated to the missions in question in terms of the use of the Coast Guard's cutters, boats, and planes.

98. See Blumenthal, *Old Fleet Asked to Fill New Mission*, A1.

99. See Inspector General, *Department of Homeland Security, Annual Review of the United States Coast Guard's Mission Performance (FY 2007)*, OIG-09-13 5 (Dec. 2008).

100. Cohen, Cuéllar, and Weingast, *Crisis Bureaucracy*, 737 n.220.

101. See Dahl, *The Federal Regulation of Waste From Cruise Ships in U.S. Waters*, 613.

102. See Inspector General, *Annual Review of Mission Performance*, 3–6.

103. *Id.*, 19–20.

104. *Id.* Curiously, government auditors failed to provide any new data on the extent of declines in resource hours dedicated to marine environmental protection and marine safety. Auditors explained the decision not to analyze resource-hour changes in those two areas on the basis that the excluded functions were largely undertaken without the use of actual Coast Guard physical resources. This rationale may have been advanced by agency officials, who may have harbored concerns about what updated analyses of resource hours would show. But it is difficult to accept. The technical system the Coast Guard uses to keep track of resource hours, after all, includes a category for both marine environmental protection and marine safety. Moreover, it is difficult to assess how the Coast Guard would be able

to accomplish marine safety and marine environmental protection missions, which depend crucially on inspections, without using its physical resources.

105. *Id.*

106. *Id.*, 15.

107. USGAO, GAO-06-816, *Coast Guard*, 15. Because the Coast Guard targets vessels, the primary measure does not reflect the compliance rate for all fishermen in those areas patrolled by the Coast Guard, as could be inferred by the description, but rather is an observed compliance rate, that is, the compliance rate of only those fishing vessels boarded by Coast Guard personnel.

108. *Id.*, 18 (discussing problems with the measures for marine environmental protection). Although government auditors found performance measures for marine safety to be sound, these are based on a five-year average of the annual number of deaths and injuries of recreational boaters, mariners, and passengers. As such, changes in Coast Guard regulatory performance in this domain are likely to take longer to become observable from an analysis of the bureau's performance measures, even if underlying compliance rates are beginning to change substantially.

109. OIRA treats rules as "economically significant" under Executive Order 12,866 when they "have an annual effect on the economy of $100 million or more, or adversely affect the economy or a sector of the economy, productivity, competition, jobs, the environment, public health or safety, or state, local, or tribal governments or communities." For an insightful analysis of the OIRA review process, see Croley, *White House Review of Agency Rulemaking*, 827–28.

110. The preceding analysis was conducted using the Government Printing Office's RegInfo database; available at http://www.reginfo.gov/public/do/eoAdvancedSearchMain.

111. See McClure, *Oil Spill Rescue Rule Keeps Seeking*.

112. Although DHS has taken some steps to preserve and expand the role of technical risk analysis in the allocation of homeland-security-related grant funds, such efforts have played out against a backdrop of pressures forcing DHS to allocate funds in accordance with external political dynamics. Two of the three major grant programs—the Law Enforcement Terrorism Prevention Program and the State Homeland Security Grant Program—have statutory baseline formulas that flatly require nearly half the money to be allocated *equally* on a state-by-state basis, with 0.75 percent of total funds going to each state and 0.25 percent of total funds allocated to a list of territories; see Reese, Cong. Res. Serv., *Homeland Security Grants*, 1. In addition, the extent to which the department has described recent changes as gradual moves to implement a more risk-based methodology suggests that the original allocation formulas more thoroughly reflected the influence of political pressures on DHS; see O'Harrow and Higham, *Politics Cast Shadow on 9-11 Funds*.

113. See Elliston, *Disaster in the Making*; see also Basavaraj, *House Approves Funding for Natural Disaster Preparedness*, 3 ("Since the consolidation of numerous federal agencies under the umbrella of DHS, many stakeholders have been concerned about the dilution of the FEMA mission of response, recovery and mitigation of all hazards—including natural disasters"). For a cogent argument explaining why it is problematic to assume that capacities to respond to natural disasters and to terrorist attacks are fungible, see Roberts, Reputation and Federal Emergency Preparedness Agencies, 1948–2003:

There are reasons to believe that terrorism is incompatible with the definition of all hazards that existed before September 11. Terrorism lacks predictability and clear definitions: the enemy is elusive and it is unclear who or what should be involved in prevention and response. Weapons could be biological, radiological, chemical, or traditional arms, and the medical and damage control elements of response overlap with law enforcement and investigative elements. *Id.*, 29.

114. See Alpert, *Senators Get an Earful on FEMA, SBA* ("[C]onstant turnover of personnel at FEMA forced them to start over multiple times in [citizens'] efforts for reimbursement or help"); Davies, *Doubts Persist About FEMA's Ability to Respond*, 42 ("FEMA lost many top professionals in the past few years, and the turnover continued after Katrina. In March [2006], a House committee reported that only 73 percent of FEMA staff positions were filled").

115. *Failure of Initiative*, 3.

116. Ripley, *Speed Read.*

117. *Failure of Initiative*, 131. The report notes:

With the creation of the Department of Homeland Security . . . and the development of the National Response Plan . . . , an additional layer of management and response authority was placed between the President and FEMA, and additional response coordinating structures were established. The Secretary of Homeland Security became the President's principal disaster advisor. . . . As part of these changes, critical response decision points were assigned to the Secretary of Homeland Security [who] . . . executed these responsibilities late, ineffectively, or not at all.

118. See *id.*, 132: "[A]bsent a catastrophic disaster designation from [Homeland Security Secretary] Chertoff, federal response officials in the field eventually made the difficult decisions to bypass established procedures and provide assistance without waiting for . . . clear direction from Washington." Moreover, "[t]he federal government stumbled into a proactive response during the first several days after Hurricane Katrina made landfall, as opposed to the Secretary making a clear and decisive choice to respond proactively." *Id.* These events, according to the congressional report, did not merely reflect personal failures on the part of the secretary, but were largely grounded in structural problems: "The White House Homeland Security Council . . . , situated at the apex of the policy coordination framework for DHS issues, itself failed to proactively de-conflict varying damage assessments." *Id.* In the weeks immediately before Katrina arrived, Secretary Chertoff had already begun planning extensive efforts to redefine the relationships between the White House, the DHS secretariat, and FEMA. These efforts also suggest the presence of pervasive structural problems in the flow of information, decisions, responses, and coordination efforts governing disaster response. For a description of those efforts, see Department of Homeland Security, Press Release, *Homeland Security Secretary Michael Chertoff Announces Six-Point Agenda for Department of Homeland Security* (July 13, 2005); available at http://www.dhs.gov/xnews/releases/press_release_0703.shtm.

119. See Office of Inspector Gen., *A Performance Review of FEMA's Disaster Management Activities in Response to Hurricane Katrina*, 23 (featuring a subsection titled, "FEMA and DHS Were Adjusting to the National Response Plan"). The report emphasizes the transition costs associated with changes in the national response plan governing federal efforts after a disaster. For a discussion of how post-Katrina oversight of allegedly emergency expenditures at DHS continued to break down even after Katrina, see Hall, *GAO* ("Homeland Security Department employees, including Secret Service agents and FEMA workers, wasted hundreds of thousands of dollars on iPods, beer-making equipment, a flat-screen TV, dog booties and clothing after Hurricane Katrina hit the Gulf Coast last fall, according to government investigators"). The referenced GAO report suggests that the degree of inappropriate expenditures considerably exceeded what would have been ordinarily expected in the aftermath of a natural disaster.

120. See Brinkley, *The Great Deluge*, 268 ("In point of fact, the ultimate responsibility for the lackluster federal response to Katrina lay entirely with Chertoff, the Secretary of Homeland Security. Under rules instituted in January 2005, Homeland Security was in charge of *all* major disasters, whether from international terrorism, Mother Nature, or infrastructure collapse").

121. See *Transportation Security Administration Arlington, Va*, 37 ("Complicating the short time frame and difficult logistics [associated with the preparation of TSA headquarters], the contractor also had to work with a newly formed government arm—TSA's Homeland Security department. Because the new department was still determining what its needs and requirements were, the construction team was constantly waiting for direction and reworking construction that had already been completed according to the original plan").

122. See Stables and Johnson, *HR2360—Fiscal 2006 Homeland Security Appropriations* ("The Federal Air Marshals become part of TSA. Although part of TSA when the department was created, the marshals were switched to Immigration and Customs Enforcement in November, 2003. As part of the departmental reorganization, the administration proposed moving them back to TSA"). This underscores the extent to which the department secretary's authority to recommend and promote internal changes within its bureaus (some of which require congressional authorization) may impose transition costs on the operation of the bureaus.

123. See *Transportation Security Administration Arlington, Va*.

124. See Mintz, *Infighting Cited at Homeland Security*.

125. See Stables and Johnson, *HR2360—Fiscal 2006 Homeland Security Appropriations*.

126. See Brill, *After*, 545; Clarke, *Against All Enemies*, 250.

127. Brill, *After*, 397.

128. See Cohen, Cuéllar, and Weingast, *Crisis Bureaucracy*, 697–99 nn.90–104.

129. See *id.*, 738–43.

130. For a detailed discussion of transition costs, see *id*. For sources acknowledging their existence, see, for example, Mintz, *Infighting Cited at Homeland Security* (noting that one of the major architects of the new department, former presidential aide Richard Falkenrath, had concluded that "many officials at the department were so inexperienced in grasping the levers of power in Washington, and so bashful about trying, that they failed to make progress on some fronts"). See also O'Hanlon et al., *Protecting the American Homeland*, xxv–xxvi (noting that the department merged "22 different agencies that contain more than 100 bureaus, branches, sub-agencies, and sections . . . including at least 80 different personnel systems"; and "[b]y far the biggest challenge Ridge and his people face[d was] to undertake this unprecedented [organizational] task while clearly keeping their eyes on the main ball—which is not to organize for homeland security but to prevent, protect, and respond to a future terrorist attack on U.S. soil"); Haynes, *Seeing Around Corners* (discussing the extent of transition costs); Kettl, *System Under Stress*, 1 ("Although the DOD reorganization involved more employees, by almost any other measure the DHS restructuring was harder. Even the large numbers vastly understate the scale and complexity of the job").

131. See Cohen, Cuéllar, and Weingast, *Crisis Bureaucracy*, 738–43.

132. Recall that because of common-pool and related collective action problems, we should expect the president to care more about efficiencies than other politicians do, unless of course there is an offsetting political rationale for doing something—which we believe there was. See *id.*, 687–89.

133. For an example of an analysis—besides that of the White House—presuming such benefits, see O'Hanlon et al., *Protecting the American Homeland*, 101–3.

134. See Cohen, Cuéllar, and Weingast, *Crisis Bureaucracy*, 707–12.

135. See, for example, Posner, *Uncertain Shield*.

136. See Zegart, *Flawed by Design*, 71 (describing long-running tensions between the Army and the Navy).

137. For a description of the differing cultures and tensions between the DEA and the FBI, see Wilson, *The Investigators*.

138. *Id.*, 242 ("The decentralization of Congress and the weakening of the seniority system has encouraged individual representatives and senators to become policy entrepreneurs, using their powers as chairmen of committees and subcommittees . . . to advance pet causes or call attention to themselves").

139. See Huber et al., *Developing More Encompassing Theories About Organizations*.

140. Brinkley, *The Great Deluge*, 333. President McKinley's take on homeland security is also mentioned in Emanuel, *Divine Wind*. Regarding the department's belated change in focus, see Hsu, *Can Congress Rescue FEMA?*

141. See Cohen, Cuéllar, and Weingast, *Crisis Bureaucracy*, 738–43.

142. For a discussion of areas in homeland security policy that are broadly discussed as priorities by experts and policymakers yet have failed to obtain increases in funding, such as securing materials that could be used to create weapons of mass destruction abroad, see Shapiro and Darken, *Homeland Security*.

143. Because the one near certainty in terms of prescriptive consequences involves transition costs, it seems reasonable that the burden for justifying the reorganization should be on those who claim that the security benefits would exceed the transition costs. And if that burden can be carried, then the weak rationales that the White House advanced are especially puzzling. We can think of no political reason why the White House would not want to offer its best rationales for the security benefits at the time when its strategy had shifted to trying to sell the department and taking credit for its creation. See Cohen, Cuéllar, and Weingast, *Crisis Bureaucracy*, 680–700.

144. See Department of Homeland Security, *Organizational Charts*.

CHAPTER 9

1. 343 U.S. 579 (1952).

2. Bellia, *The Story of the Steel Seizure Case*, 2–3.

3. See Cuéllar, *"Securing" the Nation*, 675–76. See also generally Kennedy, *Freedom from Fear*.

4. See Cuéllar, *"Securing" the Nation*, 626 n.150, 645 n.226, 682 n.347, 685 n.353.

5. See Cohen, Cuéllar, and Weingast, *Crisis Bureaucracy*, 723 (noting that legislators questioned whether FEMA's domestic policy mandate made it a good candidate for reorganization into DHS).

6. For a contrary perspective, see, for example, Gerson, *The Promise of National Security, with a Straight Face*. As we will discuss, this view consistently ignores the relationship between domestic policy generally and economic security policy in particular, as well as the conventional geostrategic account of national security against external threats.

7. For evidence supporting this claim, see Mintz and Huang, *Guns Versus Butter*.

8. Oscar R. Ewing, *More Security for You*.

9. Ewing was not the only member of the Truman administration concerned with the connection between economic and national security. For an account detailing conflict within the administration over this relationship, see Brune, *Guns and Butter*.

10. See, for example, Cuéllar, *"Securing" the Nation*, 628–29.

11. Ewing, *More Security for You*, 4.

12. See Tilly, *European Revolutions*.

13. See, for example, Gilpin, *War and Change in World Politics*.

14. Political scientist Robert Duval analyzed the relationship between U.S. defense spending and social spending, and concluded that a real trade-off exists. Specifically he concludes that an extra dollar spent on defense does indeed tend to mean a dollar less for social or other programs, unless the government makes up the difference through borrowing. Duval, *Trading Bases*, 4.

15. *Historical Budget Tables of the United States 2009*, Table 8.5.

16. *Id.*, Table 8.7.

17. Orszag, CBO Testimony Before the United States Senate Budget Committee, 2.

18. Flynn, *America the Resilient*.

19. *Id.*

20. See Flynn, *The Edge of Disaster*.

21. Flynn, *The Brittle Superpower*, 30.

22. Congressional Research Service, *Vulnerability of Concentrated Critical Infrastructure*, 4.

23. *Id.*, 5.

24. See Seib, *Deficit Balloons Into National Security Threat*.

25. Petruno, *Despite China's Jitters, Treasury Bond Market Stays Calm*.

26. Swanson, *Obama: China Should Be Confident in U.S. T-bills*.

27. Falush, *Chinese Comments Push Dollar to Fresh Lows*.

28. Javers, *Pentagon Preps for Economic Warfare*.

29. See, for example, Ryan, *Military Nutrition Research*.

30. *Id.*

31. Isaacson, Layne, and Arquilla, *Predicting Military Innovation*, 15.

32. See Easterly and Fischer, *The Soviet Economic Decline*.

33. Shelton and Dalton, *Strong Military Needs Early Education Focus*.

34. Freeman, *The "National System of Innovation" in Historical Perspective*, 13.

35. U.S. Commission on National Security in the Twenty-first Century, *The Phase III Report*.

36. For an example, see Association of American Universities, *National Defense Education and Innovation Initiative*.

37. Gingrich, *Winning the Future*.

38. For instance, the Association of American Universities noted: "As the Department of Defense has faced increasingly complex military challenges, it has relied on science and technology as a force multiplier." Association of American Universities, *National Defense Education and Innovation Initiative*, 7.

39. Military Readiness: Military Leaders for Kids. *Ready, Willing, and Unable to Serve*, 1.

40. *Id.*, 6.

41. *Id.*

42. Carpenter, *The Forging of Bureaucratic Autonomy*, 18 (2001) (reviewing definitions).

43. Tilly, *The Politics of Collective Violence*, 134.

44. Skocpol, *Protecting Soldiers and Mothers* (explaining how the degree of state institutional capacity was important as a foundation for subsequent program).

45. See Cuéllar, *"Securing" the Nation*, 628–29.

46. *Id.*

47. Pollack, *War, Revenue, and State Building*.

48. See Judt, *Postwar*.

49. *Id.*

50. See Tilly, *Coercion, Capital, and the European States*. On social capital, see Hall, *Social Capital in Britain*.

51. See Barkey, *Bandits and Bureaucrats*.

52. Tilly, *Capital, Coercion, and the European States*.

53. See, for example, Jones, *Bounded Rationality*.

54. See Fazal, *State Death in the International System*.

55. See Leffler, *A Preponderance of Power*.

56. Dryzek and Goodin, *Risk-Sharing and Social Justice*, 11.

57. Ferguson, *Empire*, 289–90.

58. See Abernethy, *The Dynamics of Global Dominance*.

59. See generally Nye, *The Decline of America's Soft Power*.

60. Kirshner, *Political Economy in Security Studies After the Cold War*, 79.

61. See Skocpol, *Protecting Soldiers and Mothers*.

62. See Kinder and Kiewiet, *Sociotropic Politics*.

63. Narizny, *Both Guns and Butter, or Neither*.

64. See Strøm, Kaare, and Müller, *The Keys to Togetherness* (analyzing the influence of "transaction costs" on formation of political coalitions).

65. See, for example, Ferguson, *The Ascent of Money*.

66. Kirshner makes this point in the context of a broader discussion of how the Cold War temporarily permitted the salience of political economy issues to recede from discussions involving national security. See Kirshner, *Political Economy in Security Studies After the Cold War*.

67. See Mintz and Huang, *Guns Versus Butter*, 738–39.

68. The White House, *National Security Strategy* (May 2010), 28 ("To allow each American to pursue the opportunity upon which our prosperity depends, we must . . . [achieve] access to quality, affordable health care so our people, businesses, and government are not constrained by rising costs; and the responsible management of our Federal budget so that we balance our priorities and are not burdened by debt").

69. See Pion-Berlin, *The Fall of Military Rule in Argentina*.

70. See Kirshner, *Political Economy in Security Studies After the Cold War*, 67.

71. Polenberg, *War and Society*, 83.

72. See *United States v. Comstock*, 560 U.S. (2010) (upholding a federal statute authorizing federal district courts to order involuntary civil commitment of sexually dangerous federal prisoners who completed their sentences). Commentators noted that this power had potentially important national security implications. See, e.g., Mahan, *Policy Sidebar*.

73. See, for example, Leuchtenburg, *Franklin D. Roosevelt and the New Deal*, 104–5 (describing the Townsend plan for old-age insurance that was far more redistributionist than the eventual social security program created by Roosevelt).

74. Federal Security Agency, *Second Annual Report*, 1.

75. See, for example, MacFarlane and Khong, *Human Security and the UN*, 129–33 (summarizing some policymakers' and theorists' attempts to expand "security" from the Cold War's focus on the military to economic, societal, and environmental factors).

76. Tilly, *European Revolutions*, 32 ("The organization of war made a fundamental difference to the character of states").

77. *Id.*, 33–35 (describing how war leads states to circumscribe and inspect the movement of capital, labor, and goods; to exert more extensive regulatory, surveillance, and educational controls over populations and commerce; and to expand the obligations that citizens owed to the state and vice versa).

78. Internal White House Memorandum, Summarizing Correspondence with M. S. Robertson, President, Department of Adult Education, National Education Association (noting the letter from Robertson requesting Roosevelt's help in furthering civil rights efforts) (Baton Rouge, La) (correspondence May 14, 1941, circa June 3, 1941); available at Franklin D. Roosevelt Presidential Library, Federal Security Agency, 1941 Folder, Official File 3700.

79. *Id.*

80. See Przeworski, *Democracy and the Market*, 33 (arguing that democratic institutions cannot sustain themselves unless they give "all relevant political forces" either a chance to win the "competition of interests and values" or the impression that "losing will not be all that bad"); Popkin, *The Rational Peasant*, 258–59 (arguing that the growth of revolutionary sentiment in Vietnamese villages can be explained by analyzing how the villagers gambled on an "improvement in the status quo"); Moore, *Social Origins of Dictatorship and Democracy*, 459 (suggesting that integrating the rural population into a nation's overall economic relations will generally tamp down on rural social unrest).

81. See Cohen, Cuéllar, and Weingast, *Crisis Bureaucracy*, 735–38. See also Flynn, *America the Vulnerable*, 14–15 (advocating a conception of security that encompasses critical infrastructure protection, public health, and natural disaster mitigation and relief).

82. See, for example, Kitrosser, *"Macro-transparency" as Structural Directive*, 1164 (questioning the Bush administration's push for secrecy in national security investigations).

83. See, for example, Chesney and Goldsmith, *Terrorism and the Convergence of Criminal and Military Detention Models*, 1121–32 (suggesting improvements in the current system of nontrial preventive detention).

84. See, for example, Golove, *United States*, 128 (2005) (arguing that Supreme Court decisions rejecting the Bush administration's detention of "enemy combatants" represent a "judicial effort to counter the radical vision of constitutional law" propounded by the administration).

85. See Cuéllar, *"Securing" the Nation*, 656–75.

86. See Cohen, Cuéllar, and Weingast, *Crisis Bureaucracy*, 681 n.24.

87. *Id.*, 696–97 n.95 (discussing the Homeland Security Act's provisions vesting in the secretary the power to decide precisely how agencies should balance legacy mandates and counterterrorism).

88. See Fehner and Holl, *Department of Energy 1977–1994*, 21–23 (describing the nuclear security and national defense organizational functions transferred to the newly created Department of Energy during the Carter administration); Cowan, *Who Needs the Energy Agency* (discussing the changes in bureau control that the creation of a new department would entail).

89. See also Zegart, *Flawed by Design*, 131–63 (discussing the political conflicts over bureaucratic control associated with crafting the Goldwater-Nichols legislation, and the changes in authority associated with the bill's passage).

90. See generally Commission on Intelligence Capabilities Regarding Weapons of Mass Destruction, *Report to the President*, March 31, 2005.

91. Cuéllar, *"Securing" the Nation*, 614 n.104.

CHAPTER 10

1. 272 U.S. 52 (1926).

2. See *id.*, 117 (reasoning that the president's obligation to execute the laws passed by Congress necessarily requires that the president be able to hire and fire administrative officers in the executive branch).

3. Hess, *Organizing the Presidency*, 3.

4. *Id.*, 305.

5. *Id.*

6. 462 U.S. 919 (1983).

7. The extent to which internal constraints on presidential control of the executive branch could substitute for power *across* branches is a central point in Neal Katyal's discussion of presidential power. See generally Katyal, *Internal Separation of Powers*. Katyal tends to think of bureaucratic fragmentation as a distinct parameter that can be essentially disentangled from traditional separation-of-powers debates. In contrast, the story of the FSA highlights the connection between the macro-level separation-of-powers questions and bureaucratic fragmentation, particularly when viewed against the backdrop of the long history of constitutional disputes over the management of executive branch architecture. To an underappreciated degree, those disputes also reflect the curious relationship between more extensive presidential control in the short term (which can be used to build agency resources, nurture agency reputations, and develop a desirable mission), and greater independence in the long run.

8. 657 F.2d 298 (D.C. Cir. 1981).

9. See *id.* at 312 (holding that the Environmental Protection Agency did not exceed its statutory authority under the Clean Air Act when it promulgated new coal-fired power plant emissions standards).

10. Compare *id.* at 406–7 (recognizing that in some instances it may be impermissible for administrative rulemakers not to "docket" the "conversations between the president or his staff and other Executive Branch officers or rulemakers" during the post-comment period of rulemaking), with *id.* at 406 ("Our form of government simply could not function effectively or rationally if key executive policymakers were isolated from each other and from the Chief Executive").

11. See *id.* at 625.

12. See, for example, Strauss, *Overseer or "The Decider"?*, 759 (2007) (arguing that the default rule in separation of powers grants the president oversight authority to ensure that laws are executed but not decisional authority to interpret statutes and promulgate rules).

13. In some respects, the doctrinal progression in this domain reflects at least some attention to the position of sustained but prudent scrutiny of presidential control of structure. Such attention is evidenced in the adoption of an increasingly functionalist separation-of-powers jurisprudence that acknowledges dynamic changes, a somewhat more flexible standing jurisprudence including, in *Massachusetts v. EPA*, 549 U.S. 497 (2007), the recognition of "procedural" injuries that might encompass the executive branch's failure to honor lawmakers' decisions to vest authority in particular inferior officers rather than the president, and a concern with placing limits on reservoirs of presidential power to affect the structure of government by pressing the limits of agency authority.

14. Cf. Bruff, *Balance of Forces*, 485–90.

15. See, for example, Kagan, *Presidential Administration*, 2301–3 (suggesting that Clinton's practice of publicly announcing regulatory actions often pushed White House staff to coordinate with the agency on the final rule and also allowed Clinton to claim credit for the agency's successes).

16. See Cuéllar, *"Securing" the Nation*, 598–637.

17. See *id.*, 655–96.

18. This is what cases such as *Myers, Humphrey's Executor*, and *Weiner v. United States*, 357 U.S. 349 (1958) (holding that the president could not remove a member of the

War Claims Commission "merely because he wanted his own appointee . . ."), are ultimately about. If they are not about the sharing of power, they make no sense at all.

19. See Cohen, Cuéllar, and Weingast, *Crisis Bureaucracy*.

20. See Schattschneider, *Party Government*, 14 (arguing that explicit party control of government was a critical component of citizens' opportunity to meaningfully engage in democratic politics). But see generally Lupia and McCubbins, *The Democratic Dilemma* (marshaling experimental evidence and theoretical arguments to bolster the case that a variety of institutional mechanisms simplify the public's task in making meaningful political decisions).

21. See Cuéllar, *"Securing" the Nation*, 656–60.

22. Here again, parallels to the creation of DHS abound. See Cohen, Cuéllar, and Weingast, *Crisis Bureaucracy*, 718 (discussing the relative absence of congressional or executive branch discussion reviewing the costs of greater centralization).

23. See, for example, Yoo, Calabresi, and Nee, *The Unitary Executive During the Third Half-Century*, 107 (arguing that Roosevelt's reorganization plan supports the idea of the unitary executive as a "constitutional custom").

24. Ronald C. Moe, *The President's Reorganization Authority*.

25. *Id.*

26. See, for example, *Hamdan v. Bush*, 548 U.S. 557 (2006).

CONCLUSION

1. Federal Security Agency, *Annual Report of the Federal Security Agency, for the Fiscal Year 1946*, xvi.

2. See generally Sunstein, *The Second Bill of Rights*.

3. *Id.*

4. Franklin D. Roosevelt, *State of the Union Message to Congress* (Jan. 11, 1944), 2.

5. *Id.*, 6.

6. See Cohen, Cuéllar, and Weingast, *Crisis Bureaucracy*, 692–93.

7. Cf. Cuéllar, *The Untold Story of al Qaeda's Administrative Law Dilemmas* (describing controversies regarding legal decision making in the Bush administration), with Polenberg, *Reorganizing Roosevelt's Government*, 55 (discussing criticisms of Roosevelt's alleged overreaching in bolstering executive power).

8. See Cohen, Cuéllar, and Weingast, *Crisis Bureaucracy*, 696–97.

9. See Knabb, Rhome, and Brown, *Tropical Cyclone Report, Hurricane Katrina, 23–30 August 2005*.

10. Cf. *id.*, 728 (discussing the combined impact of revenue neutrality and new missions), with Cuéllar, *"Securing" the Nation*, 655–96 (discussing how the FSA's broader security mission and layer of political officials contributed to capacity building).

11. See Ewing, *More Security for You*.

12. See, for example, Flynn, *The Edge of Disaster*, 170 (asserting that terrorism is only one of a "growing list of potentially catastrophic events that threatens the public" and arguing that the Bush administration did not sufficiently prepare for these other risks).

13. See Cohen, Cuéllar, and Weingast, *Crisis Bureaucracy*, 739 (discussing the relationship between bureaucratic control and the definition of "security" in the DHS context).

14. Opponents seem to have feared two things: the public attention that such an elevation would have brought to the health care issue at a time when Truman was eagerly seeking to turn it into a major subject of national debate; and the further bureaucratic resources (in terms of additional political appointees) that Truman would gain, which in turn

could facilitate efforts to use the agency's analytical and advocacy resources to promote the drive for national health insurance. See Cuéllar, *"Securing" the Nation*, 628–30 nn.157–67.

15. See, for example, Magill, *Beyond Powers and Branches in Separation of Powers Law*, 612 (arguing that separation-of-powers doctrine erroneously assumes that powers can be neatly separated when, in fact, there is no commonly accepted way to distinguish government functions in contested cases).

16. See Davidson, *Nuclear Officials Say Plants Strong Enough*.

17. See Clarke, Beers, et al., *The Forgotten Homeland*, 85–87.

Bibliography

MANUSCRIPT COLLECTIONS AND ARCHIVES

Classification File. Federal Security Agency. National Archives, College Park, MD.

Correspondence and Papers of the President's Committee on Administrative Management, Correspondence and Papers. Franklin D. Roosevelt Presidential Library.

Ewing, Oscar R. Papers. Harry S. Truman Presidential Library.

McNutt, Paul V., Federal Security Administrator. Correspondence and Papers. Franklin D. Roosevelt Presidential Library.

Miller, Watson. Archive. National Archives, College Park, MD.

Organizational Charts and Budgets. Federal Security Agency. National Archives, College Park, MD.

President's Committee on Administrative Management. Franklin D. Roosevelt Presidential Library.

President's Personal File 2836 (Paul McNutt). Franklin D. Roosevelt Presidential Library.

President's Secretary's File. Papers of Harry S. Truman. Harry S. Truman Presidential Library.

President's Secretary's Files. Federal Security Agency. Franklin D. Roosevelt Presidential Library.

War Research Service Files. National Archives, College Park, MD.

White House Confidential Files. National Security Resources Board. Harry S. Truman Presidential Library.

PUBLISHED SOURCES

Abernethy, David B. *The Dynamics of Global Dominance*. New Haven: Yale UP, 2002.

Abrams, Alan. *Tauzin Slams Coast Guard Rules, Says Ship Reforms Endangered*. Journal of Commerce, Sept. 29, 1994.

Acemoglu, Daron. *Why Not a Political Coase Theorem? Social Conflict, Commitment, and Politics*. 31 J. Comp. Econ. 633 (2003).

Ackerman, Bruce. *Constitutional Politics/Constitutional Law*. 99 Yale L. J. 453 (1989).

Adetunji, Lydia. *Bush Warns of Homeland Security Turf Battles Ahead*. Financial Times, June 8, 2002.

Agency Absorbs 8 Bureaus but Boosts Payroll. Chicago Daily Tribune, Sept. 10, 1949.

Albright, Robert C. *Arms to Get Right of Way in Congress*. Washington Post, Dec. 9, 1938.

Alien Enemies and Japanese-Americans. Comment. 51 Yale L. J. 1316 (1942).

Alpert, Bruce. *Senators Get an Earful on FEMA, SBA: Horror Tales Feature Ineptitude, Delays*. New Orleans Times-Picayune, May 20, 2006. Available at 2006 WLNR 8696865.

Alter, Jonathan. *The Defining Moment: FDR's Hundred Days and the Triumph of Hope*. New York: Simon & Schuster, 2006.

The American Navy. NY Times, Dec. 30, 1937.

Arce, Daniel G. *Taking Corporate Culture Seriously: Group Effects in a Trust Game*. 73 Southern Econ. J. 27 (2006).

Arnold, R. Douglas. *The Logic of Congressional Action* (1990).

Association of American Universities. *National Defense Education and Innovation Initiative.* January 2006.

Bach, G. L. *The Machinery and Politics of Monetary Policy-making.* 8 J. Financ. 170 (1953).

Bag Screening May Be Delayed. NJ Record, July 20, 2002.

Baldwin, Hanson W. *Fourteen Billion Dollars a Year: The World's Arms Bill.* NY Times, Aug. 21, 1939.

Balogh, Brian, et al. *Making Democracy Work: A Brief History of Twentieth Century Federal Executive Reorganization.* Miller Center of Public Affairs Working Paper in American Political Development. 2002. Available at ftp://webstorage1.mcpa.virginia.edu/apd/homeland_security/full_report.pdf.

Banks, Jeffrey S., and Joel Sobel. *Equilibrium Selection in Signaling Games.* 55 Econometrica 647 (1987).

Barkey, Karen. *Bandits and Bureaucrats: The Ottoman Route to State Centralization.* Ithaca, NY: Cornell UP, 1997.

Basavaraj, Shruti. *House Approves Funding for Natural Disaster Preparedness.* Nation's Cities Weekly, July 7, 2003.

Belair, Felix Jr. *President Decrees Three Big Offices in Centralizing 21.* NY Times, April 26, 1939.

Bellia, Patricia L. *The Story of the Steel Seizure Case.* In *Presidential Power Stories,* ed. Christopher H. Schroeder and Curtis A. Bradley. New York: Foundation Press, 2008.

Better Late than Never. Editorial. Washington Post, Jan. 5, 2006.

Blake, I. George. *Paul V. McNutt: Portrait of a Hoosier Statesman.* Indianapolis: Central, 1966.

Blumenthal, Les. *Oil Tanker Restrictions in Sound Will Remain,* Morning News Tribune (Tacoma, Wash.), Oct. 7, 2005.

———. *Old Fleet Asked to Fill New Mission.* News Tribune (Tacoma, Wash.), July 19, 2005.

Boren, Rebecca. *Coast Guard Report Is Making Waves for Miller.* Seattle Post-Intelligencer, Apr. 12, 1991.

Bressman, Lisa Schultz. *How Mead Has Muddled Judicial Review of Agency Action.* 58 Vand. L. Rev. 1443 (2005).

Brill, Steven. *After: How America Confronted the September 12 Era.* New York: Simon and Schuster, 2003.

Brinkley, Douglas. *The Great Deluge: Hurricane Katrina, New Orleans, and the Mississippi Gulf Coast.* New York: William Morrow, 2006.

Brownlow, Louis. *A General View.* 1 Pub. Admin. Rev. 101 (1941).

———. *Reconversion of the Federal Administrative Machinery from War to Peace.* 4 Pub. Admin. Rev. 309 (1944).

Bruff, Harold H. *Balance of Forces: Separation of Powers Law in the Administrative State.* Durham, NC: Carolina Academic Press, 2006.

Brune, Lester H. *Guns and Butter: The Pre-Korean War Dispute Over Budget Allocations.* 48 Am. J. Econ. Sociol. (1989).

Budget of the United States, Historical Tables, 1945–1955.

Burnell, Peter, and Andrew Reeve. *Persuasion as a Political Concept.* 14 Brit. J. Polit. Sci. 393 (1984).

Burton, Mark L., and Michael J. Hicks. *Hurricane Katrina: Preliminary Estimates of Commercial and Public Sector Damages.* 2005. Available at http://www.marshall.edu/cber/research/katrina/Katrina-Estimates.pdf.

Bush, George W. *Renewing America's Purpose: Policy Addresses of George W. Bush, July 1999–July 2000.* Bush for President and RNC, 2000.

Bush Security Plan Seeks Boost in Power. Houston Chronicle, July 16, 2002.

Caraley, Demetrios. *The Politics of Military Unification: A Study of Conflict and the Policy Process.* New York: Columbia UP, 1966.

Carpenter, Daniel P. *Adaptive Signal Processing,* * Hierarchy, and Budgetary Control in Federal Regulation.* 90 Am. Polit. Sci. Rev. 283 (1996).

———. *The Forging of Bureaucratic Autonomy: Reputations, Networks, and Policy Innovations in Executive Agencies, 1862–1928.* Princeton, NJ: Princeton UP, 2001.

Carpenter, William S. *England's New Ministry of Health.* 13 Am. Polit. Sci. Rev. 662 (1919).

Cavers, David F. *The Food, Drug, and Cosmetic Act of 1938: Its Legislative History and Its Substantive Provisions.* 6 Law & Contemp. Probs. 2 (1939).

Chang, Kelly H. *Appointing Central Bankers: The Politics of Monetary Policy in the United States and the European Monetary Union.* Cambridge: Cambridge UP, 2003.

Chesney, Robert, and Jack Goldsmith. *Terrorism and the Convergence of Criminal and Military Detention Models.* 60 Stan. L. Rev. 1079 (2008).

Chong, Dennis, and James N. Druckman. *Framing Public Opinion in Competitive Democracies.* 101 Am. Polit. Sci. Rev. 637 (2007).

Cillizza, Chris. *Bills Scold Executive Branch,* Roll Call, May 25, 2005. Available at 2005 WLNR 8280726.

Clarke, Richard A. *Against All Enemies: Inside America's War on Terror.* New York: Free Press, 2004.

Clarke, Richard A., Rand Beers, et al. *The Forgotten Homeland: A Century Foundation Task Force Report (June 28, 2006).*

Cohen, Dara, Mariano-Florentino Cuellar, and Barry Weingast. *Crisis Bureaucracy: Homeland Security and the Political Design of Legal Mandates.* 59 Stan. L. Rev. 673 (2006).

Committee Set Up on Reorganization. NY Times, Jan. 20, 1937.

Congress Divided on the Message. NY Times, Jan. 5, 1939.

The Congress from Nowhere. Editorial. NY Times, Nov. 18, 2005.

Congress Signs Off on Record Tax Bill. New Orleans Times-Picayune, Oct. 28, 1990.

Congressional Research Service. *Vulnerability of Concentrated Critical Infrastructure: Background and Policy Options.* September 12, 2008.

Congressional Research Service (CRS) Report. Immigration-Related Detention: Current Legislative Issues. Apr. 28, 2004. Available at http://www.fas.org/irp/crs/RL32369.pdf.

Cowan, Edward. *Who Needs the Energy Agency.* NY Times, May 30, 1976.

Croley, Steven. *White House Review of Agency Rulemaking: An Empirical Investigation.* 70 U. Chi. L. Rev. 821 (2003).

Cruise Ships Sail into Political Arena. Bradenton (FL) Herald, Nov. 6, 2000.

Cuéllar, Mariano-Florentino. *The Arms of Democracy: The Legacy of Economic Security Policy.* In *Shared Responsibility, Shared Risk: Governments, Markets, and Social Policy in the Twenty-First Century,* ed. Jacob Hacker and Ann O'Leary, 55–74. Oxford: Oxford UP, 2012.

———. *Review of* The Political Economies of Criminal Justice. 75 U. Chi. L. Rev. 941 (2008).

———. *"Securing" the Bureaucracy: The Federal Security Agency and the Political Design of Legal Mandates, 1939–1953.* Stanford Public Law Working Paper No. 943084. 2006. Available at SSRN: http://ssrn.com/abstract=942447.

———. *"Securing" the Nation: Law, Politics, and Organization at the Federal Security Agency, 1939–1953.* 76 U. Chi. L. Rev. 587 (2009).

———. *The Tenuous Relationship Between the Fight Against Money Laundering and the Disruption of Criminal Finance.* 93 J. Crim. L. & Criminology 311 (2003).

————. *The Untold Story of al Qaeda's Administrative Law Dilemmas.* 91 Minn. L. Rev. 1302 (2007).

Cyert, Richard M., and James G. March. *A Behavioral Theory of the Firm.* 2d ed. Wiley-Blackwell, 1992.

Dabney, Virginius. *The South Looks Abroad.* Foreign Aff. 171 (Oct. 1940).

Dahl, Meredith. *The Federal Regulation of Waste from Cruise Ships in U.S. Waters.* 9 Envtl. Law. 609 (2003).

Dam, Kenneth W. *From the* Gold Clause *Cases to the Gold Commission: A Half Century of American Monetary Law.* 50 U. Chi. L. Rev. 504 (1983).

Davidson, Keay. *Nuclear Officials Say Plants Strong Enough: Decision Angers Watchdog Groups.* San Francisco Chronicle, Jan. 30, 2007.

Davies, Frank. *Doubts Persist About FEMA's Ability to Respond.* Newark Star-Ledger, May 7, 2006.

Davis, Kenneth S. *FDR: Into the Storm, 1937–1940: A History.* New York: Random House, 1993.

Dean, James Robert Jr. *FDA at War: Securing the Food that Secured Victory.* 53 Food & Drug L. J. 453 (1998).

DeConde, Alexander. *The South and Isolationism.* 24 J. S. Hist. 332 (1958).

Deficit Balloons into National Security Threat. Wall Street Journal, February 2, 2010.

Democratic Staff of H. Appropriations Comm. 109th Cong. *A Story of Neglect: A Review of FEMA and the Army Corps of Engineers in the Aftermath of Hurricane Katrina.* 2005. Available at http://www.house.gov/appropriations_democrats/pdf/A-Story-of-Neglect.pdf.

Department of Homeland Security. *Organizational Charts.* January 29, 2007. Available at http://www.dhs.gov/xlibrary/assets/DHS_OrgChart.pdf.

————. *Performance and Accountability Report: Fiscal Year 2005.* 2005.

Department of the Treasury. Bureau of Alcohol, Tobacco, and Firearms. *Commerce in Firearms in the United States.* Feb. 2000.

Derthick, Martha. *Agency Under Stress: The Social Security Administration in American Government.* Washington, D.C.: Brookings Institution Press, 1990.

————. *Policymaking for Social Security.* Washington, D.C.: Brookings Institution, 1979.

Dickinson, Matthew J. *Bitter Harvest: FDR, Presidential Power, and the Growth of the Presidential Branch.* New York: Cambridge UP, 1997.

Doyle, John M. *HS Jurisdictional Split in Senate Seen as Maritime Industry Headache.* Aviation Week's Homeland Sec. & Def., Nov. 24, 2004. Available at 2004 WLNR 14144805.

Dryzek, John, and Robert E. Goodin. *Risk-Sharing and Social Justice: The Motivational Foundations of the Post-War Welfare State.* 16 Brit. J. Polit. Sci. 1 (1986).

Durant, Robert F. *Hazardous Waste, Regulatory Reform, and the Reagan Revolution: The Ironies of an Activist Approach to Deactivating Bureaucracy.* 53 Pub. Admin. Rev. 550 (1993).

Duval, Robert D. *Trading Bases: Resolving the Guns vs. Butter Tradeoff Puzzle via Full Specification.* Working paper, West Virginia University (Sept. 2003).

Easterly, William, and Stanley Fischer. *The Soviet Economic Decline.* 9 World Bank Economic Review 341 (1995).

Edmonson, R. G. *DHS Moving Ahead After Port Worker ID Delays.* J. Commerce, May 17, 2006. Available at 2006 WLNR 8536041.

Eggen, Dan. *D.C. May Benefit as DHS Bases Grants on Risk.* Washington Post, Jan. 4, 2006.

Elliott, E. Donald et al. *Toward a Theory of Statutory Evolution: The Federalization of Environmental Law.* 1 J.L. Econ. & Org. 313 (1985).

Elliston, Jon. *Disaster in the Making: As FEMA Weathers a Storm of Bush Administration Policy and Budget Changes, Protection from Natural Hazards May Be Trumped by "Homeland Security."* Balt. City Paper Online, Sept. 29, 2004. Available at http://www.citypaper.com/news/story.asp?id=9166.

Emanuel, Kerry. *Divine Wind: The History and Science of Hurricanes.* New York: Oxford UP, 2005.

Epstein, David, and Sharyn O'Halloran. *Delegating Powers: A Transaction Cost Politics Approach to Policy Making Under Separate Powers.* Cambridge: Cambridge UP, 1999.

Epstein, Edward. *Homeland Security in Hot Seat; Top 4 in Bush's Cabinet Try to Head Off Partisan Turf Wars.* S.F. Chronicle, July 12, 2002.

Eskridge, William N., and John Ferejohn. *A Republic of Statutes: The New American Constitution.* New Haven: Yale UP, 2010.

Executive Department Reorganization Act of June 30, 1932. Pub. L. No. 72-212, 47 Stat 413, amended by 47 Stat 1517 (1933).

Executive Reorganization Act, S 3331, 75th Cong., 3d Sess. (1938)

Ex-FEMA Chief Deflects Blame for Katrina Response. National Public Radio, Feb. 10, 2006. Available at http://www.npr.org/templates/story/story.php?storyId=5201004.

Failing on Homeland Security. Editorial. NY Times, Dec. 6, 2005.

Falush, Simon. *Chinese Comments Push Dollar to Fresh Lows.* Reuters UK, November 7, 2007.

Fazal, T. M. *State Death in the International System.* 58 Int. Organ. 311 (2004).

Fearon, James D. *Signaling Versus the Balance of Power and Interests: An Empirical Test of a Crisis Bargaining Model.* 38 J. Conflict Resolut. 236 (1994).

Federal Security Agency. *First Annual Report of the Federal Security Administrator.* Washington, D.C.: GPO, 1940.

———. *Second Annual Report.* Washington, D.C.: GPO, 1941.

———. *Annual Reports, for the Fiscal Years 1941–1942, 1942–1943.* Washington, D.C.: GPO, 1943.

———. *Annual Report, for the Fiscal Year 1944.* Washington, D.C.: GPO, 1944.

———. *Annual Report, for the Fiscal Year 1945.* Washington, D.C.: GPO, 1945.

———. *Annual Report of the Federal Security Agency, for the Fiscal Year 1946.* Washington, D.C.: GPO, 1946.

———. Community War Services, Agenda and Folder of Reference Material, Conference of Regional Directors and Assistant Regional Directors 1 (Feb. 12, 1944). Available at National Archives, Watson Miller Archive, Federal Security Agency, Community War Services Folder, Entry 10, Box 1.

———. *Employment Position Classification Sheet* (circa 1943). Available at National Archives, War Research Service Files (Entry 5A), Box 12.

———. *Organizational Charts and Budgets, FY 1946* (1946). Available at National Archives, Organizational Charts, Federal Security Agency, Entry 9, Box 1.

———. *Organizational Charts and Budgets, FY 1952* (1952). Available at National Archives, Organizational Charts, Federal Security Agency, Entry 9, Box 2.

———. *Organizational Chart* (Jan 1, 1953). Available at Harry S. Truman Presidential Library, Papers of Oscar R. Ewing, Federal Security Agency, General Correspondence, Organizational Charts, Box 29

———. *Services of the Federal Security Agency.* Washington, D.C.: GPO, 1944.

Fehner, Terrence R., and Jack M. Holl. *Department of Energy 1977–1994: A Summary History.* Washington, D.C.: U.S. Department of Energy, 1994.

Ferguson, Niall. *The Ascent of Money: A Financial History of the World*. New York: Penguin Press, 2008.

———. *Empire: The Rise and Demise of the British World Order and the Lessons for Global Power*. New York: Basic Books, 2002.

Fesler, James W. *The Brownlow Committee Fifty Years Later*. 47 Pub. Admin. Rev. 291 (1987).

Fiorina, Morris P. *Congressional Control of the Bureaucracy: A Mismatch of Incentives and Capabilities*. In *Congress Reconsidered*, ed. Lawrence C. Dodd and Bruce I. Oppenheimer, 332. 2d ed. Washington, D.C.: CQ Press, 1981.

First Annual Report to the President and the Congress of the Advisory Panel to Assess Domestic Response Capabilities for Terrorism Involving Weapons of Mass Destruction (1999). Available at http://www.rand.org/nsrd/terrpanel/terror.pdf.

Fletcher, Michael A., and Darryl Fears. *Bush Pushes Guest-worker Program*. Washington Post, Nov. 29, 2005.

Flynn, Stephen E. 2008. *America the Resilient*. Foreign Aff. (March/April 2008).

———. *America the Vulnerable: How Our Government Is Failing to Protect Us from Terrorism*. New York: HarperCollins, 2004.

———. *The Brittle Superpower*. In *Seeds of Disaster*, ed. Philip E. Auerswald et al. New York: Cambridge UP, 2006.

———. *The Edge of Disaster: Rebuilding a Resilient Nation*. New York: Random House, 2007.

Ford, Richard Thompson. *Law's Territory (A History of Jurisdiction)*, 97 Mich. L. Rev. 843 (1999).

Francis, Warren B. *President's Influence Is Slipping as Solons Labor*. LA Times, May 21, 1939.

Freeman, Chris. *The "National System of Innovation" in Historical Perspective*. 19 Camb. J. Econ. 5 (1995).

Fuchs, J. R. *Oral History Interview with Oscar R. Ewing*. Harry S. Truman Library (May 1, 1969). Available at http://www.trumanlibrary.org/oralhist/ewing3.htm. Accessed Apr. 14, 2009.

The Geneva Protocol for the Prohibition of the Use in War of Asphyxiating, Poisonous, or Other Gases, and of Bacterial Methods of Warfare, 26 UST 571, TIAS No 8061 (1925) (*Geneva Protocol*).

Gerson, Michael. *The Promise of National Security, with a Straight Face*. Washington Post, June 3, 2010.

Giddens, Anthony. *Capitalism and Modern Social Theory: An Analysis of the Writings of Marx, Durkheim, and Max Weber*. Cambridge: Cambridge UP, 1971.

Gilbert, Janice Dee. *The United States Food and Drug Administration: Purpose, History, and Function*. Monticello, IL: Vance Bibliographies, 1982.

Gillman, Todd J. *Quelling Qualms on Security*. Dallas Morning News, Jan. 9, 2005.

Gilpin, Robert. *War and Change in World Politics*. Cambridge: Cambridge UP, 1981.

Gingrich, Newt. *Winning the Future*. Washington, D.C.: Regnery Publishing, 2005.

Gold, Russell, and Ian Talley. *Exxon CEO Advocates Emissions Tax*. Wall Street Journal, Jan. 9, 2009.

Golden, Marissa Martino. *Exit, Voice, Loyalty, and Neglect: Bureaucratic Responses to Presidential Control During the Reagan Administration*. 2 J. Public Adm. Res. Theory 29 (1992).

Golove, David. *United States: The Bush Administration's "War on Terrorism" in the Supreme Court*. 3 Intl. J. Const. L. 128 (2005).

Granovetter, Mark, and Charles Tilly. *Inequality and Labor Processes*. In *Handbook of Sociology*, ed. Neil J. Smesler, 175–221. Newbury Park, CA: Sage, 1988.

Greiling Keane, Angela. *Brain Drain Pains DHS*. Traffic World, Apr. 3, 2006. Available at 2006 WLNR 5395365.

Gwynne, S. C. *Empire of the Summer Moon*. New York: Scribner, 2010.

Hall, Mimi. *GAO: TV, iPods of Post-Katrina Waste*. USA Today, July 19, 2006.

Hall, Peter A. *Social Capital in Britain*. 29 Brit. J. Polit. Sci. 417 (1999).

Harris, Stanley G. *Organizational Culture and Individual Sensemaking: A Schema-Based Perspective*. 5 Organ. Sci. 309 (1994).

Has the Wily Mr. McNutt of Indiana Been "Taken In" by Wilier Mr. Roosevelt? LA Times, July 16, 1939.

Haygood, Wil, and Ann Scott Tyson. *It Was As If All of Us Were Pronounced Dead*. Washington Post, Sept. 15, 2005. Available at http://www.washingtonpost.com/wp-dyn/content/article/2005/09/14/AR2005091402655_5.html.

Haynes, Wendy. *Seeing Around Corners: Crafting the New Department of Homeland Security*. 21 Rev. Pol'y Res. 369 (2004).

Heinrichs, Waldo. *Threshold of War: Franklin D. Roosevelt and American Entry into World War II*. New York: Oxford UP, 1988.

Hess, Stephen. *Organizing the Presidency*. Washington, D.C.: Brookings Institution, 1966.

Homeland Security Act of 2002. Pub. L. No. 107-296.

Homeland Security Council. *National Strategy for Homeland Security*. October 2007. Available at http://www.dhs.gov/xlibrary/assets/nat_strat_homelandsecurity_2007.pdf. Accessed April 14, 2009.

Homeland Security Struggles with "Extraordinary" Turnover. ExtremeTech.Com, June 10, 2005. Available at 2005 WLNR 9519206.

House Appropriators Add $1 Billion to Homeland Security Request. Defense Daily, June 24, 2003. Available at 2003 WLNR 12779928.

House Military Bill Sets Peak for Peace Time. Washington Post, Feb. 11, 1936.

House Speaker Forms Terrorism Panel. 197 Aerospace Daily & Def. Rep. 254 (2001).

Hsu, Spencer S. *Can Congress Rescue FEMA? Calls for Independence Clash with Bids to Fix Agency*. Wash. Post, June 26, 2006.

———. *Chertoff: FEMA Wasn't Ready*. Seattle Times, Oct. 20, 2005.

———. *DHS Terror Research Agency Struggling*. Washington Post, Aug. 20, 2006.

———. *Weaknesses in Nation's Emergency Preparedness Exposed Yet Again by Katrina*. Washington Post, Oct. 15, 2005.

———. *Work to Cease on "Virtual Fence" Along US-Mexico Border*. Washington Post, Mar. 16, 2008. Available at http://www.washingtonpost.com/wp-dyn/content/article/2010/03/16/AR2010031603573.html.

Huber, George P., et al. *Developing More Encompassing Theories About Organizations: The Centralization-Effectiveness Relationship as an Example*. 1 Org. Sci. 11 (1990).

Hult, Karen M. *Agency Merger and Bureaucratic Redesign*. University of Pittsburgh Press, 5 (1987).

Hunter, Kathleen. *House Adopts Revision to Coast Guard Reauthorization*. CQ Today, June 26, 2006. Available at 2006 WLNR 11408068.

Isaacson, Jeffrey A., Christopher Layne, and John Arquilla. *Predicting Military Innovation. Documented Briefing*. RAND, 1999.

Jackson, Charles O. *Food and Drug Legislation in the New Deal*. Princeton, N.J.: Princeton UP, 1970.

James, George. *A Line in the Water: In the War on Terrorism, the Coast Guard Finds Itself Stretched Thin*. NY Times, May 26, 2002, at § 14.

Javers, Eamon. *Pentagon Preps for Economic Warfare*. Politico, April 9, 2009.

Jewell, Malcolm E. *Evaluating the Decline of Southern Internationalism through Senatorial Roll Call Votes*. 21 J. Polit. 624 (1959).

Jones, Bryan. *Bounded Rationality*. 2 Annu. Rev. Polit. Sci. 297 (1999).

Jones, Charles O., and Randall Strahan. *The Effect of Energy Politics* on Congressional and Executive Organization in the 1970s*. 10 Legis. Stud. Q. 151 (1985).

Judt, Tony. *Postwar: A History of Europe Since 1945*. New York: Penguin, 2005.

Kagan, Elena. *Presidential Administration*. 114 Harv. L. Rev. 2245, 2322 (2001).

Kahneman, Daniel, and Amos Tversky. *Prospect Theory: An Analysis of Decisions under Risk*. 47 Econometrica 263 (1979).

Kashima, Tetsuden. *Judgment Without Trial: Japanese-American Imprisonment During World War II*. Seattle: U. of Washington P, 2003.

Katyal, Neal K. *Internal Separation of Powers: Checking Today's Most Dangerous Branch from Within*. 115 Yale L. J. 2313 (2006).

Katznelson, Ira. *When Affirmative Action Was White*. New York: W. W. Norton, 2005.

Kemper, Bob. *Loyalty to Bush Helps Georgian Rise*. Atlanta Journal-Constitution, Feb. 6, 2005.

Kennedy, David M. *Freedom from Fear: The American People in Depression and War, 1929–1945*. New York: Oxford UP, 1999.

Kerr, Thomas J. *Civil Defense in the U.S.: Bandaid for a Holocaust?* Westview, 1983.

Kettl, Donald F. *Overview*. In *The Department of Homeland Security's First Year: A Report Card*, ed. Donald F. Kettl, 1. New York: Century Foundation Press, 2004.

———. *System Under Stress: Homeland Security and American Politics*. Washington, D.C.: CQ Press, 2004.

Kinder, Don, and Roderick Kiewiet. *Sociotropic Politics: The American Case*. 11 Brit. J. Polit. Sci. 129 (1981).

Kingdon, John W. *Agendas, Alternatives, and Public Policies* (1995).

Kirshner, Jonathan. *Political Economy in Security Studies After the Cold War*. 5 Rev. Int'l Pol. Econ. 64 (1998).

Kitrosser, Heidi. *"Macro-transparency" as Structural Directive: A Look at the NSA Surveillance Controversy*. 91 Minn. L. Rev. 1163 (2007).

Klamper, Amy. *Congress Set for Tug-of-War Over Coast Guard Jurisdiction*. 48 Sea Power 6 (March 1, 2005).

Knabb, Richard D., Jaime R. Rhome, and Daniel Brown. *Tropical Cyclone Report, Hurricane Katrina, 23–30 August 2005*. National Hurricane Center (Dec. 20, 2005).

Kraushaar, Josh. *Veteran Operatives*. Cong. Daily, Feb. 2, 2006. Available at 2006 WLNR 1883447.

Kreps, David M. *Corporate Culture and Economic Theory*. In *Perspectives on Positive Political Economy*, ed. James E. Alt and Kenneth A. Shepsle, 90. Cambridge: Cambridge UP, 1990.

Kuklinski, James H., and Paul J. Quirk. *Reconsidering the Rational Public: Cognition, Heuristics, and Mass Opinion*. In *Elements of Reason: Cognition, Choice, and the Bonds of Rationality*, ed. Arthur Lupia et al., 153. New York: Cambridge UP, 2000.

Landis, Michele L. *Fate, Responsibility, and "Natural" Disaster Relief: Narrating the American Welfare State*, 33 L. & Socy. Rev. 257 (1999).

Lau, Richard R., and David P. Redlawsk. *Advantages and Disadvantages of Cognitive Heuristics in Political Decision Making*. 45 Am. J. Pol. Sci. 951 (2001).

Lawrence, W. H. *President Merges Housing Agencies*. NY Times, Feb. 25, 1942.

Leffler, Melvyn P. *A Preponderance of Power*. Stanford, CA: Stanford UP, 1991.

Lehrer, Eli. *The Homeland Security Bureaucracy*. 155 Pub. Int. 71 (2004).

Leuchtenburg, William E. *The FDR Years: On Roosevelt and His Legacy.* New York: Columbia UP, 1995.

———. *Franklin D. Roosevelt and the New Deal, 1932–1940.* Harper and Row, 1963.

Leviero, Anthony. *Eisenhower Offers Plan to Give FSA Status in Cabinet.* NY Times, Mar. 13, 1953.

Levinson, Daryl J., and Richard H. Pildes. *Separation of Parties, Not Powers.* 119 Harv. L. Rev. 2311 (2006).

Lewis, David E. *Presidents and the Politics of Agency Design: Political Insulation in the United States Government Bureaucracy, 1946–1997.* Stanford, CA: Stanford UP, 2003.

Linton, Fred B. *Federal Facts and Fancies.* 27 Food & Drug Rev. 191 (1943).

Lipton, Eric, and Matthew L. Wald. *Focused on 9/11, U.S. Is Seen to Lag on New Threats.* NY Times, Aug. 12, 2006.

Londregan, John, and James M. Snyder, Jr. *Comparing Committee and Floor Preferences.* In *Positive Theories of Congressional Institutions,* ed. Kenneth A. Shepsle and Barry R. Weingast. Ann Arbor: U. of Michigan P., 1995.

Looking for Fiscal Patriots. Editorial. Milwaukee Journal Sentinel, June 17, 2002.

Lovata, Linda M. *Behavioral Theories Relating to the Design of Information Systems.* 11 MIS Quarterly 147 (June 1987).

Luban, David. *On the Commander in Chief Power.* 81 S. Cal. L. Rev. 477 (2008).

Lupia, Arthur, and Mathew D. McCubbins. *The Democratic Dilemma: Can Citizens Learn What They Need to Know?* (Cambridge: Cambridge UP, 1998).

———. *The Institutional Foundations of Political Competence: How Citizens Learn What They Need to Know.* In *Elements of Reason: Cognition, Choice, and the Bounds of Rationality,* ed. Arthur Lupia et al., 47. New York: Cambridge UP, 2000.

MacFarlane, S. Neil, and Yuen Foong Khong. *Human Security and the UN: A Critical History.* Bloomington: Indiana UP, 2006.

Magill, M. Elizabeth. *Beyond Powers and Branches in Separation of Powers Law.* 150 U. Penn. L. Rev. 603 (2001).

Mahan, Halerie. *Policy Sidebar.* 5 Duke J. Const. Law & Pub. 120 (2010).

Manly, Chesly. *President Puts U.S. Agencies in 3 Supergroups: Makes First Transfer of Reorganization.* Chicago Daily Tribune, Apr. 26, 1939.

Mansfield, Harvey C. *Federal Executive Reorganization: Thirty Years of Experience.* 29 Pub. Admin. Rev. 331 (1969).

Mashaw, Jerry. *Norms, Practices, and the Paradox of Deference: A Preliminary Inquiry into Agency Statutory Interpretation.* 57 Admin. L. Rev. 501 (2005).

Mason, Julie, and Karen Masterson. *Houston Delegates at Odds: FEMA Fight Latest Flare-Up in House,* Houston Chronicle, Aug. 5, 2001.

Mayhew, David. *Congress: The Electoral Connection.* New Haven, CT: Yale UP, 1974; 2nd ed., 1975.

McClure, Robert. *Oil Spill Rescue Rule Keeps Seeking.* Seattle Post-Intelligencer, Mar. 19, 2007.

McCubbins, Mathew D., Roger G. Noll, and Barry R. Weingast. *Administrative Procedures as Instruments of Political Control.* 3 J.L. Econ. & Org. 243 (1987).

———. ("McNollgast"). *The Political Origins of the Administrative Procedure Act.* 15 J.L. Econ. & Org. 180 (1999).

———. ("McNollgast"). *Structure and Process, Politics and Policy: Administrative Arrangements and the Political Control of Agencies.* 75 Va. L. Rev. 431 (1989).

McGinley, Laurie. *Gore, Bush Would Lead Regulatory Army in Different Directions.* Wall Street Journal, Oct. 31, 2000.

McNeil, Kenneth. *Understanding Organizational Power: Building on the Weberian Legacy.* 23 Admin. Sci. Q. 65 (March 1978).

Merck, George W. *Speech on the Implications of Biological Warfare* 3–4 (May 17, 1946). Available at National Archives, War Research Service Files, Entry 5A, Box 12.

Merrill, Thomas W., and Kristin E. Hickman. Chevron's *Domain.* 89 Geo. L.J. 833 (2001).

Microsoft Allies Urge Congress to Cut Antitrust Unit's Budget. LA Times, October 10, 1999.

Migration Policy Institute. *DHS and Immigration: Taking Stock and Correcting Course.* 2009. http://www.migrationpolicy.org/pubs/DHS_Feb09.pdf.

Miles, Rufus. *The Department of Health, Education, and Welfare.* New York: Praeger, 1974.

———. *Truman Undecided, May Again Ask Agency Bill.* LA Times, Aug. 19, 1949.

Millett, John D., and Lindsay Rogers. *The Legislative Veto and the Reorganization Act of 1939.* 1 Pub. Admin. Rev. 176 (1941).

Mintz, Alex, and Chi Huang. *Guns Versus Butter: The Indirect Link.* 35 Am. J. Polit. Sci. 738 (1991).

Mintz, John. *Infighting Cited at Homeland Security: Squabbles Blamed for Reducing Effectiveness.* Washington Post, Feb. 2, 2005.

Mitchell, Alison. *A Nation Challenged: The Security Chief; Disputes Erupt on Ridge's Needs for His Job.* NY Times, Nov. 4, 2001.

Moe, Ronald C. *The President's Reorganization Authority: Review and Analysis.* Congressional Research Service Report RL 30876. 2001.

Moe, Terry M. *Control and Feedback in Economic Regulation: The Case of the NLRB.* 79 Am. Polit. Sci. Rev. 1094 (1985).

———. *Political Structure of Agencies.* In *Can the Government Govern?* ed. John E. Chubb and Paul E. Peterson. Washington, D.C.: Brookings Institution Press, 1989.

———. *Politics and the Theory of Organization.* 7 J.L. Econ. & Org. 106 (1991).

Moe, Terry M., and Scott A. Wilson. *Presidents and the Politics of Structure.* 57 Law & Contemp. Probs. 1 (1994).

Molot, Jonathan T. *Reexamining* Marbury *in the Administrative State: A Structural and Institutional Defense of Judicial Power Over Statutory Interpretation.* 96 Nw. U. L. Rev. 1239 (2002).

Moore, Barrington Jr. *Social Origins of Dictatorship and Democracy: Lord and Peasant in the Making of the Modern World.* Boston: Beacon Press, 1966.

Morrow, James D. *How Could Trade Affect Conflict?* 36 J. Peace Res. 481 (1999).

Morrow, William. *Congressional Committees.* New York: Charles Scribner's Sons, 1969.

Mullan, Fitzhugh. *Plagues and Politics: The Story of the United States Public Health Service.* New York: Basic Books, 1989.

Murray, Royce Bernstein, Mary Giovagnoli, Travis Packer, and Michele Waslin. *Second Annual DHS Progress Report.* Special Report on Immigration. Immigration Policy Center, 2011.

Nadeau, Richard, et al. *New Evidence About the Existence of a Bandwagon Effect in the Opinion Formation Process.* 14 Int'l Pol. Sci. Rev. 203 (1993).

Narizny, Kevin. *Both Guns and Butter, or Neither: Class Interests in the Political Economy of Rearmament.* 97 Am. Pol. Sci. Rev. 203 (2003).

National Archives and Records Service. General Services Administration. *United States Government Organization Manual, 1950–1951.* Washington, D.C.: GPO, 1951.

Nat'l Comm'n on Terrorist Attacks upon the U.S.: *The 9/11 Commission Report* (2004) [hereinafter *Commission Report*].

New Orleans 80 Percent Flooded, Dike Breach Letting in Lake Water-Officials. Forbes.com, Aug. 30, 2005.

Newport, Frank. *The American Public Reacts.* Gallup Poll News Service, Sept. 24, 2001. Available at http://www.galluppoll.com/content/Default.aspx?ci=4900.

———. *Americans Approve of Proposed Department of Homeland Security.* Gallup Poll News Service, June 10, 2002. Available at http://www.galluppoll.com/content/Default .aspx?ci=6163.

No Quick Homeland Security Fix. Editorial. Chicago Tribune, July 17, 2002.

Nye, Joseph. *The Decline of America's Soft Power.* Foreign Aff. (May/June 2004).

Nzelibe, Jide. *The Fable of the Nationalist President and the Parochial Congress.* 53 UCLA L. Rev. 1217 (2006).

O'Connell, Anne Joseph. *The Architecture of Smart Intelligence: Structuring and Overseeing Agencies.* 94 Cal. L. Rev. 1655 (Dec. 2006).

O'Hanlon, Michael E., et al. *Protecting the American Homeland: One Year On.* Washington, D.C.: Brookings Institution Press, 2003.

O'Harrow, Robert Jr., and Scott Higham. *Politics Cast Shadow on 9-11 Funds.* Cincinnati Post, Dec. 26, 2005.

Office of Inspector Gen. Dep't of Homeland Sec. *A Performance Review of FEMA's Disaster Management Activities in Response to Hurricane Katrina.* 2006.

Office of Management and Budget. *Analytical Perspectives. Budget of the United States Government, Fiscal Year 2004.* 2003.

———. *Analytical Perspectives. Budget of the United States Government, Fiscal Year 2005.* 2004.

———. *Analytical Perspectives. Budget of the United States Government, Fiscal Year 2006.* 2005.

———. *Analytical Perspectives. Budget of the United States Government, Fiscal Year 2007.* 2006.

———. *Budget of the United States, 1980.* Washington, D.C.: GPO, 1979.

———. *Budget of the United States Government, Fiscal Year 2003.*

———. *Historical Tables. Budget of the United States Government. Fiscal Year 2007.* 2006.

———. Public Budget Database, Budget Authority. http://www.whitehouse.gov/omb/budget/ fy2007/db.html.

Office of Performance Budgeting. U.S. Dep't of Treasury. *The Budget in Brief: FY 2004.* 2003. Available at http://www.ustreas.gov/offices/management/budget/budgetinbrief/ fy2004/fy2004bib.pdf.

Office of the Sec'y of Def. U.S. Dept. of Def. *Quadrennial Defense Review* (1997). Available at http://www.fas.org/man/docs/qdr/.

Oppenheimer, Reuben. *The Supreme Court and Administrative Law.* 37 Colum. L. Rev. 1 (1937).

Orszag, Peter. CBO Testimony Before the United States Senate Budget Committee. June 21, 2007.

Our Autocratic State. Editorial. Chicago Daily Tribune, Apr. 27, 1939.

Patterson, James T. *A Conservative Coalition Forms in Congress, 1933–1939.* 52 J. Am. Hist. 757 (1966).

Perrow, Charles. *Complex Organizations: A Critical Essay.* New York: Random House, 1986.

Petruno, Thomas. *Despite China's Jitters, Treasury Bond Market Stays Calm.* LA Times, March 13, 2009.

Pinter, Nicholas. *One Step Forward, Two Steps Back on U.S. Floodplains.* 308 Science 207 (2005).

Pion-Berlin, David. *The Fall of Military Rule in Argentina: 1976–1983*. 27 J. Interam. Stud. World 55 (1985).

Poen, Monte M. *Harry S. Truman Versus the Medical Lobby: The Genesis of Medicare*. Columbia: U. of Missouri P., 1979.

Polenberg, Richard. *Reorganizing Roosevelt's Government: The Controversy over Executive Reorganization, 1936–1939*. Cambridge, MA: Harvard UP, 1966.

———. *War and Society: The United States, 1941–1945*. Philadelphia: Lippincott, 1972.

Pollack, Sheldon D. *War, Revenue, and State Building: Financing the Development of the American State*. Ithaca, NY: Cornell UP, 2009.

Popkin, Samuel L. *The Rational Peasant: The Political Economy of Rural Society in Vietnam*. Berkeley: U. California P., 1979.

Posen, Barry. *The Sources of Military Doctrine: France, Britain, and Germany Between the World Wars*. Ithaca, NY: Cornell UP, 1984.

Powell, Robert. Defending Against Terrorist Attacks with Limited Resources. Aug. 2005. Unpublished manuscript, on file with author.

Preston, Mark, and Susan Crabtree. *Hill Confronts Reorganization; Turf Battles Erupt Over New Department*. Roll Call, June 10, 2002.

Przeworski, Adam. *Democracy and the Market: Political and Economic Reforms in Eastern Europe and Latin America*. New York: Cambridge UP, 1991.

Quadagno, Jill. *One Nation, Uninsured*. New York: Oxford UP, 2005.

Reese, Shawn. Cong. Res. Serv. *Homeland Security Grants: Evolution of Program Guidance and Grant Allocation Methods*. 2006.

Reeves, Richard. *President Nixon: Alone in the White House*. New York: Simon and Schuster, 2001.

Reorganization Act of 1939. Pub. L. No. 76-19, 53 Stat 561.

Richman, Daniel C. *Federal Criminal Law, Congressional Delegation and Enforcement Discretion*. 46 UCLA L. Rev. 757 (1999).

———. *"Project Exile" and the Allocation of Federal Law Enforcement Authority*. 43 Ariz. L. Rev. 369 (2001).

Riddick, Floyd M. *American Government and Politics: Third Session of the Seventy-sixth Congress, January 3, 1940 to January 3, 1941*. 35 Am. Polit. Sci. Rev. 284 (1941).

Ridge, Tom. *U.S. Is More Secure*. USA Today, Feb. 2, 2004.

Riker, William H. *The Art of Political Manipulation*. New Haven: Yale UP, 1986.

Ringquist, Evan J. *Political Control and Policy Impact in EPA's Office of Water Quality*. 39 Am. J. Pol. Sci. 336 (1995).

Ripley, Amanda. *Speed Read: The White House Katrina Report*. Time.com, Feb. 23, 2006. http://www.time.com/time/nation/article/0,8599,1167076,00.html.

Risky Funding. Editorial. Washington Post, Nov. 21, 2005.

Rivers, Douglas, and Nancy L. Rose. *Passing the President's Program: Public Opinion and Presidential Influence in Congress*. 29 Am. J. Polit. Sci. 183 (1985).

Roberts, Patrick. *The Master of Disaster as Bureaucratic Entrepreneur*. 38 PS: Poli. Sci. & Pol. 331 (2005).

———. Reputation and Federal Emergency Preparedness Agencies, 1948–2003. Sept. 2, 2004. Unpublished manuscript. Available at http://www.training.fema.gov/EMIWeb/downloads/RobertsPfema 8 20 04 apsa.pdf.

Romer, Thomas and Barry R. Weingast. *Political Foundations of the Thrift Debacle*. In *Politics and Economics in the Eighties*, ed. Alberto Alesina and Geoffrey Carliner, 175–214. Chicago: U. of Chicago Press, 1991.

Roosevelt, Franklin D. *Message of the President: Reorganization Plan No. 1 of 1939*. April 25, 1939. Reprinted in 5 U.S.C. App.

Rosenberg, James N. *Reorganization Yesterday, Today, Tomorrow*. 25 Va. L. Rev. 129 (1938).

Rothenberg, Lawrence S. *Regulation, Organizations, and Politics: Motor Freight Policy at the Interstate Commerce Commission*. Ann Arbor: U Michigan P, 1994.

Ryan, Donna H. *Military Nutrition Research: Eight Tasks to Address Medical Factors Limiting Soldier Effectiveness*. October 2005. Pennington Biomedical Research Center, Louisiana State University. Prepared for the U.S. Army Medical Research and Material Command.

Saad, Lydia. *Personal Impact on Americans' Lives*. Gallup Poll News Serv., Sept. 24, 2001. Available at http://www.galluppoll.com/content/?ci=4900.

Scalia, Antonin. *Deference to Administrative Interpretations of Law*. 1989 Duke L.J. 511 (1989).

———. *Judicial Deference to Administrative Interpretations of Law*. 1989 Duke L.J. 511.

Schattschneider, E. E. *Party Government*. New York: Farrar and Rinehart, 1942.

Schlesinger, Mark, and Richard R. Lau. *The Meaning and Measure of Policy Metaphors*. 94 Am. Polit. Sci. Rev. 611 (2000).

Schneider, Saundra K. *Administrative Breakdowns in the Governmental Response to Hurricane Katrina*. 65 Pub. Admin. Rev. 515 (Oct. 2005).

Seib, Gerald F. *Deficit Balloons Into National Security Threat*. Wall Street Journal, February 2, 2010.

Select Bipartisan Comm. to Investigate the Preparation for and Response to Hurricane Katrina, *A Failure of Initiative: Final Report*. H.R. Rep. No. 109-377. 2006. [hereinafter *Failure of Initiative*]

Selznick, Philip. *An Approach to a Theory of Bureaucracy*. 8 Am. Sociol. Rev. 50 (1943).

Shapiro, Jacob N., and Rudolph Darken. *Homeland Security: A New Strategic Paradigm?* In *Strategy in the Contemporary World*, ed. John Baylis et al. 2d ed. New York: Oxford UP, 2007.

Shelton, Hugh, and John Dalton. *Strong Military Needs Early Education Focus*. Politico, January 8, 2009.

Short, Lloyd M. *Adjusting the Departmental System*. 41 Am. Polit. Sci. Rev. 48 (1947).

Shull, Bernard. *The Fourth Branch: The Federal Reserve's Unlikely Rise to Power and Influence*. Westport, CT: Praeger, 2005.

Skocpol, Theda. 1995. *Protecting Soldiers and Mothers: The Political Origins of Social Policy in the United States*. Cambridge, MA: Belknap Press of Harvard UP, 1992.

Skowronek, Stephen. *Building a New American State: The Expansion of National Administrative Capacities, 1877–1920*. Cambridge: Cambridge UP, 1982.

Smith, Jean Edward. *FDR*. New York: Random House, 2007.

Stables, Eleanor, and Toni Johnson. *HR2360—Fiscal 2006 Homeland Security Appropriations*, CQ BillAnalysis, Apr. 3, 2006. Available at 2006 WLNR 5945020.

Staff of H. Comm. on Energy and Commerce. 107th Cong. The Recommendations of the Committee on Energy and Commerce to the Select Committee on Homeland Security Concerning H.R. 5005 (2002).

Strang, David, and John W. Meyer. *Institutional Conditions for Diffusion*. 22 Theory & Society 487 (1993).

Strauss, Peter L. *Overseer or "The Decider"? The President in Administrative Law*, 75 Geo. Wash. L. Rev. 696 (2007).

Strøm, Kaare, and Wolfgang C. Müller. *The Keys to Togetherness: Coalition Agreements in Parliamentary Democracies*. 5 J. Legis. Stud. 255 (1999).

Sullivan, Laura. *FEMA Official Says Agency Heads Ignored Warnings.* National Public Radio, Sept. 16, 2005. http://www.npr.org/templates/story/story.php?storyId=4849706. Accessed Dec. 18, 2011.

Sundquist, James L. *Dynamics of the Party System: Alignment and Realignment of Parties in the United States.* Washington, D.C.: Brookings 1973.

Sunstein, Cass R. *Beyond* Marbury: *The Executive's Power to Say What the Law Is.* 115 Yale L.J. 2580 (2006).

———. *The Second Bill of Rights: Roosevelt's Unfinished Revolution and Why We Need It More Than Ever.* New York: Basic Books, 2004.

Susman, Thomas M. *Congressional Oversight of Homeland Security.* Admin. & Reg. News, Fall 2004.

Sutton, Victoria. *Biodefense: Who's in Charge?* 13 Health Matrix 117 (2003).

Swain, Donald. *The Rise of a Research Empire: NIH, 1930 to 1950.* Science 1233 (Dec. 14, 1962).

Swaine, Edward T. *Unsigning.* 55 Stan. L. Rev. 2061 (2003).

Swanson, Ian. *Obama: China Should Be Confident in U.S. T-bills.* The Hill, March 14, 2009.

Szanton, Peter. *Federal Reorganization: What Have We Learned?* London: Chatham House Publishers, 1981.

Take Time on Homeland Plan. Editorial. Hartford Courant, June 20, 2002.

Terrorism and U.S. Government Capabilities: Hearing Before the Subcomm. on Commerce, State, and the Judiciary of the S. Comm. on Appropriations. 107th Cong. 2001.

Terrorist Attacks: Public Opinion from April 1995–January 2001. Gallup Poll News Serv., Sept. 11, 2001. Available at http://www.galluppoll.com/content/ default.aspx?ci=4876.

Tetlock, Philip E. *Expert Political Judgment: How Good Is It? How Can We Know?* Princeton, N.J.: Princeton UP, 2005.

Teton, Alfred B. *Reorganization Revisited.* 48 Yale L. J. 573 (1939).

Theoharis, Athan G. *The FBI and American Democracy: A Brief Critical History.* Lawrence: UP of Kansas, 2004.

Thessin, Jonathan. Note. *Recent Developments: Department of Homeland Security,* 40 Harv. J. on Legis. 513 (2003).

Thomas, Dorothy Swaine. *Some Social Aspects of Japanese-American Demography.* 94 P. Am. Philos. Soc. (1950).

Tilly, Charles. *Coercion, Capital, and the European States.* Malden, MA: Blackwell, 1992.

———. *European Revolutions: 1492–1992.* Oxford: Blackwell, 1993.

———. *The Politics of Collective Violence.* New York: Cambridge UP, 2003.

Ting, Michael M. *A Theory of Jurisdictional Assignments in Bureaucracies.* 46 Am. J. Polit. Sci. 364 (2002).

To Safeguard Defense. Editorial. Washington Post, Dec. 2, 1938.

TPM Hurricane Katrina Timeline. September 20, 2005. talkingpointsmemo.com.

Trading with the Enemy Act. Pub. L. No. 65-91. 40 Stat 411 (1917), codified in various sections of 50 U.S.C. App.

Transportation Security Administration Arlington, Va. Mid-Atlantic Construction, Dec. 1, 2005.

Truman, Harry S. *Memoirs by Harry S. Truman.* Vol. 2: *Years of Trial and Hope.* New York: Doubleday, 1956.

———. *State of the Union Address.* Jan. 5, 1949. Available at http://www.presidency.ucsb.edu/ws/index.php?pid=13293. Accessed Apr. 14, 2009.

Truman Seeks Rise in Nation's Health. NY Times, Jan. 31, 1948.

Truman Undecided, May Again Ask Agency Bill. LA Times, Aug. 19, 1949.

Tulane Maritime Law Center Newsletter. Spring 2006.

United States Government Manual. 1939. Office of Government Reports. U.S. Information Service. *United States Government Manual, October 1939.* Washington, D.C.: GPO, 1939.

———. 1940. Office of Government Reports. U.S. Information Service. *United States Government Manual, Fall 1940.* Washington, D.C.: GPO, 1940.

———. 1941. Office of Government Reports. U.S. Information Service. *United States Government Manual, September 1941.* Washington, D.C.: GPO, 1941.

———. 1942. Bureau of Public Inquiries. Office of War Information. *United States Government Manual, Fall 1942.* Washington, D.C.: GPO, 1942.

———. 1943–1944. Division of Public Inquiries. Office of War Information. *United States Government Manual, Winter 1943–1944.* Washington, D.C.: GPO, 1942.

———. 1945. Division of Public Inquiries, Government Information Service, Bureau of the Budget. *United States Government Manual, 1945.* 2nd ed. Washington, D.C.: GPO, 1945.

———. 1946. Division of Public Inquiries, Government Information Service, Bureau of the Budget. *United States Government Manual, 1946.* Washington, D.C.: GPO, 1946.

———. 1948. Division of the Federal Register. National Archives. *United States Government Manual, 1948.* Washington, D.C.: GPO, 1948.

———. 2000–2001. Office of the Federal Register. National Archives and Records Administration. *United States Government Manual: 2000–2001.* Washington, D.C.: GPO, 2001.

———. 2001–2002. Office of the Federal Register. National Archives and Records Administration. *United States Government Manual 2001–2002.* Washington, D.C.: GPO, 2002.

———.2007–2008. Office of the Federal Register. National Archives and Records Administration. *United States Government Manual 2007–2008.* Washington, D.C.: GPO, 2008.

Uniting and Strengthening America by Providing Appropriate Tools Required to Intercept and Obstruct Terrorism Act (USA PATRIOT Act) of 2001. Pub. L. No. 107-56, 115 Stat. 272 (codified in scattered sections of the U.S.C.).

U.S. Census Bureau. *Statistical Abstract of the United States.* 119th ed. Washington, D.C.: GPO, 1999.

———. *Statistical Abstract of the United States 2003: Mini-historical Statistics* 94 table HS-50. Available at http://www.census.gov/statab/hist/HS-50.pdf. Accessed Apr. 14, 2009.

U.S. Commission on National Security in the Twenty-First Century. *The Phase III Report: Road Map for National Security: Imperative for Change.* February 15, 2001.

———. *Seeking a National Strategy: A Concert for Preserving Security and Promoting Freedom.* 2000. Available at http://www.au.af.mil/au/awc/awcgate/nssg/phaseII.pdf goal.

U.S. Department of Homeland Security. *The Budget for Fiscal Year 2004.* 2003.

———. Homeland Security Centers of Excellence. July 31, 2006. Available at http://www.dhs.gov/xres/programs/editorial_0498.shtm.

U.S. Department of Labor. *Memorandum on Proposal to Transfer the US Employment Service to the Social Security Board* (1939). Available at Franklin D. Roosevelt Presidential Library, Correspondence and Papers of the President's Committee on Administrative Management, Correspondence and Papers: Reorganization, Reorganization Plan I Folder, Box 24.

U.S. Gen. Accounting Office. Customs Service: Comments on Strategic Plan and Resource Allocation Process (1997). (Statement of Norman Rabkin, Dir., Admin. of Justice Issues, Gen. Gov't Div.). Available at http://www.gao.gov/archive/1998/gg98015t.pdf.

U.S. Government Accountability Office (US GAO). *Coast Guard: Non-Homeland Security Performance Measures Are Generally Sound, but Opportunities for Improvement Exist* GAO-06-816 (Aug. 2006).

———. *Influenza Pandemic: Lessons from the H1N1 Pandemic Should Be Incorporated into Future Planning*. Rep't. to Cong. Requesters, GAO 11632 1 (June 2011).

———. *Homeland Security: Management Challenges Facing Federal Leadership*. Dec. 2002. GAO-03-260. Available at http://www.gao.gov/new.items/d03260.pdf.

———. *Major Management Challenges and Program Risks: Department of Homeland Security* (Jan. 2003). Available at http://www.gao.gov/pas/2003/d03102.pdf.

———. *Secure Border Initiative: DHS Needs to Follow Through on Plans to Reassess and Better Manage Key Technology Program*. 2010. Available at http://www.gao.gov/new.items/d10840t.pdf.

Vizzard, William J. *In the Cross Fire: A Political History of the Bureau of Alcohol, Tobacco, and Firearms*. Boulder: Lynne Rienner 1997.

Walcott, Charles E., and Karen M. Hult. *Governing the White House: From Hoover Through LBJ*. Lawrence: UP of Kansas, 1995.

Wallis, John Joseph. *Employment, Politics, and Economic Recovery during the Great Depression*. 69 Rev. Econ. & Stat. 516 (1987).

Walsh, Bill. *House Panel Strips Millions from FEMA Budget; Vitter Supports Cuts to Disaster Relief*. New Orleans Times-Picayune, June 20, 2001.

Walz, Jay. *Welfare Agency Has Grown Fast*. NY Times, Mar. 1, 1953.

Wamsley, Gary L., and Aaron D. Schroeder. *Escalating in a Quagmire: The Changing Dynamics of the Emergency Management Policy Subsystem*. 56 Pub. Admin. Rev. 235 (1996).

Weber, Max. *Economy and Society: An Outline of Interpretive Sociology*. Ed. Guenther Roth and Claus Wittich. Trans. Ephraim Fischhoff et al. New York: Bedminster Press, 1968.

Weingast, Barry R. *Bureaucratic Discretion or Congressional Control? Regulatory Policymaking by the Federal Trade Commission*. 91 J. Polit. Econ. 765 (1983).

———. *Caught in the Middle: The President, Congress, and the Political-Bureaucratic System*. In *Institutions of American Democracy: The Executive Branch*, ed. Joel D. Aberbach and Mark A. Peterson, 312–342. New York: Oxford UP, 2005.

———. *Reflections on Distributive Politics and Universalism*. 47 Polit. Res. Quart. 319 (1994).

———. *Regulation, Reregulation, and Deregulation: The Political Foundations of Agency Clientele Relationships*. 44 Law & Contemp. Probs. 147 (1981).

White House. Office of the Press Secretary. *Remarks by the President at the Signing of H.R. 5005, the Homeland Security Act of 2002* (Nov. 25, 2002). Available at http://georgewbush-whitehouse.archives.gov/news/releases/2002/11/print/20021125-6.html.

———. *Proposed Homeland Security Act of 2002*. June 2002. [hereinafter *President's Plan*]. Available at http://www.whitehouse.gov/deptofhomeland/bill/hsl-bill.pdf.

Wilner, Frank N. *User Charges Proposed*. Traffic World, Feb. 8, 1999. Available at 1999 WLNR 5024660.

Wilson, James Q. *Bureaucracy: What Government Agencies Do and Why They Do It*. New York: Basic Books, 1989.

———. *The Investigators: Managing FBI and Narcotics Agents*. New York: Basic Books, 1978.

Wise, Charles R., and Rania Nader. *Organizing the Federal System for Homeland Security: Problems, Issues, and Dilemmas*. 62 Pub. Admin. Rev. 44 (2002).

Wolfensberger, Donald R. *Congress and Policymaking in an Age of Terrorism*. In *Congress Reconsidered*, ed. Lawrence C. Dodd and Bruce I. Oppenheimer, 343. 8th ed. Washington, D.C.: CQ Press, 2005.

Wombell, James A. Army Support During the Hurricane Katrina Disaster (2009), 45, http://www.cgsc.edu/carl/download/csipubs/wombell.pdf.

Wood, B. Dan, and Richard W. Waterman. *The Dynamics of Political Control of the Bureaucracy.* 85 Am. Polit. Sci. Rev. 801 (1991).

World Health Organization. Statement by Dr. Keiji Kukuda on Behalf of WHO at the Council of Europe Hearing on Pandemic (H1N1) 2009. *Global Alert and Response* (Jan. 26, 2010).

Wright, Gavin. *The Political Economy of New Deal Spending: An Econometric Analysis.* 56 Rev. Econ. & Stat. 30 (1974).

Wright, Lawrence. *The Looming Tower.* New York: Knopf, 2006.

Yoo, Christopher S., Steven G. Calabresi, and Laurence D. Nee. *The Unitary Executive During the Third Half-Century, 1889–1945.* 80 Notre Dame L. Rev. 1 (2004).

Zegart, Amy B. *Flawed by Design: The Evolution of the CIA, JCS, and NSC.* Stanford, CA: Stanford UP, 1999.

———. *September 11 and the Adaptation Failure of U.S. Intelligence Agencies.* 29 Int'l Security 78 (Spring 2005).

Index

Note: Page numbers followed by *f* or *t* indicate figures and tables, respectively. Federal cabinet departments are listed under "Department of . . ."